A HISTORY OF NIGER 1850–1?

D0879325

THE PUBLISHER WISHES TO THANK THE NORWEGIAN
RESEARCH COUNCIL FOR SCIENCE AND THE HUMANITIES FOR
ITS GENEROUS SUBVENTION IN SUPPORT OF THE PUBLICATION
OF THIS BOOK.

A HISTORY OF NIGER
1850–1960

FINN FUGLESTAD

CAMBRIDGE UNIVERSITY PRESS

CAMBRIDGE
LONDON   NEW YORK   NEW ROCHELLE
MELBOURNE   SYDNEY

CAMBRIDGE UNIVERSITY PRESS
Cambridge, New York, Melbourne, Madrid, Cape Town, Singapore, São Paulo, Delhi

Cambridge University Press
The Edinburgh Building, Cambridge CB2 8RU, UK

Published in the United States of America by Cambridge University Press, New York

www.cambridge.org
Information on this title: www.cambridge.org/9780521252683

© Cambridge University Press 1983

First published 1983
This digitally printed version 2008

A catalogue record for this publication is available from the British Library

Library of Congress Catalogue Card Number: 83–1809

ISBN 978-0-521-25268-3 hardback
ISBN 978-0-521-10139-4 paperback

Contents

Contents

Maps

Acknowledgments

This book is the direct, although in many ways remote, descendant of a thesis written under the very stimulating supervision of Professor J. D. Fage and submitted to the University of Birmingham in 1977. Second thoughts and new evidence made it necessary to rewrite the original manuscript almost entirely. Only the introduction, most of chapter 6 and a few sections in chapters 3 and 4 have been left unaltered. If the book is at all readable, this is due to a number of people who agreed to correct my increasingly faltering English, and to whom I am as a consequence deeply indebted. They are Mrs Marion Johnson and Dr Peter Mitchell of the University of Birmingham; Dr Patricia Fryer and Dr Humphrey J. Fisher of the University of London; Mr and Mrs Francis Peters of the University of Trondheim; Mrs Toril Swan of the University of Tromsø; Dr Stephen Ellis of St Anthony's College, Oxford; Elizabeth O'Beirne-Ranelagh of Cambridge University Press and above all Mr Arnold Hughes and Professor J. D. Fage of the University of Birmingham who, between them, corrected and commented upon the final version. I owe a special debt of gratitude to Professor Fage.

My thanks are also due to the fifty-one Nigeriens, Europeans and Americans whose hospitality and friendship made it possible for me to travel through the length and breadth of Niger between 1969 and 1972, to the French Secrétariat d'Etat (now Ministère) de la Coopération which was kind enough to appoint me to a position in West Africa in 1968; to the authorities of the Republic of Niger (especially Harou Kouka and Léopold Kaziendé, the then Ministers of Education and Public Works, the latter also acting as Minister of the Interior) who gave me free access to the archives and who also provided me with a living between 1970 and 1972; to the thirty-two Nigeriens, forty-six Frenchmen and one Frenchwoman who agreed to answer my questions; to a considerable number of French, British, Norwegian, Senegalese and Nigerien librarians and archivists; to the British Council and especially that most remarkable of institutions, the Norwegian Research Council for Science and the Humanities, for generous financial support.

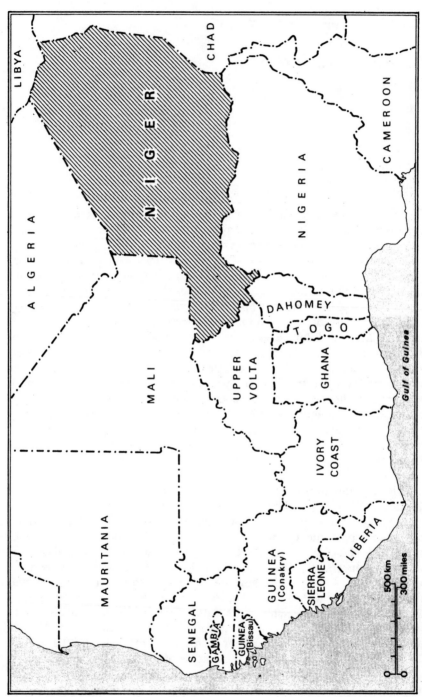

1 Niger in West Africa.

Introduction

The present-day Republic of Niger is one of the largest, hottest, poorest, most thinly populated, most rural, and most landlocked states of the world. It was also one of the world's least known countries until the severe drought of the 1970s brought the gruesome plight of the people living immediately south of the Sahara to the attention of Europe and North America. But even now the name 'Niger', as applied to a state, means very little to the majority of people. Most jump to the conclusion that there is a mistake somewhere, and that what is really being referred to is Nigeria. It is in this respect of some significance that European languages are inadequate when it comes to distinguishing between a person from Nigeria and one from Niger. In this book the problem has been 'solved' by applying the French adjective 'Nigerien' to the latter.

Since Niger is such an unknown quantity, a preliminary presentation seems necessary. The former French territory of Niger, since 1960 an independent republic, is situated in that part of the West African interior which is commonly referred to as the Central Sudan, although in fact two-thirds of the country is properly speaking part of the Central Sahara. The distance to the Guinea coast is 700 km, to Dakar 1,900 km and to the Mediterranean 1,200 km. Niger covers 1,187,000 square km, approximately five times the size of Great Britain and twice that of France. The only reliable, but unfortunately incomplete, population census of Niger dates from 1960, and gives the figure of 2,876,000 inhabitants for the whole of the country. This figure is the result of a census of the sedentary population and an estimate of the number of nomads and oasis dwellers.[1] More recent figures, which are no more than very rough estimates, give a total population of more than four million.[2] The population is composed of what are commonly called 'ethnic groups'. By far the most important group numerically is the Hausa, which makes up between 45 and 48 per cent of the total population. The Zerma/Songhay (also called Jerma, Djerma or Zaberma/ Sonrai) make up about 20 per cent, and the Kanuri (or Beri-Beri) between 6 and 8 per cent. These three groups are all to be found in the southern third of Niger. Their common attributes are that they are mainly negroid and mostly

1

2 Places referred to in the text.

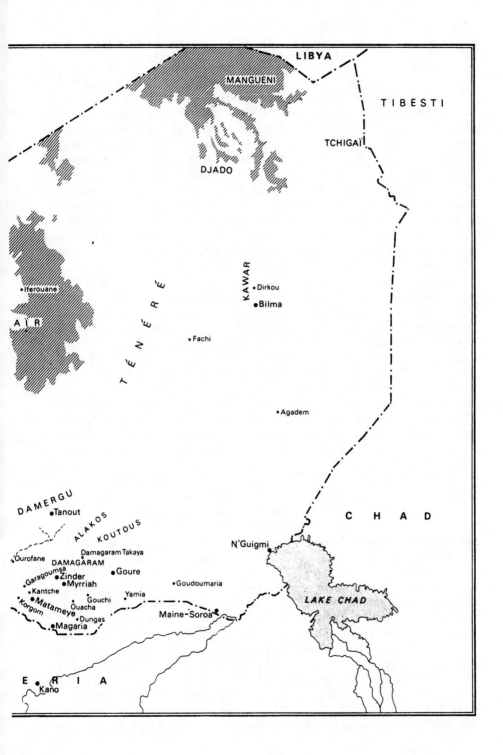

involved in agriculture. That enigmatic people, the Fulani (11 to 13 per cent of the population), are distinct from the other inhabitants of southern Niger in many ways: they are newcomers to the area (the majority arrived from Northern Nigeria during the colonial period), they are markedly caucasoid in their physical makeup, and many of them are still nomads. Even among those who have become sedentary, animal husbandry is still an important economic activity. The reputedly white-skinned desert nomads, the Tuareg, who have – more than any other African people – captivated European imagination, are, as we shall see later, very difficult to define, and even harder to classify. Suffice it to say for the moment that all categories of Tuareg put together make up between 10 and 12 per cent of Niger's population. (This percentage was probably much higher at the beginning of the century.) The Tubu (or Teda-Daza) in the east, the few Arabs in the south-east, and the Gurmantche who live close to the Voltaic border make up altogether about 2 to 3 per cent of the population.

Because of the relatively strong Tuareg element, Niger can be said to have been, and to some extent still to be, one of the least black countries in West Africa. This leads to another important point, namely that although the Nigerien population is composed of few ethnic groups compared to many of the other states in West Africa, its main characteristic is nevertheless its heterogeneity, since it is comprised of not only different ethnic groups, but also different races, and above all opposed, yet complementary, ways of life and civilizations. The extremes are symbolized by the proud Tuareg warrior of the desert and the toiling Hausa farmer of the south. Although the former despises manual work, and can think of nothing more contemptible than his southern neighbour, he cannot do without the latter; and before the colonial era the Hausa farmer was dependent upon the Tuareg for certain goods and commodities such as salt.

Given the distribution of the ethnic groups, for the purpose of the present work Niger can conveniently be divided into six regions: (1) The West (i.e. the present-day *Départements* of Dosso and Niamey, corresponding to the pre-1956 *cercles* of Tillabery, Dosso and Niamey). This region is mainly inhabited by the Zerma/Songhay, together with two hausaphone groups, the Mawri and the Sudie, and a number of mainly sedentary Fulani. There are also a few Tuareg around Tera, in the *dallol* Bosso and along the river valley. (2) The Centre (i.e. the *Département/cercle* of Tahoua, with the exception of the *sous-préfecture* of Tchin-Tabaradene, formerly the *subdivision nomade* of Tahoua). Here the population is composed mainly of Hausa and (in many cases sedentary) Tuareg. (3) The East (i.e. the *Départements/cercles* of Maradi and Zinder, with the exception of the *sous-préfecture* of Goure), a region predominantly Hausa. (4) The Far East or Kanuriland (i.e. the southern half of the *sous-préfecture* of Goure, and the southern third of the *Département* of Diffa, formerly the *cercle* of N'Guigmi). (5) The nearly empty North-East (i.e. the northern half of the *sous-préfecture* of Goure and the northern two-thirds of the *Département* of Diffa, along with the *sous-*

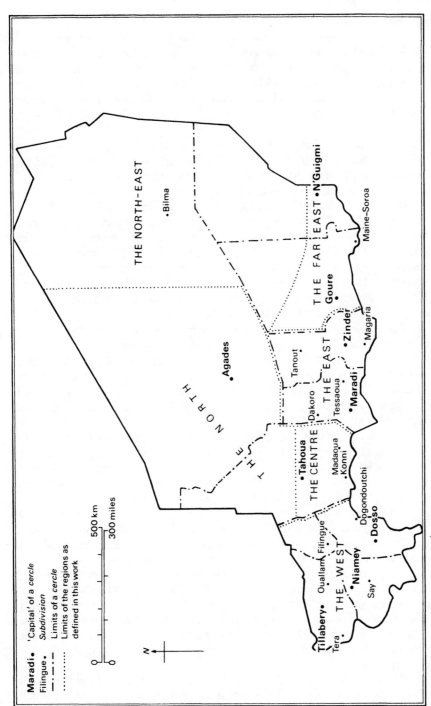

3 Administrative divisions of Niger before 1956.

préfecture/subdivision of Bilma, and also – up to 1929 – the Tibesti massif).
(6) Finally the North or the land of the Tuareg (i.e. the *sous-préfecture* of
Tchin-Tabaradene and the *Département/cercle* of Agades, with the exception
of the *sous-préfecture* of Bilma). Two other terms will also be used
frequently: Hausaland, defined here as including the East, most of the Centre
and also the region inhabited by the Mawri in the West, and the 'sedentary
south', that is to say most of the Far East, the East, the Centre and the West.

In 1922, when the colony of Niger was established (having been a military
territory), it was oriented much further to the east than the present republic.
The river Niger formed the western border, and to the east the Tibesti massif
belonged to the colony. Tibesti was transferred to Chad in 1929.[3] To the
west the frontier changed a number of times. In 1932 the *cercles* of Fada
N'Gurma and Dori, previously part of Upper Volta, were incorporated into
Niger. When they were restored to Upper Volta in 1947, Niger retained the
right bank of the river, i.e. the Songhay–Fulani bank.[4] This book is mainly
concerned with the regions within the borders of the Republic of Niger as
they are today, thus theoretically excluding Fada N'Gurma, Dori and
Tibesti. However, it is difficult (for reasons that will become apparent later)
not to devote some attention to Tibesti.

The new colony, carved out by the French at the turn of the century, was
named after the river which flows through the present-day republic for only
about 550 of its 4,200 km. The name Niger is derived not from the Latin
word for black, but from the Tamacheq (the language of the Tuareg) name
of the river, *Eguerew n'eguerew*, meaning literally 'the river of rivers'.[5] All
the indigenous peoples living along the river call it 'river of rivers' or 'great
river', in Songhay *Issa Beri*.

The main features of the geography of Niger have already been mentioned, and only a few points which are necessary for the comprehension of
the history of the regions of present-day Niger need be added.[6] From a
topographical point of view, Niger is essentially a flat and monotonous
country. The few mountainous regions, Djado, Manguemi, and especially
Aïr, all situated in the northern, Saharan part of the country, are no more
than isolated features of the landscape. But the Aïr massif in particular
considerably influences the climate of neighbouring regions. Thus rainfall is
extremely rare east of the massif, but adequate to the west. To the east lies
the nearly impassable desert of the Ténéré, where no one can survive for long
outside the oases of Kawar. But west of Aïr, in the regions known as Azawak
and Tamesna, zones of temporary grassland during the rainy season attract
a considerable number of nomads and their cattle. In the south, there are
two small hilly regions, Koutoss in the Far East and Adar in the Centre. The
latter has adequate supplies of water and is therefore relatively densely
populated.

In the region defined as the West there are a number of so-called fossil
valleys, relics of the Quaternary, when these parts of Africa had a much

wetter climate than at present. During the Quaternary, the river Niger drained a fairly important area, and absorbed a number of minor rivers or affluents which have long since dried out, or are no more than intermittent at best. The most important of these wide and shallow but steep-sided fossil valleys, all situated on the east of the river, are – from north to south – the *dallol* Bosso, or Boboye (called Azawak north of Filingue), the lesser *dallol* Fogha, and the *dallol* Mawri. The reason why there are no fossil valleys on the right bank is because of the composition of the rocks, which are mainly granitic. The next valley, not yet a fossil valley, is that of the Rima, an affluent of the Niger and situated mainly in Nigeria. The volume of water now flowing through it is not enough to explain the valley, which must therefore be in the process of becoming fossilized. This process is virtually over in the case of some of the affluents of the Rima, such as the intermittent rivers and corresponding valleys of Maradi, Tarka, Kaba and Eliki, as well as the valleys of Adar and of the neighbouring regions of Majya and Doutchi. The important point to note for our purpose is that all these valleys, whether fossil or in the process of becoming fossil, and of course the Niger river valley, are privileged spots, where rain water tends to accumulate and where underground water is close to the surface.

The terrain is nowhere an obstacle to traffic, whether of horsemen or camel-riders, friendly traders, conquering warriors, or marauding raiders. Indeed, the Central Sudan has always been characterized by the frequent movement and mingling of peoples, a fact which accounts for the extreme flexibility of its ethnic boundaries.

The climate of Niger is usually described as hot and dry. But anyone who has lived in Niger during the dry season knows that the nights of December and January are very chilly indeed. Temperatures below 7 or 8°C are quite common. In the northern regions, frost may even occur. However, if the months of December and January are chilly, April and May are equally hot, with temperatures often approaching 50°C, especially in the North and the North-East. The seasonal (and also diurnal) range of temperature is thus exceptionally wide, and increases from south to north. But life in Niger is first and foremost conditioned by that very rare commodity, water. Away from the river valleys and the old river beds of the *dallols*, the country is essentially dependent upon rainfall. Map 4 shows a simple pattern of rainfall decreasing from south to north. Gaya on the Dahomean border has on average 800 mm per annum, but Bilma in the extreme North-East only has 25 mm. Considering the pattern of temperature and rainfall distribution, Niger can be divided into four climatic zones, of which by far the largest is the desert zone. The southern limit of the desert zone is approximately 15 to 16° north, and this is the effective northern limit of year-round livestock rearing outside the oases and a few privileged spots west of Aïr and in Aïr itself. Next comes the very much smaller northern Sahelian zone, the exclusive domain of the nomads. Between the isohyets of 300 and 800 mm lies the southern Sahelian and the northern Sudanic zone, an area compris-

7

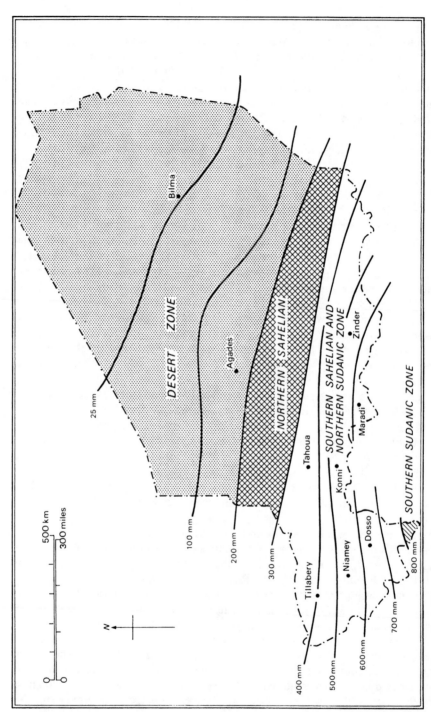

4 Vegetation and rainfall.

ing approximately one-third to one-quarter of the total land surface of Niger, to which permanent cropping is confined. Finally, the southern Sudanic zone, where rainfall averages more than 800 mm per annum, is only a small area in the extreme south (the region of Gaya).

Thus rainfall is both scanty and irregular even in regions where agriculture constitutes the main economic activity. Although the southern Sahelian and northern Sudanic zone is a useful climatic division, the importance of the isohyets of 400 and 500 mm must nevertheless be stressed. The isohyet of 500 mm in particular marks a sudden increase in the annual variability of rainfall which is very detrimental to permanent agriculture. North of this limit, the country was virtually empty before the colonial period. Although the demographic expansion and later the extension of groundnut cultivation in the south have forced an increasing movement northwards both of peasants and of the nomadic Fulani and their cattle, it should be borne in mind that agriculture, while possible in this region, can only support a limited number of people. Even south of the isohyet of 500 mm there are, outside the valleys, large areas where the soil is so poor and thin as to be virtually unproductive; in other areas, either because of shortage of soil moisture or low organic contents, the soil needs to lie fallow for long periods. The very existence of agricultural societies in Niger rests on a very delicate balance, which drought, late or early rainfall, or a too rapid demographic expansion can easily upset. Given this balance, Niger can only support a small population.

The calendar year is divided into three seasons: the rainy season lasting from about July to September in the south, the dry and increasingly chilly season from October to January, and the dry and very hot season from February to July. Thus the main bulk of farm-work is limited to only three or four months a year.

After the dramatic drought of the 1970s, the question has been asked whether the climate of this part of Africa is deteriorating, and whether the same can be said of the environment. Although this is a rather controversial subject among geographers, there seems nevertheless to be a certain consensus on one particular point, namely that nature's capacity to regenerate has not been destroyed in the regions affected by the drought. Rather there is a discrepancy between what man is expecting from the environment and what the environment is able to produce.

Historically, however, it can be seen that since about 1800 the Central Sudan has experienced a cycle of low rainfall which compares unfavourably with a previous 'wet' cycle through the sixteenth to eighteenth centuries.[7]

SOURCES AND GENERAL ORIENTATION

This book is a general modern history of Niger based extensively on written sources and concentrating on the colonial period. Niger as defined by its colonial (or more precisely post-1947) borders is, as indicated earlier, the appropriate unit of study in this period. The name Niger will also be used in a purely geographical sense to describe the same area during earlier periods.[8]

My original intention was to investigate the history of nationalism and of the nationalist movement in Niger. However, having immersed myself in Nigerien history, I came to realize that no genuine nationalism, let alone any nationalist movement, existed in Niger before 1960 at the earliest. (I am no longer convinced, either, that the people of Niger wanted political independence, or that the very notion of political independence made any sense to them.) This somewhat controversial conclusion – it is one of the major conclusions of this book – was not reached without serious thought. Indeed, it clashed with my own preconceived notions of modern African history. Worse, it turned out to be but one of several such unexpected conclusions. As I continued my research, this time with the aim of writing a monographic survey of Niger during the colonial period, I found myself questioning many of the more widely held generalizations, models, theories and assumptions pertaining to this period. None of them proved to be of much relevance to the study I had undertaken. My personal experience thus induces me to argue that colonial history is a subject which has often been approached with answers in mind, rather than with questions in hand. Perhaps the truth is that the tendency towards generalization and theorizing, particularly inevitable in such an emotionally loaded subject as colonial history, has outdistanced the progress of primary research. This implies that colonial history still remains a subject very incompletely investigated. Thus, although I thought that, by opting for a subject in the field of colonial history I would be walking on well-trodden ground, I soon realized, much to my dismay, that I had embarked upon a pioneering thesis: the first work based on primary research to attempt an overall appraisal of the colonial past of a single West African country.[9] Although this point should not be overemphasized, it does compel me to devote more space than would otherwise have been appropriate to a number of considerations of a general character.

A few examples are needed to illustrate some of these points. It is clear that the colonial regime was a regime imposed exclusively by force. It is less clear, however, that it was also maintained exclusively by force. Furthermore, and if we leave aside the complex problem of definition, few scholars would deny that notions such as political oppression and economic exploitation are relevant for the study of the colonial past. Certainly, both political oppression and economic exploitation occurred in Niger during the colonial period. But they did not occur throughout the whole of that period, nor, in my opinion, to the degree one would expect. In fact, I am no longer convinced that the colonial period compares unfavourably on these points with the preceding or even with the succeeding periods. It is my contention that these notions can in no way be looked upon as characteristic of, or defining, that period. It does not necessarily follow, however, that the colonial regime lacked the will to pursue an oppressive and exploitative policy. Rather, it lacked the means to do so. The colonial regime in Niger (but only in Niger?) was weak, always desperately short of men and funds, and dependent on the at least tacit support of local groups for its survival. I support the theory that the Europeans conquered Africa mainly for economic motives; but they soon realized that Africa in general, and the West African hinterland in particular, was not the Eldorado they had believed it to be, and so lost interest, leaving the colonial administrations to muddle through with very limited means. Nevertheless, it is the case that the impact of the colonial administration in Niger before 1946 was in many instances negative, if not destructive, to the extent that during certain periods the colonial administration can be classified as one of Niger's major scourges, along with drought and locusts. The main factors responsible seem to have been the incompetence and ignorance of the French colonialists coupled with the basic problem of simply making the colonial administration function. Frequently the French decided upon measures which turned out to have exactly the opposite effect of the one hoped for, and their supreme arrogance and self-confidence took a beating on the light soil of Niger. However, the impact of the colonial administration must not be exaggerated; the degree of African influence on the course of events remained significant, even during the darkest hours of colonial rule.

Although I finally completed my survey of Niger in colonial times, I came to the conclusion that this period did not stand out as a distinct period in African history. Nor should it in my opinion be treated as *one* period. There is an enormous difference between for instance the 1911–22 and the 1946–60 periods. The former has much in common with the pre-colonial era, while it is debatable whether the latter should be classified as belonging to the colonial era at all. I have time and again been struck by the rapidly changing nature of French rule, and also by the extremely uneven impact of that rule during the sixty or so years of colonialism. This is the main reason for the strictly chronological ordering of this book. Furthermore, and without wishing to be provocative, I am no longer certain of the main characteristics of the colonial period compared with the pre-colonial era.

Is alien rule a characteristic of the colonial period? Obviously, but not without important qualifications. It must be remembered that although many groups in Niger have, as we shall see, a particularly long and distinguished record of resistance to alien conquerors, quite a few regions in Niger and in Africa generally had long been accustomed to being ruled by foreigners – whether fellow-Africans or Europeans makes little difference. Indeed, it seems legitimate to argue that the nineteenth century witnessed a sort of pre-colonial internal partition of black Africa. Is the penetration of the capitalist world economy a characteristic? This penetration was modest in Niger. Moreover, many regions of Niger had been integrated into this world economy long before the arrival of the first French officials. Are significant structural changes a characteristic? Such changes are not all that obvious in the case of Niger. Is one characteristic the imposition of a dominant ideology stressing and exalting the inherent superiority of the new ruling group (the French), and instilling into the Africans a sort of slave mentality, an enduring inferiority complex? Such a type of ideology was nothing new in Niger or elsewhere in Africa. Indeed, virtually all the pre-colonial ruling elites had attempted to do exactly the same. It is far from certain, therefore, that the imposition of colonial rule led to any lasting trauma, or to any trauma which was not already there.

Instead I would like to argue, first, that the colonial period needs to be viewed in a very wide context. This is because many of the more significant long-term trends observable during this period have origins in the pre-colonial past. In other words, I do not believe that 'an abrupt discontinuity was imposed by the experience of colonial rule'.[10] (In spite of this, although this book attempts to cover the period 1850–1960 – and even beyond – it is primarily concerned with the colonial era.) I would then argue that the study of colonial history is – as has been more than hinted at above and especially in the discussion of the relevance of the notions of exploitation and political oppression – mainly a study in ambiguity. Perhaps the most clear-cut illustration of this is in the position of the French officers who conquered West Africa and of the administrators who later ruled it, or at least were under the impression that they ruled it. Before 1946 these officers and administrators at times behaved in a most ruthless, brutal, arrogant, if not downright despotic manner, and considered the Africans to be inferior human beings. On the other hand, these same officers and administrators were the representatives of a government committed to democracy and human rights, to the principles of *liberté, égalité, fraternité*, however imperfectly implemented at home. Furthermore, most French officials in Africa belonged to the middle class, a class strongly attached to the revolutionary tradition of 1789 and 1848, and consequently strongly at-tached to what the French call the *régime républicain*. It would be inappro-priate to translate *républicain* as 'republican' since this notion carries, as is well known, quite specific connotations for the French. Indeed, the opposite of a *régime républicain* is an oppressive regime, a feudal and despotic one; in other words a classic colonial regime. Thus the officials found themselves in an ambiguous, if not paradoxical situation, one which was increasingly difficult to sustain as the Europeans began, especially after the First World War, to lose confidence in their own superiority. Colonialism came to an end *inter alia* because it was incompatible with other European ideologies.

Although as mentioned earlier no genuine nationalism existed in Niger before 1960, this tells us little or nothing about the nature of the political struggle after 1946. The essential point in my opinion is that by analysing this struggle (along with a great many other significant phenomena in modern African history) exclusively within the context of conventional western conceptual categories – nationalism, independence, class struggle, voting patterns, liberal versus conservative parties etc. – one is likely to misunderstand its real nature. What happened in 1946 was that an alien political institutional framework was superimposed upon a tradition and a culture with which this framework had relatively few points in common. The result was a hybrid; an ambiguous political system.

Another example can be taken from the earlier days of the colonial era. The conquest of the regions of Niger appeared to be a struggle between a group of aliens and the indigenes. A deeper analysis reveals, however, that the conquest of Niger may be defined as a three-dimensional or even four-dimensional struggle, between an African army commanded by French officers, a group which I have chosen to call the 'pre-colonial imperialists', another group composed of latter-day 'adventurers' such as Rābīh and Ahmad Chekou, and the indigenous population. Similarly, the revolts of the Zerma/Songhay in 1905–6 and of the Tuareg in 1915–18 were not simply cases of the oppressed rising against the oppressors. The Tuareg revolt in particular has a conservative, if not reactionary dimension (to use two western conceptual categories), in that one of the motives of the Tuareg was to reestablish their own brand of oppression over those black communities which the French had wrested from their control. Perhaps we should look upon what happened in 1915–18 as the final clash between two rival imperialist 'powers'. Those who chose not to resist and not to revolt against the French were, seen from a certain angle, 'quislings'. But at the same time they merit recognition as modernizers and reformers in the sense that they in many instances were able to perceive and to take advantage of the new opportunities offered by colonial rule. As such, they paved the way for the future.

Thus while attempting to highlight the ambiguous character of the colonial period, I have also argued that the essence of history, and above all of colonial history, is complexity. This complexity stems in part from what is perhaps (although yet again not without important qualifications) a unique characteristic of colonial history: the fact that the rulers and the ruled belonged to significantly different cultures. This in turn is the main reason why one of the most vexing problems in colonial history has to do with values and norms. One may argue that value judgments of some kind or other are implicit in every kind of historical writing, and that they escape unquestioned only when widely accepted within the academic community. This is certainly not the case in colonial history, a field characterized by an almost total lack of consensus not only as to what values but also as to what norms and considerations should constitute the basis for an evaluation and/or appreciation both of the colonial period as a whole and of that period's component elements. For instance, it could be argued that when the Europeans built railways, roads and harbours (or forced the Africans to do so), it was primarily in order to improve communications and to provide hitherto isolated regions with an easy access to the world market, and so to provide the local population with new economic opportunities. But it could also be argued that it was done, first, in order to facilitate political-military control, and second, to tap and exploit new resources and new people for the benefit of the world capitalist system. Furthermore, when the French did not build railways and built only a few roads (as in Niger), then they may be accused of having failed to fulfil their obligations towards the colonized. When one of the present-day progressive African governments, for instance that of Angola, cracks down on the chiefs, the argument is that it is necessary in order to wipe out a reactionary element that stands in the way of progress. Surely the French should benefit from the same justification for the same actions. However, in their case we perhaps see an attempt to dispose of the society's natural leaders, that is to dispose of an institution which was the result of a long-term harmonious (Burkean) evolution. When, as happened during certain periods, the French instead governed through the chiefs (as did the British in Northern Nigeria), it could then be argued that they allied themselves with the most conservative elements of society, thus arresting the normal process of social and political change. But an equally good argument is that by governing through the chiefs the Europeans simply respected the natural order of things.

These examples, which could be multiplied indefinitely, only prove that in the field of colonial history there is room for endless disagreement. Truth, like beauty, is in the eye of the beholder.

I have often been asked: why Niger?; and I am tempted to answer, as explorers and mountaineers have done, because it is *there*. The question implies that the history of Niger is of limited interest, and that I would have been better off studying a less peripheral African country. Indeed, much of what has been said above may lead to the objection that Niger constitutes an atypical case from which no general conclusions should be drawn. After all, the colonial history of black Africa abounds in particularly clear-cut examples of economic exploitation, political oppression, virulent nationalism, wars of liberation etc. South Africa, the Portuguese territories, Rhodesia-Zimbabwe, Kenya, King Leopold's Congo, and parts of French Equatorial Africa during the inter-war years are well-known cases in point. It is also true that Niger is (or rather was, before the beginnings of the uranium boom and the Libyan involvement in Chad) something of a no-man's-land. But although the regions of present-day Niger constituted in many ways an assembly of borderlands during the pre-colonial era, it could nevertheless be argued that this peripheralization was the result of an historical process which can be dated to the colonial period, and so deserves to rank as an important theme in the colonial history of Niger. More importantly, if we add up all those countries and regions of Africa which at one period or another could be considered peripheral, in my opinion we are dealing with a very substantial slice of Africa. It was only logical and natural that the scholars interested in colonial history should have felt attracted initially by the spectacular, but now the time has come to analyse closely the main historical trends in a country which did *not* experience a major uprising after 1920; a country where the economic penetration of international capitalism remained slight before 1960; a country which was not ruled *de jure* or *de*

14

facto by an exploitative and racist settler community; a country which never experienced any virulent nationalism let alone a stiff uphill struggle for freedom and independence. Of course, it is absurd to ask what country is most representative for the evolution of Africa generally, Niger or, say, Rhodesia-Zimbabwe. They represent two different facets of this evolution. Therefore, any balanced appreciation of the colonial past requires that both be taken into account. I am inclined to argue, nevertheless, that precisely because the history of Niger after 1920 is unspectacular, it serves much better than that of Rhodesia-Zimbabwe to illustrate the ambiguous, complex and controversial character of the colonial period.

Chapter 1 and parts of chapter 2 of this book represent a synthesis of the abundant printed primary and secondary sources pertaining to the Central Sudan. The subsequent chapters, however, are based primarily on archival sources, that is to say on the archives of the French administration.

The French administrative records can conveniently be divided into three categories. The first category, the records emanating from the local administrators, i.e. the *Commandants de cercle* and the *chefs de subdivision*, is to be found in the archives of Niger.[11] The second, the records of the former Government General of French West Africa and of the former Ministry of Overseas France (*France d'Outre-Mer*, before 1937 the Ministry of Colonies) are in the Dakar and Paris archives respectively, with some overlapping. (There is a near-complete microfilm set of the Dakar archives in Aix-en-Provence.) The third category, material emanating from the Governor and the various agencies which constituted the government of colonial Niger, can be found in nearly all the archives mentioned above.

Before about 1920 the administrative services in Niger were thinly spread. In fact, a fully fledged local administration, complete with administrative records, was only established some time during the 1920s. In addition, first, the Federal authorities were quite heavily involved in Nigerien affairs up to 1922, when Niger finally achieved the same status as the other colonies of French West Africa; secondly, during this period Niger was of considerable strategic importance; thirdly, the first decades of the colonial period witnessed a number of spectacular events that were of concern both to Federal and metropolitan authorities; fourthly, post-1940 material is not open to consultation in the archives of France and Senegal. All this explains why chapters 2 and 3 draw heavily upon material from the archives in Paris, Aix-en-Provence and Dakar, whereas subsequent chapters are based mostly – virtually exclusively in the last chapter – on material from the local archives in Niger.

There is relatively little in the way of complementary sources. The material from Northern Nigeria in the Public Record Office, London and in Rhodes House, Oxford, although it has provided me with useful supplementary information and also with many alternative viewpoints, is obviously of limited relevance to the study of the history of Niger. The anthropological material, indispensable though it is, is somewhat uneven. Furthermore, it is often difficult to fit into a strict chronological framework. As for eyewitness and travellers' accounts, they are few and far between.[12] Finally, there are the oral sources. I have conducted interviews with forty-seven Frenchmen who lived in Niger before 1960 mostly as administrators, and with thirty-two Nigeriens who were prominent in politics during the 1946–60 period. However, the main purpose of these interviews was not to gather facts or precise information, but to acquire a feel for the *ambiance* of the colonial period, a period which in terms of mentalities and attitudes is already very remote. To this end the interviews proved useful. Moreover, they turned out to be extremely revealing from one particular and rather unexpected viewpoint. They made me aware of the fact that the French administrators and the indigenous politicians (i.e. the *évolués*) after 1946 constituted in many ways a fraternity, a sort of old boys' network. The members of these two groups had, it seemed to me, more similarities than differences. Certainly I never came across anything in the way of an apologetic attitude, still less one of remorse, among the French. Nor did I find much in the way of bitterness among the Nigeriens. Perhaps a different picture might have emerged had I been able to interview more former members of the Sawaba, the party that held power briefly in 1957–8 before being outlawed in 1959. Those former Sawaba members who I did interview, six altogether but none of the top leaders, were certainly bitter, but this bitterness seemed to me to be directed primarily against their Nigerien opponents rather than against the French.

At the time I conducted my interviews (between 1969 and 1972) the political events of the 1957–64 period were still burning issues. Consequently many of my Nigerien informants insisted, before allowing themselves to be interviewed, that they should remain anonymous. I have abided by this although it has had the effect of diminishing greatly the value of these interviews as primary sources. They have been used, therefore, with considerable caution, and most of my references to oral sources are in chapter 6, covering the 1945–60 period, and are generally anecdotes and/or hearsay of a political or para-political character, biographical details concerning certain prominent personages, and other such 'inside' information. Naturally, only information corroborated by several informants has been taken into account. Thus the complementary sources are such that they do not really offer resistance to, or control of the main source.

On the strength of my very limited experience of the Northern Nigeria correspondence, I am inclined to argue that the French administrative records, although often less informative and less detailed, are far more reliable than the British. This has something to do, paradoxically, with the fact that the French administrators changed assignments more frequently and constituted a far less close-knit corporation than did their British counterparts. Indeed, the perpetual tug-of-war characteristic of the French colonial service (in particular between the military officers, whether turned administrators or not, and their civilian colleagues) meant that no matter what a *Commandant* overlooked, chose to disregard or failed to notice during his tour of duty, one of his successors was bound to discover it. In fact, many an official took a malicious pleasure in disclosing, even in denouncing, the goings on under his predecessors. This point can be taken one step further: anyone wishing to denounce French colonial rule in Africa does not have to look further than the French administrative records (at least those dating from about the mid-1920s onwards) for material to substantiate his case. Time and again during my archival research I came across administrative reports containing very harsh, even devastating criticism, not only of the handling of certain situations, or of certain aspects of colonial rule, but also in some cases of the very system itself. Of course the majority of the reports were somewhat less self-critical. It should also be remembered, when evaluating the French sources, that the aloofness so characteristic of the British officials in many parts of Africa was alien to the mentality of their French colleagues. In particular, the French often established close relations with the indigenous members of the opposite sex, many of them learning the local language through 'the pillow method'!

However, it is still true that the material at our disposal presents us with a problem, since it emanates in the main from an alien ruling group. But this is in my opinion simply the quintessential problem of all *detailed* historical reconstruction. Such detailed reconstruction requires a heavy reliance upon written sources, and written sources do in general reflect the point of view of the ruling classes[13] – classes which have often been, as in colonial Africa (whether of foreign origin or not), culturally distinct from the masses. Furthermore, it is only once the chronological framework and other such basic matters have been satisfactorily dealt with that it is possible in my opinion to conduct detailed studies on more limited subjects, studies based on written as well as on oral sources and making use of the full methodological panoply of the social sciences. I submit, therefore, that a general study such as this fulfils the useful purpose of presenting a framework within which monographs can be produced and debates conducted. Of course, one may argue that a general work covering some hundred years in the history of a country is feasible only to the extent that it can be based upon a series of prior minor studies. As yet only very few such studies exist in the field of Nigerien history.

Thus in the context of this book it is difficult to satisfy the current widely shared desire to give a voice to the silent and inarticulate, that is to write the history of the Nigerien masses.[14] Although I have occasionally tried to do just that – admittedly by often stretching the evidence rather too far – I wish to make it clear that my treatment of the perception of the colonized in particular is hypothetical and in some instances even speculative, and that it should be looked upon as such. The nature of the sources imposes severe limits on this endeavour which is therefore essentially exploratory.

We must conclude that the French administrative records, however biased and selective they may be, constitute the principal source for the reconstruction of the colonial history of Niger[15] (and of a host of other African countries). Nothing can alter this basic fact. Having conducted an exhaustive search of these records, I am satisfied that they do indeed provide a firm basis for such a reconstruction.

Anyone taking up a subject such as mine must first deal with the basics, that is the chronological framework. Given the neglect from which colonial history is suffering, this is a much more formidable and challenging task than is commonly realized, and of necessity it constitutes the primary task of this work. The branching out to more fundamental topics requires consideration of a number of necessarily interrelated themes. The first theme is the complexity and above all the ambiguity of the colonial period, a theme which provides in a sense the backcloth of this study. The second theme is a comparison between the various regions and ethnic groups of Niger. It is my contention that such a comparative approach significantly helps to highlight the main evolutionary trends of Nigerien history.

The third theme is the changing nature of colonial rule, together with the general impact of that type of rule and the interaction between the French and the Nigeriens; that is, the interaction between on the one hand an alien group which possessed the necessary means of destruction, i.e. the necessary technological superiority to impose itself as rulers, and on the other the indigenes. To what extent were the ruled influenced by the rulers and *vice versa*? To what extent did the rulers try to impose the mental, as well as military, political and economic mechanisms of subordination and exploitation, and how successful were they? The implication is that the colonial situation ought to be viewed as a situation in which the Europeans and the indigenes are united in one analytical field. A related theme here is that of resistance in all its various guises.

The fourth theme is change, especially in the social and economic spheres, whether leading to basic structural changes or not. Obviously, religious change also constitutes an important theme in the history of Niger. However, although this theme will be frequently touched upon in the following chapters, the evidence does not permit a detailed reconstruction of the religious history of Niger during the colonial period.

The fifth theme is a comparison between the pre- and post-1946 periods, together with the emergence and nature of politics after 1946. The underlying assumption here is that 1946 is probably the most significant date in the history of colonial Niger, if not in the history of French Africa generally.

1

Peoples and societies of Niger: early history to 1850

The pre-colonial history of Niger covers a wide spectrum of societies, ranging from so-called segmentary, 'acephalous' ones to what certain authors have qualified as 'states'. There were also, subsisting within certain 'states', small groups of people who had not only maintained their independence, but who were often ethnically distinct from the surrounding population. It may seem appropriate therefore to distinguish between territorial entities – such as the multi-ethnic but predominantly Hausa 'states' – and 'biological' entities. But although this distinction is useful in some cases, it is not in the final analysis very meaningful. In particular, it tends to blur two of the main characteristics of pre-colonial West African history generally; first, that people were always more important than land, and second, that even in the most articulated polities descent remained the core of a man's identity.

A frequent problem in presenting a survey of the pre-colonial history of a modern West African state is that the present-day frontiers are often artificial in that they cut across ethnic boundaries and/or pre-colonial political entities. This is not quite the case with Niger. True, it is an artificial unit, carved out by the French at the turn of the century. But this artificiality stems primarily from the fact that the French brought together within a single grouping peoples who had little experience of coexisting within the same borders – borders that do make sense, at least from an historical point of view. Consider the main section of the border with Nigeria; although it cuts across ethnic boundaries, it nevertheless approximates to the nineteenth-century demarcation line between the regions which were permanently incorporated into the Sokoto Caliphate after 1804, and the regions or entities which were able either to withstand the onslaught of the jihad, either to free themselves from Sokoto rule, or because they were too peripheral to attract the attention of the conquerors.[1] (Before 1804 present-day Nigerien Hausaland corresponded to the northern, outlying provinces of the main Hausa states.) Consider the northern, Algerian border which corresponds roughly to another 'traditional' demarcation line, that between the Kel Ahaggar and the Aïr Tuareg. Consider the Malian border which not only divides the territory of the eastern Iwillimidden or Kel Dinnik, a distinct confederacy since the eighteenth century,[2] from that of the western Iwillimidden or Kel Attaram of Mali, but which can also claim to separate the Songhay, heartland from the more marginal regions which at no time played a significant part in the history of the Songhay empire. Consider finally the border with Upper Volta which marks, very approximately, the westernmost extension of the Songhay people. In fact, only the Dahomean and Chadian borders, and the eastern quarter of the Nigerian border, can be considered to be completely artificial.

It should be clear by now that sedentary Niger at least is an assembly of borderlands, of regions that have always been peripheral to the main centres of this part of Africa. This would suggest, first, that the sedentary societies of this area were more loosely knit, less articulated, more 'anarchistic' than neighbouring societies, and second, that many regions within the frontiers of present-day Niger were probably thinly populated, with vast areas of wasteland or bush, at least until the nineteenth century.

The Tuareg and the North are quite another matter, however. It is important to remember that the main bulk of the Tuareg people live not in Algeria, but in Niger. They live mainly south and west of the Aïr massif, Aïr itself being very sparsely populated.[3] Here, and in Aïr – in contrast to the rest of Niger – many archaeological remains have been found, and also abundant evidence of agriculture. This region must therefore have been much more densely populated and also of greater importance in a relatively recent past; *and* the population then must have been composed of a majority of sedentary agriculturalists (who perhaps also practised animal husbandry). The present-day inhabitants of the oases of In Gall and Teguidda-n-tesemt, who are perhaps descendants of this ancient sedentary population, speak a language defined as a mixture of Songhay and Tamacheq, but which is closely related to archaic Songhay.[4] The agriculturalists of Aïr and of the regions west and south of Aïr were therefore like the Songhay, Nilo-Saharan speakers.[5]

It would be interesting to know when agriculture ceased here and why. Was it due to climatic deterioration or the depredations of the incoming Tuareg, or both? It would also be interesting to know what happened to the Nilo-Saharans. Did they migrate to the south where they were eventually absorbed by the Hausa? Or could it be that their nineteenth-century descendants constituted the main bulk of the numerically very important servile strata of Tuareg society?

In the south-eastern part of Niger (the region defined earlier as the Far East), in Kanuriland, the ruins of Garoumele near N'Guigmi and the proximity of the former Bornoan capital of Ngasargamu[6] suggest that this region also may have played a more prominent role earlier than it did at the time of the arrival of the French.

HAUSALAND AND KANURILAND

Early Hausa society[7]

As a starting-point for a rapid overview of Hausa history we may assume that 'ancient' Hausa society ('ancient' being best left undefined chronologically) was made up of small kindreds, which we may call 'sibs' or 'clans' (*dangi* in Hausa). Several such kindreds probably constituted small confederacies or communities under the diffuse and essentially ritual authority of the head of the most ancient kindred. This leader, or 'priest-chief', the intercessor between the local deities, the ancestors and the humans, was in reality no more than the *primus inter pares* of the kindred-heads. One could perhaps argue that the 'priest-chief', by virtue of his real or putative descent from the chief ancestor(s) and first settler(s), had been entrusted with the responsibility for maintaining the initial 'pact' (referred to in certain myths as a 'marriage') between the local deities (including the earth) and the ancestor(s). According to this sacred 'pact', the humans had been granted – in the case of agriculturalists – usufructuary rights to the land, provided they performed the necessary rituals and sacrifices prescribed by the effective 'owners of the land', i.e. the deities. This same logic also applied to fishermen, blacksmiths, hunters, salt-diggers etc. Each occupational craft, perhaps corresponding to one or several kindreds, had its own deities who were the proprietors of the water, the iron, the salt etc. There could thus be a number of 'priest-chiefs' within a given community, depending upon the number of occupational crafts represented.

Paraphrasing T. O. Ranger[8] one feels tempted to argue that much of the history of Hausaland can be seen in terms of the differing relationships between the custodians of indigenous traditions and beliefs and the incoming political authorities, producing a richly varied situation. It seems that the arrival of new groups often led to the establishment of what has been called a 'dual institutional structure' or a 'contrapuntal paramountcy'. Such a structure or paramountcy is defined (slightly incorrectly but nevertheless appropriately for our purpose) as one of power-sharing between the head of the incoming group (usually referred to as the first 'chief' or 'king') who appropriates the political power, and the priest-chiefs, who retain their ritual control, over the land in particular. Indeed, any aspiring ruler needed the consent or sanction of the custodians of the indigenous population (that is, in the last analysis, the local deities). This was because the position of these custodians was inalienable, in the sense that it had been sanctified and thus constituted the cornerstone in the system established by the original 'pact' between the deities and the humans. It must be remembered that we are dealing with a type of society in which religious beliefs are paramount, both in the sense that they permeate every aspect of individual and social life, and in the sense that changes have to be explained and legitimized in religious terms.[9]

In polities characterized by a 'dual institutional structure' or a 'contrapuntal paramountcy' the indigenous priest-chief was often entrusted with the responsibility of choosing and probably also of deposing the king, especially in times of failing harvests and military defeats, or if the king fell ill, grew old etc. – if, that is, his 'force' or 'luck' (*nasara k'arfi* or *arzika* in Hausa) declined, a token of the fact that he no longer had the favour of the deities.

How do some of the better-known Hausa myths and legends fit into this pattern? We could suggest that Queen Daura of the Bayajida legend[10] personified the institution of 'priest-chief', whereas Bayajida personified an incoming political authority. Then perhaps their 'marriage' referred in reality to a *modus vivendi* agreed upon between the intruders and the autochthones, leading in turn to the establishment of a 'contrapuntal paramountcy'. Another mythical figure in Hausa history is Barbushe, who by virtue of his descent from the local founding ancestor (Dala) 'owned' the cult connected with Dala hill at Kano. The *Kano Chronicle*'s[11] account of the early social fabric of Kano, which presents us with eleven clan-heads among whom Barbushe was no doubt paramount, would seem to imply that Barbushe too personified the institution of priest-chief.[12] If so, one is led to conjecture that the tale of the incoming Kutumbawa under their chief Bagauda who, still according to the *Kano Chronicle*, became the first *sarkin* Kano, referred to the establishment of a political authority and a dual institutional structure; but *not* a contrapuntal paramountcy. The expression 'contrapuntal paramountcy' should be applied exclusively to those cases where the king and the priest-chiefs worked within the same system for the same ends. This was certainly not so in Kano, where the relations between the newcomers and the indigenous population continued to be characterized by hostility and even confrontation, centring, not surprisingly, on religious issues. The claim set forward in the 'Song of Bagauda'[13] that Bagauda was the first settler in Kano is significant in this respect. It smacks very much of propaganda intended to erode the very foundation of the power-basis of the priest-chiefs, their ritual control over the land.

It may also be conjectured that the *durbi* or head of the Durbawa – the indigenous population of the region of Katsina – occupied a position very similar to that of Queen Daura or Barbushe,[14] as does the *saranuyia* or 'queen' of Lougou and the *baura* or chief of the village of Bagaji among the hausaphone Mawri of Arewa in present-day Western Niger.[15] The *saranuyia* and the *baura* are among the nine representatives of the indigenous population (called Gube or Gubawa) on the twelve-member 'state' council in charge of electing the ruler or *sarkin* Arewa from among the members of the lineages descended from the Bornoan intruders (i.e. the Mawri proper). These intruders, after their leader had according to legend married a daughter of the *baura*, probably established their political authority over this region some time during the seventeenth century.

The ancient social-religious fabric of the Hausa people survived, or is easily perceptible underneath later superimposed layers, in many parts of Hausaland, especially on the 'northern fringes' (present-day Nigerien Hausaland) and in other peripheral regions.[16] The people who have remained attached to this ancestral type of society and the corresponding religious beliefs are usually referred to as *anna* (or *azna*), 'owners-masters of the land', or *yan kasa*, literally 'children of the earth'.[17] They may be known locally as Durbawa (in Katsina), Magusawa (in Kano), Gubawa (in Arewa) and so on. In general they are classified as *talakawa* or 'ordinary' people, the poor people of the countryside, as opposed to the town-dwellers and the ruling elite (or *sarauta*).

The abortive Wangara 'revolution' of the fifteenth and sixteenth centuries

Different layers of society were, as noted above, superimposed on the ancient society, some at a very early date. But the real shake-up probably occurred some time during the fifteenth and sixteenth centuries. Before this came the influx of the Wangarawa, traders and clerics of Mande origin. It is not clear when the Wangarawa arrived in Hausaland, but a fair assumption is that their arrival antedates the second half of the fourteenth century. This assumption is based on indirect and rather tenuous evidence: the travel accounts of Ibn Battuta.[18] In A.D. 1353 Ibn Battuta visited the 'kingdom' of Takedda which held sway over the region west of the Aïr massif, including the oases of In Gall, Teguidda-n-tesemt and Azelik, among others. Ibn Battuta's account, corroborated by recent research,[19] makes it clear that Takedda possessed important copper mines.[20] The copper extracted there was apparently used as currency throughout the Sahel and the Sudan.[21] (Whether Takedda also exported salt is a matter of controversy).[22] Copper mining generated trade, and it seems from Ibn Battuta's account that Takedda was the hub of an important inter-regional network of trade-routes, linking Songhayland with Gobir in Hausaland, the Maghrib and even Egypt.[23] My contention here is that the Wangarawa, venturing east and south from communities already established in Songhayland,[24] arrived in Hausaland via the 'kingdom' of Takedda. This would explain why we find the Wangarawa already firmly entrenched in Hausaland by the middle of the fifteenth century. I have argued elsewhere[25] that these Wangarawa, familiar as they were with the more sophisticated and articulated polities further west, were responsible for establishing or encouraging the emergence of state-like institutional structures designed primarily to protect and promote their commercial interests, presumably because no one else had been able to do so. For example, in those polities, such as Kano and probably also Gobir, where the chiefs or kings were of alien extraction, the Wangarawa strongly backed these chiefs against the local priest-chiefs. As a consequence their influence became predominant. However, in those polities where only the institution of priest-chief existed, the Wangarawa tried to impose rulers of their own. This was probably the case in Katsina, where the first *sarkin* Katsina, Muhammed Korau (died 1493/4 or 1496/7)[26] – responsible according to the legend for having slain the incumbent *durbi*[27] – is reported to have been of the stock of the Wangarawa.[28] Everywhere these Wangarawa aimed at a full-scale religious-political revolution, to wreck the power-base of the indigenous priest-chiefs by imposing a universal religion, Islam. However, they do not appear to have been successful in the long run. Instead many of the rulers tempered their pro-Muslim zeal and tried to operate a rapprochement with the priest-chiefs. This led in several instances to the emergence of what looks very much like a dual institutional structure, and to the changing of the institution of kingship in the direction of the sacred kingship model. A case in point is Katsina where a later *durbi* was elevated to what was in reality the second highest position in the official hierarchy.[29] However, it probably also led to considerable strife not only between Muslims and pagans, but also within the Muslim community between partisans and adversaries of this policy of compromise. Furthermore, there developed a stark dichotomy between, on the one hand, a basically egalitarian, pagan and rural society, and on the other a Muslim, hierarchized, trade-oriented, urban and cosmopolitan society,[30] possibly also a slave-ridden society.[31] It is probable that the Hausa 'kings' never wielded much power outside the walls of their respective capitals or *birane*. This lack of internal cohesion may help to explain the many wars between the Hausa polities; why no single polity was never able to impose a permanent hegemony over Hausaland, although they all tried; and also why Borno was able to impose its nominal suzerainty over virtually the whole of Hausaland.[32]

The Torodbe-Fulani jihad and its consequences

The second major shake-up in Hausa history occurred after 1804 and is known as the Fulani jihad. It led to the establishment of the Sokoto Caliphate. The jihad was proclaimed by the famous Usuman dan Fodio, a member of the Qādiriyya brotherhood, and the local head of the Torodbe clerisy,[33] or Muslim clerical clan of professional teachers.[34] According to J. R. Willis it 'evolved out of that mass of rootless people who perceived in Islam a source of cultural identity'.[35] Thus, although the Torodbe had adopted the Fulani language, they belonged to no particular ethnic group. Perhaps it would be more correct, therefore, to refer to the Torodbe-Fulani jihad; a jihad which may be looked upon as the 'second round' in the struggle between the Muslims and the custodians of indigenous religious beliefs in the Central Sudan.

The Hausa polities, unable to present a common front, fell an easy prey to dan Fodio and his followers, many of whom were probably recruited from among the overtaxed and therefore disgruntled small Fulani cattle-herders.[36] Quite a few Tuareg also fought with dan Fodio.[37] But Borno resisted the onslaught. Furthermore, and although Konni and adjacent entities of the Centre had to pay tribute to the ruler (or *sarkin Musulmi*) of the Sokoto Caliphate,[38] none of the regions of present-day Niger were permanently incorporated into this new empire. In fact, one of the consequences of the Torodbe-Fulani jihad was to detach the northern outer 'fringes' from the rest of Hausaland. It could be argued, therefore, that the jihad constituted the starting-point of the history of Nigerien Hausaland proper.

The jihad triggered off sizeable migrations to the south and even more to the north. Those opposed to the new Torodbe-Fulani 'order', whether for political or religious reasons, fled the Hausa heartland. Among them were many members of the deposed pre-jihad dynasties of Katsina, Gobir, Kano and Zaria. The consequences were twofold. First, there was a considerable increase of the population of the northern fringes, which led in turn to a number of significant changes. In the Maradi–Tessaoua region,[39] for instance, the forest, which had previously covered the Maradi valley, was partially cleared and the area occupied by farmland considerably extended. Agriculture became the dominant economic activity and the population, which had hitherto lived in small scattered hamlets, was now grouped into fairly large and often fortified villages. Second, some of the princes who had been deposed by the Torodbe-Fulani founded a number of new polities, one in the south at Abuja where the *sarkin* Zazzau found refuge,[40] and two on the northern fringes. Around 1819 the *sarkin* Katsina-in-exile was able, thanks to the connivance of the local population, to establish himself as the independent ruler of the northern provinces of his former realm (i.e. the region of Maradi–Tessaoua).[41] It thus came about that the northern rump of Katsina was liberated from the Torodbe-Fulani and emerged as an independent entity, ruled by the legitimate *sarkin* Katsina, as opposed to the Torodbe-Fulani *sarki* in Katsina proper. The *durbi*, the paramount priest-chief of the pre-jihad Katsina kingdom who also settled down in Maradi, seems to have acquired a dominant position over the local priest-chiefs (although the head of the latter, the *maradi*, probably retained considerable power).[42]

Much the same happened some twenty years later a few kilometres further west. Here, at Tibiri, the *sarkin* Gobir-in-exile established the capital of his 'rump' state. As for the paramount priest-chief of the pre-jihad Gobir kingdom, the *sarkin* Anna, he acquired a position similar to that of the *durbi* in Maradi.[43]

Surprisingly, given their small size and limited resources, Maradi and Tibiri proved to be a very serious threat to the Torodbe-Fulani rulers of the Sokoto Caliphate. Indeed, these exiled loyalists of the north, these 'irreconcilables' or 'die-hards' as they have been called,[44] were able to launch an impressive number of raids deep into the Hausa heartland; which on several occasions were repelled only within a short distance of such important urban centres as Katsina and Sokoto. Even the resounding defeat inflicted upon the 'die-hards' at the battle of Bawakuke in 1835 was not enough to put an end to the state of permanent warfare. After a few years' lull, Maradi and Tibiri resumed their raiding activities, apparently on an even greater scale than before.[45]

The Bornoan sphere

Maradi and Tibiri were joined, especially after the middle of the nineteenth century, by an emerging Hausa polity east of Maradi: Damagaram, originally situated within the Bornoan sphere of influence. Damagaram's rise to the position of a medium-sized power of considerable importance in the Central Sudan will be investigated more fully in the next chapter. However, since the ascendancy of Damagaram is clearly linked with the decline of the Borno empire, a few comments concerning the history of the latter would seem appropriate at this stage.

In its sixteenth-century heyday Borno controlled roughly the eastern third of present-day Niger.[46] This area comprised in addition to the hausaphone province of what was to become Damagaram (and which we have included in the region defined as the East), the North-East – i.e. the domain of the Tubu nomads,[47] with the exception of the Kawar oases whose inhabitants are kanuriphone – and the Far East. The Far East, or Kanuriland, is in reality an area of considerable ethnic complexity. Even if we leave out the Arabs and the Daza (the southern 'cousins' of the Tubu) and concentrate on the Kanuri, it is noticeable that the term 'Kanuri' does not correspond to any homogeneous group. In fact, the literature refers to no less than seven ethnic groups: the Sugurti, the Kanembu, the Budduma of the Lake Chad islands,[48] the Dietko, the Mobeur, the Manga (probably the most numerous) and the Dagera.

The Far East is today a particularly desolate region, a no-man's land. This has not always been so. Before 1808 the Far East was probably one of the most important provinces of the Borno empire. Two factors may explain this: first, because of its situation on the edge of the desert, the Far East took an active part in what has been termed the 'desert-side economy'.[49] In particular, this region was the terminus for the important trans-Saharan trade route via Kawar and the string of oases between Kawar and the sedentary south.[50] Second, the Far East, as well as Kawar, possessed a considerable number of salt-producing sites. It is possible that Borno was the principal supplier of salt throughout the Central Sudan and the Sahara, and that the salt trade constituted one of the empire's main sources of revenue[51] (second in importance only to the slave trade?). However, some time during the nineteenth century the oases between the sedentary south and Kawar disappeared. It is not known whether ecological or human factors or both were to blame. It could be conjectured that Borno's hold over the trans-Saharan route via Kawar was tenuous due to the presence of Tuareg and especially Tubu nomads and raiders; and that the Great Drought of about 1738–56[52] – the prelude to the present 'dry' cycle which set in around 1800 – had a very adverse effect upon the might of Borno, first, by upsetting the delicate ecological balance characteristic of this region, and second, by unleashing the Tuareg nomads whose raids became increasingly frequent and devastating.[53] It is probable that these raids were not conducted exclusively to secure food for the impoverished people of the desert. Indeed, the raids of the Tuareg, by laying waste the Far East and thus contributing to the decline of Borno, had the effect of eliminating from the Central Sahara a power too prominent for the taste of the desert nomads. It had the additional effect of partially diverting trade from the old Fezzan–Kawar– Gazargamu route to two other routes, one further east,[54] the other further west and largely controlled by the Tuareg, i.e. the route between North Africa and Katsina in Hausaland via Agades and Tessaoua. This was by no means a new trade route, but its importance is likely to have increased considerably due to the decline of trade further east. Furthermore, these developments cut off communications between the salt-producing oases of Kawar and metropolitan Borno, leaving the people of Kawar with little choice but to acknowledge the suzerainty of the Tuareg. This in turn gave a new impetus to the inter-regional commercial circuit between Kawar and Hausaland.[55] Henceforth, huge caravans (the so-called *azalai*) journeyed back and forth between Kawar and Agades twice a year, while a multitude of smaller caravans travelled between Aïr and Hausaland, and the regions of Damergu and Damagaram in particular. The responsibility for provisioning a number of additional oases in millet and other foodstuffs goes a long way to explain the apparent change of emphasis in favour of agriculture perceptible in the economy of certain Tuareg confederacies during the eighteenth and nineteenth centuries.

As noted earlier, the Borno empire withstood the Torodbe-Fulani onslaught, but at a price. It was only the remarkable statesmanship of Muhammad al-Kānemī, the cleric, that saved the day for the Bornoans. After al-Kānemī's death, the strife between his descendants and the princes of the legitimate Saifawa dynasty, together with the wars against Borno's eastern neighbours, contributed to undermine further an already compromised situation.[56]

Further west, the position of Katsina as the main southern terminus of the trans-Saharan trade was soon to be challenged by Kano. Of the component emirates of the Sokoto Caliphate, Katsina had suffered the most from the raids of the northern 'die-hards'. The chronic state of warfare proved detrimental to trade, inducing the foreign (i.e. North African) merchants to move to Kano, which took over Katsina's position as the principal emporium of the Central Sudan.[57] But Kano is situated much further south than Katsina, and so there was a need for a relay station or halting place somewhere closer to the edge of the desert. This is the function that Zinder, the capital of Damagaram, was able to perform and to monopolize. Thus Zinder emerged as a 'new [local] centre for the collection and distribution of the natural products of the Sudan'.[58] These 'natural products' included a considerable number of slaves. The paradox, then, is that although Damagaram often sided with Maradi and Gobir–Tibiri, it benefited from the state of warfare generated by the hostility between these two polities and the Torodbe-Fulani emirates.

THE TUAREG, THE NORTH AND THE CENTRE

Tuareg society

The history of the sedentary south clearly cannot be treated in isolation from that of the north and the Tuareg. Indeed, the Hausa, the Kanuri and the

Tuareg interacted, as has already been demonstrated, within a larger composite society and economy. According to P. Lovejoy and S. Baier,[59] Tuareg society, constructed like a pyramid with nobles on top and various levels of dependents and servile groups below, was dominated by a few aristocratic leaders who were in effect like managers of large firms. These managers invested in such diverse activities as animal husbandry, trade, agriculture and also in raiding (especially when, as often happened, no power in the sedentary south was strong enough to hold them at bay). This high diversification of the Tuareg economy was a necessity, for the Tuareg – 'bred to disaster' – live in a hostile natural environment and cannot afford to rely upon one economic activity alone. Diversity is their strategy for survival.[60]

The Tuareg define themselves as the Kel Tamacheq, those who speak the Tamacheq language.[61] Although their social structure varies from region to region, the following general remarks may be offered. On the top of the pyramid we find the veiled, often fair-skinned nobles or *imajeghen* (sing. *amajegh*) – nearly always nomads. These *imajeghen* have always been few in number. But they were the 'tiny inner core' around which the Tuareg 'people' have been constituted. The *imajeghen* are grouped into apparently impervious kindreds often called 'tribes'. Each of these 'tribes' (*tawchitt*), under the authority of an *ar'holla*, has attached to it one or several vassal 'tribes' made up either of *ineslemen* ('those of Islam', i.e. the Muslim clerics) or of *imghad*.[62] The latter may, in some cases at least, have originally been small stock-breeders and raisers who were subsequently conquered and reduced to the status of vassals by the incoming and camel-riding *imajeghen*. Some *imghad* may also have been former *imajeghen* who were defeated in war and taken prisoner. The relations between noble and vassal 'tribes' have been described as essentially corporate.[63]

In the lower social categories the picture is not altogether clear.[64] However, if we leave aside the *enaden* or artisans, the most useful distinction seems to be between the *iklan* and the *ighawellan* (which includes the *iklan-n-egef* of the Kel Dinnik and the *iderfan*). The former, the *captifs de case* or domestic slaves, were regarded as personal property nearly on the same level as cattle. The latter, referred to as 'freed slaves', were quite another matter. In charge of the herds, and especially in charge of the farming estates the Tuareg had established in the south, the *ighawellan* often constituted semi-autonomous communities of their own. These communities 'provided a safety valve for the nomads in times of scarcity',[65] for instance during drought and famine. There are several points to note: first, that both slaves and 'freed slaves' are in most cases more markedly negroid than the other Tuareg; second, that the *ighawellan* living in the south are in the process of being assimilated by the Hausa and the Zerma/Songhay; third, that both slaves and 'freed slaves' are often referred to as *bugaje* (sing. *buzu*), a Hausa term, or *bella*, the corresponding Zerma term; and finally, that the proportion of slaves and 'freed slaves' increases from north to south (while that of the *imghad* decreases), reaching 70 to 90 per cent among the Kel Gress and the Tuareg of Imanan.

Tuareg 'tribes' are usually grouped into larger confederacies which vary considerably in size. The most important numerically since the nineteenth century have been the Kel Owi, the Kel Gress and the Kel Dinnik. Mention should be made, among the smaller confederacies, of the Kel Fadei and the Kel Ferouane in particular; also of the Kel Attaram of Mali and the Kel Ahaggar and Taitoq of Southern Algeria. One of the *ar'holla* acts as head of each confederacy. The title varies, but the most commonly used are *amenukal*, *tambari* and/or *ttebel* (the title of *anastafidet* applies exclusively to the head of the Kel Owi).[66] *Tambari* and *ttebel* are not only titles but also the generic terms for 'drum', the insignia of the chief.

Few if any of these chiefs wield any significant power. Matters of importance are in fact decided by the *ameni* or assembly of all 'free' men (i.e. the *imajeghen*?). But the extent to which the decisions of these assemblies were respected is very much open to debate.

Main trends in Tuareg history

Tuareg history is partially that of a continuous migration southwards. The same scenario has apparently been repeated time and again: a new group or confederacy arrives and pushes already established groups out of the Central Sahara and south towards the Sudan. In the fourteenth century the now nearly extinct Massufa and Igdalen were already the masters of the famous kingdom of Takedda west of Aïr.[67] As has already been noted, Takedda's might was based on the export of copper and on the kingdom's position at the intersection of a number of important trade routes. Takedda also controlled the region of In Gall, vitally important to the Tuareg. Indeed, most nomads converge with their animals towards In Gall once a year for the indispensable *cure salée*, or *tanekert* in Tamacheq.[68] Agriculture may also still have been an important economic activity at the time of the kingdom of Takedda.

It is not clear why, how and when the kingdom of Takedda disappeared. Nor is it possible as yet to tell how that very strange institution known as the sultanate of Agades fits into the overall picture.[69] Perhaps the copper mines were worked out, or the climate changed, or perhaps we should seek an explanation in the shift of trade-routes which occurred during the fifteenth and sixteenth centuries. Briefly, the trade-route between the Niger river valley and Takedda probably declined, especially after the collapse of the Songhay empire in 1591. At the same time a direct route was established from the Maghrib to Hausaland via Agades, thus bypassing Takedda. It should be noted, furthermore, that the Tuareg confederacies associated with the foundation of the sultanate of Agades (confederacies of which only relics survive today) were distinct from those which controlled the kingdom of Takedda.[70] This would seem to imply some sort of rivalry or struggle between various Tuareg groups for the control of trade.[71] Whatever the case, the following characteristics of the sultanate should be noted: first, the sultan, in his capacity as *amīr al-mu'minīn* or 'commander of the faithful', is the spiritual leader or head of the Tuareg,[72] a position of little meaning since, with the exception of the *ineslemen*, most Tuareg have always been rather lukewarm Muslims at best.[73] Second, the sultan has not only been described as a 'slave-king' but also as a 'non-Tuareg',[74] and as a 'fantoche sans prestige, ni autorité'.[75] These assertions are based upon the fact that only sons of one of the sultan's black concubines can succeed to the throne.[76] Third, although the sultan's writ was nominal among the nomads, he has always been considered, in some degree, the effective suzerain of the sedentary population of Agades and the other desert oases. Fourth, the sultanate was clearly linked with trade from which the sultan derived a handsome income. This is in a sense symbolized by the title of his principal minister, the *sarkin turawa*, a Hausa title meaning literally 'chief of the foreigners', i.e. the North African traders. Fifth, during the first half of the nineteenth century the dynasty of the sultans settled down at Doguerawa in western Gobir. Since then, only the sultans and his closest relatives have resided in Agades.[77]

Given these characteristics, one may speculate that the establishment of the sultanate of Agades had something to do with the need for a 'power' capable of maintaining a minimum of order in the oases and of regulating trade, perhaps also of arbitrating in conflicts between the confederacies. In other words, an administrative infrastructure was needed which, although rudimentary, nevertheless took care of certain functions that were vital to the Tuareg economy; but it had to be sufficiently weak not to represent a threat to the independence of the confederacies and the 'tribes'. Hence the strange rule of succession mentioned above, probably designed to make certain that none of the rival groups would be able to gain control of the sultanate, through for instance an astute matrimonial policy.[78]

Tuareg and Hausa in the Centre

It was probably during the seventeenth century that a group of Tuareg from Aïr, known as the Lissawan and commanded according to tradition by a certain Agabba, a son of the sultan of Agades, conquered the relatively fertile hilly region of Adar, the northernmost part of Hausaland. The indigenous population, the Adarawa, were pagans (or *anna*), and their society was very similar to the ancestral Hausa society described above.[79] The Tuareg established their capital at Illela in western Adar, which became the seat of the *sarkin* Adar, always chosen from among the descendants of Agabba. The subsequent evolution of Adar seems to have been unique, in the sense that the *sarkin* Adar, who remained the nominal vassal of the sultan of Agades, was more and more identified with the autochthonous, animistic population, whereas real power passed to one of his three (Lissawan) governors, the *amatazza* of Keita.

The Kel Gress, masters of Aïr during at least the first half of the eighteenth century, seem to have been slowly pushed out by a new incoming confederacy, that of the Kel Owi (or Kel Ewey), during the second half of the century. As a consequence, the Kel Gress began to migrate to the south-west and to infiltrate the region of Gobir Tudu to the south-east of Adar, around the 1770s.[80] Gobir Tudu, situated immediately to the south-east of Adar, was then an outlying province of the pre-jihad polity of Gobir. However, Tuareg other than those from Aïr have been important in the history of the Centre. These are the Tuareg of the north-west, most of whom seem to have sojourned at some stage in or around the massif known as Adrar of the Iforas in present-day northern Mali and southern Algeria. The history of the Tuareg of the north-west is characterized by the same slow migration southwards (in their case to the south-east, towards Azawak and Adar) as that of their eastern 'brethren'. On the eve of the Torodbe-Fulani jihad, two confederacies were in competition in the region of Azawak north of Adar, the Tamesguidda and the newly arrived Kel Dinnik.[81] Many of the Kel Dinnik *ineslemen* appear to have been profoundly influenced by the jihad of dan Fodio. According to H. T. Norris, they saw in the concept of the jihad a class struggle whereby they, the *ineslemen*, could assert their total independence from the *imajeghen* and establish a new order. The matter came to a head in 1809 when their leader, the famous Muhammad al-Jaylānī, declared a jihad of his own.[82] What followed was a many-sided struggle for the control of Adar, Gobir Tudu and adjacent regions, involving not only the Kel Dinnik, the Tamesguidda, the Lissawan, the Adarawa and the Kel Gress, but also the 'rump' states of Tibiri and Maradi and the Sokoto Caliphate. The end result was that the Tamesguidda, the Lissawan, the Adarawa, Tibiri and Maradi were all defeated, leaving the Kel Gress (who had sought the alliance of Sokoto against Tibiri) in control of Gobir Tudu, and the Kel Dinnik (among whom the *ineslemen* apparently could not liberate themselves entirely from the *imajeghen*) in control of Azawak and most of Adar. The latter region was ruled through a puppet *sarkin* Adar established at Tahoua. However, the competition between the Kel Gress and the Kel Dinnik soon degenerated into intermittent warfare.[83]

The Kel Dinnik never settled down in Adar. Furthermore, their domination was destructive in that they contented themselves simply with exacting as high a tribute as possible from the various local communities, whether the now sedentary Lissawan or the indigenous Adarawa. By contrast the Kel Gress turned Gobir Tudu into a prosperous region which attracted immigrants from far away, setting into motion a wholesale internal migration. Wide tracts of land, hitherto wilderness, over which the *imajeghen* had acquired rights of ownership, were cleared and brought under cultivation by the 'freed slaves' or *ighawellan* and other clients. As for the few scattered Hausa communities already in the region, they benefited, it seems, from a fairly lenient and indirect system of rule whereby the *imajeghen* governed through the Hausa village chiefs. Those villages which had fought alongside the Kel Gress enjoyed the privileged position of allies. A considerable portion of the produce of both the *ighawellan* and the Hausa communities

31

was channelled in the form of land rent and tribute into the hands of the *imajeghen*, who were thus able to attain an increasingly predominant position in the desert-side economy, supplying the oasis-dwellers (especially those of Kawar), the nomads of the north, and perhaps some of the urban centres of the southern areas, with food-stuffs and other commodities. The caravans of the Kel Gress became a familiar sight throughout the Central Sudan and Sahara in the nineteenth century. Not surprisingly, this prosperity led to an intense competition among the *imajeghen* as to who could attract the greatest number of tributaries and clients.

The Kel Owi and Damergu

The Kel Owi, having pushed the Kel Gress from the north, came under pressure themselves from the Kel Ferouane and especially the Kel Fadei. The sphere of influence of the Kel Owi shifted southwards and came to include the relatively fertile region of Damergu through which passed the new trade-route from Agades to Zinder.[84] In Damergu the Kel Owi pursued a policy very similar to that of the Kel Gress in Gobir Tudu, the only notable difference being that whereas the Kel Gress *imajeghen* relied heavily upon the *ighawellan*, the Kel Owi favoured and encouraged the establishment of communities of 'free' agriculturalists, most of whom appear to have been kanuriphone refugees from the Far East. These agriculturalists, benefiting from the security provided by the Kel Owi, turned Damergu into a region with a considerable grain surplus. This security was challenged now and then by more raid-oriented tribes such as the Imuzurag and the Iskazkazen, both theoretically members of the Kel Owi confederacy.

Thus the Kel Owi emerged as the main rivals of the Kel Gress in the economic sphere. Both economies underwent a change of emphasis in favour of agriculture, probably during the eighteenth and nineteenth centuries. It is possible that the conquest and colonization of Damergu, Gobir Tudu and Adar became a necessity as agriculture became impracticable further north. This is of course pure speculation, but the possibility that the Great Drought of the mid eighteenth century dealt the final blow to agriculture in the north, thus forcing the Tuareg to seek to gain control over regions situated further south, should not be overlooked. Is it mere coincidence that the first raids of the Kel Dinnik against Adar and the first incursions of the Kel Gress into Gobir Tudu correspond with the period of the Great Drought?

The possibility that the Napoleonic Wars in Europe (and also in Egypt) strongly influenced the course of events in the Central Sudan has never been investigated. Since trade in the Mediterranean came to a standstill as a result of the wars, they presumably had a detrimental effect upon trans-Saharan trade also. If so, the Central Sudan and Sahara would have experienced a severe economic depression around 1800. Such a depression coming hard on the heals of the Great Drought might be among the causes of the decline of Borno and the success of the Torodbe-Fulani jihad.

THE WEST

General characteristics

The main function historically of the West, or at least of the middle Niger river valley, seems to have been as a transit zone. It has witnessed a succession of both large- and small-scale migrations throughout its history, along with a constant ethnic shaping and reshaping as groups merged or crystallized (especially when moving out of the area) or split up; the West can be seen as both ethnic cradle and graveyard.[85] Although usually described as the country of the Zerma/Songhay, it should nevertheless be noted that many people of the West look upon themselves not as Zerma or Songhay, but as Gabda, Kado, Dendi, Sorko, Wogo, Gurmey, Gube, Tienga, Kurfey, Kalle, Sabiri or Toulmey.[86] The question as to whether we are dealing here with 'proto-groups', i.e. with the component parts of the ethnic group we call today the Zerma/Songhay, with more or less assimilated residual groups of the original ancient population of the West, or with Zerma/Songhay who have broken away from the main group and developed certain particular traits, or a combination of all three alternatives, is beyond the scope of the present study. What should be noted here is, first, that we need two words to designate the principal ethnic group of the West; are they *two* ethnic groups, or two groups slowly merging, or one group splitting up into two? Secondly, those sub-groups such as the Gabda and Gube that have been able to preserve to a certain extent their cultural (and ethnic?) particularity are to be found on what we may call the 'outer fringes' of the West, i.e. the regions furthest away from the river valley. Whether this implies that these groups were pushed out from the centre, or whether they were able to preserve their separate identity precisely because they lived on the 'outer fringes', or some combination of both, is difficult to say.

In the southern half of the West the Gurmantche, the Tienga, the Sabiri, the Gabda, the Kalle and the Gube can probably be classified as indigenous. In the northern half, the most ancient element of the population seems to have been the Kado, a name which applies today to the pagan Songhay, just as the name *anna* applies to the pagan Hausa. Among the Kado there was originally a clear distinction between the peasants (Gabiri) or 'masters of the soil', and the fishermen (Sorko) or 'masters of the river/water', to whom we might perhaps add the hunters (Gow), 'masters of the bush'. As for the Zerma, their cradle seems to have been the arid plateau of Zermaganda. The politico-religious institutions of these groups were generally very similar to those of ancient Hausaland. Kindred groups lived in hamlets and small villages under the diffuse authority of priest-chiefs. The most common titles seem to have been *labukoy*, 'chief of the land', among the farmers, and *hikoy*, or 'chief of the water', among the fishermen. As among the *anna*, the position of the priest-chief depended upon his or her 'luck', 'force', or 'chance', *bon-kaney*; that is to say his or her ability to please the deities upon whom the welfare of the community depended. For, as in ancient Hausaland, the

33

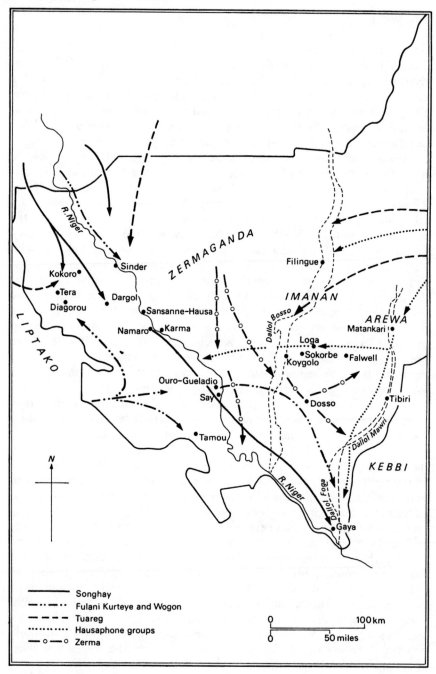

5 Migrations in Western Niger.

deities were considered to be the ultimate 'owners' of the soil, the water, the bush etc. and had conceded only usufructuary rights to the humans.[87]

The demise of the Songhay empire and its consequences

Before 1591 the West was a peripheral and unimportant province of the Songhay empire. However, after the Moroccan invasion the northern half of the West came into its own in the sense that it served as a zone of refuge for all, and especially the members of the Songhay aristocracy, who were determined to carry on the resistance against the Moroccan invaders and perhaps too against Islam. There was a 'rump' Songhay empire which the Moroccans were never able to conquer.

But once the Moroccan danger had faded away, the Songhay noblemen – the Maiga, the descendants of the *askiyas* – were unable to maintain a united front. The 'rump' empire split into a number of small unities: Kokoro, Karma, Ayoro, Gorouol, Namaro, Tera and above all, Dargol, paramount among the so-called 'free' Songhay successor-states.[88]

The massive influx of members of the former ruling class of the Songhay heartland naturally had a profound impact upon the local social fabric. In the first place it led in several instances to the establishment of an institutional structure closely resembling that defined earlier as the 'dual institutional structure' and/or 'contrapuntal paramountcy'. Second, and more important, it contributed to the emergence of a new ideal, that of the noble warrior-lord who held manual work in contempt and whose status and position in society was determined by the number of cattle, slaves and other dependents he possessed. The result was a hierarchical and aristocratic society characterized by a clear-cut distinction between noblemen (*koy-ize*), free men (*boro-kini, boran*) and non-free (*horso, cire-banya*). The non-free probably made up about two-thirds of the population on the eve of the colonial conquest.[89]

Another group of people from the Songhay heartland also led by descendants of the *askiyas*, the Dendi, migrated much further south and settled in the region of Gaya where they subjugated and partially assimilated the indigenous Tienga. The Tienga as a separate group survived in the cantons of Yelou and Bania and especially in the *dallol* Fogha where they controlled the extraction of salt.[90]

Other regions of the West also witnessed migrations, often on a large scale during the seventeenth and eighteenth centuries. The Zerma began to disperse from their semi-arid homeland in the north-east, pouring down towards the river, and especially into the *dallol* Bosso, and then further south-east on to the Djigui (or Dosso) plateau.[91] In conformity with a pattern familiar by now, the *sandi* or priest-chief of the indigenous population (the Sabiri) became the premier dignitary of the court of the *zermakoy* of Dosso, without whose approval no new *zermakoy* could be installed.[92] Much the same happened, as noted earlier, in the *dallol* Mawri further east as a consequence of the encounter between the proto-Mawri and the indigenous, hausaphone Gube (or Gubawa). The Gube proper survived as an ethnic group, although adopting, curiously enough, the language of the Zerma, in the northern part of the Djigui plateau around Loga. Here they became the neighbours of the Gadba of Falwell. Later on some Mawri groups, which also eventually became zermaphone, settled down at Sokorbe, immediately to the south of Loga.[93]

The coming of the Fulani and the Tuareg

The slow infiltration of Fulani herdsmen into the Gueladio–Tamou–Lamor-de–Say region, gained momentum during the eighteenth century. From this region, some Fulani moved northwards in the early years of the nineteenth century, settling down in Diagorou, south of Tera. From Diagorou, they made incursions into the Songhay states, Dargol, and especially Tera, which was raided for the first time in 1838. Another and much more important group moved across the river, and established itself in the middle *dallol* Bosso, where the town of Tamkalle was founded. Finally, a small group of Fulani invaded the *dallol* Fogha, where they subdued the indigenous Tienga.[94] All the Fulani of the West seem to have become sedentary fairly quickly.

From the north two mixed groups, but of predominantly Fulani stock, poured down the river valley during the first half of the nineteenth century. The Kurtey settled down in the Sinder region around 1830, followed some ten to twenty years later by the Wogo, subduing the indigenous Songhay/-Kado. Their frequent slave-raids earned them the reputation of 'men thieves'.[95]

The Songhay states of the North, increasingly harassed by the Fulani emirate of Liptako in the West (established about 1810), by the Fulani of Diagorou and later by the Kurtey, apparently sought the protection of the Tenguereguedech, the Logomaten and other Tuareg of the Niger bend. The Tuareg protection seems to have been effective, especially against the Fulani of Liptako. But the Songhay realized too late that the Tuareg were dangerous allies aiming for a predominant position. Indeed, with the exception of Dargol, most of the northern third of the West seems to have been reduced to a state of vassaldom.[96]

Songhayland was, however, not the only region of the West which witnessed an influx of Tuareg in the nineteenth century. Events in and around Adar caused a certain number of Lissawan, Kel Dinnik and other Tuareg to establish themselves in the Tagazar and, especially, Imanan regions of the upper *dallol* Bosso. In Imanan at least the Tuareg adopted a policy reminiscent of that of the Kel Gress in Gobir Tudu and the Kel Owi in Damergu.[97] They had been preceded by the hausaphone Sudie of Kurfey, also originally from Adar, who now found themselves 'squeezed' between two groups of Tuareg.[98] These successive migrations into the *dallol* Bosso of the Fulani, the Sudie and the Tuareg had the effect of pushing out many of the earlier inhabitants, the Kalle in particular, and of splitting the Zerma in two, the Zerma of Dosso being more or less cut off from their kinsmen of the Zermaganda.

In the southern two-thirds of the West in the first half of the nineteenth century, we see the attempt by the Fulani to establish their hegemony over that region illustrated by the careers of two famous clerics, Mahaman Diobbo and his companion Boubacar Loukoudji. Diobbo was a native of Jenne, a town he is reported to have left for Gao around 1810, before settling finally in Say.[99] Because of his reputation as a learned and peaceful man, Diobbo soon gained an ascendancy over the Fulani in the Say region, who recognized him as their overlord. Say became not only a seat of learning but also very soon an important economic centre, through which east–west trade and especially trade along the river was channelled (thanks to apparently close relations between the Fulani of Say and the Sorko).[100] By the time Diobbo died (*c*. 1840) he was by far the single most important chief of the West, and could claim allegiance from a host of lesser chiefs of the right bank and the river valley, Fulani as well as Zerma and Songhay. Diobbo in turn considered himself to be a vassal of the *sarkin Musulmi* in Sokoto. But Diobbo's rise to political prominence in the West raises many questions which still remain unresolved. It is not clear how he was able to achieve his dominant position (bearing in mind that he never made use of force). Nor has it been explained why many Zerma and Songhay chiefs, some of them animists, should so willingly agree to pay tribute to Say.

Boubacar Loukoudji, Diobbo's companion and the leader of the Fulani who settled down in the middle *dallol* Bosso, represented a more militant brand of Islam. Boubacar and especially his son, Dambo (who took the title of *lamido*), established close ties with the Sokoto Caliphate, specifically with the Emir of Gwandu. The Zerma, the Mawri, the Dendi and also the Kebbawa (of present-day Northern Nigeria) were caught in the middle and by about 1830–5 the first three had been reduced to a state of vassaldom, compelled to pay, we are told, exorbitant tributes.[101]

CONCLUSION

There are, as has been noted, many similarities between the early socio-politico-religious fabric of the Hausa and of the Zerma/Songhay. This is not as surprising as it looks at first glance, since such a fabric may well be typical of early West Africa in general.

Both the West and what became Nigerien Hausaland came into prominence as zones of refuge, but at very different dates: the West after the Moroccan conquest of the Songhay empire in 1591, Hausaland after the Torodbe-Fulani jihad of 1804. In both cases the refugees were not only people who had lost out in the political and military struggle of their respective heartlands, but also people who were not prepared to accept the religion of the new rulers, Islam. It could perhaps be argued, therefore, that both regions became bastions of traditionalism in the face of alien conquerors attempting to impose an alien religion.

The restructuring of Zerma/Songhay society after 1591 does not seem in the long run to have had many beneficial effects. Thus, although the people of the West were able to withstand the Moroccans, later they fell a relatively easy prey to new incoming (and predominantly Muslim) groups. By the 1850s at the latest, virtually the whole of the West had been subdued by, or was paying tribute to, the Tuareg and the Fulani, and also a foreign power, the Gwandu emirate of the Sokoto Caliphate. In Hausaland, on the other hand, the influx of refugees from the south instilled into the local society a dynamism which was, surprisingly, to turn these outer fringes into formidable opponents of the Sokoto Caliphate.

The Tuareg role in the history of the Central Sudan is ambiguous. Certainly, the Tuareg were, especially in the West and the Centre, quick to impose their domination over communities of sedentary agriculturalists whenever the opportunity presented itself. In many instances new land was cleared and the area under cultivation extended as a result of Tuareg endeavour. Perhaps the most characteristic development in Tuareg history after about 1700 is the growing intermixture with the sedentary population of the south together with the increasing involvement in trade and especially agriculture.

In the Far East the slow decline of the Borno empire favoured the emergence of a number of relatively new entities. The most important of these was Damagaram, which soon joined Maradi and Gobir/Tibiri in their struggle against the Sokoto Caliphate.

2

The revolutionary years, 1850–1908

By the mid nineteenth century, Tuareg domination in the northern third of the West seems to have been relatively complete. Among the Songhay states only Dargol and Anzourou were able to maintain a somewhat shaky and at times fictitious independence.[1] The river valley, however, looked increasingly like a political jigsaw. The Kurtey and the Wogo, although nominally suzerain, were themselves the nominal vassals of the *alfaize* of Say, and effective overlordship had in fact passed to the Tuareg.[2] In the southern two-thirds (with the exception of Zermaganda and the upper *dallol* Bosso) the Fulani had established their hegemony, whether the pacific and nominal hegemony of the *alfaize* of Say, or the more militant and oppressive brand represented by the *lamido* of Tamkalle (in the *dallol* Bosso) and his overlord, the Emir of Gwandu.

Tuareg rule over the Songhay is reputed to have been harsh,[3] but their rule of the river valley down to Karma relatively easy-going (*débonnaire*).[4] This rather lenient Tuareg domination over the river valley, strong enough to guarantee peace, together with the increasing insecurity and instability further south, probably explains why trade was apparently diverted from Say to Sinder and especially to Sansanne-Hausa during the second half of the century. Sansanne-Hausa emerged as by far the most important market of the West, and also as the main link between Hausaland and the regions within the Niger bend. Figures dating from 1898–9 suggest that the volume of trade passing through Sansanne-Hausa was two and a half times that passing through Say.[5]

It can be deduced from this that although the *alfaize* of Say remained the nominal overlord over wide regions of the West, his position and power declined sharply during the second half of the century. Effective power on the right bank had passed to the *lamido* of Ouro-Gueladio, another Fulani chief.[6] Ouro-Gueladio was a new polity named after its founder Gueladio, the famous Masina *ardo* who, after having assisted *shehu* Ahmad in establishing the Fulani Caliphate of Hamdallahi in 1818, revolted some six

39

years later and was eventually driven out.[7] It seems, however, that the position of the *lamido* of Ouro-Gueladio was successfully challenged by yet another Fulani chief, the *diaoru* of Tamou, in the very last years of the pre-colonial era.[8]

The end of Fulani rule

In the south-eastern part of the West in the second half of the century, there were frequent attempts by the Zerma, the Mawri and the Dendi to free themselves from Fulani rule.[9] The third and successful revolt erupted in 1856. The initiative came from a certain Karfe, a Mawri war-chief of one of the petty chiefdoms of the lower *dallol* Mawri.[10] Karfe was soon joined by Dauda and by the *kanta* of Kebbi, who managed to escape from Sokoto, where he had lived in captivity since his overthrow by the Torodbe-Fulani, to join the forces of the rebels and to assume command. The war dragged on for ten years and came to an end only in 1866 when Kebbi (in present-day Northern Nigeria) and Gwandu agreed upon a treaty (the *Lafiya Toga*) which recognized the near-complete victory of the rebels. The Fulani were expelled from the middle *dallol* Bosso, and the Zerma, the Mawri, the Dendi, and the Kebbawa recovered their independence. Karfe, as a token of the *kanta*'s indebtedness to him, was made *samna* or war-chief of Kebbi. He settled down in Tibiri in the lower *dallol* Mawri, where he became for all practical purposes the head of an independent political entity.[11] But the price the rebels had to pay for their victory was a heavy one, according to Jean Rouch, who argues that the whole region was ruined.[12]

The common front against the Fulani and the victory of 1866 might logically be seen as the first steps towards a unification of the south-east and the establishment of a political entity of some magnitude, comprising for instance Dosso, Kebbi, Arewa, Dendi and adjacent regions. But such an entity never materialized, possibly because the energy of the rebels had been spent fighting the Fulani and/or, as has been argued, because 'les forces en présence s'équilibrèrent'.[13] It is nevertheless possible to look upon the various entities of the south-east as constituting after 1866 a loose 'confederacy'. When Tuareg raids against the exposed Gube of Loga, Gabda of Falwell and Sudie of Filingue became increasingly frequent towards the end of the century, the 'confederacy' came to their rescue. It was the war-chief (*wonkoy*) of Dosso, Issa Korombe (established at Koygolo on the left 'bank' of the *dallol* Bosso), who led the 'war' against the Tuareg. He had little success. Instead, the continuous raids and counter-raids exhausted, if possible, the south-east even more.[14]

Political, social and religious evolution

The many wars of the nineteenth century against the Fulani and the Tuareg seem to have led first – and rather surprisingly – to the (partial?) islamization of the Zerma,[15] secondly to a general, albeit moderate, strengthening of already existing and previously embryonic political institutions, and finally to migrations westwards. Many of the Zerma who fled their ravaged homeland to seek fortune elsewhere, adopted – strange as it might seem – a particularly militant brand of Islam, which served as justification for their raids against various pagan or superficially islamized groups. These Zerma were the antithesis of peaceful exiles in search of a shelter; they were power-hungry and rapacious warriors, who served as mercenaries wherever their services were needed, turning against their masters whenever the opportunity arose. The Zerma warriors seem to have been particularly active in what is today northern Ghana and the south of the Upper Volta, where they earned themselves the nickname of 'cavaliers of the Vulture'. In Gurunsi they seized power altogether and are said to have completely exploited the local population.[16]

The many wars of the nineteenth century contributed, as we have seen, to the strengthening of certain pre-existing political institutions, and in particular benefited the Fulani *lamido* of Ouro-Guéladio, the *zermakoy* of Dosso, the *samna* of Tibiri and the *sarkin* Arewa of Matankari. In the case of the *zermakoy* of Dosso, little more than a village-chief during the first half of the century, there is some evidence to suggest that he gained a certain ascendancy over the other communities of the Djigui plateau.[17] It is also possible that he emerged as the leader of a loose coalition of the *gabdakoy* of Falwell, the *gubekoy* of Loga and perhaps also the *mawrikoy* of Sokorbe. (However, none of these chiefs ever paid tribute to Dosso.) But although Dosso represented 'le seul point organisé' in this part of the West, as the French found out,[18] the *zermakoy* was at the end of the century still no more than an insignificant rustic princeling.[19] This was true of *all* the chiefs of the West. Indeed, the process of crystallization and development of articulated political entities had made little progress by the time the French arrived.

The wars of the nineteenth century seem to have given rise to, or rather to have accentuated, the 'war-lord' aspect of Zerma, Songhay and Fulani societies. As a corollary, the condition of bondsmen and slaves probably deteriorated further.[20] It is difficult to determine whether this was linked with an economic decline which forced the nobility to exploit the servile strata of the population more harshly.

We know little if anything about the progress of Islam in the West during the nineteenth century, although we may presume that the influence and action of the *alfaize* of Say in particular had some impact upon the peoples of the West. What we do know is that the Mawri, the Sudie, the Gube, the Gabda, the Kalle, the Zerma of Zermaganda and the Gurmantche remained staunch animists. One tentative conclusion from this is that the central regions of the West, i.e. the river valley, parts of Songhayland, the Say–Guéladio region and parts of the south-east, witnessed the emergence of a partially islamized war-lord society, increasingly dependent upon the institution of slavery, whereas the societies of the 'outer fringes' remained to a considerable extent unchanged – egalitarian, animistic, clan-based and acephalous. For even in those societies where there was a war-chief (as among the Sudie) or a sort of 'overall' priest-chief (Gabda, Gube, Kalle and Mawri of Sokorbe?), these institutions were often subordinated to and/or rotated among the clan or lineage-elders, and were in any case endowed with little power.

THE CHANGING CONDITIONS OF TRADE AND THEIR IMPACT

The history of the rest of the Central Sudan in the second half of the nineteenth century is largely dominated by the vicissitudes of trade, particularly trans-Saharan trade. These vicissitudes can be partially explained by the course of events in the Maghrib, especially in Tripolitania which rapidly became practically the only northern terminus.[21] Here the rather lax rule of the Karamanli dynasty was replaced in 1835–6 by 'direct' and much more efficient Turkish rule.[22] During the next decades the Turks, perhaps with the aim of channelling the benefits of trade into their own hands, pursued an expansionist policy directed southwards. In particular the town of Ghadames, the home base for the merchants who controlled trans-Saharan trade, and the strategically important region of the Fezzan came under Turkish control.[23] Towards the end of the century and during the first years of the twentieth century the Turks also became interested, as we shall see, in regions even further south, most notably Kawar and Tibesti.

In 1855 the slave trade was abolished throughout the Ottoman empire.[24] Although contraband in slaves probably continued until the end of the century, the Turks were successful in putting an end to the slave trade as a large-scale and profitable commercial enterprise.[25] However, the end of the slave trade did not mean the end of trans-Saharan trade. A number of authors have convincingly demonstrated[26] that far from continuously declining throughout the nineteenth century, as an earlier generation of scholars believed, trans-Saharan trade experienced a spectacular recovery after the 1840s. This recovery, which became a wholesale boom after about 1873, lasted until approximately 1884.[27] Newbury argues that the final and relatively sharp decline occurred after 1884 and that it was a consequence of the general economic crisis in Europe at that time. Miège and Baier on the other hand are agreed that although the decline in the 1880s was real enough, it was halted in the 1890s when trade eventually stabilized at around half the early 1880s level. The final decline began during the first decade of the twentieth century as far as the Tripolitania–Hausaland axis is concerned, and even later with regards to the eastern-most route between Benghazi and Wadai.[28]

The recovery of trans-Saharan trade after the 1840s can be explained by the fact that the Central Sudan and Sahara 'developed its own brand of "legitimate" commerce';[29] first in ivory, later in ostrich feathers, and finally (during the 1890s) in hides and goat-skins.[30] According to Stephen Baier the export of ostrich feathers from the Central Sudan to Tripoli increased in value eightfold between 1870 and 1884 before declining sharply.[31]

We have little evidence of what impact the change to 'legitimate' trade had on the societies of the Central Sudan. But it seems unlikely that slave-raiding diminished drastically during the second half of the century, or that, as has been suggested,[32] trade in this period had a broader social basis than the slave trade. What seems to have happened was that the slave trade was diverted southwards,[33] and that the domestic demand for slaves increased sharply. This latter development is linked with internal changes which affected the local social fabric. Briefly, there developed, especially within the Sokoto Caliphate, but also in Damagaram, a plantation economy which required large supplies of slaves.[34] Slaves were also recruited to fill the many new *appointive* positions created in the rapidly expanding administrations of the polities of the Central Sudan.[35] And finally slaves came to make up the main bulk of the standing armies, composed mainly of infantry, which many rulers sought to organize and which progressively replaced the 'feudal' (mainly cavalry) levies of the past. All this implies that during the second half of the nineteenth century many Central Sudanic rulers were able to strengthen their position at the expense of their vassals. There was during this period an evolution towards a more arbitrary and despotic rule throughout the Central Sudan, an evolution to which the rapidly rising demand for slaves bears witness.[36]

The picture with regard to imported goods is slightly more confusing. We know that such diverse objects as small glass-ware, side arms, saddles, perfume and haberdashery continued to be imported. We also know that tea and sugar became increasingly popular during the nineteenth century,[37] as did bleached and unbleached calico from Manchester. Indeed, Marion Johnson has convincingly argued that calico constituted the main bulk of the southward-bound merchandise. These imports ruined the local handicraft industry in Tripolitania,[38] and it can be assumed that they had much the same effect south of the Sahara. The Turkish authorities forbade the southwards export of firearms, and although it did not stop sporadic contraband trade in such arms, the Turkish embargo had important consequences. It meant that firearms became a rare commodity, and the further south one went the fewer firearms there were. Thus the Kel Ahaggar (and also the Awlād Sulaymān Arabs) probably possessed more firearms than the southern Tuareg. Maradi, Gobir/Tibiri and especially Damagaram saw to it that no firearms at all filtered through to the emirates of the Sokoto Caliphate.[39] Furthermore, since the coastal Guinea states had for a long time pursued a policy similar to that of the Turks, refusing to export firearms to the inland polities, the Sokoto Caliphate was at least until the 1870s at some disadvantage from a military-technological point of view compared with its neighbours both to the south and to the north.[40]

There are indications that many caravans returned empty from the north, and that the Kano–Tripoli route seems to have become increasingly a one-way route.[41] We may hypothesize from this that imports did not match exports in volume and even in value. If this were the case, the implication is that the Central Sudan had a favourable balance of trade. If so, was the surplus used to finance the expanding administrations and the new standing armies of many of the Central Sudanic polities and/or to pay for merchandise imported from the south? The latter theory is supported by the testimony of the mid-nineteenth-century British traveller Richardson, who noted that Hausaland exported slaves to Nupe and imported large quantities of *American* goods from the south. According to Richardson trade with the south was conducted on such a scale that the merchants from the north were slowly driven out of the market.[42]

THE CENTRAL SUDAN AND SAHARA TO THE 1890S

In addition to the factors already discussed, the Central Sudan and Sahara during the second half of the nineteenth century is characterized, first, by the absence of large-scale droughts and the succession of a number of rather 'wet' years between 1875 and 1895[43] (in spite of the fact that climatic conditions were, as we have seen, generally less favourable than during the preceding centuries); second, by the meteoric rise of Damagaram; and third by the continuous warfare between the Kel Dinnik and Kel Gress Tuareg, as well as between, on the one hand, the Hausa 'rump' states of Tibiri and Maradi, now joined by Damagaram, and, on the other, some of the increasingly autonomous emirates of the Sokoto Caliphate.

The Sokoto Caliphate
The cluster of emirates known as the Sokoto Caliphate remained the dominant power in the Central Sudan, and continued to have considerable influence on the evolution and the events of the regions which became Niger. But it was a power 'increasingly subject to stress and strain which were affecting its political and economic health';[44] a power already on the decline, as exemplified by the severe defeat inflicted upon the emirate of Gwandu and its allies in the West in 1866. It was above all a power which had undergone drastic changes since the days of Usuman dan Fodio. After dan Fodio's death (and in some instances even before), 'deviations from Islamic models and from the Shehu's instructions developed rapidly and grew apace', according to M. G. Smith.[45] This was in a sense inevitable. As Smith says, the 'simple government of learned men based on the consensus of the *jema'a* [set up by dan Fodio] could not continue indefinitely' given the size of the empire.[46] More fundamentally, the ambiguities characteristic of Torodbe-Fulani rule turned on a central dichotomy which Smith has summarized as follows: 'Had the conquerors recognized [the Hausa] as Muslims and sought to rule purely by Muslim law, they might then have found it difficult to justify the jihad.' Consequently the Torodbe-Fulani 'asserted the heathenism of all Hausa, against historical data and their own observations'.[47] Smith argues that the Muslim Hausa (or Habe) considered Torodbe-Fulani rule to be both oppressive and illegitimate. The attitude of the *rural* Hausa, the

majority of whom remained attached to their ancestral religious beliefs and whose numbers do not seem to have diminished to any significant extent during the nineteenth century, must have been even more hostile. There is no evidence, as Hull has pointed out,[48] of an Islamic revival following the jihad. Can it therefore be argued that the jihad was, in the last analysis, a failure?

In any case, Murray Last's somewhat idealistic picture of a ruling class essentially devoted to Islamic religion and scholarship[49] has recently been challenged by J. Smaldone, who also argues that Torodbe-Fulani rule became increasingly oppressive.[50] E. Ayandele said much the same several years earlier, and stated that the Torodbe-Fulani constituted 'a leisurely aristocratic class [of absentee landlords][51] who had lands to till and capital to invest [and who] considered it beyond their dignity to do manual work'.[52] One of the factors involved here was the fundamental change in rights of ownership to the land which must rank as one of the major consequences of the jihad and the imposition of Islam as the official state religion. The concepts embodied in Islam were incompatible with the notion of usufructuary rights prevalent in Hausaland. The new rulers therefore had no qualms in appropriating a fair portion of the land, which they distributed to their followers as fiefs.[53] Large tracts of land were also exploited directly by an army of slaves,[54] slaves that were 'recruited systematically . . . by raids on local non-Muslim people'.[55] This gave rise to an odd system of landlordism, reminiscent both of the medieval European feudal system and of the American plantation system.

These economic trends were paralleled by important changes on the military side. The 'Raiding Citizen Army' of the early days of the Caliphate was progressively replaced by mounted feudal levies under the command of the fief-holders or *hakimai*. The predominant position of these *hakimai*, both in the military and political fields, lasted to the late 1870s when the large-scale importation of firearms enabled the emirs to establish standing (infantry) armies composed mainly of slaves. This reversal of the internal power-balance found its expression in the bureaucratization which became such a characteristic feature of the two last decades of the century.[56] As noted earlier, the various bureaucracies were heavily staffed with slaves. These palace slaves (or *batakuli*), as they came to be called, displayed an increasingly arrogant attitude towards the *talakawa* or rural poor (at least in the Katsina emirate).[57]

Three conclusions can be drawn. First, as Smaldone has made abundantly clear, the emirates of the Sokoto Caliphate became predatory 'states' organized for war. These wars became increasingly destructive, aimed principally at securing slaves.[58] Second, although heeding Marc-Henri Piault's warning that 'la relative concentration des captifs entre les mains du pouvoir (a) pu donner l'impression aux voyageurs européens nécessairement en contact et avant tout, sinon exclusivement avec le pouvoir, d'une société esclavagiste',[59] there can be no doubt that metropolitan Hausa society in the second half of the nineteenth century was indeed thoroughly slave-ridden.[60] Third, because of the insatiable demand for slaves and funds, the gulf between the ruling elite and the masses seems to have grown ever wider. Direct taxes increased steeply, according to Hull[61] and Smith.[62] The demand for slaves may not have been answered by raids against non-Muslim groups, so that many 'ordinary' people may have been press-ganged into the armies or sold into bondage.[63]

There are two reasons why the history of the Sokoto Caliphate has a bearing on that of the regions further north. The first is that the emirates of the Caliphate dominated the Central Sudanic scene during the second half of the nineteenth century; and the second is that the only explanation for the fact that the tiny entities of the northern fringes continued to pose a serious threat to some of these emirates is in terms of the Caliphate's internal weaknesses. Up to the 1870s the 'die-hards' of the north held a military-technological advantage over their southern neighbours, but the influx of firearms into the Sokoto Caliphate from the 1870s onwards does not appear to have upset the military balance. In fact, the situation of the Sokoto Caliphate was such that the northern fringe entities could count on the active support of many local groups and could also take advantage of internal dissensions which often degenerated into civil warfare. The history of the Sokoto Caliphate in these years is studded with revolts, rebellions, secessions, civil wars and other disturbances.[64]

It is beyond the scope of this work to give a detailed account of the wars between the Sokoto Caliphate and the northern 'die-hards', now assisted by Damagaram. Suffice it to say that the latter seem to have been particularly daring and successful during the reign of Dan Baskore, *sarkin* Katsina of Maradi (1857–79), and again in the early 1890s, when the 'die-hards' joined forces with Zamfara and the other towns situated within the proper domain of the *sarkin Musulmi* in their near-successful revolt against Sokoto.

These wars proved utterly devastating to some of the emirates of the Sokoto Caliphate, Katsina in particular (but *not*, as far as one can see, to the northern fringe entities). Perhaps the most tangible proof of this is the fact that many regions were in a state of permanent turmoil, and that large areas were turned into uninhabited wilderness as the population gathered together in secure clusters.[65]

It is tempting to conclude that the 'die-hards' of the north paved the way for the British conquest. It is equally tempting to argue that the British and especially Lord Lugard and his predilection for 'Indirect Rule' in a sense saved the Sokoto Caliphate from disintegration.

The rise of Damagaram

Damagaram's rise to prominence was dramatic, taking place within the space of a few decades during the second reign of *sarki* Tanimune (1851–84).[66] The fact that this was also the peak period of trans-Saharan trade during the nineteenth century is no coincidence. Clearly Damagaram owed its position to Zinder's function as an important halting-place along the by now dominant trade-route between Kano and Agades, and also as the terminus for the salt trade with Kawar.[67] This can be seen in the relationship that eventually emerged between the Tuareg and Damagaram. After an initial phase of hostility during the formative years of Damagaram, when the arms of the *sarki* and his followers provided the sedentary agriculturalists with adequate protection against the depredations of raiders from the north, the antagonists decided to put the sword aside and to cooperate. One of the results was that the Tuareg, and especially the Kel Owi of Damergu, Damagaram's neighbours to the north, were permitted to establish some of their *bugaje* communities on estates which enjoyed extra-territorial rights inside Damagaram itself.[68] (Similar estates seem also to have been established in the Katsina and Kano emirates.)[69]

There is no satisfactory answer to the question of why Damagaram, very much an upstart polity, and not the traditionally dominant power in this region, the very ancient Sossebaki empire[70] and its successor-states, was able to take advantage of the shift in trade-routes. However, it should be noted that Damagaram represented in a sense a new type of polity in this region, one nearly exclusively militaristic in character. This was evident from the outset. Damagaram seems to have been founded by a group of kanuriphone Dagera from the east who were able to offer the local population protection against raiders from the north (the Tuareg) as well as from the south (some of the emirates of the Sokoto Caliphate). These newcomers thus attracted a large following and were able subsequently to embark upon a particularly bellicose expansionist policy. By the middle of the century the people of Damagaram had reduced all the Sossebaki polities, together with such entities as Magaria, Korgom and Kantche, to a state of vassaldom.[71] Tanimune, who became *sarki* for the second time in 1851, and who was possibly the first ruler of the Central Sudan to grasp the importance of firearms,[72] continued the expansionist policy of his predecessors. He directed his efforts principally against his eastern neighbour, the kanuriphone polity of Mounio, famous for its many salt-extracting sites. The war came to an end some time during the mid-1870s with the complete defeat of Mounio and its incorporation into Damagaram – together with such lesser polities as Gamou and Koutoss.[73] Although both Damagaram and Mounio were nominal vassals of the *maï* of Borno, and the ruler of Mounio even ranked as one of the *maï*'s most loyal and favoured vassals according to Nachtigal,[74] Borno found itself in too advanced a state of decay to intervene.[75]

There are conflicting views about the relations between Damagaram and Kano. Adeleye has argued that Tanimune 'was the terror of Kano'.[76] Landeroin's account, on the other hand, leaves the impression that although Tanimune made an early attempt at expanding southwards, he did not press too hard in the face of stiff opposition.[77] (In the south-east Damagaram defeated Hadejia twice but refrained nevertheless from conquering that emirate.)[78] In fact, although Damagaram supported Maradi and Gobir/Tibiri in their struggle, relations between Damagaram and Kano seem to have been tolerably peaceful up to about 1893. After all, it was in the interest of both parties to maintain a climate of security conducive to trade.

The evolution of Damagaram closely paralleled that of the southern emirates. In Damagaram too a plantation system emerged based on the extensive use of slaves. Slaves may also have made up the main bulk of the labour force on the 'ranches' which Tanimune established in order to encourage the breeding and raising of ostriches. But slaves were employed in a number of other occupations as well. The artisan guilds, the army and the expanding bureaucracy were all heavily staffed with slaves. Finally slaves also constituted a critical export commodity.[79] Thus slavery was of prime importance in nineteenth-century Damagaram, as was slave-raiding, not only against neighbouring entities but also against those communities and peoples in Damagaram itself who remained attached to their ancestral beliefs and who as a consequence represented a threat to Tanimune's staunch pro-Muslim policy.[80] It should be pointed out, however, that since the region of Damagaram was situated very close to the desert-edge and had in the past suffered from the depredations of its neighbours, the population was perhaps fairly sparse by the beginning of the nineteenth century. It may be, therefore, to paraphrase H. J. Fisher, that this population needed constant replenishment and supplementation through slave-raids. Furthermore, raids may have been the *only* way through which the population increase essential to state growth could be achieved. Whatever the case, the important point is that Damagaram came to resemble its southern neighbours more and more. The nineteenth-century history of Tibiri/Gobir and Maradi has not yet been investigated in any detail, so we do not know whether they followed a similar pattern. However, a fair guess would be that since these polities were situated in an economic backwater, and since they were in a sense committed to 'traditionalism', they did not undergo, or at least not to the same degree, the transformations so characteristic of their eastern and southern neighbours.

Adar, Gobir Tudu and neighbouring regions

Conditions in Adar continued to be characterized by a state of near-permanent warfare between the Kel Dinnik and the Kel Gress (of Gobir Tudu). The Kel Dinnik seem to have become increasingly aggressive. They are reputed to have raided not only the Kel Gress, but also such far-off regions as Aïr, Damergu, Damagaram, the Niger river valley and even the domain of the Kel Attaram of present-day Mali.[81] In the face of such intense raiding the Kel Gress and the Kel Aïr united and were able to inflict several defeats upon the Kel Dinnik in the 1870s.[82] Moreover, from the 1880s onwards, the Kel Dinnik found themselves faced with a new and, as it turned out, formidable raiding 'power', that of the Kel Ahaggar.[83]

It may be conjectured that this raiding activity of the Kel Dinnik was in some way linked with the internal antagonism between the *ineslemen* and the *imajeghen*. It may further be conjectured that the raids enabled the *imajeghen* to recover the predominant position which they had temporarily lost to the *ineslemen* in 1809. However, it could equally well be argued that the Kel Dinnik were at a disadvantage from an economic point of view compared with the Kel Gress, the Kel Owi and other Tuareg, and that they sought to compensate for this through raiding. In other words, since the Kel Dinnik had failed to operate the economic changes perceptible within other Tuareg societies, raiding continued to be of prime economic importance to them.

The Kel Ahaggar raided both the Kel Dinnik and the Aïr Tuareg.[84] The latter, together with their vassals, especially the oasis-dwellers of Kawar, came under pressure from another direction as well, the east. It seems that the Tubu and the Awlād Sulaymān Arabs intensified their raiding activities during the second half of the nineteenth century. In particular the Kawar oases and the *azalaï* were attacked on a number of occasions in the 1870s, the 1880s and the 1890s. Bands of raiders also pushed further westwards.[85]

Although the Kel Gress were by and large able to hold the Kel Dinnik at bay, and although their economy apparently continued to flourish, they were torn by internal dissension during the second half of the nineteenth century. Its cause was the intense competition among the *imajeghen* of the various tribes as to who could attract the greatest number of tributaries and clients. The *imajeghen* of the Tohadji tribe appear to have been the most successful in this, so that their chief (or *ar'holla*) came to eclipse in wealth and power the *ar'holla* of the Tatmakaret, who in his capacity as *tambari* was the nominal head of the confederation of the Kel Gress. It is no coincidence therefore that it was *ar'holla* Budal of the Tohadji (*c*. 1855–75) who made an unsuccessful attempt at moulding the region and the people of Gobir Tudu into some sort of centralized kingdom. Budal, who proclaimed himself *amenukal*, was able to build up a cross-tribal clientele especially of some of the poorer *imajeghen* and also apparently of some *ighawellan*. With this backing he tried to force the *imajeghen* into absolute and permanent submission. The result was a state of civil war which dragged on intermittently until the arrival of the French.[86]

ADVENTURERS AND INVADERS, 1891–1903

The French and the British
In the 1890s new adventurers, invaders and powers appeared on the Central Sudanic and Saharan scene. Two of these were France and Great Britain. In fact, in 1890 France and Britain had, unknown to the inhabitants of the Central Sudan and Sahara, already divided this region between them on paper. The British received the lion's share, by duping the French into recognizing their claim (unfounded, as it turned out) to exercise control over the Sokoto Caliphate through Sir George Goldie's Royal Niger Company. This claim was based on a treaty with Sokoto which we now know to be a fake.[87] According to the Franco-British agreement of 1890, the British were

49

to receive all land south of a straight line between Say and Barwa on Lake Chad (that is, present-day Northern Nigeria and a fair slice of the sedentary south of modern Niger), and the French all land to the north of this line.[88] The French, dissatisfied with the 'light soil' allotted to them, sent out a mission under Captain P. L. Monteil to reconnoitre and explore the regions between the river Niger and Lake Chad, and to determine the real extent of British influence. Monteil, escorted by only a handful of *tirailleurs sénégalais*, was able to travel peacefully for twenty-seven months among Africans who little suspected that he was the fore-runner of an army of invaders. Monteil went from Saint Louis to Say and then to N'Guigmi, via Dosso, Argungu, Kano – three places situated south of the Say–Barwa line – and Zinder, before returning to France via Tripoli. Monteil's mission is important in several respects. First, he exposed the myth of the 'powerful' Niger Company; second, he demonstrated that there was no practicable route between the river Niger and Lake Chad north of the Say–Barwa line; third, and above all, his was the first official French mission in what was to become Niger. As such it can be seen as ushering in the era of colonial conquest. The fact that Monteil signed protectorate treaties both with the chief of Ouro-Gueladio and with the *alfaize* of Say may be considered proof of this.[89] Monteil's mission was followed by three other exploratory missions, all of them confined to the West, and all of them launched not by the French of the Western Sudan, but by the French in Dahomey. (The region of the West was, as we shall see, the object of rivalry between the Western Sudan and Dahomey.) These missions were those of Baud and Vergoz in 1895, of Toutée in the same year, and of Hourst in 1895–6.[90]

By the early 1890s the French, as well as the British, were committed to the conquest of the Central Sudan and Sahara. It would seem appropriate at this juncture, therefore, to insert a few general remarks regarding the nature, aim and motives of the colonial conquest of these regions. Yehoshua Rash has argued that the conquest of the future Niger constituted a 'poussée coloniale tardive et à bout de souffle',[91] a rather drab affair carried out by reluctant, disillusioned and bored officers who met with little if any resistance among the indigenous population.[92] It will be argued that this opinion is not substantiated by the available evidence. On the other hand, it is clear that the conquest of the Central Sudan and Sahara was of a different nature altogether from that of the regions further west. The era when the Marine (later Colonial) Infantry, in spite of official reluctance, could carve out what has been described[93] as a private empire in the Western Sudan clearly belonged to the past.[94] By the time interest began to focus on the Niger area, the imperialist powers were firmly committed to colonial conquest. Frontiers had been drawn on the map, zones of influence delineated and explorers-turned-treaty-makers had ventured forth, before, finally, the army was ordered in. In fact, it looks very much as if the conquest of the Niger area was willed and planned by the superior authorities in Paris. This is not to deny that the initiative often came from the military, especially from those who had taken part in the conquest of the Western Sudan. But they had no longer any difficulty in persuading the government in Paris to adopt their projects.

Why this interest in such a decidedly out-of-the-way region? Part of the answer is that it did not look like a backwater to the French at the end of the nineteenth century. They had illusions about the importance of trade and the wealth of the Central Sudan and Sahara.[95] T. W. Roberts has argued that the myth of an interior rich in resources and population was simply an explanation and justification for advances undertaken for quite other reasons.[96] However, Roberts fails to make clear what those other reasons were. Certainly, to the military who took part in the conquest, the Central (like the Western) Sudan was an area for ribbons, crosses and medals. It is difficult, however, to imagine that an enterprise of such magnitude was undertaken primarily to provide a handful of officers with opportunities to cover themselves with glory and to obtain quick promotion.

Apart from economic considerations, the Central Sudan, and in particular the region around Lake Chad, was of considerable importance to the French from a strategic and geopolitical point of view. It presented so to speak, the 'missing link' between the emerging colonial empires of northern, western and equatorial Africa. The powerful attraction exercised upon the official mind by that old dream of a French colonial empire stretching not only from the shores of the Mediterranean to the Congo, but also from Saint Louis on the Atlantic to the Red Sea, should not be underestimated. The fact that this dream lingered on in many minds helps to explain decisions and events which would otherwise remain partially incomprehensible.

From a more general point of view it can be argued that a colonial conquest, once under way, is to a certain extent carried forward by its own inner logic. Colonial powers in their inevitable quest for safe and stable frontiers cannot afford to leave any blank spots on the map; they cannot risk regions outside their control becoming refuges for potential opponents, or bases for military action against their possessions. The absence of natural boundaries and the close intercourse between the peoples of West Africa made the conquest of the Niger region inevitable once the French had committed themselves to colonial expansion in the Western Sudan and North Africa. It follows that if the French had not ventured forth, someone else would have.

Rābīh and the Sanūsīya

During this time, the Central Sudan saw a host of other adventurers and invaders, the most important of them being Rābīh Fadlallāh. The story of Rābīh, which belongs mainly to the history of the Sudan, Chad and Nigeria, is only of peripheral concern to the student of Niger. However, since his action had considerable influence on the situation in the Central Sudan, the subject cannot be eschewed altogether. Rābīh Fadlallāh, a native of Darfur, began his career as a captain in the army of al-Zubayr Rahma, the merchant-prince who controlled the Bahr al-Ghazal from about 1865 onwards (after 1874 officially in the name of the Khedive), and who went on to conquer Darfur in 1874, before being ousted by the khedival forces.[97] Rābīh escaped, and eventually made his way eastwards with a considerable force. Having set his sights on the sultanate of Wadai, he operated for many years in the regions south of that sultanate. Wadai was then the southern terminus of the very important trans-Saharan route via Kufra to Benghazi, a route controlled by yet another rising 'power', the *sufi* order or brotherhood of the Sanūsīya. The Sanūsīya, originally a Cyrenaic brotherhood, began during the last decades of the nineteenth century to extend its influence to the south and south-west.[98] It even encompassed the eastern half of the Niger region, where a *zawīya* or 'lodge' was set up at Djadjidouna in Damergu.[99] Most of the traders in Zinder are reported to have adhered to the Sanūsīya.[100] According to the members of the Foureau-Lamy mission, the brotherhood had also made considerable inroads among the Tuareg.[101] It was, however, Wadai and adjacent regions (Kanem in particular) which primarily attracted the attention of the Sanūsīya, who for obvious commercial reasons established a close alliance with Wadai.[102] Perhaps this is why Rābīh, after having defeated and despoiled Wadai, refrained from conquering that sultanate (or was unable to do so),[103] and instead headed westwards where the moribund Bornoan empire fell an easy prey to him in 1893.[104]

Rābīh's conquest of Borno indirectly benefited Damagaram in several ways. First, *sarki* Ahmadu, who ascended the throne of Damagaram in 1893, relinquished his last formal ties with Borno. Second, a large section of the former Bornoan army sought refuge in Damagaram, and were incorporated by Ahmadu into his army which was thus considerably strengthened.[105] Third, and most important, Ahmadu took advantage of the fact that Rābīh's victory threw the rulers of the southern emirates into a state of near panic. These rulers had good reason to fear Rābīh, who led a modern army almost wholly equipped with firearms,[106] and who carried out his conquests in the name of the Sudanese Mahdi who had arisen in 1882.[107] It is certain, furthermore, that Rābīh intended to march further westwards, towards Kano.[108] Rābīh's presence induced many of the petty potentates of north-eastern Hausaland to look to Damagaram for protection. Thus Ahmadu was able to conquer and to reduce to a state of vassaldom the polities of Hadejia, Nguru, Gumel and parts of Daura.[109] He reversed the policy of his predecessors and embarked upon an expansionist and bellicose policy. The ultimate target was Kano, whose strength had been sapped by the recent prolonged civil war. After an initial defeat in 1896 which took a particularly heavy toll, Ahmadu returned south in 1898. This time the Damagaram army completely routed that of Kano, and Ahmadu was able to lay siege to the town itself. Inexplicably, however, Ahmadu lifted the siege and returned home at the very moment when his enterprise seemed to be on the verge of success.[110]

Ahmadu's policy may have been dictated by the need to compensate for the losses incurred by the decline in trade. If so, it can only be described as a failure. Although there is no direct evidence to this effect, it is quite possible that the state of warfare proved detrimental to trade. It is the best explanation for the fact that Ahmadu's policy earned him the enmity of the trading community of Zinder and especially that of its unofficial head, the wealthy and powerful Mallam Yaro.[111] Ahmadu's support for the raid-oriented Imuzurag Tuareg of Damergu against the other Kel Owi did not help to improve matters.[112] Neither did his very cool reception of an envoy of the Sanūsīya brotherhood in 1897–8.[113]

The rise of k'aura Assao

West of Damagaram, in Maradi and Gobir-Tibiri, a local adventurer by the name of Assao rose to power in the 1890s. This was surprising because Assao was a Fulani. Perhaps the implication is that the northern 'die-hards' did not wage war against the Fulani as such, but only against the Sokoto Caliphate. In any case, a dynastic struggle in Maradi provided Assao with his opportunity. This struggle led to the secession of the Tessaoua region which was definitively separated from Maradi in 1897. The ruler of Tessaoua, a member of the old Katsina-Laka dynasty, also styled himself *sarkin* Katsina. In this situation of virtual civil war Assao was appointed *k'aura* or war-chief of Maradi, apparently as a result of public pressure. From this position he was able to exercise *de facto* power, much to the dismay of the *de jure* ruler, the *sarkin* Katsina of Maradi, who sought the aid of his neighbour, the *sarkin* Gobir of Tibiri, against his own war-chief. Both rulers were defeated by Assao and his men at the battle of Chikadji in 1898. After this *k'aura* Assao became for all practical purposes the ruler of a new polity encompassing Maradi as well as Gobir-Tibiri.[114]

It is reported that Assao received a helping hand from Katsina at the battle of Chikadji. But when he was established he turned against Katsina, thus continuing the traditional policy of Gobir and Maradi towards the southern emirates.[115]

Ahmad Chekou and other adventurers in the West

In the West, another newcomer appeared on the scene in the 1890s. He was Ahmad Chekou, the son and successor of al-Hājj 'Umar at the head of the Segu Tukolor empire. After the defeat of the Tukolor empire at the hands of the French in 1893, Ahmad trekked eastwards in the company of another famous victim of the French advance, Ali Bori N'Diaye, the former *buurba Jolof* who had rallied Segu in 1890.[116] There followed three years of vicissitudes before Ahmad Chekou, Ali Bori N'Diaye and their men established themselves in the West. They could count on the support of the exiled Fulani of Tamkalle under their chief Bayero, and of the Tuareg of Tagazar. The *alfaize* of Say and the chief of Ouro-Guéladio also adopted a favourable attitude. But the Zerma of the river valley and the 'allies' of the south-east, including the Sudie of Kurfey, did not. Having liberated themselves from the Gwandu emirate and its local allies, they were in no mood to submit to another Muslim prince. After a devastating war, Ahmad Chekou and his men had to seek refuge in Sokoto, where Ahmad died in 1898.[117] According to Smaldone, Ahmad controlled 10,000 warriors or more. Their arrival, Smaldone argues, strengthened the military capability of the Caliphate.[118]

The beginnings of the French conquest

Even before Ahmad had been expelled, a new 'scourge' appeared on the horizon: a seven-hundred-man strong column of the French under the command of Major Destenave. This column was sent out from Masina in the Western Sudan in 1896 in order to establish French rule over the emirate of Liptako and its capital Dori[119] (in present-day Upper Volta). But once in Dori, the French had to venture further east in order to eradicate the threat which the Fulani of Diagorou and the Logomaten Tuareg represented to their new possessions. Such action, it was believed, would also encourage trade between Hausaland and the Niger bend country, via Sansanné-Hausa and Songhayland.[120] The presence of Ahmad Chekou in the West may also have been one of the causes of this eastwards thrust.

Destenave seems to have achieved most, if not all, of his objectives. But although the column reached the river, which was considered a suitable natural frontier for the time being, it established only one permanent post (in 1897), at Say. The *alfaize*, who had for a time flirted with Ahmad Chekou, was deposed, and his successor, probably hand-picked by the French, made his official submission.[121] After having defeated the Fulani of Ouro-Gueladio, who as a consequence of their resistance saw their power and influence severely restricted,[122] the French were able to persuade the initially hesitant Fulani of Tamou and Torodi to submit.[123] But further north the retreat of the Destenave column proved disastrous to the Songhay/Kado, over whom the local Fulani and Tuareg were soon able to reassert their hold. The Songhay/Kado chiefs of this region made regular requests to the French in Dori to return.[124]

The Destenave column constitutes in many ways the last episode in the conquest of the Western Sudan. The conquest of the Central Sudan proper, that is the regions east of the river, only began in earnest in January 1899. In the meantime yet another treaty-making and exploratory Monteil-type mission appeared on the scene, the Cazémajou mission, sent out in 1897. However, Captain Cazémajou's objectives were far more ambitious from a political-military point of view than those of Monteil had been. In fact, Cazémajou was to prepare the way for conquest, first, by trying to persuade the *sarkin* Damagaram to sign a protectorate treaty, and second by concluding some sort of alliance with Rābīh.[125] Both the French and the British saw in Rābīh a 'potential joker in the expansionist pack equally capable of upsetting their own calculations as ... those of their rivals'.[126] The British had tried unsuccessfully on several occasions to establish cordial relations with the new ruler of Borno.[127] These British overtures were not unknown to the French, who feared a vast British pincer-movement against Lake Chad from the Lower Niger in the south-west and the Upper Nile in the north-east.[128] (They were also apprehensive about possible Turkish moves in the regions south of the Fezzan.)[129] Such a scheme, if realized, would of course spell the end of the French dream of a vast trans-African empire linked together by the Lake Chad region. Hence the Casémajou mission to forestall any possible British threat.

Cazémajou was welcomed with open arms by the trading community in Zinder. Mallam Yaro even provided the French with quarters. But *sarki* Ahmadu, who had just returned from his expedition against Kano, harboured strong suspicions – with good reason as we have seen – of possible collusion between the French and Rābīh. He resolved therefore to execute Cazémajou, a resolution which was carried out during Cazémajou's visit to the palace on 5 May 1898. (Astonishingly, Cazémajou's tiny escort was able to return in good order to Say.)

Scandal: the Voulet–Chanoine mission
The task of avenging the assassination of Cazémajou fell to the Voulet–Chanoine mission. This was not strictly speaking a 'mission', but a sizeable military column, the first such column to venture into the regions east of the river Niger. Before then, small detachments, sent out by the French in Dahomey, had penetrated the regions north and east of the river. In fact, the 'Dahomeans' had established a post at Dosso in November 1898. This was with the approval of the local population, but rather to the dismay of the *zermakoy* who had requested the protection of the French, not their presence. The French *did* provide the Zerma with adequate protection, notably by routing the Tuareg of Tagazar who were forced to submit.[130] A small garrison of *tirailleurs* was also established at Kirtachi on the river.[131] In order to secure their rear the French had completed the 'pacification' of the right bank during the second half of 1898. The principal column sent out, led by Major Crave, was able to expel the Logomaten Tuareg and to inflict a resounding defeat upon the Fulani of Diagorou. Crave also established a number of permanent posts on the river and on the river islands to serve as a bulwark against the Tuareg.[132] The Resident in Say noticed during the ceremony of enthronement of the new *alfaize* in 1890 that many of the chiefs of the left (and then unoccupied) bank took the trouble to travel to Say and to pay allegiance to the new French protégé, and hence, indirectly, to the French themselves. The incumbent Resident and his successors deduced that the *alfaize* was the effective overlord of both banks, and that the inhabitants of the left bank were, by virtue of their allegiance to the *alfaize*, French subjects.[133]

The Voulet–Chanoine expedition and the Voulet–Chanoine 'affair' can only be properly understood in a very much wider context than that of the conquest of Niger.[134] The first important point to note is that this expedition was only one of three expeditions sent out towards Lake Chad. The two others were the Foureau–Lamy mission, which was to cross the Sahara (via Aïr) and to join the Voulet–Chanoine expedition in Zinder,[135] and the Gentil mission coming up from the Congo.[136] According to the original scheme,[137] the French forces would, once in the region of Lake Chad (and once Rābiḥ had been disposed of), push eastwards and eventually join up with the Marchand mission, which was on its way from the Congo to the Bahr al-Ghazal,[138] and also with the Bonchamps mission en route westwards from Djibouti.[139] Clearly, the French were bent on more than the partition of the (eastern) Sudan, the main objective of the Marchand mission, and more than forestalling any link-up between Lord Kitchener and his fellow countrymen in Nigeria. They were also intent on making a reality of their old dream of a colonial empire stretching from Dakar to Djibouti and from Algiers to Brazzaville.[140] It was a daring, even reckless, policy contrived in ministerial offices in Paris, although probably instigated by those who were to become the commanding officers of the various expeditions. It was above all a policy contrived with supreme disregard for logistic problems and for the actual state of affairs in the regions to be traversed or occupied. It was finally a policy which left even the boldest officers of the Western Sudan breathless. Brigadier-General de Trentinian, their chief, disapproved strongly of the projected Voulet–Chanoine expedition. This was, one suspects, primarily because Captain Voulet, the commanding officer, was to receive his orders directly from Paris, and that as a consequence the responsibility for the conquest of the African interior had been taken out of the hands of the officers on the spot in the Western Sudan.[141]

In fact the whole project was thwarted by the diplomatic-political evolution. First, the firm stand adopted by Joseph Chamberlain, the British Secretary of State for the Colonies, in the face of the French pretensions in the Central Sudan more or less forced the French to back down. A new and this time (it was believed) definitive line of demarcation was agreed upon; a line as disadvantageous to the French, if not more so, as the Say–Barwa line. Indeed, the Convention of 14 June 1898 stipulated that all land within a circle of 100 miles radius around Sokoto was to be included in the British sphere of influence (that is, the present-day Nigerien regions of eastern Arewa, Adar, Konni, Gobir Tudu, Gobir–Tibiri and Maradi). Further east, Magaria and a stretch of Kanuriland north of the Komadougou-Yobe river also fell to the British. The French were left with Damagaram and – or so they thought – a practicable route between the Niger and Lake Chad.[142] The second important factor in this context is the change of government in Paris on 28 June 1898, and in particular the arrival of Théophile Delcassé at the Quai d'Orsay. Delcassé, who was determined to pursue a policy of détente with Britain,[143] objected strongly to the original instructions issued to Voulet. He considered them too risky and above all not in conformity with the spirit of the Convention that had just been signed.[144] As a consequence of Delcassé's determined opposition, the Voulet–Chanoine expedition was seriously delayed, and the instructions were modified. The final instructions stipulated that Voulet, whatever happened, was to stay clear of the British zone of influence; where, it is worth recalling, not a single British soldier had yet penetrated. Above all, these instructions made no mention of Marchand and the Upper Nile.[145] The ultimate objective of all three expeditions was then to be the Lake Chad region. But it does not follow that the colonial party had completely surrendered to Delcassé. The possibility that the sizeable French forces, once assembled in the Lake Chad region, could be used for a variety of purposes, especially if the domestic and international situation were to change in the interval, may not have escaped the attention of the promoters of the three expeditions. After all, Marchand was still on his way towards the Upper Nile and the Convention of 14 June 1898 had not yet been ratified (this only happened in March 1899). But, in September 1898, *before* Captain Voulet sailed for Africa, Marchand's fiasco at Fashoda on the Nile occurred, a fiasco which was to turn public opinion against colonial adventures.[146]

The Voulet–Chanoine expedition set out from Sansanne-Hausa on the left bank of the river Niger in January 1899. Almost immediately it ran into difficulties. Since the expedition had at its disposal scandalously inadequate resources, and since the whole enterprise was based on a misunderstanding and a miscalculation, this was inevitable.[147] The misunderstanding concerned the inhabitants of the left bank, and the claim that they were French subjects by virtue of the fact that their chiefs had paid allegiance to the *alfaize*. Since the left bank had not yet been occupied, let alone pacified, this claim was unfounded. The local inhabitants may have looked to Say for protection and may have perceived the Resident and the French as potential allies, but it was one thing to seek French protection, and quite another to provide a very sizeable French military column with all sorts of provisions. The miscalculation was to believe that a seventeen-hundred-man strong column could live off the country in a region already ravaged by a series of raids and wars and probably also suffering from severe drought. (There is enough evidence to suggest that the period 1899–1904 was one of inadequate rainfall throughout the Central Sudan and especially in the Lake Chad basin.)[148] The inhabitants of the left bank, to whom the Voulet–Chanoine expedition probably looked like another version of the hordes of Ahmad Chekou, put up an unremitting and desperate fight against the advance of the column. This totally unexpected resistance, notably in the form of a scorched earth policy, forced Voulet to resort to extremes simply in order to get through. His victims, or their relatives, complained to their nominal overlord, the *alfaize*, who in turn alerted the Resident. The latter protested vehemently against what he considered to be abuses committed against French subjects. Voulet retaliated by accusing the Resident of having provided him with inaccurate information.

57

A detailed account of the progress of the Voulet–Chanoine expedition is to be found elsewhere.[149] Here we may note that because the expedition had to stay close to the river, it was seriously delayed. Only south of Kirtachi did Voulet decide to make a thrust towards the north-east, into the *dallol* Fogha and then the *dallol* Mawri, through a region close to Dosso. It is noteworthy that the Resident in Dosso, Lieutenant Cornu (or indeed the French in Dahomey), never lodged a single complaint against the expedition. Perhaps this was because Cornu, unlike his colleague in Say, did not hold any illusions about the true allegiance of the inhabitants of the region. Pushing north-eastwards and finally eastwards (thus 'violating' the British zone of influence) and leaving behind a trail of devastation and desolation, the expedition sacked northern Arewa (where the *saranuyia*'s village of Lougou was burnt down) and the town of Birnin Konni, before heading towards the sultanate of Tessaoua. By this time, it had grown into a horde of some 3,000 people, including a considerable number of women taken as captives. By this time also, the fate of Voulet and Chanoine had been sealed, far away from the battlefield in the Central Sudan. The key figure in the drama now unfolding was a certain Lieutenant Peteau, dishonourably discharged from the expedition when it was still in the vicinity of Say. After his return to the Western Sudan, he wrote a letter to his fiancée in France, denouncing the methods used by Voulet, and alleging that Voulet and Chanoine were responsible for a number of atrocities. (Peteau, no saint himself, had been responsible, as it turned out, for at least two summary executions and the burning down of several villages.) This letter, inexplicably, found its way to the desk of a *député* and then to the desk of the Minister of Colonies, A. Guillain, who communicated its contents to his colleagues. On the strength of a single private letter written by an officer after his dishonourable discharge, the government decided to replace Voulet and Chanoine at the head of the expedition and to have both men arrested and court-martialled in order to test Peteau's allegations. Not only did the use of the conditional mood quickly disappear from the official correspondence, but Lieutenant-Colonel Klobb received the order to take over command of the expedition on 16 May, *before* the first official reports concerning Peteau's allegations had been sent from Saint-Louis. Indeed, the principal report, written by Major Crave, who was the commanding officer of the right bank and as such the superior of the Resident in Say, and who therefore had good reason to support Peteau's version, gave 'l'impression de riguers excessives plutôt que de cruautés honteuses' according to the acting Governor of the Sudan, another of Peteau's supporters.[150] According to the Minister, the report confirmed 'non dans tous les détails, mais dans leurs grandes lignes les indications données' by Peteau.[151] It is perhaps significant that the report itself has disappeared from the archives, but there is enough evidence to warrant the conclusion that the government had been moved by considerations which had nothing to do with the plight of the people of the Central Sudan. It must be appreciated that Peteau's letter arrived at the height of the

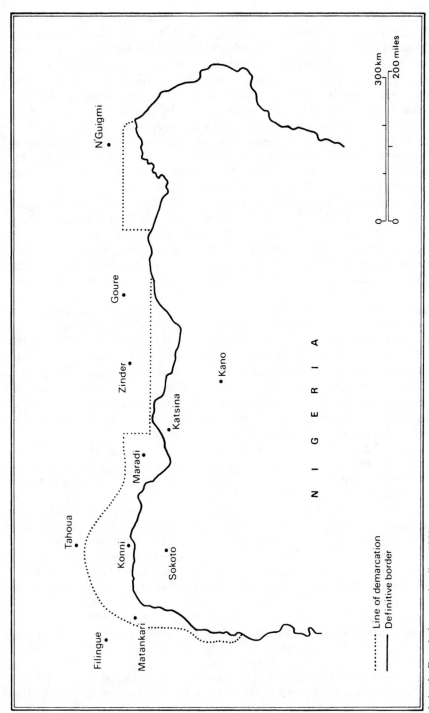

6 Anglo-French demarcation line, 1898.

Dreyfus affair, at the height of a crisis of such a magnitude that it threatened the very existence of the republican regime.[152] It was also a time when the colonial party and the very principle of colonial expansion were under heavy attack as a consequence of the fiasco at Fashoda. Given these factors, two theories (which may well be complementary) are possible. The first is that the government had in mind to prevent any inconsiderate action on Voulet's behalf once Lake Chad had been reached. If by chance Voulet decided to push further east (and the officers of the Colonial Infantry were notorious for their insubordinate attitude), then he was bound to violate the new French–British demarcation line between Wadai and Darfur established by the Additional Declaration of 21 March 1899, a declaration which Voulet had no knowledge of. The second theory is that the nervous ministers acted to prevent even the possibility of a new scandal which would certainly have been one too many. This they could do since all the promoters of the Voulet–Chanoine expedition had either died, resigned or been eliminated from office during the preceding months. (The list includes notably, Félix Faure, the President of the Republic who had recently died, and General Chanoine – the Captain's father – who had just resigned after a short stint as a markedly anti-Dreyfus Minister of War.) The question remaining is why Klobb was instructed to make as speedy a progress as possible towards Lake Chad. Was this in order to make certain that the British would respect their undertaking to leave the region north and east of Lake Chad to the French?

Lieutenant-Colonel Klobb caught up with the expedition on 14 July 1899. To Voulet, who *had* committed condemnable acts (but then what officer taking part in the conquest of West Africa had not?),[153] the arrival of Klobb meant the end of his career and probable disgrace if not worse. He ordered his *tirailleurs* to open fire on Klobb's party. Klobb was killed. Then the rank and file revolted and both Voulet and Chanoine were slain.

From the point of view of the Dupuy cabinet and of the military establishment of the Western Sudan this tragic end presented several advantages. First, there would be no court-martial, no muck-raking. Second, since the killing of Klobb made it evident to everyone that Voulet and Chanoine were insane, and since both were dead, they could safely be denounced by everyone. In short, this tragic end provided the government, the colonial party and the military with a golden opportunity to exculpate themselves by putting all the blame on the madness of two individuals. Even better, since the other officers who had taken part in the conquest of West Africa were not madmen, it followed logically that *they* had not resorted to the same extremes as Voulet and Chanoine. Thus the Voulet–Chanoine expedition served to justify and to legitimize *a posteriori* the methods in use in the Western Sudan. Furthermore, from the point of view of the military in West Africa, it had now been proved that an expedition launched without their approval and over their heads could not but fail.

The question of whether Voulet and Chanoine did resort to extremes compared with the other officers responsible for the conquest of West Africa rests I believe not on *what* they did but *when*. What was tolerable ten months earlier was no longer so in the summer of 1899.

The assassination of Klobb masked the fact that the disaster of the Voulet–Chanoine expedition was caused in the last analysis by the determined resistance of the people of the Central Sudan. It may be argued that the whole episode represents one of the most glorious pages in the history of African resistance against the imposition of colonial rule. If this most important point had been overlooked by the historians, it is not only because of the assassination of Klobb, but also because there was on the African side no easily identifiable leader of the stature of, say, a Samori Toure or an al-Hājj 'Umar.

The resistance against the Voulet–Chanoine expedition probably took a heavy toll (perhaps five thousand or more casualties). Vast regions, the river valley in particular, had been thoroughly devastated. After the terrible sack of Birnin Konni, which must have created a profound impression throughout Hausaland, it would take a great deal of courage to try and resist the French.

The Joalland–Meynier and Foureau–Lamy missions

The Voulet–Chanoine expedition was over, but the Central African mission was not. The remaining French officers – Lieutenants Meynier (Klobb's second-in-command), Pallier and Joalland (all soon to be promoted to Captain) – were somehow able to put the pieces together again, and to continue towards the east. This was only possible because Zinder was just a few kilometres away, and because the *tirailleurs* were looking forward to the booty they expected to collect after the fall of that important town.[154]

The mighty Damagaram inexplicably collapsed in the face of the horde which went under the official name of the Central African mission. After a brief battle (at Tirmini on 30 July) *sarki* Ahmadu fled, only to be captured and killed a short while afterwards, and his army then disintegrated.[155] Was this because the news of the sack of Birnin Konni sapped the will to resist? Or had the war against Kano exhausted the men and resources of Damagaram? Had Ahmadu's policies generated so much resentment among his subjects (and especially among the traders) that they came to look upon the French as the lesser of two evils? It may be significant that a *coup d'état* was in preparation in Zinder, only failing to take place because of the arrival of the French.[156] It *is* certainly significant that Mallam Yaro and the trading community openly sided with the French *and* that the Kel Owi Tuareg of Damergu quickly submitted. Mallam Yaro in particular became a trusted ally of the French.[157]

While all this was happening in the south, the Foureau–Lamy mission was struggling on its way through the Sahara in the face of very stiff opposition. The Tuareg refused all contact. Their tactics 'consistait à faire le vide absolu autour [des Français], [à] éloigner les troupeaux ... [et] les denrées alimentaires, [à] disparaître enfin eux-mêmes'. To the French this was sabotage, and vigorous action was needed. 'L'heure de la répression a sonné', remarked Major Lamy in his diary.[158] It may be that the Foureau–Lamy mission was forced to resort to the same 'questionable' methods as the Voulet–Chanoine expedition in order to get through. Certainly summary executions occurred on several occasions,[159] but since Lamy had no Peteau among his men, the question will have to remain unanswered. But it took the mission, whose progress considerably upset the flow of trade,[160] some eight months to travel the stretch from Iferouane in northern Aïr to Zinder, a distance of some 500 kilometres. South of Agades it was led astray by its guides, with the result that many of its members nearly died of thirst. When the mission finally arrived in the vicinity of Zinder, it was a half-naked band on foot, stripped of everything, and saved only by a rescue party sent out by the Central African mission. The Foureau–Lamy mission finally reached Zinder on 2 November 1899.[161]

Once in Zinder, Major Lamy assumed command of the combined forces of the two missions, or rather of the forces still left. Many of the *tirailleurs* of the Central African mission, frustrated by the French refusal to allow them to sack Zinder, mutinied. Lieutenant Pallier took it upon himself to escort the most unruly elements back to Say. He left Zinder with 650 *tirailleurs*, auxiliaries and carriers and 700–800 female 'slaves' who constituted the booty of the *tirailleurs*. After a long and strenuous journey they arrived at Say on 14 November 1899.[162]

After Lamy had conquered the sultanate of Tessaoua (which offered very stiff resistance),[163] he ventured eastwards to join Joalland and Meynier who had preceded him, and they joined forces with Major Gentil coming up from the Congo. Together they converged on Rābīh who, no longer useful from a diplomatic point of view, now constituted the main obstacle to French domination in the Lake Chad basin. Although Rābīh was defeated and killed at Kousseri[164] on 22 April 1900 – only after he had inflicted heavy casualties (twenty dead including Lamy) on the French – it was not a wholly conclusive battle. Rābīh had not been able to gather a sizeable army at Kousseri, and his son Fad-el-Allah still had at his disposal enough men and resources to continue the struggle against the French.[165] He even had considerable diplomatic support. Indeed, the British thought of appointing him Emir of Borno in order to counter-balance what had suddenly become a dangerously preponderant French influence in the Lake Chad region.[166] However, Fad-el-Allah was killed by the French late in 1901.[167] Lamy's campaign had succeeded in fulfilling the old dream of uniting France's Northern, West, and Equatorial African possessions.

The Péroz expedition and the establishment of the Territory of Niger
The first and most spectacular but inconclusive phase of the conquest of the Central Sudan was over. The second and conclusive phase was to be distinctly unspectacular, and also very slow. This slowness must be attrib-

uted, first, to African resistance, and second, to the cautious attitude of the French government which sought to avoid anything that smacked of a repetition of the Voulet–Chanoine expedition.[168]

In 1900 Niger came into being as an entity – at least on paper. By the decree of 23 July all land beyond the river Niger (thus excluding Say and the right bank), and north of what the French considered the unfavourable demarcation line of 1898–9, became the 3rd Military Territory of Niger, placed under the authority of the Lieutenant-Governor of the newly created colony of Upper Senegal and Niger[169] (formerly Sudan). The first commander of the new territory, Lieutenant-Colonel Péroz, arrived at Say on 5 December.[170] By then the French controlled most of the West, together with the Tessaoua–Damagaram region, an isolated French outpost surrounded on all sides by vast stretches of land outside European control. To the west, the nearest permanent post was still Dosso. Between Dosso and Zinder, there was no French presence, only occasional small parties passing rapidly through from time to time along the path of destruction and desolation left behind by the Voulet–Chanoine expedition. The West was 'pacified' before the arrival of Péroz by a number of small detachments. The traumatic experience of the Voulet–Chanoine expedition had broken the will to resist, and so these detachments encountered little opposition. Even the Logomaten Tuareg submitted quickly to the French.[171] The exceptions were the pagan Gube of Loga and the Gabda of Falwell. It took three successive military expeditions, the first having suffered eighteen casualties, the second being forced to retreat after a fierce four hours battle, and the last numbering some 600 men, to conquer the rather insignificant villages of Loga and especially Sargadje, both completely destroyed in November 1900.[172] Among those eager to collaborate, we find first and foremost the Sudie of Filingue,[173] and the exiled Fulani from the *dallol* Bosso. The latter were allowed to resettle in the region of Tamkalle much to the dismay of the Zerma of Dosso and Koygolo.[174] In Dosso itself a party led by a certain Aouta (soon to become *zermakoy*) sought the favour and support of the French.[175]

It is unnecessary to relate in detail the very slow progress and fanning out of the thousand-man strong Péroz column.[176] Instead we must concentrate on some of the more fundamental elements. The first point to note is that Péroz's initial task was not to conquer Niger but to establish a line of communications between the Sudan and the French in Chad. However, by the time Péroz was in a position to do this, the government in Paris changed its mind and ordered Péroz not to establish any permanent posts east of Zinder. Since the government had good reason to suspect that Péroz would not abide by this order, he was recalled at the end of 1901.[177] The second point to stress is that Péroz was severely handicapped in his action by the obligation imposed upon him to respect the Anglo-French line of demarcation scrupulously and to avoid any disputes with the British.[178] This forced him to adopt a route too far to the north, via Filingue, Tahoua and El

Hassane north of Tessaoua; a semi-desert route which, as it turned out, was impracticable during the long dry season, and which as a consequence put a heavy strain on men and beasts.[179] After a number of small detachments had nearly perished on the stretch between Filingue and El Hassane, and Zinder had been cut off from the West for long periods,[180] the French finally swallowed their pride and applied to the British government for permission to cross through its zone. This permission was granted – parsimoniously, for only six months at a time.[181] (The absurdity of a situation in which a European government granted permission with regard to an African territory it did not control and to which it had no legitimate claim was never seen at the time.) It had been demonstrated that the 3rd Military Territory was not a viable entity.

Thirdly, Péroz was also severely handicapped, like Voulet before him, by an almost appalling lack of funds and means. Thus, like Voulet before him, he had to *vivre sur le pays*, to muddle through as best he could, 'sans moyens aucuns', as he expressed it himself.[182] This implied the operation of large-scale requisitions for which he was unable to pay. It was the West, the base for French expansion, and as such the corridor of access to the east, which bore the brunt of these requisitions, footing the bill for the conquest of modern Niger.[183] Its resources were taxed to their uttermost limit, and probably beyond. Requisitions and drought produced localized famine in many parts of the West during these years.[184] Péroz's successor, Lieutenant-Colonel Noël, was appalled by the naked misery he saw there,[185] and also by the magnitude of the southward-bound exoduses.[186] (The Kel Dinnik, the Kel Owi and other Tuareg, whose camels were indispensable to the French, also suffered heavily from the requisitions.)[187] The miracle, and a miracle the inhabitants of the West would have preferred to do without, is that Péroz was successful.

The fourth point is that Péroz was not always able to control his subordinates, and in particular to prevent some of them from resorting to questionable methods *à la* Voulet–Chanoine. For instance, a certain Lieu-tenant Figeac, turned loose on the Tuareg, '[se] livrait à une série d'opéra-tions militaires caractérisées surtout par des salves meurtrières jetées sur les groupes d'habitants qui fuyaient devant lui. Le commandant du territoire n'avait de nouvelles de cet officier que par le bruit et l'émotion que cette agression avait causée dans le pays.' This quotation is from Péroz's own official report.[188] Another lieutenant was believed to have attacked and completely destroyed a large village,[189] which demonstrates that the 'ex-cesses' of the Voulet–Chanoine expedition were in conformity with the nature and logic of colonial conquest.

It is probable that Péroz contributed indirectly to the acceleration of the British conquest of what is now Northern Nigeria. The effective occupation of large tracts of the French zone provided Sir Frederick Lugard with a number of excellent arguments to his superiors in London in favour of a northwards thrust.[190]

The first Tuareg revolt and its consequences

In the Centre, and in conformity with the nineteenth-century pattern, the sedentary Lissawan Tuareg and the hausaphone inhabitants of Adar and Gobir Tudu quickly submitted and even assisted the French against the Kel Dinnik and Kel Gress Tuareg.[191] The Kel Gress proved to be the most unremitting opponents of the French in this region. After Péroz's second-in-command, Major Gouraud, had inflicted upon them two heavy defeats at the battles of Zanguebe and Galmi (the latter well inside the British zone),[192] several factions submitted. But many Kel Gress, especially the *imajeghen*, retreated north and eastwards, determined to escape the French. Those who submitted had to pay a war levy (*impôt de guerre*) and were to provide the French regularly with supplies and transport. These were conditions which nearly all Tuareg nomads and semi-nomads had to subscribe to before their submission was accepted. Finally, by the convention of Tamaske (2 November 1901), the French put an end to the tributary status of the Adarawa and expelled both the Kel Gress and the Kel Dinnik from Adar. The sedentary Hausa of Gobir Tudu also obtained their independence from the Kel Gress. As for the sedentary Lissawan Tuareg, they were allowed to remain in the Tamaske region over which their chief, the *amatazza*, retained command.

The 'dissident' Kel Gress found ready allies among the Tamesguidda of Tarka and particularly among the Imuzurag and Izkazkazen Tuareg of Damergu, who were out to revenge their recent defeat at the hands of the French in the battle of Tanamari.[193] Before long, the rebels controlled the regions between Aïr and Damagaram, as well as land west and especially east of that line. Plundering the Kel Owi caravans and the sedentary communities of unoccupied Kanuriland (the Far East), entrenching themselves firmly in the hills of Koutoss and Alakoss, and finally joining the Sanūsī in Kanem and Borku further east, they posed a serious threat to the French not only in Niger, but also in Chad.[194] The town of Zinder, the easternmost French post in Niger and the capital of the 3rd Military Territory, was particularly exposed.

The decisive battles during this first Tuareg revolt took place not in Niger but at the Sanūsī *zawīya* or lodge of Bir-Alali in Kanem in January and December 1902. The second of these two battles was won by the French,[195] and as a result some of the Tuareg followed the retreating Sanūsī forces northwards. Among them was a certain Kaocen, an Izkazkazen Tuareg from Damergu, the future leader of the second Tuareg revolt in 1916–17.[196] But the main retreat was westwards into Niger. Deprived however of the support of the Sanūsīya, and no longer able to count on safe refuges east and north of the lake, the Tuareg were slowly but surely squeezed between a number of small French detachments. By 1903 most of the rebels had submitted[197] or had fled to Nigeria.[198]

This first Tuareg revolt had demonstrated the vulnerability of the French positions in the east. The practical consequences were first the transfer of the capital of the 3rd Military Territory from Zinder to Niamey on the river

Niger,[199] and second the extension of French rule both northwards and eastwards. The northward extension was also made necessary by the mounting insecurity in Aïr as evidenced by the many attacks on the trade caravans, including the *azalaï* which the French had for some time been providing with an escort.[200] (The main cause of these attacks appears to have been the French advance in southern Algeria and the subsequent closing down of markets which more or less forced the Kel Ahaggar Tuareg to try their luck further south.)[201] Posts were established at Goure in 1903, at N'Guigmi on the shores of Lake Chad and at Agades in 1904.[202] The French saw their position further strengthened by the British drive towards Kano and Sokoto in the early months of 1903,[203] a drive which was to deprive the Kel Gress of their refuge in the south. More important, the British finally agreed to have a second look at the border problem. The Convention of 1904 (which was part of the *Entente Cordiale*), stipulated that certain regions south of the line of demarcation, such as southern Adar, Maradi and Gobir, were to become French. But this would only take place after a mixed French–British commission had delimited the new border.[204] In fact, although the commission did not complete its work until 1909, the French were allowed to take possession of the new regions in 1907–8.[205] But the agreement had the rather curious consequence of artificially prolonging the independence of certain African polities, notably the realm of *k'aura* Assao, which now found itself in the uncomfortable position of being surrounded by European possessions.

The 'Great Withdrawal' was to take place in 1905. On orders from superior authorities, all posts north of Damergu and east of Goure were evacuated by the French in April and May.[206] The Minister did however authorize so-called 'intermittent' occupation, and the French continued to escort the *azalaï* and other caravans.[207] But they were not able to stop the Aïr Tuareg from taking a terrible revenge on the towns and oases accused of having displayed a conciliatory attitude towards the French. In Gall was sacked and the inhabitants of Teguidda massacred.[208]

By this time the French had put an end to the ephemeral existence of the 3rd Military Territory. The new territory, created in accordance with the decree of 26 December 1904,[209] was a rather strange entity. Composed of the former 1st and 3rd Military Territoires, and baptized *Territoire Militaire du Niger*, it stretched – on paper at least – from west of Timbuctu to Lake Chad, and included the left bank of the river Niger. It was an enormous territory, governed from Niamey, and centred on the West, that region where French rule was apparently the most solidly established.

THE FIRST YEARS OF THE FRENCH PRESENCE

Early changes in the West and the Zerma/Songhay revolts (1905–6)
The first basic problem confronting the French in Niger as elsewhere was the necessity of establishing some sort of local administration. This administra-

tion would have to rely upon whatever institutional framework existed already, first, because the French never had the necessary means and men to establish so-called 'direct rule'; and secondly, because coercive force had to be converted into legitimate authority accepted by the Africans and therefore mediated through their own pre-existing institutions. The difficulty was that these institutions were in French eyes more or less feudal in character, and thus theoretically incompatible with the nature and aims of French rule. It was a dilemma the French never managed to solve. In the final analysis the whole problem boiled down to where suitable intermediaries could be found to be appointed *chefs de canton*. Since the French aimed at establishing a uniform administration, all the canton chiefs were to be put on equal footing and to be given (theoretically) identical duties, obligations and prerogatives. In the West, it was obvious, in certain cases at least, whom the French would have to appoint. Thus the Songhay *amirus*, the Fulani *lamidos* and the *alfaize* of Say were appointed *chefs de canton*. In other more or less 'acephalous' regions of the West, the French 'solved' the problem by appointing priest-chiefs, or – in the case of the Zermaganda, Koygolo and Kurfey-Filingue – war-chiefs. In regions where a dual institutional structure had come into being, the 'political' chief was appointed, and the religious chiefs completely overlooked. However, in many parts of the West the French were forced to modify their initial approach, in order to maintain and cement the alliances they had contracted with a number of local leaders, factions and groups. The *cas célèbre* in this context is Dosso, where the French went out of their way to strengthen the position of the *zermakoy* (to the detriment, most notably, of the *sandi*), and in particular the position of Aouta, the strong man of Dosso. After Aouta had become *zermakoy* in 1902, the French made him the head of an entity consisting of Dosso and a certain number of regions and groups not previously under the jurisdiction of the *zermakoy*: the zermaphone Mawri of Sokorbe, the Gabda of Falwell, and Kiota, situated on the 'right bank' of the *dallol* Bosso and the seat of another *zermakoy*.[210] Parts of the *dallol* Bosso itself and the nearly uninhabited region south of Dosso down to the river may also have been incorporated into the domain of Dosso. Not content with this, the French systematically looked the other way when Aouta and his warriors raided neighbouring regions such as Loga and Gaya, where they are said to have captured slaves and cattle.[211] Aouta also tried to persuade the French to incorporate the *dallol* Fogha, Arewa and Dendi into his realm; with some success, it seems, since he was permitted to levy certain taxes among the inhabitants of the *dallol* Fogha and Dendi.[212] Aouta was thus able to achieve what his predecessors had probably been striving for over the better part of half a century, a predominant position for Dosso in the south-eastern half of the West, and perhaps even more significant, an internal transformation of the office of *zermakoy* into what may be described as a hereditary monarchy, conferred on Aouta and his direct descendants.

The case of Kurfey-Filingue is less clear cut but nevertheless highly instructive.[213] The region of Filingue was the gateway to the east as long as the French had to pass north of Adar, and for this reason it was of vital strategical importance during the first years of the colonial era. The French therefore felt the need to have an ally they could count on in this region. The ally was to be Gado Namalaya, the *mayaki* or head of the Sudie cavalry, whom the French appointed *chef de canton* as they did many other war-chiefs in other parts of the West. But in the case of Gado, as in that of Aouta, the French closed their eyes to his extensive raiding activities.[214] The booty which Gado collected enabled him to establish his new-found position on a firm basis, and to emerge as both the *de jure* and *de facto sarkin* Filingue, as he now called himself. Gado, hitherto a war-chief whose function it was to carry out the decision of the clan or lineage heads, had become the undisputed master of the Sudie.

After 1903 the region around Niamey, the new capital, also became of prime importance. Here the French found themselves faced with a seemingly intricate and bewildering situation which induced them to mould the whole region into one huge canton. However, not only was Karma, a traditional Songhay polity, incorporated into the completely artificial canton of Ni-amey, but a certain Bagniou, former guide of the Voulet–Chanoine expedi-tion and a man without any traditional or legitimate claims to the position of chief, was appointed *chef de canton*. It was not long before Bagniou and his subordinate, the chief of Karma, found themselves at odds.[215]

Slavery was not a major preoccupation with the French during the early days of colonial rule. In theory, slavery was incompatible with French law. But French law applied only to citizens and not to the African subjects, and this subtlety provided the officers on the spot with an excellent excuse for doing little or nothing. The exception was the *bugaje* communities which the Tuareg had implanted in certain southern regions, especially the East. Many of these communities were, for obvious political reasons, made independent of their Tuareg overlords and put under the authority of the sedentary canton chiefs.[216] In the West, however, it seems that many slaves simply ran away from their masters and settled down on hitherto uncleared land. Since this led to localized troubles, the French were frequently forced to intervene between the former slaves, now called 'non-free', and their masters.[217] However, the superior authorities in Dakar and especially in Paris advocated a different policy. Through a federal decree issued on 12 December 1905, which stipulated heavy penalties for all forms of slave trade,[218] they signalled to the men on the spot the necessity of taking more positive action. As a consequence, the Governor of Upper Senegal and Niger proclaimed in a famous *circulaire* of June 1906 the incompatibility of slavery with French rule.[219] The result was immediate and devastating. Almost instantly the majority of slaves deserted their Tuareg, Zerma and Songhay masters (and also, it seems, the religion of their masters, at least when this religion was Islam).[220] In the face of this monumental threat to their very life style, the nobles of the West adopted a strategy which was to prove quite successful. It involved the institution of *labukoy* or earth-priest. The *chefs de canton*, whether they had been earth-priests previously or not, tended to take the title of *labukoy* for themselves. They then reinterpreted customary law to their own advantage. According to this reinterpretation, with which the French apparently found no fault, the *labukoy* was not only the 'owner of the land' in the traditional sense of that term, but the authentic landlord of all vacant land. Thus the nobility of the West was soon able to reassert its hold over the former slaves, who were slowly reduced to the status of rent-paying tenants, cultivating land belonging to the nobility. This new concept of land tenure paved the way for the formation of large estates in the West, and their corollary, a landless rural proletariat. But it also resulted in a near-permanent and pernicious climate of social tension and unrest and in a long series of land disputes.[221] Naturally, this was a slow process, and we are anticipating somewhat the course of events, as we are when making the obvious point that it was among the former 'slaves' of the West that the French recruited most of their auxiliaries (including those former slaves parked in so-called 'freedom villages' before 1910).[222] In other words the French provided at least some of these slaves with new opportunities, and the West underwent a process of status reversal during the colonial period.

As already noted, former slaves (before 1906, runaway slaves) also constituted the majority of those who took part in the internal migration which was one of the major features of the early colonial period in the West. However, other social categories were also among those who were responsible for the clearing and settling of vast areas of hitherto uninhabited bush, and who did so mainly in order to escape the authoritarian rule of the new canton chiefs. For instance, among the people from Dosso who settled down in the Kobkitanda and Sambera regions on the river bank (and separated from Dosso by nearly 60 kilometres of no-man's-land), there seems to have been an important contingent of Sabiri.[223] The Sabiri constituted, as noted earlier, the most ancient population of Dosso. As such, they and their chief, the *sandi*, occupied a privileged position before the advent of Aouta *zermakoy*. It is probable, therefore, that their southwards migration should be interpreted as a protest against the internal changes that had taken place in Dosso. But as already seen the settlers in Sambera and Kobkitanda were denied their autonomy and became instead subjects of the very ruler whose authority many of them had tried to escape, the *zermakoy* of Dosso.

It can be deduced from the above that although, curiously enough, the official French policy during this early period was not to tamper with the internal affairs of the regions they had subdued,[224] the colonial conquest and its aftermath nevertheless had a profound impact upon the societies of the West. Three main factors may be identified, the first being the need to establish a local administration. This induced the French to simplify to a dangerous degree the extremely intricate situation which prevailed in the West prior to their arrival. The second factor was the need for the French to find allies, and third, the degree to which local leaders, groups and factions were able to adjust themselves to the colonial situation, and to perceive the advantages that could be derived from it. The outcome was a complete realignment of the pre-colonial *rapports de force*, not only between but also within the various entities and societies of the West. Internally (and institutionally), the most significant transformation concerned the rapid withering away of whatever systems of checks and balances had existed previously. The French, by recognizing the *chefs de canton* as the sole intermediaries between themselves and the indigenous population, and by ignoring for instance the state councils (where such existed), relegated other officials or priest-chiefs to the role of insignificant subordinates without any official status. Their position was further undermined and that of the *chefs de canton* further strengthened by the tendency of the French to base succession on a fairly strict hereditary principle to the near-total exclusion of whatever other principles – not infrequently rotational – had prevailed during the pre-colonial period. Externally, although the French manipulated the local chiefs, they were in turn manipulated by those very same chiefs. Thus, although the French 'débarassa [l'Ouest] des maîtres Peul et Touareg',[225] they enabled other rulers and groups to exercise a form of subimperialism over former rivals.

Whether these war-chiefs, priest-chiefs and former French auxiliaries, now 'promoted' to the rank of *chef de canton*, tried to establish their new-found position on as firm a basis as possible, or whether they were simply out to 'make the most of it', to profit from the new situation as long as they could count on French support, the result was the same. 'Ces chefs, forts de notre appui, ont' (in the words of Michel Sellier, himself an administrator) 'exigé, pillé, menacé.'[226]

When we consider the multiple abuses and the exorbitant requisitions and taxes (against a background of drought and famine); the fact that the early years of colonial rule witnessed, as we have seen, the emergence of an authoritarian society and, worse still, a society in which authority was exercised arbitrarily (at the level both of the African *chefferies* and of the French); and finally the grave social tension as evidenced by the exodus of the slaves; we have the explanation for the trouble which occurred in several parts of the West between 1902 and 1906. It began in the region of Karma in 1902, spread to Liddo in the lower *dallol* Mawri in 1903, to Kiota in the same year, and to Falwell, the Zermaganda and Arewa in 1904.[227] In the following year the inhabitants of Sambera and Kobkitanda revolted. Refusing to pay taxes and to have anything more to do with the *zermakoy*, they put up a vigorous resistance to the French and their auxiliaries, the warriors of Aouta *zermakoy* and *lamido* Bayero. Both villages were completely destroyed and a considerable number of rebels killed (although we do not know how many).[228] The Sambera–Kobkitanda revolt was a local affair, which had erupted in an isolated part of the West. Quite another matter, however, was the revolt of the Zerma/Songhay on the left bank in January 1906. Triggered off by the *amiru* of Karma, Oumarou, who was able to rally all the villages from Sorbon-Hausa to Boubon, it took the French completely by surprise. The rebels, of whom some 1,200 seem to have been armed, destroyed the main telegraph line, sacked a river convoy, massacred a small French unit on tour and prepared to march on the virtually defenceless Niamey. This was a revolt which had erupted in the very heart of the Military Territory, only a few kilometres north-west of the capital, in a region believed to be particularly tranquil. However, the rebels failed to conquer the colonial capital and instead gave the French time to gather together the necessary troops. (The detachment coming in from Dori was attacked on the right bank, where it seems that the local population was ready to support the rebels.)[229] The clash between the French column, composed of some 300 *tirailleurs* as well as the inevitable Zerma, Fulani and Sudie auxiliaries from Dosso, Birnin Gaoure (formerly Tamkalle) and Filingue, and the rebels occurred on 16, 17 and 18 January. The rebels, having suffered heavy casualties (about seventy dead), retreated northwards to Zermaganda, where the inhabitants of some eighteen villages under the leadership of the chief of Simiri, Lande, joined them. A second French column was attacked on 3 March. However, the battle proved disastrous to the rebels, of whom thirty were killed including Lande, and most of them surrendered.[230] Oumarou and a small party of stalwarts were able to retreat northwards, but not for very long. Tracked down by Gado Namalaya and his men, they were ambushed and killed somewhere in northern Zermaganda.[231]

A third revolt seems to have been on the brink of erupting among the zermaphone Mawri of Sokorbe in March–April 1906. A so-called 'military demonstration' was deemed necessary and carried out.[232]

Early changes in the Centre and the East, and the plot in Zinder
The Centre and the East fitted the pre-conceived schema of the French much better than did the West. Here at least there were organized states, governed by princes who could be classified as 'oriental despots'. And even in regions where the political organization was somewhat more fluid, the main characteristic of the society was the existence of a 'feudal' and in some cases conquering aristocracy (the Tuareg) which pressurized and exploited the rural masses. Even better, some of the princes in the East were also 'imperialists' who had subdued alien entities. Given this situation it was evident what line of conduct the French, as the self-proclaimed 'liberators' of the Africans, as the opponents of 'feudalism' and 'tyranny', would have to adopt; they would have to curtail the power of the princes and the feudal lords, and to 'liberate' subdued or vassal states from 'foreign' rule. The main 'victims' of the French were the Tuareg and especially the *sarkin* Damagaram. His domains were soon reduced to Damagaram proper. The French liberated *maï* Moussa Kosso, who had spent twenty-nine years in captivity in Zinder, and restored him to the throne of Mounio. The rulers of Magaria, Kantche and the Sossebaki states were all made independent of the *sarkin*

Damagaram.[233] (In the south, the French for a while contemplated exploiting the *sarkin* Damagaram's claim to overlordship of such polities as Nguru, Hadejia and Daura to their own advantage. But since this claim was of quite recent origin, and since these polities were evidently situated outside their zone, the firm stand adopted by the British soon induced the French to abandon the project.)[234] In Adar, as already noted, the French made the local Hausa chiefs independent of their Tuareg overlords. This even included the *sarkin* Tahoua who was not a traditional chief at all but a puppet imposed by the Kel Dinnik. Among the Gobirawa of Gobir Tudu and the Kanuri of Damergu, formerly under 'direct' Tuareg rule, the situation was different, since they did not possess any institutions beyond the village level. Here the French created what can be considered to be artificial units or cantons, and usually appointed the chief of the most important village as *chef de canton*.[235] For the nomads, or at least those who had already submitted, the French adopted a uniform administrative system. Thus both the Tuareg and the Fulani, the latter previously under the jurisdiction of the Hausa princes, were formed into *groupements* and placed outside the authority of the *chefs de canton*. Although the French tried strictly to delimit the grazing zones and the corridors of transhumance, the result was nevertheless a rather awkward situation, pregnant with conflicts, in which a portion of the population living permanently or intermittently within a given canton escaped the authority of the *chef de canton*.[236]

In the case of the rural Hausa, it may be tentatively suggested that their conditions improved as a result of the arrival of the French. The main factors relevant here seem to be the curtailing of the power of the ruling class or *sarauta*, the nature of Hausa society, and above all the geopolitical position of Hausaland. Indeed, the proximity of the frontier compelled the French to adopt a rather low-key approach as far as taxes and requisitions were concerned, simply in order to prevent migrations to the south. Besides, being for the moment the most peripheral region under French rule, the East (as opposed to the West and certain parts of the Centre) did not serve as a corridor of access. Although the French in Niger and Chad continued to collaborate closely, the attempt made in 1904 to use Niger as a basis for the provisioning of Chad in men and supplies does not seem to have been renewed before 1908.[237] Hence the need for requisition was less substantial here than further west. In addition, slaves were apparently few in number outside Damagaram and perhaps a few other polities, and the basically egalitarian nature of the rural society of Nigerien Hausaland (as opposed to that of metropolitan Hausaland) meant that the East escaped the social tensions which characterized the West during the first years of colonial rule.

The attitude of the rural Hausa towards the French seems to have been ambiguous. Outside the regions pacified by Major Lamy, the French met little opposition. Nor was there anywhere any enthusiasm or any attempt by particular groups, factions or individuals to take advantage of the new situation. Indeed, the Hausa countryside remained remarkably quiet and undisturbed during the first fifteen years or so of colonial rule. The only exceptions were Yamia east of Zinder where a localized revolt erupted in 1901,[238] the Gangara region south of Tessaoua, where an abortive revolt broke out in 1902 (followed, according to the British, by an exodus southwards of some 5,000 persons),[239] and certain parts of Adar and Gobir Tudu, where there seem to have been violent clashes between the *anna* and the Tuareg in 1903.[240]

In the East, the main challenge to the French did not originate (as in the West) from what can perhaps be described as the 'grass-roots' level but, logically enough, from the 'ruling class' or *sarauta*, and – perhaps more surprisingly – from the trading community, in other words, from urban Hausaland. It all began in 1901 when the French, realizing how poorly informed they were about the state of affairs in Damagaram, rid themselves of most of their auxiliaries, suspected of being in the service of Ahmadu II, the new *sarkin* Damagaram. At the end of the same year Ahmadu II sent out a certain *sarki* Shau Sule to collect taxes. According to Major Gouraud, the then Resident in Zinder, *sarki* Shau Sule and his men 'mettaient le pays en coup reglé', burning down villages and executing recalcitrant subjects.[241] The French were in no mood to tolerate such practices (which were probably all too common in the pre-colonial era) and *sarki* Shau Sule ended his days in front of a firing squad. The immediate consequence was, as Gouraud put it, that 'les réclamations pleuvaient',[242] and that many members of the *sarauta*, including the *sarkin* Damagaram himself, had to hand an impressive quantity of cattle and goods back to what the French, and the local Muslim judge, considered to be their rightful owners, the people of Damagaram.[243] Thus the *sarauta* instantly lost its hold over the country. A 'revolution' had taken place, with the consequence that the resources of Damagaram would no longer be channelled in a sufficient proportion towards the court; and, incidentally, that the numerous state or palace slaves, whose responsibility it was to collect taxes, and who were entitled to commissions on the sums they collected, would soon be reduced to a state of beggary.[244] Consequently, the *sarki* and the court dignitaries now lacked the necessary capital to engage in long-distance trade, or even to maintain the central administration of the polity. The taxes imposed by the French absorbed an increasing proportion of the profits derived from the steadily declining trade, and so it is not surprising that the agitation in Zinder in February 1904 was most acute among the traders, the Muslim clerics and the palace slaves.[245]

However, thanks in part to the widespread popular support they enjoyed in Zinder for the time being, the French were able to set up a network of informers. From this they discovered in time a plot designed to liberate Damagaram from the Europeans. Behind the plot was, it seems, a powerful alliance comprising the *sarauta*, including the palace slaves, and also the trading community under its leader, that once faithful ally of the French, Mallam Yaro. A total of sixteen arrests were made between the end of March and June 1906. Ahmadu II, Mallam Yaro and four others were exiled to the Ivory Coast[246] and the state of Damagaram dismantled.[247] Outlying regions, such as Bande and Dan Tchiao, became independent under the *sarkin Bare* (or chief archer of Damagaram) and the *waziri* (chief of customs).[248] Simultaneously the French had to effect numerous *tournées de police* throughout the region in order to make clear to the *talakawa* that the execution of *sarki* Shau Sule and the arrest of Ahmadu II did not mean the end to *all* superior authority.[249] What was left of metropolitan Damagaram was divided into three provinces, the province of Zinder being placed under the authority of Bellama, a former palace slave and a eunuch. His nomination is said to have provoked an exodus of some 3,000 persons.[250]

In Mounio, Damagaram's recently restored eastern neighbour, *maï* Suleiman (the successor of Moussa Kosso), also conspired against the French, possibly in connection with the plotters in Zinder. As a result, the *maï* himself and his realm suffered the same fate as Ahmadu II and Damagaram.[251]

The disturbances in the Central Sudan 1905–6: a comparative analysis
The plotters and conspirators in Zinder and Mounio achieved nothing, except to precipitate the ultimate and final fall of both states. This is in stark contrast to the rebels in the West who do seem to have obtained, indirectly, a certain number of positive results. Indeed, the evidence suggests that the revolts of 1905–6 'opened the eyes' of the French; they revealed to the French the extent to which they had been led astray by their allies and protégés, especially by Bagniou.[252] The canton of Niamey was abolished in 1908, and that of Karma restored.[253] The *sarkin* Filingue seems to have moderated his raiding activities after 1906. As for the *zermakoy* of Dosso, he slowly lost his grip over Falwell, Sokorbe and even Sambera, which were eventually to become cantons themselves.

Northern Nigeria was also the theatre of revolts in 1906.[254] In February 'Lugard's ramshackle empire was suddenly threatened by a rebellion of Hausa peasants at Satiru armed with hoes and axes',[255] peasants who annihilated a whole company of mounted infantry.[256] This happened at a time when nearly all available troops were engaged in restoring order in Munshi (i.e. Tiv) country much further south.[257] The British, who were taken completely by surprise, had good reason to fear that the Satiru revolt was the prelude to a general rising throughout the north. Although there was widespread unrest in many parts of Northern Nigeria, especially in the old Mahdist stronghold of Bauchi,[258] no such general rising did in fact occur, mainly because of the firm stand of the *sarkin Musulmi* and the other Fulani emirs[259] (except for the Emir of Gwandu).[260] This stand provided the British with the necessary time to recall the detachments in the south. The fear generated among the British *and* the Fulani emirs by the Satiru rising is evident in the particularly brutal and ferocious way in which it was suppressed. The Resident in Sokoto (Major Burdon) used the word 'slaughter' in his official report,[261] and told the French blandly that the rebels (who numbered about 5,000 according to an eyewitness account)[262] had been practically exterminated.[263] The village of Satiru was razed to the ground. 'No wall or tree [was] left standing.'[264]

In April 1906 Lugard deemed it necessary to send a military expedition against the emirate of Hadejia, a former vassal of Damagaram, which had assumed 'an aggressive demeanour'.[265] Two smaller detachments had also to be sent to restore order in parts of the emirate of Kano.[266] The question is whether there was a link between all these plots, conspiracies, unrests and revolts. Much has been made in this context of the presence both at Kobkitanda and at Satiru of a certain blind Mahdist cleric by the name of Saibou or Mallam Shuaibu or Dan Makafo, who was beheaded in the market place of Sokoto on 12 March 1906.[267] The French concluded that they were up against a vast Mahdist conspiracy designed to oust the Europeans from Central Sudan.[268] It may well be that such a scheme actually existed. It may also be that Mahdist clerics were instrumental in articulating and in voicing the grievances of the discontent. There is little doubt that Mahdists took an active part in all the disturbances listed above. On the other hand, the Mahdist conspiracy theory is too convenient to be entirely convincing, and does not tell the whole story. It may be argued that the disturbances of 1905–6 erupted as a logical consequence of the European policies in the Central Sudan, more precisely as a consequence of the Europeans' quest for local allies. For instance, in the case of Satiru, most of the rebels were runaway slaves[269] who had been denied their freedom by the British.[270] Their revolt was probably directed as much against their immediate master, the *sarkin Musulmi* of Sokoto, and more generally the Fulani 'establishment', as against the British or the British–Fulani alliance.[271] This alliance must have come as a shock to the Hausa peasantry which 'seems to have endeavoured to overthrow the Fulani rulers subsequent to the latters' defeat in the military confrontation with the British'.[272] This analysis applies also in the Sambera–Kobkitanda revolts, directed as much against the local allies of the French as against the French themselves. In both Damagaram and Hadejia the *sarauta*, and in particular the palace slaves, reacted against what they considered to be an attempt by the Europeans to dismantle the state machinery.

The extension of French rule north and east after 1906
In the spring and summer of 1906 French official policy was completely reversed. The Minister of Colonies, Georges Leygues, now ordered the immediate establishment of French posts in a number of distant places in southern Algeria and Niger, including N'Guigmi, Agades and Bilma.[273] The officers in the field lost no time, and the orders had been carried out by July 1906.[274] This haste was not determined by local conditions, such as for instance the plight of the oasis-dwellers, but – it is tempting to say, as usual – by imperial rivalry. To the authorities in Paris there was in fact little doubt

that a German scientific mission, officially designed to explore the Tripolitanian hinterland, had in reality been instructed to push as far as Lake Chad, and to establish German rule over the ancient and hitherto unoccupied Fezzan–Bilma–Borno route. The creation of a sort of German 'corridor' stretching from Cameroon in the south to the Turkish possessions in the north would naturally cut off the French colonial empires in north and western Africa from Chad and therefore had to be thwarted.[275]

The new posts established in Agades and Bilma were, according to Paris, temporary, that is they were to be maintained only as long as German (and Turkish) ambitions posed a threat to the North and the North-East.[276] But the officers on the spot, as well as the Governor-General in Dakar, advocated the opposite viewpoint,[277] and did their best to consolidate the positions already acquired. The posts of Agades, Bilma and N'Guigmi were to be permanent.

Once in Agades and Bilma the French were confronted with the formidable task of pacifying the North and the North-East. This forced them to operate, probably for the first time, large-scale requisitions among the peoples of the Centre and especially of the East; requisitions for which the French were unable to pay. (As usual, the government in Paris refused to grant the funds necessary to implement its own orders.)[278] As happened again and again throughout the colonial history of Niger, this stepping-up of the French demands coincided with a period of drought, which lasted to about 1909, and possibly also of famine.[279]

Fortunately for the French, the Aïr Tuareg, who had probably suffered severely from the drought of 1898/9–1904, as well as from the numerous raids perpetuated by the Tubu, the Awlād Sulaymān and the Kel Ahaggar, and who now had to cope with yet another drought, were not in a position to offer any active, armed resistance. On the other hand, they – especially the Kel Fadei – had no intention of submitting to the French.[280] The pacification of the North took, therefore, the shape of numerous small detachments sent out to ambush and kill as many 'dissident' Tuareg as possible, to sack their camps, and to capture their cattle. After two years of these brutal methods, the Aïr Tuareg had had enough and most submitted. The routes were safe once more.[281] It only remained for the French to pacify the North-East.

CONCLUSION

I have in the second half of this chapter tried to expose and put to rest two related and intertwined myths. The first is that the people of Niger offered little resistance to the French; the second that the difficulties experienced by the most important of the French expeditions, the Voulet–Chanoine 'mission', were due mainly to the insanity of the principal officers together with inadequate planning, lack of means and internal division among the French. In reality, the Voulet–Chanoine mission was a disaster primarily because it ran into a population which was determined to resist its advance. Several other French missions or expeditions, notably the Foureau–Lamy mission, encountered equally determined opposition.

Seen in a broader perspective, the resistance against the French constituted, as we have seen, one of the final episodes in a particularly long and distinguished tradition of resistance against foreign conquerors as well as against the pretensions of neighbouring expansionist realms. In the West this tradition dated back to the collapse of the Songhay empire at the end of the sixteenth century; in Hausaland to the establishment of the Sokoto Caliphate more than two hundred years later. Towards the end of the nineteenth century the people of many parts of the West were able to liberate themselves from Fulani rule and to defeat Ahmad Chekou, Ali Bori and their men. Further east, the Hausa not only withstood the attempts of the Torodbe-Fulani rulers of the Hausa heartland to subdue them, but also posed a significant threat to the position of these rulers. The Hausa were particularly strong in Damagaram, the only large polity to emerge in the area during the pre-colonial era.

However, even in the earliest phase of the colonial period its ambiguous and complex nature is evident. For in spite of the tradition of resistance referred to above, a number of individuals and groups, in the West in particular, were quick to perceive the advantages presented by an alliance with the French. In fact the first major revolts were directed as much against these individuals and groups as against the French; or perhaps against the changes brought about by the many local alliances between certain groups and the French; against the emergence of an authoritarian and autocratic society. Perhaps the French were simply one conqueror too many.

What also stands out very clearly is the difference between the Zerma/Songhay and the Hausa. The former represent the extremes: staunch resistance and early rebellion, but also close collaboration. The latter, on the other hand, may be qualified as 'middle-of-the-roaders', reluctant both to collaborate and to revolt; or at least reluctant to revolt with arms in hand. Instead, after the initial shock of the Voulet–Chanoine mission, the Hausa opposed the French with a particular kind of passive resistance, and a successful one from the point of view of the 'traditionalists', since Hausa society remained (as we shall see) relatively impermeable to French influence. This difference may be attributed in part to the changes brought about by the French. Whereas the coming of the French in the West had the effect of accelerating the evolution towards an authoritarian society, and thus of accentuating social antagonisms, it had the opposite effect in Hausaland. The French severely circumscribed the power of the Hausa *sarauta*, including that of Damagaram, and in so doing reversed the dominant trend of the second half of the nineteenth century. That period, in part because of significant changes in international trade and economic conditions generally, had witnessed in many regions of Hausaland, Damagaram included, a growing opposition between rulers and ruled; between an increasingly slave-ridden and increasingly predatory society on the one hand, and the basically egalitarian society of the rural *talakawa* on the other.

It may also be, quite simply, that the 'hundred years' war' against the Sokoto Caliphate and the Voulet–Chanoine mission had sapped the will of the Hausa to resist and to revolt.

The Tuareg, as the leading pre-colonial imperialists and because of their engagement in trans-Saharan trade, a trade which was now doomed, stood to lose the most from French rule. While it is true that many of the trade-oriented Tuareg sought to accommodate the French, it was clear by 1908 that the Tuareg way of life was incompatible with French rule, as the revolt of 1901–3 had already demonstrated. But the repression which followed did not break the strength of the Tuareg.

3

The decisive years, 1908–22

By approximately 1908 all the regions which later became the Republic of Niger had been brought under more or less effective French control. The exception was the huge but very sparsely populated North-East where conditions remained unsettled. The French claimed that the Turks were at least partly responsible for this. After 1907 the Turks tried to tighten their grip over the Central Sahara, Tibesti in particular, establishing small garrisons at Bardai, Zaouar and Yao in 1911.[1] According to the French, they also encouraged their Arab and Tubu subjects to raid French territory.[2] However, after the French had apparently soundly defeated the raiders in 1908,[3] 1909[4] and 1910,[5] and after a series of successful French retaliatory raids,[6] the situation improved markedly. Furthermore, and although one party of raiders reached as far south-west as the outskirts of the *cercle* of Zinder in 1911,[7] the main bulk of the population of Niger was scarcely affected by what went on in the North-East. The time had come, it seemed, for the French – now partially relieved of military preoccupations – to increase their activity by pursuing a stronger internal policy. That purely military considerations were no longer paramount is illustrated by the fact that the regular military forces stationed in Niger were reduced to a mere thousand men in 1910.[8] However, because of reinforcements over the years, there were some 1,600 men by the autumn of 1916.[9] Governor and Colonel Venel's policy ('ne toucher aux groupements préexistants que d'une main légère et très adroite')[10] was reversed and the years after 1908, and especially after 1911, witnessed what Pierre Bonte has called 'une accélération de la politique colonisatrice'. Henceforth 'l'administration pense agir en profondeur'.[11] This 'new' French approach led to a number of important changes, although only rarely were they what the French had anticipated. This was not simply because of the severe drought and famine of 1913–15; the disruptive effects of external events, the First World War in particular, must also be taken into account. But basically the French miscalculated, in that they overestimated their own efficiency and the means at their disposal, and underestimated the combativeness of the Africans. Or rather, they failed to realize that the majority of the people of Niger had not yet fully acquiesced to colonial rule. Many Nigeriens were still determined to have a say in the shaping of their own future, so that the very assumption that it was no longer necessary to rule by the sword alone, although perhaps correct in the case of the Zerma/Songhay of the West, proved to be a fallacy in the case of the other peoples of Niger.

The year 1908 marked the end of the initial period of colonial conquest and ushered in a few years of relative peace. It is therefore appropriate here to give an overview of the formal institutional, administrative and legal system that the French sought to set up in Niger, and which was of course identical to the systems already established in the other colonies of French West Africa. But first a few words about territorial changes. The borders of the 'new' Military Territory of Niger, which was established on 1 January 1912, corresponded closely to those of the former 3rd Military Territory before 1905. Having been shorn earlier of Timbuctu and Gao,[12] it included all the land between the river Niger and Lake Chad. However, by contrast with the old 3rd Military Territory, the 'new' territory was granted autonomous status, in the sense that its Governor received his orders directly from the Governor-General in Dakar. Finally, Zinder recovered its former dignity as capital.[13]

Early French colonial administration was entirely bureaucratic. Legislative and executive power devolved from the President of the Republic (and not Parliament) through the Minister of Colonies and the Governor-General of French West Africa in Dakar to the Governor and his district officers. The top man on the spot in Niger, the Governor (entitled Commissioner or *Commissaire* before 1922), was up to 1922 usually a lieutenant-colonel or full colonel. Responsible to the Governor were a small number of departmental heads and, in particular, the seven *Commandants de cercle* of Niamey, Madaoua (later Tahoua), Zinder, Goure, N'Guigmi, Agades and Bilma. Six of the *Commandants* were army officers, usually of the rank of captain, the seventh, the *Commandant* of Niamey, being, after 1913 at least, a civilian. After Niger achieved the status of a civilian-governed colony in 1922, the military remained in charge only of the *cercle* of Agades. The *cercles* were in turn subdivided into a varying number of *secteurs* (later renamed *subdivisions*), four at the most, administered by officers of lieutenant rank. Finally, a *secteur* comprised indigenous political entities such as provinces, cantons, tribes and/or 'groups' (*groupements*), under the authority of so-called 'traditional' chiefs. Provinces, fairly large entities subdivided into cantons, were the exception. Most *chefs de secteur* (later *chefs de subdivision*) in the south had under their authority between three and eight cantons, and one or two *groupements* of Fulani and/or Tuareg nomads or semi-nomads. Provinces and cantons were territorially defined entities, tribes and 'groups' were ethnically defined entities.[14]

The cornerstone of French rule in Niger, as elsewhere in Africa, was the notion of 'subject' or *sujet*. As *sujets* the Africans were governed, not by law, but by so-called administrative decrees, all of which emanated in theory from the President of the Republic. This implies that the Africans enjoyed none of the rights embodied in the Constitution of the Third Republic. Nor were they called upon to assume any of the duties defined by that Constitution.

What the status of *sujet* really meant was spelt out by the decree of 21 November 1904. This decree defined a number of special legal provisions known collectively as the *indigénat*. The most notorious of these provisions stipulated that any *sujet* could be tried on the spot by the local French administrator and sentenced to a maximum of fifteen days' imprisonment and fifty francs in fines. The decree listed a total of twenty-six offences. Among these was the refusal by a *sujet* to carry out, or even to carry out in a careless or reluctant manner, requisitions ordered by the administration. Other offences listed were the non-payment of taxes and fines; a disrespectful attitude towards the administrators; disrespectful speeches or even remarks made or uttered in public, together with songs intended to undermine the respect due to the French; and a non-collaborative attitude, that is, the withholding of information from the French. Finally, festivities and public celebrations of any sort were not allowed to continue beyond the time specified by the local district officer.[15]

As for that other notorious institution, forced labour, it was limited by the decree of 1912 to no more than five days a year for every fit adult person of male sex.[16] In matters both of criminal and civil law, the *sujets* came under the jurisdiction of the *cercle* courts, presided over by the *Commandants*, who also acted as public prosecutors. In his capacity of judge, the *Commandant* was assisted by two native assessors whose task it was to advise him on the local customary law, which was the law he was supposed to apply. There was no limit to the sentence a *cercle* court could impose, even including capital punishment. However, all sentences exceeding five years of imprisonment had to be officially confirmed by the Dakar-based *Chambre d'Homologation*, a sort of Supreme Court.[17]

Any appreciation of this institutional system, not only in Niger but throughout French Africa, must first point out that it contained no built-in checks or balances. Apart from the restraints imposed upon all French citizens by criminal law, the administrators could do pretty much as they pleased. To say that no institutional channels existed through which the Africans could voice their grievances is to blur the main point. Faced with the *Commandant*, i.e. the local chief administrative officer, law-maker (in the sense that he could interpret local customary law as he wished), judge, police chief, military commander, prison superintendent, tax-collector, chief medical officer and much more, the average African was powerless. He was left with three alternatives: to obey, to migrate somewhere else if possible, or to revolt. Indeed, as can be seen from the provisions regarding requisitions, a mere tacit acquiescence to French rule would not do. The French required nothing short of active collaboration. The administrators on the spot in

Niger wielded, if anything, even more power than their colleagues in other parts of French West Africa, because the difficulties of communication within their territory made it practically impossible for superior authorities to keep a watchful eye on the local administration and to see that directives and orders were carried out at the local level.

The institution of forced labour and the provision by which any African could, without trial, be fined or imprisoned for a limited number of days have received much attention, but it was the stipulations regarding requisitions that proved most detrimental to the Africans, and which were in a sense the most questionable. These stipulations implied, as has already been seen, that the French could – legally – tax the resources of the Africans at will. Bearing in mind that requisitions could mean anything from the forceful seizure of food-stuffs and animals, at prices set by the French, to forced labour in disguise, these stipulations constituted little more than a licence to plunder.

The French system thus appears potentially despotic and arbitrary. Only the sometimes hypothetical benevolence and humanitarianism of the administrators, together with lack of means and the fear of revolts, constituted potential checks.

THE 'NEW' FRENCH POLICY

The collapse of trans-Saharan trade and the Tuareg economy
After 1907 trans-Saharan trade was reduced to a trickle.[18] It collapsed altogether in 1911 as a consequence of the outbreak of the Turkish–Italian war in the north and the extension of the Nigerian railway to Kano in the south. The railway extension led to a drastic cut in transportation costs, from 1,230 francs per ton via the desert to Zinder to a mere 350 francs via Nigeria.[19] The collapse of trans-Saharan trade had apparently little adverse effect upon the Tuareg economy. One reason for this was that, due to increasing security, the inter-regional trade between the Sahara and the Sudan, as opposed to the long-distance trans-Saharan trade, survived and between 1907 and 1913 even recovered from its previous all-time low. Salt from the Kawar oases continued to be in considerable demand throughout the Sudan, and the oasis-dwellers still needed millet from the south.[20] More important were the repercussions of developments in Northern Nigeria. The almost instant boom triggered off by the railway – as people turned to groundnut cultivation[21] – not only increased the need for local transportation, i.e. from the producers and/or the local markets to the railway termini, but also provided expanding markets for grain and animals from the north. The Tuareg, including the *bugaje*, benefited considerably from this.[22] Small wonder therefore that when around 1913–14 the decision-makers in Dakar and Paris thought of resurrecting the trans-Saharan trade, they found that the officers posted in Niger were against it, and that the Tuareg were not interested.[23]

Apparently the French also provided the Tuareg transporters with new opportunities. An expanding administration which by now maintained garrisons in such far-off places as N'Guigmi, Agades and, in particular, Bilma, found itself increasingly dependent upon Tuareg transport. Apparently the Tuareg carried out transport on behalf of the French, up to 1913 at least, on a regular basis. The French did not resort to requisitions in this matter; in fact it seems that they paid the Tuareg quite well for their services.[24]

Although the evidence is patchy, the same was apparently true of the provision of men and supplies to Chad, provisioning which was carried out, intermittently, through Niger (after 1913 through Nigeria). In 1908, and possibly also in 1911, the French did requisition camels, pack bullocks and food-stuffs for this purpose, especially among the Kel Gress Tuareg of the Centre and the Kanuri of the Far East,[25] but these requisition drives seem to have been exceptional. In 1912–13, for instance, the French paid more than 185,000 francs to the transporters who took part in the provisioning of Chad, an operation which that year involved 2,600 camels and 2,100 oxen.[26]

The 'new' economic policy and its consequences
Perhaps the most important factor responsible for the expansion of the extra-subsistence sector in parts of Niger was the 'new' economic policy inaugurated by the French. This 'new' policy, which was based on illusions about the economic future of Niger,[27] consisted simply of imposing heavier taxes. From the rather poor evidence, it seems fairly certain that the rate of the poll tax doubled between 1914 and 1915[28] and that it trebled during the period 1906 to 1916 as a whole.[29] Furthermore, certainly by 1911 it was no longer possible for the Nigeriens to pay their taxes in kind or in cowries, a currency which, as a consequence, disappeared altogether around 1914.[30] From 1916 onwards, the French insisted that taxes should be paid exclusively in francs, among other reasons to check the continuous deterioration of the local exchange rate between the franc and sterling.[31] However, this tells only part of the story. More significant, curiously enough, are the extremely rough figures for the population of Niger. According to official censuses there were some 851,000 Nigeriens in 1911, and 960,000 in 1913. Then the population dropped to 884,000 in 1914 and to 883,000 in 1916. However, the figure for 1921 was a huge 1,084,000.[32] Taking the figures for 1911 and 1921 only, we arrive at a very high and, for reasons that will be explained later, improbable growth rate. And the growth rate which can be deduced for 1916 to 1921 is simply absurd. Even the decrease between 1913 and 1916 is far too moderate. Indeed, from what we know of the period between 1911 and 1921 – a period characterized by probably the most severe drought in the history of Niger, by a major and very disruptive revolt together with a series of minor disturbances, and by several large-scale exoduses southwards – a very steep *decrease* in population would be expected for the period as a whole, not just for the years between 1913 and

1916. Since, naturally, the censuses provided the basis for the tax rolls, the implication of all this is simply that more taxes had to be paid. People who certainly did find themselves on the tax rolls of the French for the first time were the Fulani nomads.[33]

Political aspects: the attempt to establish direct rule

If the tax burden increased substantially, the total amount of wealth, goods or money which the average Nigerien had to part with increased even more sharply. The extra amounts went into the pockets of two categories of people. In the first category we find those African (and usually non-Nigerien) auxiliaries (soldiers in particular) whom the French sent out to collect taxes without supervision. This method, like similar methods in Northern Nigeria earlier,[34] led – or so the British alleged – to 'surreptitious' levies, in other words extortion.[35] In the second category we find the chiefs, or rather a new brand of particularly rapacious chiefs who came to power after 1908, especially in Hausaland and Kanuriland. Here, then, we have the second, *political*, dimension of the 'new', French policy; a new approach discernible in the French attitude towards the Hausa, Kanuri and Tuareg chiefs, and more generally towards the problem of local administration in the North, the Centre, the East, and the Far East. Up to 1911, the French approach in these parts of Niger had been to a certain extent indirect. But during the post-1911 period, there is enough evidence available to suggest that the French were attempting to establish what may be described as direct rule, even contemplating the outright abolition of the institution of province and canton chiefs.[36] In the case of the Tuareg nomads, the French had hitherto respected the pre-existing tribal entities as well as the position and status of the Tuareg warriors and nobles, the *imajeghen*. After 1911, however, they apparently tried their best to circumscribe the influence of the *imajeghen* and to encourage instead the economic and especially the political ascendancy of the *ineslemen*, or clerics.[37] The idea was to undermine decisively the 'martial spirit' of the Tuareg, in order to forestall another revolt. The French also tried to extend to the nomads what we may call the 'canton system'. In other words they set out to break up the pre-existing tribal entities, and to group the Tuareg into evenly sized 'administrative tribes', not infrequently, at least among the Tuareg of Azawak and Gobir Tudu, under the authority of *ineslemen*.[38]

In Hausaland and Kanuriland up to 1911 the French had tried with some success to circumscribe the power of the *sarauta*, and to 'liberate' subdued entities. Now, after 1911, they began to split up the basic, traditional entities (as had already happened with Damagaram and Mounio in 1906), and to replace them by 'administrative', i.e. artificial, entities. Hence the pre-colonial realms of Gobir and Maradi were in the end split into no less than six entities;[39] the *subdivision* of Magaria, which corresponded to three pre-colonial entities, was split into seven cantons and one Fulani *groupement*; the territory corresponding to the sultanate of Tessaoua was split into twelve cantons, roughly half of which remained (until 1927) under the nominal authority of the *sarkin* Katsina or 'sultan' of Tessaoua; in 1913 the Tamaske region, formerly under the authority of the *amatazza* of the Lissawan, was divided into three autonomous cantons. Further west, the hausaphone *subdivision* of Dogondoutchi (Arewa) was split into seven cantons, as opposed to a pre-colonial figure of three; the *subdivision* of Gaya counted at one stage no less than eleven cantons, as opposed to five. Finally, the Zermaganda region was split into five cantons between 1906 and 1924, as opposed to a 'normal' figure of three.[40]

The most important element in this 'crush' and 'destroy' strategy was, however, the extremely harsh manner in which the French dealt with individual chiefs. They were simply deposed, and not infrequently imprisoned, at random and at will. Even the slightest mistake or the most extravagant denunciation could be fatal to the local incumbent chief.[41] Among the more prominent victims were the *sarkin* Gobir in 1911; his successor in 1912; the *alfaize* of Say in 1913; the *zermakoy* of Tondikandia, the *sarkin* Myrriah, the *tazard* of Tessaoua, the chief of Ouacha and one of the province-chiefs of Damagaram in 1914; the *amiru* of Tera and the *sarkin* Tahoua in 1915; the chief of Karakara in 1916; a third *sarkin* Gobir and the chief of Gouchi in 1917; the chief of Korgom, the *amatazza* of Keita and the *sarkin* Tahoua in 1918; the Sultan of Agades and the *amenukal* of the Kel Fadei in 1919; the *maï* of Yamia/Boune, the chief of Olleleoua, the province-chief of Zinder and the *maï* of Goure in 1921; the *sarkin* Magaria and the *sarkin* Maradi in 1922; three chiefs of Laba between 1909 and 1915, all eight successive chiefs of Aguie up to 1924; one, possibly two, chiefs of Konni in 1917–18;[42] and finally a total of fifteen canton chiefs in the Damagaram region deposed in the late 1910s according to Gamory-Dubordeau.[43] It is significant that relatively few chiefs from the West figure in this list.

When a vacancy had to be filled, the French would usually appoint the most 'collaborative' of the pretenders, not infrequently the most incompetent and insignificant of the lot. In several cases the French even appointed individuals whose claims to legitimacy were less than obvious, if not nonexistent. The more prominent examples are a former soldier of Fulani stock who was appointed chief of the Songhay canton of Tera in 1915;[44] a Tuareg who was placed at the head of the Hausa canton of Eastern Gobir between 1916 and 1924;[45] and finally two former court-dignitaries of low rank and a former palace slave who were appointed province-chiefs in the Damagaram region.

It was all very well to try and establish direct rule in Niger. But the French did not have the necessary means to do so, especially after the outbreak of the First World War and the subsequent mobilization which led to a desperate shortage of personnel. The Governor found himself in the rather uncomfortable position of having to appoint warrant officers to head *subdivisions*;[46] men, that is, hardly suitable to exercise the great power and responsibility such offices entailed. (In one case the corrupting temptations of absolute power proved too strong, and the local *chef de subdivision*, an adjutant, together with his sergeant-major deputy, had to be recalled and imprisoned.) But there were not even enough warrant officers to fill all the vacancies, and at least one *subdivision* remained ungoverned for more than a year.[47]

The result was that the French found themselves in a vicious circle. The shortage of personnel together with the increasing administrative burden (which was partly a consequence of the 'new' policy, partly a consequence of external events which will be discussed later) forced them to rely more heavily upon the chiefs than before. But the shortage of personnel also meant that they were unable to exercise any firm day-to-day control over the chiefs, and so they were left with little choice but to make occasional displays of authority, resorting to heavy-handed methods to demonstrate that they were still in command. This was all the more necessary since the French had promoted candidates who proved themselves to be totally inept as chiefs, and who were above all useless as intermediaries, simply because they enjoyed little if any prestige among their own 'subjects'. But the frequent depositions only made things worse by making the incumbents realize just how precarious their position was. Small wonder then, that most chiefs tried their best to profit as much as they could from their position as long as it lasted.

Among the many cases which came to light partly because of the famine in 1913–15, Tchikouma, one of the province-chiefs of Damagaram between 1907 and 1914, is a typical example. As a consequence of his plunderings, some thirty villages were said to have disappeared altogether. Among other things, Tchikouma requisitioned millet not only on behalf of the administration, but also on behalf of himself. And, although the French paid 0.30 francs for each kilo, the money never found its way back to the producers. When the famine struck, Tchikouma was able to sell his stocks of millet for 0.80 francs a kilo. The French, who never thought themselves responsible for what had been going on, described Tchikouma's reign as one of organized brigandage and robbery. It was also a reign of terror, in which the chief's envoys saw to it – through systematic acts of intimidation – that no complaints reached the ears of the French.[48]

The situation which developed after 1911 provided ample opportunity for local antagonists to settle accounts. It was a time of intrigues when men fought for power and influence, that is, for the support of the French. In the case of Maradi, the *sarkin* Fulani, Moussa, son of *k'aura* Assao, was able to have a number of chiefs deposed and to emerge himself as the *de facto* (and later *de jure*) ruler of both Maradi and Gobir.[49] In the case of Damagaram, Bellama, the palace slave turned province-chief, tried his best, and with considerable success, to discredit the other province-chiefs, while at the same time defending himself against the intrigues masterminded by a certain Barma Mustapha. Barma, a former quite high-ranking court-dignitary, had 'endeared' himself to the French by being of considerable help during the recruitment drive of 1915–16.[50] But Bellama was soon able to reverse the situation and to have Barma imprisoned and subsequently banished (*interdit de séjour*) for four years. Bellama's hour of glory came in 1918 when the two other provinces of Damagaram were incorporated into his own, making him the *de facto sarkin* Damagaram. However, Barma, after returning home in 1920, set about to gather evidence about the alleged extortions and abuses committed by Bellama. The French, forced to investigate the matter, found that Bellama had made use of much the same methods as Tchikouma, and deposed him in 1921. After this, Barma Mustapha was appointed *sarkin* Damagaram in 1922,[51] sixteen years after the deposition of *sarki* Ahmadu II.

The 'new' economic policy: further consequences

Returning to the economic aspects of the 'new' French policy after 1908, let us look at how the Nigeriens reacted to the higher tax burden, and how they went about finding the necessary cash to pay taxes. Among the peoples of the south there was a very marked difference between the Zerma/Songhay on the one hand, and the Hausa, the Fulani, and possibly also the Kanuri, on the other. The young Zerma/Songhay began to go as seasonal labourers to the Gold Coast, mainly to the Kumasi region, following in the footsteps, as it were (but pushing further south than), their nineteenth-century warrior ancestors who had conquered the Mamprussi–Dagomba region. This seasonal migration, which during its early stages involved mainly former slaves but which soon spread to other social categories, may have begun as early as 1902. It really got under way around 1910–11 and soared after 1919, partially as a consequence of the economic development of the Gold Coast under the governorship of Sir Gordon Guggisberg.[52] Labour migration reveals many structural similarities with long-distance trading, and especially with raiding. It is probable therefore that there occurred among the 'adventurous' Zerma/Songhay a form of culture transfer in favour of migrant labour. In particular, the long and at times perilous journey to the Gold Coast became part of a 'modernized' initiation ritual.[53]

The Hausa, the Fulani, the Kanuri and the *bugaje*, on the other hand, appear to have responded to the new demands by increasing their production and by commercializing their surpluses to a greater extent than earlier. They found a ready market for their produce, and especially their cattle, in Northern Nigeria, thus enabling a fair number of the Hausa south of the border to concentrate on groundnut cultivation at the expense of the subsistence sector.[54] One 'by-product' of this cash-crop expansion was the squeezing out of a fair number of the Fulani nomads, who now – a hundred years after they had helped establish the Sokoto Caliphate – were more or less forced to trek northwards into Niger. This trend apparently got under way, significantly enough, around 1910.[55] In Nigerien Hausaland, the change from an extra-subsistence economy centred on long-distance trade involving only a few items to one encompassing a great many more people probably led to a decentralization of the market economy. This in turn had a detrimental effect upon the local urban centres. The sharp drop in the population of Zinder from 15,000 in 1912 to a mere 5,000 in 1922 is probably an indication of this trend.[56] Angus Buchanan, who visited the town in 1920, noted that 'many of the dwellings [were] forsaken' and remarked that there hung over the place 'a certain melancholy atmosphere of decline'.[57]

As the peoples of the Centre, East and Far East were forced (although they probably also found it in their interest) to produce a more substantial surplus and to sell it in the markets, they became more and more dependent upon the regional commercial network and its nucleus, the towns of Northern Nigeria. This is the main reason why the establishment in 1914 of a customs barrier along the economically non-existent frontier between Niger and Nigeria can only be qualified as an absurdity, even from a French point of view.[58] Furthermore, it was erected in the middle of the very severe famine of 1913–15. The customs barrier's function was quite simply to channel some of the surplus into the hands of the French. However, if anything it prevented or at least retarded the expansion of the extra-subsistence sector of the economy. Indeed, it could be argued that the customs barrier had the effect of denying the Nigeriens access to some of the opportunities which would have enabled them to meet the new tax burden. What was perhaps even more damaging was the arbitrary way in which the customs officials carried out their duties. They inaugurated what a later French report described as an era of official and systematic plundering of the local population.[59]

The increased tax burden and the corresponding and necessary expansion of the extra-subsistence sector of the economy led to the clearing of new land. The French were unaware of this at the time, and so documentation is once more far from satisfactory. The clearing of new land was, as pointed out earlier, a process which had started in the very first years of the French presence in Niger and which was originally linked with the emancipation of the slaves in the West. It spread quickly to the Centre and the East, where the African farmers now enjoyed access to much exploitable land, as the French *pax* enabled them to use areas previously left empty for reasons of defence. Since concentration made people increasingly vulnerable to tax and labour demands, and since many people disliked living in large villages which impeded cultivation and restricted personal freedom, settlements broke up in many areas of the sedentary south.[60] Whereas up to about the first decade of the nineteenth century this internal migration and colonization had affected mainly the many unoccupied areas between the earlier compact villages, during and after that time people all over Niger began to move to more remote and previously very sparsely populated regions. Examples are the Birnin Lalle-Dakoro region and the Tarka valley north of Maradi;[61] the regions east and north of the Zermaganda, where the original villages were turned into what has been described as 'rotten boroughs';[62] eastern Adar, where a great many of the Kel Gress *ighawellan* settled down, thus severing their ties with the *imajeghen*;[63] and, although somewhat later, the Bambeye region west of Tahoua.[64]

THE GREAT FAMINE AND OTHER CALAMITIES

The Löffler column and the occupation of Tibesti

From 1913 onwards a number of disasters, some natural, some man-made, hit the peoples of Niger. The beginnings, in 1913, were curiously enough a direct consequence of the Italian–Turkish war. In Libya the Turks, hard pressed by the Italians, evacuated Tibesti and the Fezzan in 1912–13, leaving behind considerable stocks of arms, which they probably hoped the local population would make good use of in resisting the advancing Italians.[65] The Turkish withdrawal came in one sense as a relief to the French, who had been uneasy about possible Turkish ambitions in Chad. On the other hand, it presented them with a two-fold problem. First, the Turkish withdrawal and the conversion of the Fezzan and Tibesti into what from the French point of view looked like a no-man's-land could, and apparently did, have an adverse effect upon the security of the North-East.[66] Secondly, the French feared that the Italians, who had not subscribed to the Franco-British agreement of 1898–9 stipulating that Tibesti lay within the French sphere of interest, would claim Tibesti as part of their Turkish 'heritage'. French occupation of this arid and mountainous but nevertheless strategically important region would have the advantage of presenting the Italians with a *fait accompli*, thereby forestalling any further Italian ambitions in this part of Africa.[67]

The task of occupying the western slopes of Tibesti, which was as far as the French government was prepared to go initially,[68] fell to the French in Niger. To send out a sizeable enough column to occupy and especially to pacify such a large and distant region as Tibesti was, of course, a costly enterprise, so costly that the French had to reverse their previous policy towards the Tuareg and to resort, this time, to requisitions. Once more the Africans had to foot the bill of the imperial conquest.

When the column of 310 men under Captain Löffler set out on its thirteen-months, strenuous odyssey from Zinder in September 1913, it contained some 650 camels. It had been preceded by several caravans carrying supplies, as well as by a small unit whose task it was to occupy Djado, north of Bilma.[69] It is not known how many camels there were in these caravans, but they were all requisitioned. And the French, being in a hurry, pushed the camels too hard, so that few animals returned. If the Tuareg were compensated at all for their losses, it was only several years later and only inadequately. The French paid 75 francs per camel, which seems a fair enough sum, but does not take into account the fact that the Tuareg lost considerable profits by not being able to take part in transportation in Northern Nigeria, and also the fact that it takes quite a long time to reconstitute a camel-herd.[70] The result was disastrous to the Tuareg economy.

To send a column to Tibesti was one thing; to maintain even small garrisons in an environment naturally inhospitable to man some 1,400 km from the main regions of supply was quite another. It required large-scale requisitions of camels, millet, and even of men as conveyors. We know that in the autumn of 1916 *alone*, the French requisitioned a total of 1,550 camels from the *cercles* of Madaoua/Tahoua, Zinder and Agades.[71] The occupation of Tibesti taxed the resources of both the French and the Tuareg to their uttermost limits, and contributed significantly to the general anti-French attitude of the Tuareg nomads.[72] The French officers in charge locally became increasingly aware of the difficulties of maintaining a presence in the North-East, and in their correspondence with superior authorities found themselves advocating withdrawal. Even the Governor-General was sympathetic towards their viewpoint.[73]

The Great Drought and its consequences

The occupation of the western slopes of Tibesti was particularly ill-timed. It took place during perhaps the worst drought in the history of Niger. This drought is linked with the sharp climatic deterioration that set in at the turn of the century with, as we have seen, a number of very dry years throughout the Central Sudan up to 1903–4. Rainfall was again deficient in many parts of Niger (the Centre in particular)[74] and Northern Nigeria[75] during 1907–9. The situation got much worse, however, after 1911 when Niger, together with, it seems, a great many regions of Africa, experienced a most severe four-year drought.[76] Rainfall was abnormally low, close to or less than half the average in some regions both in 1913 and 1914, the peak years.[77] In fact, the rainfall figures for 1913–14 are the lowest ever registered in Niger, the late 1960s and early 1970s included.[78] On top of this, the western parts of Niger seem to have been ravaged by an invasion of locusts.[79] Undeterred, the Governor wrote in his annual report for 1913 that 'la situation économique du territoire est des plus satisfaisantes'.[80] He was wrong. The stage was already set for the Great Famine (*gande beri* in Zerma/Songhay,[81] *rafowa manga* in Fulani[82] and *kakalaba* – 'hollow belly' – in Hausa).[83] Naturally, the Great Famine of 1913–15 was chiefly due to drought. But (to paraphrase John Iliffe) drought causes famine when reserves are low, recuperative powers are weakened, outside relief is difficult to obtain and transport and communication are defective. In all these ways the attitude and policy of the French made the famine more general, more intense and more prolonged.

We cannot, for lack of evidence, quantify the severity of the Great Famine. A later Governor evoked the 'effrayants ravages de la famine' and gave vivid descriptions of the horrors to be seen everywhere in 1914, when 'les cadavres d'enfants et de vieillards ... emplissaient les villages'.[84] We know that whole villages were abandoned and that large tracts of land were laid waste.[85] But such non-quantifiable descriptions are no substitute for facts and figures. On the other hand, perhaps this dearth of evidence is in itself revealing. It implies that the French paid scant attention to the plight of the Nigeriens. Certainly, they never contemplated launching anything in the way of a relief programme. The record of the British in Northern Nigeria is only slightly less dismal; although Lugard sent rice to the regions most severely hit,[86] the official contention that the famine was limited to the area of Kano[87] is inconsistent with an eyewitness account according to which people 'died like flies on every road'.[88]

What figures there are convey some idea of the magnitude of the disaster. Stephen Baier has advanced the figure of 85,000 dead out of a total population of 350,000 for the *cercle* of Zinder[89] – one of the worst hit according to a French report.[90] In addition, the local *Commandant* reported that an estimated 32,000 fled to Nigeria.[91] Price figures are also relevant in this respect. Périé reports that the price of millet per bag in Maradi soared from 1.50 francs to 15, and then to a staggering 20 francs in August 1914.[92] This led among other things to a sharp depreciation in the price of cattle, which was in 1914 five hundred times less, in terms of millet, than in good years.[93]

In the annual report for 1914 the Commissioner wrote that 'malgré la misère . . . les impôts sont rentrés sans difficulté. Les obligations imposées aux populations par les gros ravitaillements . . . du cercle de Bilma et du Tibesti ont pesé lourdement . . . elles ont été acceptées . . . sans aucun murmure'.[94] The first part of his statement was incorrect. According to official figures, tax revenues amounted to 1,113,000 francs in 1914, compared with 1,633,000 francs in the preceding year,[95] when the rates were much lower. But the fact that the French were able to squeeze more than a million francs out of the impoverished and hunger-stricken peoples of Niger can only be described as a major performance. However, the point here is that the Commissioner's statement shows that, in the face of the terrible plight of the Nigeriens, the French officers on the spot in 1913–15 were hardly sympathetic.

The French, by now desperately short of funds and equally desperately under-staffed, were determined, famine or no famine, and as long as no formal orders to withdraw from the posts in the North-East had been issued, to satisfy the needs of their garrisons in Bilma, Tibesti and other remote places before thinking about anything else. The result was a nightmarish situation in which the local administrators had to make increasing use of the whole range of sanctions embodied in the *indigénat* in order to get the necessary quantities of millet.[96] Such harsh action, combined with the attempts of chiefs and traders to exploit the situation as best they could, accelerated the southward exodus already under way. And the action was not totally efficient; the French were unable to provide their garrisons with the necessary supplies, and more generally unable to prevent the political consequences of the Great Famine from spreading northward. The threat of starvation became a very real one to the troops posted in the North-East and in Tibesti, troops who, again because of the shortage in personnel, could not expect to be relieved. The French feared a general mutiny.[97] As for the indigenous populations of those remote regions, the threat of famine turned into grim reality when the inter-regional trade between the south and the oases broke down in the autumn of 1914, because the peasants of Hausaland had no more millet to part with.[98]

Prelude to the Tuareg revolts: unrest in the Sahara and elsewhere
In the North the impact of the drought seems to have been felt very early. The Tuareg of the Adrar of the Iforas region were reported as early as 1912 to have descended southwards en masse in search of pastures. They were followed by the Kel Ahaggar.[99] This brought the southern Tuareg under pressure, as they were pushed or migrated further towards the Sudan.[100] In particular this seems to have been the case with the Kel Attaram of Menaka, who trekked southwards towards the river Niger and the *dallol* Bosso in 1914. In the latter region, tension built up with the Sudie. The French, under the impression that a revolt was in the making, decided to establish a garrison at Filingue and to have Firhoun, the turbulent *amenukal* of the Kel Attaram, arrested and exiled to Timbuctu.[101]

While the situation in Niger was steadily deteriorating, events on the international scene began to make their impact felt throughout the Central Sahara. After the outbreak of the war in Europe in 1914, the Turkish Sultan, in his capacity as Caliph, declared holy war on the enemies of the Sublime Porte. In Libya the Italians, who had only recently conquered the Fezzan, were forced to retreat northwards (and certain garrisons had to seek refuge in Algeria), leaving behind – as the Turks had before them – important quantities of arms. But although the Sanūsī offensive in the direction of the Suez Canal was easily checked by the British, the defeat of the Italians, the Holy War declared by the Caliph, and the substantial reduction in French forces throughout western and northern Africa all had a profound impact upon the nomads of the Sahara. Disturbances, uprisings and revolts are reported throughout the war years in a number of widely scattered places, such as Southern Tunisia, Southern Algeria, Darfur and Wadai.[102] In Niger, in the *cercle* of Agades, the mutiny of some of the Tuareg auxiliaries in June and July 1915, although serious enough for the French to declare a state of emergency, was quickly quelled.[103] And a raiding party from as far north as Timbuctu, although causing considerable damage in the region of Madaoua, was forced to retreat north in December 1915.[104] Furthermore, there were increasingly persistent rumours in 1915 and 1916 – which the French apparently chose to ignore – that Sanūsī attacks not only on the exposed garrisons of Tibesti and Kawar but also on the garrison of Agades were imminent.[105]

The Sahara was not the only region where the colonial powers ran into difficulties during the war years. Much further south, an important faction of the population of Upper Volta and Northern Dahomey rose against the

French.[106] Many minor uprisings also occurred in Nigeria,[107] notably among the pagan population of Kano.[108] The French were confident that the revolt in Northern Dahomey would not spill over into Niger.[109] But when the Tuareg inside the Niger bend, including the Tuareg of the Tera region, rose in January 1916, forcing the French to abandon the post of Tera and sending waves of refugees into Niger, there was a real fear that the Tuareg of Tillabery, Imanan and Tagazza might join in.[110] However, an appropriate display of military might and the obligation imposed upon the Tuareg chiefs to take up residence in Tillabery seem to have been sufficient to persuade the local Tuareg to remain aloof.[111]

The first recruitment drive in the sedentary south and its consequences
By then, it seemed as if other regions of Niger, Hausaland and Kanuriland were on the brink of revolt. The apparent cause was the recruitment of native troops, which began all over French West Africa in the autumn of 1915. Niger was asked to provide 1,200 men. But the officers in charge in Niger thought they could do better than that, and set out to recruit a contingent of 2,500 men.[112] Several aspects of this first recruitment drive need to be stressed. It took place at the worst possible time, during the crucial harvest of 1915. It was carried out in a hurry, without any preparations whatsoever, and without any attempt to explain what it was all about; the French simply assumed that the Nigerien peasants were more than willing to fight for the *mère patrie* in the trenches in France. Worst of all, the recruitment was carried out through the chiefs, which in the case of Hausaland and Kanuriland meant that only those unable to pay were in danger of being incorporated into the army.[113] In the West, however, the recruitment does not seem to have presented any difficulties.[114] One of the reasons for this is that the chiefs of the West collaborated closely with the French, and even recruited for the French not only among their dependents but also among their own families. The Gao family of Matankari alone (the family of the *sarkin* Arewa) provided the French with a total of fifteen soldiers during the years 1915–18.[115] And in Dosso, not only did the *zermakoy* support the French as best he could, but his own son and heir apparent, Saidou, enlisted and went on to serve gallantly at Verdun and the Chemin des Dames before returning home as lieutenant of the French army.[116] This attitude of the western chiefs obviously did much to strengthen their alliance with the French. But from what we know of the Zerma/Songhay, considering their rather adventurous and 'martial' spirit, it seems that the prospect of fighting a war, even in distant Europe, did not strike them as being too distasteful.

A majority of the recruits from the West appear to have been former slaves,[117] as was the case in most parts of French West Africa, as Kersaint-Gilly has pointed out.[118] But whether the sway of the chiefs over the populations of servile origin was such that they could be forced to enlist, or whether the former slaves themselves seized upon the opportunity offered by the recruitment to improve upon their position, or both, is difficult to tell.

The more egalitarian rural societies of Hausaland and Kanuriland were firmly opposed to recruitment, so much so that the French had to resort to force. The peasants of the Centre, the East and the Far East, press-ganged into the army – faced, according to an *official* report, with 'rafles ... vols et abus de toute sorte commis par les agents des chefs et par les tirailleurs qu'il avait fallu envoyer dans les villages pour avoir des recrues' – were on the brink of open revolt.[119] The worst incidents seem to have occurred in the Madaoua, Konni, Maine-Soroa and N'Guigmi regions. Several envoys of the chiefs were slaughtered, and there were mass desertions of freshly enrolled recruits in a number of places. The French had to send out small detachments on 'punitive expeditions'.[120] But revolt was too distasteful a business to the peaceful but obstinate peasants of the East, who instead responded as usual by voting against the French with their feet. In other words, the recruitment drive of 1915–16 triggered off yet another large-scale exodus southwards. It is, of course, impossible to tell how many left Niger this time, but officials in Zinder guessed at the startling figure of one hundred thousand.[121]

The French were finally able to recruit 2,798 soldiers.[122] Of these an important proportion came from the West. There was no recruitment among the Tuareg.[123] These figures agree with those advanced by Marc Michel, but not with those of Michael Crowder.[124] Of the 2,798 recruits finally enlisted, 292 deserted,[125] and it is not known how many of the remaining 2,506 actually saw action in Europe.

Mounting unrest

The recruitment drive of 1915–16 was barely over when the French found themselves faced with a revolt in the West. Firhoun, the *amenukal* of the Kel Attaram, had managed to escape from his exile in Timbuctu in February 1916. Returning home to the Menaka region, he declared Holy War against the French, rallied most of the Kel Attaram, together with some Awlād Djerir Arabs, but only a few Nigerien Tuareg,[126] and headed south towards the fertile *dallol* Bosso. What he did not know, however, was that the French were ready for him, having only recently reinforced their garrison at Filingue. Also ready were the Sudie warriors under Gado Namalaya. After a fierce battle on 9 April, Firhoun was forced to retreat northward. The rebels, squeezed between detachments sent out from Kidal (in the Sudan), from Niamey and Tahoua, as well as from Southern Algeria, were finally massacred at the Anderamboukane waterhole (on the frontier between Niger and Sudan) on 9 May 1916.[127] At the same time a French column was pacifying the right bank, a task which seems to have been completed by June 1916.[128]

The calm was to be short-lived. Throughout 1916 a series of isolated and, as such, seemingly insignificant incidents were a prelude of what was to come. The first of these incidents, which occurred as early as March, was serious enough, costing the lives of nearly all the soldiers who made up the small liaison unit of the *cercle* of Kawar-Tibesti (Bilma). They were massacred somewhere in the Bilma region, according to the French by Sanūsī warriors.[129] In July a raiding party of Awlād Djerir Arabs came within 30 km of Tahoua before being forced to retreat.[130] And in August the officers-in-command of the small garrisons in Tibesti, fearing an imminent Sanūsī attack, and no longer able to maintain discipline among their half-starved and disgruntled men, took it upon themselves to evacuate Tibesti and to repatriate their men into Chad. Although their superiors had long been in favour of withdrawal from Tibesti, they could only disapprove of an action carried out on the initiative of junior officers, who were in fact disobeying formal orders.[131] Lieutenant Colonel Mourin, the Governor, fearing that the withdrawal might deal a severe blow to French prestige, decided to go east to make a personal appraisal of the situation. He was strongly backed by his superiors;[132] in fact, the French government was, for diplomatic and strategic reasons, not prepared to accept the *fait accompli*, and ordered the reoccupation of at least one of the garrisons, that of Zaouar, in November.[133] A small detachment under Second Lieutenant Mesplegh was sent out in December,[134] but received orders to withdraw a year later.

In the meantime the situation in the North had steadily deteriorated. In September a small French detachment on tour in northern Aïr ran into a band of Tuareg dissidents and was forced to return south. A column of some fifty men was sent out and they defeated the dissidents at In-Taggaren, killing thirty men and 200 camels.[135] In October there was another alert in the Madaoua–Tahoua region, when a raiding party heading southwards was eventually forced to return north.[136] However, by then small marauding bands of dissidents were becoming increasingly numerous throughout the North and the North–East. The situation had become highly explosive,[137] but it was external intervention which ignited the powder-keg.

THE REVOLTS IN THE NORTH

The Kaocen column and the siege of the French garrison in Agades
When Captain Sabatié took over as *Commandant* of Agades in early December 1916, both Captain Bosch, his predecessor, and the Sultan of Agades, Tegama – considered to be a reliable ally of the French – urged Sabatié to disperse his troops throughout the *cercle*, in order to deal with the many small marauding bands. But Sabatié, perhaps aware of the rumours of an impending Sanūsī attack, did exactly the opposite and ordered units already on patrol to return to Agades. Sabatié also saw to it that the blockhouse situated one and a half kilometres outside the town was amply provided with supplies and ammunition and even ordered trenches to be dug around it.[138] In doing this, Sabatié probably saved the French from a major

disaster. For when he arrived in Agades, preparations for an attack on the French were already far advanced. Tegama, while earning himself the confidence of Captain Bosch,[139] had established close contacts with the Sanūsī war-lords in the Fezzan.[140] Together they had devised a simple but astute plan. First, they would persuade the French to disperse their troops. Then, while the French were away, an important column sent out by the Sanūsīya would arrive in Agades. By then, Tegama hoped, the Tuareg nomads, who were already in a state of latent or in some cases open revolt, would have rallied to his cause. The next step would be to deal with the various small French units one by one as they returned to Agades. After this, Tegama planned to march on Zinder, and eventually on Kano.[141]

The Sanūsī column arrived as planned at Agades (via Djado and Iferouane) on 13 December. It was composed, it seems, of 600 to 800 men, most of whom were deserters from the French and especially Italian Saharan units, and it looked like a regular army complete with artillery.[142] The commander-in-chief was no other than Kaocen, one of the last of the 'rebels' from 1901–3 still at large (see chapter 2), who had taken a prominent part in the Sanūsī conquest of the Fezzan and had also been active against the French in many parts of the Sahara.[143]

The arrival of Kaocen and his men in Agades produced the desired effect upon the Aïr Tuareg who rallied to the rebels almost to a man.[144] But as already noted, Captain Sabatié had refused to heed Tegama's (and Captain Bosch's) advice. On 13 December most of the troops had already returned to Agades. Although the French did not attempt to resist Kaocen and his men, they were nevertheless able to retreat to the block-house, which the 'rebels' attacked on a number of occasions but were never able to capture.[145] The units still out on patrol, however, suffered a horrible fate. The exception was a detachment of fifty-one men under Lieutenant Fons, which was somehow able to join the besieged garrison of Agades on 15 December without suffering a single casualty.[146] Another detachment under Second Lieutenant Soudan was less fortunate, however, and was massacred at the gates of Agades.[147] And on 28 December, the meharist section escorting the *azalaï* back from Bilma (the first since 1913) rode into an ambush and was annihilated. Fifty-three of the sixty men died in the ambush or were later executed in Agades.[148]

News of the events in Agades reached the French in Zinder on 21 December and threw them into a state of panic.[149] At that time the French were so dangerously short of troops that the south, and Zinder in particular, were virtually defenceless, and could certainly not have withstood an attack of between 5,000 and 8,000 well-armed rebels. In December 1916 the French had on paper some 1,600 men. But this included the two units which had already been wiped out as well as the besieged garrison of Agades. Of the remaining, eighty men were on their way to Tibesti, another 140 (the former Tibesti garrisons) were in Chad; and 110 men made up the garrison of Bilma. Troops had also been sent to Northern Dahomey to help quell the revolt there.[150] In short, the French, who had only 250 to 300 men in the Zinder–Tanout region, needed assistance from external quarters, not only from the other colonies in French West Africa, but also – and perhaps above all – from the British across the border. Sir Frederick Lugard, the Governor-General, acted swiftly, aware of the threat that the Tuareg rebels – now a cause for international concern – posed to Northern Nigeria. As soon as he received the official request for assistance from Dakar (on 8 January), he ordered four companies with artillery to move into Niger.[151] At the same time he applied for and was granted reinforcements from Sierra Leone.[152] The British troops took up position in the vicinities of Tahoua, Madaoua and Tessaoua;[153] in other words, those regions of the sedentary south where there was a particularly heavy concentration of Tuareg. This swift action may well have saved the day for the French, in that it dissuaded the Kel Gress of Madaoua from joining the rebellion.[154] The southern Tuareg, as well as those of the West, bore the brunt of the requisitions of camels necessary to fight the rebels.[155] As for the possibility that the disgruntled Hausa peasants would take advantage of the situation by staging a revolt of their own, the display of European solidarity probably had what was called in colonial jargon a 'positive effect'. The sedentary Hausa and Kanuri opted, as far as one can see and as far as they had a choice, for the lesser of two evils: the French. We know for instance that the Hausa of Kantche fought bravely against a band of Tuareg heading north on 15 January,[156] and that the Kanuri of Damergu put up a spirited resistance against marauding rebels searching for food.[157] But the French–British force could not prevent the Tuareg of Damergu from going north to join the rebels. Nor could it prevent the revolt from spreading to the Kel Dinnik. But although the Kel Dinnik were in a state of rebellion, they did not join forces with the Aïr Tuareg. Their *amenukal*, El Horar, had only contempt for Kaocen, whom he considered a slave. Instead they staged their own revolt, directed as much against the Lissawan Tuareg, considered to be traitors, as against the French. The Tamaske–Keita region is reported to have been thoroughly plundered and sacked, and the *amatazza* was killed.[158]

Lugard not only sent troops, but saw to it that French reinforcements, more than 1,200 men, arriving at Lagos by boat from Dakar and Equatorial Africa, were dispatched by rail to Kano as quickly as possible.[159] The strategic importance of the Nigerian Railway was thus demonstrated, although Lugard's suggestion of using aeroplanes against the rebels was not taken seriously by the French[160] – possibly because it did not fit in with the somewhat romantic image of desert warfare. The rebels, having lost the opportunity to push southward and seize Zinder, allowed the French the necessary time to recover from the initial shock and to set in motion a formidable military machine which no rebels, however determined or daring, could stop. For that a much more sophisticated military organization and, above all, better equipment than the rebels actually possessed would have been needed. The question is why the rebels did not take advantage of the

97

situation when the French were still on the defensive. Possibly the rebels believed that time was on their side, that they simply had to sit back and wait for the Germans (and the Turks) to defeat the French (and the British). More prosaically, it is possible that Tegama and Kaocen were uneasy about the potential threat which the besieged garrison represented should they choose to lift the siege and head southwards.

The French counter-attack

A detailed account of the military operations in 1917–18 can be found elsewhere.[161] Here we shall concentrate on some of the major events. Three columns were sent out against the rebels, the most important being under the personal command of the Governor, Lieutenant-Colonel Mourin, and consisting of 828 men and 400 carriers. When it set out from Zinder on 8 February,[162] it contained 1,800 camels, all hastily requisitioned – from the Kel Gress in particular (and only reimbursed three years later).[163] On the same day, the Berger column of 600 men set out from Menaka in French Sudan towards Ih Gall.[164] Finally, a smaller column under Captain Sadoux was to deal with the situation in and to the north of the Tahoua region.[165] The remainder of the French and British forces served as a screen in the south for the north-bound columns. The Mourin and Berger columns had to fight three major battles against the rebels, who suffered a total of 120 casualties. On 3 March the Mourin column arrived in a near-deserted Agades, exactly three months and ten days after the siege had begun. It was followed by the Berger column, which had previously bombarded and besieged In Gall, on 18 March.[166] The revenge taken by the French was terrible. According to oral testimony gathered by André Salifou, those men who had not fled In Gall and Agades were exterminated.[167] The well-informed British traveller Dugal Campbell who visited Agades in the 1920s supports this, stating that 'every male caught paid the last price'.[168]

The recapture of Agades and its consequences

After 18 March the French had about 1,500 men in Agades. However, the needs of this sizeable army for provisions and camels were such that there was limited time before the major part of it would have to retreat south and west again.[169] The French thus had a compelling need to wipe out the rebels as quickly as possible, and to win an early and decisive victory. But in spite of two major battles, which cost the rebels about 170 men,[170] and in spite of the fact that many Tuareg, most notably the Damergu Tuareg and the Kel Ferouane,[171] were already opting out, a decisive victory eluded the French. When the main body of Mourin's army, the former Berger and Mourin columns, was forced to evacuate Aïr in July 1917, the rebels, although their numbers had been reduced considerably, were still in control of most of the area.[172]

In the Tahoua region the first, indecisive, engagement with the rebels occurred on 22 February, when eighty-five rebels were killed.[173] This defeat was enough to persuade the *ineslemen* to abandon the revolt.[174] On 7 April at Tanout (roughly half-way between Tahoua and In Gall, not the Tanout in Damergu) the French suddenly found themselves faced with the majority of the rebels, who for reasons unknown surrendered, and so no battle took place. Nevertheless the French proceeded to execute summarily most of the rebels made prisoner, nearly all of whom were *imajeghen*.[175] 'La fine fleur de l'aristocratie Kel Dinnik disparut' at Tanout.[176]

In order to deal with the few small marauding parties still left, and to make certain that the revolt had been definitively crushed, the French now turned the Kel Gress and the Lissawan loose on their traditional enemies, letting them sack and plunder the Kel Dinnik at will.[177] A French administrator wrote in 1950 that 'Ils ne furent ni les guides, ni les conseillers les moins fanatiques, ni les auxiliaires les moins féroces dans la poursuite et la répression.'[178] The Kel Dinnik having been crushed, there still remained the threat of raids from further north, as demonstrated by a band of Awlād Djerir Arabs who came within 30 km of Tahoua in October before being forced back.[179]

The French strategy towards the rebels in Aïr consisted first of all in trying to starve them out, by establishing a line of defence from west of Tahoua to the Koutoss hills, strong enough to deny the rebels access to the south;[180] and by systematically destroying the oases in the North.[181] Then those Tuareg who submitted were forced to move south of this line.[182] In Damagaram alone there was an increase of 2,423 in the number of Tuareg on the tax-rolls in 1918 compared with the previous year.[183] But many Tuareg moved even further south with their camels, into Northern Nigeria, thus provoking a severe shortage of transport animals in Niger.[184] Finally, the detachments left in Aïr, assisted by an increasing number of Tuareg auxiliaries, were under orders simply to hunt down and kill as many rebels as possible.

The French were indirectly helped by events in the Fezzan, where a party of ill-defined pro-Turkish 'adventurers' had ousted the Sanūsī,[185] thus cutting Kaocen off from his base. Kaocen had nowhere to go but to the south to find food for his men. In August 1917 the rebels suddenly burst into Damergu, sacking and plundering even northern Damagaram. A detachment of some sixty men, sent out in great haste, was cut to pieces on 29 August. French defence in the south broke down, and Kaocen and his men were able to hold out in the region east of Damergu and north of Goure for some time, before being forced to return northward again.[186] But they did not stay there long. In October and November incursions of rebels were reported in the Koutoss region and in Damergu.[187] But it was a losing battle; after the French had sent reinforcements to Aïr, and after another three months of savage and ruthless repression,[188] Kaocen, Tegama and their men, by now only a handful of rebels, left Aïr for Tibesti in March 1918,[189] fifteen months after the outbreak of the revolt.

THE SEDENTARY SOUTH, 1916–19

The situation after the Great Famine

After the terrible years of 1913 and 1914, the harvests of 1915 and 1916 seem to have been average or above average throughout the Central Sudan (with the apparent exception of the Far East in 1915).[190] In fact, judging by the level of Lake Chad the year 1915 inaugurated a cycle of favourable climatic conditions.[191] The improvement in the food situation together with the promise that there would be no more recruiting encouraged a few people to return from Nigeria,[192] but not many. The French were forced to admit that most had settled south of the border for good.[193]

The people of the sedentary south seem to have been poorly rewarded for their loyalty during the Tuareg revolts. Although the evidence is not altogether satisfactory, the significant concentration of military forces in Niger during 1917–18 apparently meant that the peoples of the south were faced with increasing requisitions.[194] What is certain is that the sedentary population in Niger, as indeed throughout French West Africa, was forced to produce food (groundnuts?) for metropolitan France. How and to what extent we do not know, only that certain 'natives' had to be 'disciplined' for not having fulfilled instructions in this matter.[195]

The second recruitment drive

The French government began to press for more African troops, issuing the decree of 14 January 1918 which established compulsory military service in French West Africa.[196] The Governor, although he had been told that there would be no further recruitment in his territory, was now asked to provide a contingent of a thousand men, a figure subsequently raised to 2,500.[197] But this time the French in Niger would not have it, arguing that further recruitment would yet again bring the country to the brink of revolt and would also trigger off new large-scale migrations. But in Dakar, Governor-General Joost Van Vollenoven, who had tried his best to withstand the demands from Paris, had been replaced by the more amenable and 'martial' G. Angoulvant.[198] Angoulvant sent the Governor of Niger, Lieutenant Colonel Méchet, a telegram which deserves to be fully quoted:

> C'est en pleine connaissance des difficultés que vous signalez, que le Gouverne-ment de la République a décidé de demander aux colonies ouest-africaines de fournir un nouvel et important effort militaire ... Quelle que soit l'importance des difficultés qui se présentent, il faut les affronter ... Lorsqu'il y va de l'intéret supérieur du pays, ce qui paraît irréalisable devient réalisable.

And he added that he would contact the Governor-General of Nigeria and ask him to take the necessary steps to expel any fugitives from his territory.[199] But Méchet was adamant:

> Je suis en conscience obligé de maintenir intégralement mes objections initiales.

La situation du territoire est nullement comparable à celle des autres colonies ouest-africaines. La presque-totalité des troupes est encore employée à lutter contre les rebelles. Les troupes ne sont pas disponibles pour appuyer les opérations de récrutement. Les unités sont épuisées ... Le ravitaillement d'Agades et de Bilma présente de très grosses difficultés. Et la réception et l'alimentation de 4000 tirailleurs venant du Tchad ne seront pas assurées dans des régions pauvres et troublées. Je décline la responsabilité de l'accomplissement de taches multiples et absolument inconciliables. S'il est passé outre ces considérations, j'exécuterais ordre formel, mais je pense que la France paiera ...[200]

Later Méchet went even further: 'je ne puis accepter la responsabilité du commandement du territoire si la décision de procéder à des opérations de récrutement est maintenue'.[201] These were harsh words indeed. But Méchet had his way. Instead of 2,500 men, Niger was asked to provide from 700 to 800.[202] In spite of this low figure, and the fact that this time the recruitment was not carried out through the mediation of the chiefs and that the French were more lavish with their funds than in 1915–16,[203] the recruitment drive of 1918 had much the same effect upon Hausaland and Kanuriland as the previous one, although everything went smoothly in the West.[204] In Damagaram several villages revolted and two African envoys were killed. In the *subdivision* of Tessaoua another envoy was killed and two grievously wounded; the cantons of Dungass, Ouacha and Gouschi in the *subdivision* of Magaria were in a state of virtual rebellion. Further east, in Kanuriland, people either fled to Nigeria or into the hilly regions to the north. The French had to send out small detachments in all directions, as in 1915–16. In the end 877 recruits were incorporated into the army.[205]

There were to be no more large-scale recruitment drives in Niger. For although universal peace-time conscription was established in 1919,[206] the French only levied very small contingents during the following years. However, even these small-scale recruitment drives led to so much unrest that the French decided, in the early 1920s, to discontinue the practice altogether.[207] Taking the two recruitment drives of 1915–16 and 1918 together, Niger contributed 3,675 soldiers to the war in Europe, or less than 0.5 per cent of the total population. This was the lowest percentage in the whole of French West Africa. One of the reasons for this was obviously the Tuareg revolts, but it seems to substantiate Marc Michel's point that there is no correlation between the recruitment drives between 1915 and 1918 and the many revolts which erupted in French West Africa during this period.[208] In Niger there was no rebellion in the West, the region most seriously affected by the recruitment drives.[209] Less affected were the Hausa/Kanuri, who were twice on the threshold of open rebellion. And the Tuareg were not affected at all by the recruitment drives, but rose nevertheless against the French. We must conclude that the incidence of recruitment was not a cause for revolt, but a consequence of it, the French being careful not to press too hard for recruits in troubled regions or in regions considered to be hostile.

AFTERMATH, 1918–22

The revision of French policy

By 1918 at the latest the French found themselves at a dead end. Their 'new' approach, which we have dated to about 1908 and which gained momentum after 1911, was submerged by the turmoil of the 1913–18 period. More specifically it had cut short the nascent prosperity triggered off by the boom in Northern Nigeria and, in consequence, thwarted the economic reorientation under way. It can be argued that this 'new' approach was largely responsible for the disturbances, unrests and revolts of the decade. It imposed considerable hardship upon the Nigeriens at a time when climatic and other conditions ought to have induced the French to show restraint.

By 1918 the French were left with little choice but to try and 'muddle through' as best they could; in practical terms, to change their policy and to make concessions. First that monument to stupidity, the customs barrier, was abolished in 1918, officially and not surprisingly because the cost of maintenance exceeded the receipts from duties and tariffs.[210] In 1920 it was once more made legal to pay taxes in sterling.[211] Then the French decided (or were forced) to treat the chiefs more leniently. After 1918 a *Commandant* who wished to make use of the sanctions of the *indigénat* against a local chief could only do so with the prior written consent of the Governor.[212] This local measure was followed by a federal decree which exempted chiefs – and also former servicemen – from the *indigénat* altogether.[213] In addition, an advisory board composed of chiefs and *notables* and known as the *Conseil des Notables* was set up in each *cercle* in 1919.[214]

The year 1919 also marked the very timid beginnings of what could perhaps be called an 'economic development' policy. This was the establishment of officially sponsored and controlled cooperatives known as *Sociétés Indigènes de Prévoyance* (SIP) in some of the *cercles*. However, since membership and membership fees were compulsory and since the *Commandant* was the ex-officio president, the SIP's proved rather inefficient, and became for all practical purposes simply another branch of the administration.[215]

The measures enumerated above could be assumed to have a beneficial effect, with the consequence that the general overall situation would improve after 1918. With both the revolts and the recruitment drives over this might have been expected. But the picture that emerges from the official reports for the period 1918–22 is far from rosy. The reports contain the all too familiar tale of drought, requisitions and migrations – although perhaps on a less grand scale than during the previous years. They also convey the image of an administration with only a shaky grip of the situation. The added dimension (or perhaps just one that the French began to pay attention to after 1918) was that the enfeebled people of Niger fell victim to a number of devastating epidemics. An epidemic of malaria among the Tuareg in 1918 claimed, according to official estimates, about a thousand victims – mainly women and children. How many succumbed to the famine which followed in its train is unknown.[216] However, this was minor compared with the flu epidemic which ravaged the whole of Niger between October 1918 and February 1919. The French made a very rough estimate of 16,000 casualties.[217] An epidemic of cerebro-spinal meningitis in 1921, the first known of what was to become a very long series indeed, cost 1,700 lives in the *cercle* of Niamey.[218]

As for the supply of food-stuffs, only the harvest of 1920 seems to have been above average.[219] Apparently 1917–18, 1919 and 1921–2 were all bad years with localized famines.[220] The French, in an attempt to remedy the desperate situation of the Tuareg, levied sizeable requisitions of millet and cattle in the sedentary south in 1919, 1920 and 1921, requisitions that provoked yet another southward exodus among the Hausa.[221]

The last sequel of the Tuareg revolts: the Tegama affair
Once again it was in the North that the French were confronted with an alarming situation; what on the surface looks like the last convulsions of the revolts. For although the French had been able to quell the revolts, they had *not* been able to restore orderly peaceful conditions. Several small bands of what from the French viewpoint were outlaws and 'irregulars' still roamed the country. The severe French repression had generated a climate of fear and distrust highly detrimental to the policy of reconciliation inaugurated by the new *Commandant* of Agades, Captain Vitali. The nomads of French Sudan, Southern Algeria and the Nigerien North-East felt increasingly tempted to take advantage of the chaotic conditions prevailing in Aïr and adjacent regions. As a result there was a marked recrudescence of raids and acts of brigandage throughout the North in 1919. Conditions continued to remain unsettled until approximately 1921.[222]

Captain Vitali, convinced of the complicity of both the chief of the Kel Fadei and the 'new' Sultan of Agades, Ibrahim (Tegama's predecessor and successor), had them deposed, arrested and deported.[223] This rash action led to 'la ruine de l'ordre politique' and placed the French in a position where they had to admit their 'impuissance à faire exécuter nos ordres'.[224] They had no choice but to maintain the state of emergency.[225] Then, in the midst of what looked like a new Tuareg revolt, Captain Vitali found himself confronted with a particularly thorny and delicate problem represented by the former Sultan, Tegama, who had been captured in May 1919.[226] This problem is of particular interest because it highlights certain aspects of the Tuareg revolts,[227] and certain aspects of colonial rule in Niger generally. The authorities in Zinder wanted Tegama to be judged as a criminal by the tribunal of the *cercle* of Agades – presided over ex officio by the *Commandant de cercle* – and to have him sentenced to death and executed in public. But Vitali was of a different opinion, and he advanced a number of well-founded arguments. Was it wise, Vitali asked, to transfer Tegama to Agades and to indict him before a local court, considering the insurrectionary mood once again manifest among certain nomad tribes? Besides, in a region where nearly every single inhabitant had taken part in the revolts at one stage or another, no one could be relied upon to testify against Tegama, let alone to officiate as assessors. Furthermore, a public trial would give Tegama a splendid opportunity to incriminate a number of his former allies turned enemies, whom the French would then have to indict. The trial of Tegama promised to be the first of a long series of trials, the consequences of which might prove politically disastrous. More fundamentally, how could the *cercle* tribunal sentence Tegama to death, since it was supposed to judge according to the Muslim code of law, which held that it was Tegama's prerogative, in the capacity as *amīr-al-muminīn*, to declare and fight holy wars?[228] Instead Vitali proposed a more elegant solution, to indict Tegama for treason before a military court. But the superior authorities in Zinder and Dakar remained adamant, and ordered Vitali to undertake the necessary judicial proceedings. Faced with what he must have considered to be an impossible situation, Vitali 'persuaded' some of his *tirailleurs* to put Tegama to death in secret, and to disguise the murder as suicide. The authorities in Zinder quickly realized what had actually happened, but they refrained from indicting Vitali, who was simply transferred to another post.[229] The other prominent leader of the revolt, Kaocen, was killed in 1919 trying to recapture the Fezzan for the Sanūsīya.[230]

The Tuareg revolts: concluding remarks

The role of Tegama in the Aïr revolt was, I have argued elsewhere,[231] as the real instigator of that revolt. But this does not fit in with what we know about the institution of the Agades sultanate, or about the attitude of Tegama's predecessors towards the French. The Sultan of Agades, this *roi-captif* as we have presented him, the sovereign of the oasis-dwellers, would be expected to side with the French against the nomads, as Tegama's predecessors did in the past. Was it religious motives or more political ones that induced Tegama to change sides? Did he believe that a successful revolt would enable him to emerge as the effective ruler of the Tuareg? Whatever the case, Tegama's role raises two further and inter-related questions. First, why did the Tuareg of Aïr and Damergu respond almost to a man to Tegama's call; and second, what importance are we to ascribe to Kaocen and the Sanūsīya? It is clear that by 1916 the Tuareg had ample cause for complaint; French action after 1911 – the occupation of Tibesti in particular – had proved highly detrimental to their economy. But more fundamentally, the record of Franco-Tuareg relations before 1916 shows that the Tuareg submitted only when they had no alternative. I would argue that the Tuareg way of life, their ethos, their whole civilization, were incompatible with colonial rule. It may be that the Tuareg still aimed in 1916 at recovering their independence, and Tegama, Kaocen and their Sanūsī warriors presented them with an opportunity of achieving just that. Given the numerical strength of the Kaocen column and the apparently weak position of the French, and the general state of affairs in the Central Sahara in 1916,

Kaocen's – and Tegama's – cause probably looked like a winning one. This, I believe, decided the opportunist Tuareg of Aïr and Damergu, very few of whom were members of the Sanūsīya in 1916, to join in.

In view of the Islamic militancy of Tegama, Kaocen and some of their men, however, H. T. Norris is in a sense correct in pinning the label jihad on the revolt of 1916–17.[232] He may also be correct in criticizing my earlier view that the revolt was caused to a considerable extent by the French pro-*ineslemen* policy.[233] On the other hand the fact that the rise of the *ineslemen* from a lower and semi-vassal status among the Kel Dinnik, and the Kel Dinnik *only*, dates back to the seventeenth century, is not in itself enough, as Norris seems to believe,[234] to invalidate my theory. It simply means that as far as the Kel Dinnik are concerned, the French contributed to accelerate a process already in motion. After all, as Norris himself notes,[235] the French brought about the final ·freedom of the *ineslemen* from the *imajeghen*. However, Norris's views raise a number of questions, the most important of which concerns precisely the Kel Dinnik *ineslemen*. Given their traditional Islamic militancy (as already noted they had fought a major jihad in the nineteenth century) and their extremely hostile attitude towards the French,[236] it is hard to explain why they did not join the jihad (if that is what it was) in Aïr, and why they opted out of the rebellion in Azawak and the Tahoua region (a rebellion Norris fails to mention) at an early stage. Could it be because they were reluctant to jeopardize their new-found freedom, and/or because their traditional opposition towards the *imajeghen* was more pronounced than their hostility towards the French or their willingness to fight a jihad? If so, this confirms my earlier contention that Tuareg society was the opposite of homogeneous, and suggests that the French policy exacerbated local antagonisms and tensions and so contributed indirectly, in a way that remains to be defined, to the outbreak of the revolts.

My point here is that religious motives were not paramount among the rank and file Tuareg. The rebels aimed quite simply, I would argue, at reestablishing the situation which prevailed before the coming of the French.[237] There is therefore a reactionary dimension to the Tuareg revolts. This viewpoint is incompatible with André Salifou's contention that the rebels of 1916–17 represented the first generation of Nigerien nationalists.[238] In my view the principal weakness of the rebels was the opposition between on the one hand Tegama, Kaocen and the Sanūsī warriors – who constituted the foreign element *and* the inner hard core of the revolt, the die-hards who were thinking in terms of 'holy war' – and on the other the Nigerien Tuareg, many of whom opted out as soon as the Berger and Mourin columns reached Agades. Another weakness resided in the fact that Kaocen and Tegama were only able to rally the Aïr and Damergu Tuareg. The Kel Gress remained aloof, as did the Kel Ahaggar of Southern Algeria under their *amenukal* Moussa Ag Amastane.[239] The Kel Attaram and the Kel Dinnik staged their own revolts.

The revolt in the North proved disastrous to the Aïr and Damergu

Tuareg. They lost nearly all their camels, together with the estates, pastures and trading contacts they controlled in the south. In addition the *bugaje* were emancipated en masse.[240] From a more general point of view, the revolts had the effect of pushing the Tuareg out to the periphery. They were no longer to play a significant role in the history of Niger.

The North-East after 1918–19

In the North-East the French were back to square one, confronted with a situation very reminiscent of that around 1908. They were faced with the task of reconquering the whole of the North-East, and as in the years after 1908, the French now feared that the situation in the Fezzan would help to make that task particularly gruelling and time-consuming. In 1917, the Sanūsīya and the Italians had agreed upon a sort of *modus vivendi* by which the brotherhood was recognized as a temporal power (an emirate) under formal Italian overlordship. Hence the Fezzan, which the Sanūsīya was finally able to reconquer, became an Italian protectorate under effective Sanūsī rule.[241] This *modus vivendi* presented the French with an awkward situation, since the Sanūsī as Italian subjects were theoretically their allies. But what the French feared, and rightly so as it turned out, was that the Fezzan would become yet again a refuge zone for Tubu, Arab and Tuareg raiders, whom the Sanūsīya had every reason to encourage since they considered Tibesti to be part of their territory, as the French were perfectly aware. The latter in fact suspected the Italians of encouraging the Sanūsī claim, in view of a possible future extension of their colonial empire.[242] Given these conditions it is not surprising that the history of the North-East after 1918 is punctuated by a series of increasingly savage raids and equally savage French counter-raids.[243] It was only with the eruption of the second Italo-Sanūsī war in 1923 and the Italian reconquest of the Fezzan in 1930 that peaceful conditions were restored in the ravaged North-East.[244] By then Tibesti had been ceded to Chad.

4

Summing up and looking ahead

The societies of the Hausa and the Zerma/Songhay may have showed similarities in a remote past, but they showed a number of significant differences at the end of the nineteenth century. In simple terms, Hausa society was, on the eve of the colonial conquest, made up of peasants and traders, and Zerma/Songhay of warriors and dependants (or slaves). But both Nigerien Hausaland and the West came into prominence as refuge zones, the West after 1591, Hausaland much later, after 1804. In both cases new political entities were set up by members of dynasties that had been deposed and expelled from their respective 'heartlands'.

Due to rapidly changing conditions, the last decades of the nineteenth century witnessed the arrival of a number of adventurers and the rise to prominence of new entities and groups, and especially of a new brand of rulers, personified by men like Rābīh, *k'aura* Assao, Ahmad Chekou, *sarki* Tanimune of Damagaram and *ar'holla* Budal of the Kel Gress. In one sense these new groups and rulers paved the way for the Europeans; from this perspective, the colonial conquest may be seen as the culminating episode in a long series of invasions, conquests and upheavals. In another sense, their presence blurred the issue when the Europeans appeared on the horizon, so that the colonial conquest took the shape of a many-sided struggle between 'traditional' rulers, the pre-colonial 'imperialists', the nomads and the Europeans. It could be argued that the disturbances of 1905–6 both in Niger and in Northern Nigeria constituted the last chapter of this struggle, in that they were directed against yet another group of 'new' rulers, now promoted by the French, such as Aouta, *zermakoy* of Dosso, and *sarki* Gado Namalaya of Filingue, or against pre-colonial 'imperialists' whose position had been bolstered by the British, the Fulani rulers of Central Hausaland.

In the final analysis, the French could hardly have asked for more favourable conditions for easy conquest than the ones which prevailed in the Central Sudan in the 1890s. The Kel Gress were torn by internal strife, as were the people of Damergu and Damagaram. Maradi and Gobir had barely recovered from decades of warfare; in Adar the indigenous population was becoming increasingly hostile to the inefficient and oppressive overlordship of the Kel Dinnik. The same situation prevailed in the northern part of the West, among the Songhay. As for the Zerma, the Mawri, the Dendi and other peoples of the West, they had been utterly exhausted by the wars against the Sokoto Caliphate, the Tuareg, the hordes of Ahmad Chekou and the Voulet–Chanoine expedition. Their societies were in the process of disintegrating. In the Centre, the East, the North and the North-East, the decline of trans-Saharan trade was sapping the economic basis of the might of the Tuareg, the Tubu and the state of Damagaram. Finally, nearly the whole of the Central Sudan experienced severe drought between about 1899 and 1904 and again in 1907–9. It is hardly surprising therefore that the French were able to conquer these regions. A conquest it was, a successful aggression, simply because the aggressors had a superior technology. As such, it conforms to a historical 'law' which is that the peoples which at any time have the most advanced technology tend to dominate. This is not to deny that a number of chiefs, in the West in particular, asked for French support and even intervention, but they did not necessarily ask for French *rule*. Similarly, many people in Zinder and in the oases of the North were apparently favourably disposed towards the French. They hoped that the French would restore peace and the conditions beneficial to trade. But many of them turned against the French when they realized what colonial rule actually implied.

A military conquest in itself rarely constitutes a firm basis upon which to establish a new type of regime. It is one thing to conquer a given region, quite another to hold on to it. I would therefore argue that the imposition of colonial rule implies something more than a military conquest, a point I shall return to shortly. Similarly, armed resistance is only one type of resistance, as illustrated by a comparison between the Zerma/Songhay and the Hausa. As we have seen, the former presented a whole range of responses to the French conquest and the imposition of colonial rule, from the fiercest armed resistance to the most outspoken collaborative attitude. In general, however, the Zerma/Songhay put up some of the stiffest initial resistance against the French, and were also the first to rise against colonial rule. But after the 1905–6 revolts had been put down, the French experienced no more difficulties in the West. The Zerma/Songhay remained totally unaffected by the upheavals and troubles around them during the 1911–19 period. By contrast, the rural Hausa who – in spite of the heroic struggle of Maradi, Gobir and Damagaram against the Sokoto Caliphate – did not in general delight in war, put up little resistance during the initial phase of colonial conquest. Nor did they revolt against colonial rule, with the exception of small-scale and localized acts of rebellion especially in 1916–18. But *passive* resistance was much more general and tenacious in Hausaland than in the West. Although the French tried hard after 1911 to transform Hausa society, they were not successful. The Hausa opposed the 'new' French approach with their traditional inertia, or simply by walking away from it all; either by seeking refuge in remote regions, or by migrating to Northern Nigeria where there was an abundance of good land laid waste by the wars of the previous century.[1] It is anyone's guess how many Hausa (and Tuareg and Kanuri) who, for one reason or another and notably the Great Famine of 1913–15, crossed the border and settled down in the south, thus reversing the nineteenth-century trend. Rumours, denied both in London and Paris, were that a total of two to three million people from French West Africa 'escaped' to the British territories up to the 1920s.[2] These figures are of course speculative. But the very fact that migrations into British West Africa caught the eye of journalists and parliamentarians who were not particularly interested in African affairs suggests that the influx into British West Africa of people from the French territories must have been quite substantial.

The passive resistance of the Hausa was much more efficient than the armed resistance and rebellion of the Zerma/Songhay and the Tuareg. Indeed, Hausa society remained relatively unaffected by the French presence long after 1922. Even the Hausa chiefs managed somehow to retain the reasonably powerful position in spite of French 'crush-and-destroy' policy of the 1911–19 period. (After all, many of the 'legitimate' chiefs had been out of office during that period and could not be blamed for the errors or abuses committed.) But when the process of decolonization was set in motion, the French naturally turned to those people with whom they had the closest affinities, the *évolués*. And these *évolués* came mostly from the ethnic group which had proved most receptive to French ways, the Zerma/Songhay (and among the Zerma/Songhay mostly from the lowest social stratum, the former slaves). The Hausa proved to be no match for the Zerma/Songhay in the competition for power and influence within the European type of political system set up by the French in 1946. However, the contrast between the Zerma/Songhay and the Hausa was not confined to the political sphere. It is also very much in evidence in the *economic* sphere, or rather, it is brought out by a comparison between politics and economics. Briefly, although the Zerma/Songhay virtually monopolized the political scene after 1946, the Hausa became the principal contributors to the public purse. Between the wars, only the Hausa took up cash-crop farming. But the startling and in a sense self-contradictory point is that in Hausaland cash-crop farming did not lead, as far as one can see, to the breakdown of the traditional system of land-tenure or to the emergence of anything resembling rural capitalism. In fact, it was in the West, a labour-exporting region, that freehold property and its corollary, the notion of land as a marketable commodity, first made their appearance.[3]

Because they proved receptive to French ways, and because they lived in a region the French paid close attention to after 1927, the Zerma/Songhay continued to suffer much more severely than the other peoples of Niger from forced labour, requisitions and the other more questionable aspects of colonial rule. Thus the Zerma/Songhay were both the victims and beneficiaries of colonial rule.

However, the principal victims of colonial rule in Niger were without doubt the Tuareg and Tubu nomads. Although the French displayed a marked predilection for the Tuareg, this could not hide the fact that the very life of the Tuareg and the prominent position they had acquired during the nineteenth century were incompatible with colonial rule. (In the case of the Tubu, whose social system was based on warfare,[4] this is even more clear-cut.) It is important to realize in this context that French power was, by definition, a sedentary power, and that colonial conquest constituted the final episode in the century-old struggle between the sedentary populations and the nomads of the West African interior; an episode which proved fatal to the nomads. The destiny of the Tuareg under colonial rule may be seen in the context of the geopolitical position of Niger and the initial impact of the colonial conquest on the economy of the Central Sudan and Sahara. We have earlier stressed the peripheral character of most of the regions of modern Niger during the pre-colonial era. But we have also noted that some of these regions, precisely because of their peripheral character, served as transit zones between some of the more prominent centres of West Africa. Zinder was a commercial 'crossroads', second to Kano but nevertheless of considerable importance. So further west were Say and later Sansanne-Hausa. The French, moreover, were inclined to consider the Sahara as a sort of *mare nostrum* and the Sahel as its southern shore. They not only considered the Central Sudan and the Central Sahara to be of vital strategic importance, but also had high hopes of the economic potential of Niger. By 1922 all that was over. The combined effects of colonial conquest, the collapse of trans-Saharan trade, the extension northwards of the Nigerian railway, the revolts and repressions of 1915–18, and, last but not least, growing French disenchantment, had turned the Sahara into a barrier and Niger into a sort of *cul-de-sac*, a gloomy no-man's-land. This was reflected in the publicity given to Niger: the assassination of Cazémajou, the position and wealth of Zinder, the Voulet–Chanoine expedition, the Zerma/Songhay uprisings of 1905–6 and the Tuareg revolts of 1915–18 (although not the famine of 1913–15) all made the headlines. But after 1918 Niger, together with the rest of Africa, disappeared from the newspapers altogether. The epic and heroic era of colonial conquest had come to an end, and Africa ceased to be fashionable. Niger in particular was increasingly looked upon as the most unpromising part of West Africa, a sort of *colonie pénitencière* to which officials were 'exiled' whenever they made themselves undesirable elsewhere. These trends proved particularly detrimental to the Tuareg nomads who had constituted the human link between North Africa and the Central Sudan, and who now found themselves pushed out onto the periphery. Seen in this perspective, it is not at all clear whether the revolts and repressions of 1915–18 constitute a cause or a consequence, or whether they simply contributed to the acceleration of an evolution set in motion earlier. What *is* certain is that these events definitively broke the power of the nomads.

The relative prosperity enjoyed at least by the Tuareg and the Hausa between about 1908 and 1913 is therefore a point of some interest in a comparative perspective. In certain recent works on south-eastern Africa[5] the idea that the colonial conquest did not turn out to be as counter-productive as first appeared seems to be gaining ground. According to these arguments, the colonial regime in its first years provided Africans with new opportunities which they were successful in exploiting. It was only several years later, under the combined impact of natural disasters (rinderpest, drought etc.) and of a more aggressive colonial policy, that the real change occurred, a change which paved the way for structural underdevelopment. The history of the West, where the cost of the initial phase of colonial conquest was staggeringly high, does not fit into this pattern, but (with the exception of the problematic contention regarding structural underdevelopment) the history of the Centre, the East and the North certainly does. The problem therefore is to determine whether the relative prosperity of the 1908–13 period (and of the corresponding periods in other African territories) was simply coincidental, or whether it came to an end as a consequence of more long-term structural changes. Although the evidence is inconclusive, it is difficult to point to any structural changes in the case of Niger.

Several factors contributed to the acceleration of the marginalization of the Tuareg, and also of the Tubu, after 1919. First, as a consequence of the low population growth among the Tuareg and the Tubu (compared with the Zerma/Songhay and the Hausa), their numerical importance declined.[6] Second, the exchange rate between cattle and millet deteriorated steadily (to the detriment of cattle) throughout the colonial period.[7] Third, the herds of the nomads were ravaged by rinderpest and bovine pleuro-pneumonia at least until the 1930s. Fourth, whatever profits the Tuareg derived from transportation declined rapidly during the 1930s when lorries began to take over.[8] Fifth, during the second half or last third of the colonial period, the Tuareg nomads found themselves increasingly in competition with the Fulani for pastures and water, as the latter trekked further and further northwards over the years. This in turn was a direct consequence of the gradual extension of cultivated land in the south (see chapter 6). Finally, after 1946 the Tuareg chose to remain aloof from politics, with the result that their interests were neglected. The overall picture, then, is that of a society on the defensive, in a state of gradual decline. Perhaps the surge of mental diseases among the Tuareg[9] may be considered as an indication or a consequence of this decline.

Two of the factors given above also apply to the sedentary Kanuri of the Far East: their growth-rate was probably much lower than the average in Niger,[10] and they too took very little interest in politics after 1946. It would seem, therefore, that after 1922 Niger gradually became a predominantly sedentary and black country, and that the history of the last thirty-eight years or so of colonial rule is in essence that of the Zerma/Songhay, the Hausa and the French.

Returning to the theme of the nature and impact of colonial rule and the interaction between the French and the Nigeriens, I have earlier made the contention that the military conquest of Niger should be looked upon as but *one* of the actions, although by far the most important, which eventually resulted in the imposition and establishment of colonial rule. I would argue that colonial rule was not based exclusively on force and coercion and that coercion had by about the 1920s been replaced to a large extent by consent. This line of argument is impossible to substantiate and even difficult to back up with convincing evidence. It could of course be said that no regime based purely on force can survive, as did the French regime in Niger, for roughly sixty years. To this it may be objected, first, that the South African regime has survived for just that long; second, that the French controlled means of coercion that were vastly more efficient than anything seen in Niger before; and third, that the colonial regime in Niger did not in the final analysis last for sixty years. The period of conquest and consolidation lingered on until 1922, if not beyond, and the process of decolonization was set in motion in 1946. This leaves us with only some twenty-four years or so to account for. On the other hand, although the French had superior means of coercion (that is to say, an impressive army whose rank-and-file was composed – the point is worth repeating – exclusively of *Africans*), they did not have to resort to these means after 1919. In fact, there is a stark and in many ways puzzling contrast between the pre- and post-1919 periods. Whereas the years before 1919 were marked by several revolts and uprisings, and considerable unrest and difficulties of all sorts, the post-1919 period can be described as one of near-total calm and quiet. In the case of the Tuareg, the explanation is obvious. Having been thoroughly and completely crushed by the French, they had no alternative but to keep quiet and hope for the best. But the Tuareg had to be crushed precisely because a majority among them did not accept colonial rule. This may not have been the case among the sedentary population, who never staged a general revolt against the French, and who refused to join the Tuareg in 1915–18. With the exception of the Tuareg revolts, there is in Niger nothing resembling a war of independence or liberation. Was this because the ethnic, social and religious diversity made it impossible to form a common front against the French? Or simply because most people realized the futility of armed opposition? But a general uprising in 1916–18 might well have succeeded, or at the very least have forced the French to reconquer Niger. On the other hand, it must be remembered that there were in Niger in 1921 only some 220 resident non-Africans, all sexes, ages, grades and occupations included;[11] not a very impressive or intimidating number.

If one accepts the theory that the people of Niger had by 1922 at the latest accepted colonial rule, and even that the French administrators were perceived as being the legitimate rulers of the land, then a number of otherwise incomprehensible circumstances becomes intelligible. But if they had come to be looked upon as the legitimate rulers, how had the French been able to achieve such a startling result (which was *not*, it must be stressed, the consequence of any determined or coherent policy)? Obviously, their absolute belief in their own superiority and the fact that they were always victorious in the end could not but have a profound impact upon the Africans. It led the latter, inevitably, to question their own values, their own political system, society and civilization. Things were falling apart, to paraphrase Chinua Achebe. This is the quintessence of colonial rule, and its most subtle, damaging and long-lasting aspect: the cultural, historical, and even psychological alienation of the Africans; the fact that the French had been able to persuade not only themselves, not only their fellow-Europeans, but even the Africans, that the latter had no history, no civilization, and that they were barbarians predestined to be ruled by the white man. There was a complete disregard for African values, culture and history.[12] These then, were the main ingredients of what many would term the new dominant ideology, the ideology of the colonial regime. But this type of ideology was in no way peculiar to colonial rule or even to the Europeans. Indeed, nearly all the pre-colonial ruling elites had developed similar ideologies; the *imajeghen* of the Tuareg,[13] the Fulani of Northern Nigeria[14] and the *koy-ize* of the Zerma/Songhay[15] are those cases where we have adequate information. The main ingredients were the same everywhere: the ideologies extolled the superior virtues and the superior culture of the rulers who, as a consequence, assumed the stature of *natural* rulers, and who, as a further consequence, were able to instil into their subjects what can only be described as a slave mentality. (The phenomenon is of course universal and still in evidence even in Western Europe, although in a more subtle form.) Perhaps these pre-existing 'ideologies of superiority', which in the case of Northern Nigeria exercised a particularly powerful attraction for the British and made them feel almost at home, help to explain the imposition and adoption of a colonial ideology. The paradox here is that the Europeans began to lose faith in the ideological justification for colonial rule long before the Nigeriens did.

Given the sacral nature of African society, any ideology needs to be wrapped in a religious clothing, to have a religious dimension. In the case of the pre-colonial rulers this dimension is clear. They had been invested by supranatural powers with a mandate, and been endowed with *arzika, bon-kaney, k'arfi* or *dadi n'kay* (translated earlier as 'force' or 'luck') to enable them to exercise this mandate. In my view the notions of 'force' and 'luck' are invaluable for an understanding of the French position in Niger: there occurred at the level of these concepts a form of transfer in favour of the French. After all, by 1922 the French could point to an impressive record. They had conquered the Central Sudan and Sahara, crushed the Zerma/Son-ghay and Tuareg revolts, uncovered the plot in Zinder, quelled a number of localized rebellions and had more generally displayed an awesome military superiority. From the African point of view, was this because the French possessed an extraordinary 'luck', an unparalleled 'force', which could only emanate from supranatural powers? Does it follow that colonial servitude lost some of its sting since authority now rested with those to whom faith had attributed the power of safe-guarding the existence of society?

This theory helps to explain the startling contrast between the pre- and post-1922 periods. It also explains why the Zerma/Songhay, unlike the other peoples of Niger, remained quiet after 1906 – the French, first through the Voulet–Chanoine expedition, and then by crushing the revolts of 1905–6, displayed much earlier there than further east the full scale of their 'force'. And it adds another dimension to the difficulties experienced by the French in 1914–18, which may be explained partially in terms of the grave doubts raised in many minds by the drought of 1913–15, which was seen as a token of the diminishing French 'force'. Finally, our theory gives at least some clues to the understanding of the somewhat strange reaction of the Nigeriens both to the defeat of the French in 1940 and to the Reforms of 1946, and also of the more puzzling aspects of the political struggle after 1946. It may be objected that the spread of Islam made the categories of 'force' and 'luck' obsolete for analytical purposes, but this is not necessarily so, since popular and especially *sufi* Islam contains a very similar concept, that of *baraka*.[16]

The concepts of 'luck' and 'force' should perhaps also be taken into account in analysing another aspect of colonial history, the fact that the Africans who led the resistance and later the revolts against the French are long since forgotten in Niger. It is perhaps because they all lost in the end, and African traditions easily forget the losers, who are clearly not endowed with the necessary *arzika, bon-kaney, dadi n'kay, k'arfi* or *baraka*. Therefore, their legitimacy as leaders was questionable. But it may also be because the 'heroes' of the pre-1919 period were not Nigeriens, but Zerma/Songhay, Tuareg or Hausa. Whatever power-basis they controlled, it was ethnic in character. For a politician of the post-1946 era to evoke their memory would have been tantamount to 'tribalism'. And since nearly all those politicians were from the sedentary south, one could hardly expect them to look upon men such as Tegama and Kaocen with much sympathy. It is also important to realize that the *évolués*, although they frequently invoked African civilization, culture, history and values, did not look to the past but very much to the future. *And* they opposed colonial rule in the name of not African, but of western, European concepts, notions and traditions, and first and foremost the French revolutionary tradition. They did so not primarily in order to attain freedom or independence, but for equality. Indeed, the fight of the pan-African *Rassemblement Démocratique Africain* after 1946 was not so much a fight against colonial rule as a fight against the colonial administration, not so much in order to abolish that institution as to take possession of its functions (perhaps to capture the 'force' and/or 'luck' of the French?). And when these men felt the need to affirm their own originality, their specificity *vis-à-vis* the Europeans, they did not turn to what we could call 'Old' Africa, but to the Muslim religion and culture.

As the people of Niger tried to comprehend the colonial phenomenon in the light of their own conceptual framework, so the French adjusted themselves, perhaps unconsciously, to this same framework. In practical terms this means that after the attempt to establish direct rule during the

1908–19 period had failed, the French, instead of reverting to indirect rule, developed a type of rule which one is tempted to describe as basically African. Indeed, the impression prevails that the *Commandants* tended increasingly to administer their *cercles* as if they were *chefferies*, and as if the *Commandants* were African chiefs. As Pierre Alexandre has argued, 'on ne commande à l'Afrique qu'en lui obéissant', which implies that 'les commandants devinrent des rois nègres'.[17] This evolution towards what we may call the 'indigenous chieftaincy-model' had one considerable advantage: it solved the contradiction between the French distaste for indirect rule and the shortage of personnel and means. It led to the emergence of a particular breed of bush-administrators – mainly batchelors, who felt more at ease in the African countryside than in France, who more than often spoke the local tongue (thanks to their African mistresses), who knew everyone, and in particular everything that went on. At ease in the tortuous labyrinths of 'traditional' African politics, they were not only aware of local intrigues and cabals, but were often instrumental in launching them. In short, the French administrators were in a real sense incorporated into the local social landscape. Most of them loved every minute of it. Here they were, Frenchmen often of rather modest origins, who rode around their respective districts (as opposed to their colleagues further south, who often had to *walk*), wielding nearly unlimited power, and issuing orders to aristocrats. But the other side of the coin is that the French administrators became very much attached to the 'old' or 'traditional' Africa. They heartily despised the *évolués*, and they took little interest in economic matters.[18]

Among other long-term trends the most significant is the internal migration and colonization which, during the pre-colonial era, had been conducted mainly under the auspices of the Tuareg. After the arrival of the French, it changed character and became what I call a 'Land and Freedom' movement. It came to affect the whole of the sedentary south and continued unabated throughout the colonial period. This internal migration was an aspect of African resistance to colonial rule, and a successful one at that, since the pioneers (if so they can be called), especially those who settled down in relatively distant regions, usually remained outside the reach of the French for several years. And when they *were* brought under colonial rule, they suffered less heavily from the *indigénat*, forced labour and requisitions than did the more densely populated areas.

The internal migration substantially modified the pattern of population distribution. In Hausaland it tended increasingly to conform to the pre-jihad pattern when the population lived in small, scattered hamlets. This trend is probably the main factor responsible for the rapidly decreasing fauna in the West[19] and perhaps also elsewhere. Another consequence was that the local societies became even more fragmented than before. This seems also to have been the case among the Tuareg (whether nomads or not), whose confederations and tribes were slowly breaking up into smaller autonomous entities.[20]

With regard to the process of modernization, the record of the first twenty-five years of the French presence in Niger is depressingly dismal. In 1921–2 a grand total of ten primary school teachers, five doctors and *one* veterinarian (none of them Nigeriens) resided in Niger. (The number of children attending French schools was 674.)[21] In other words, health, education, veterinary and other services were in 1922 either non-existent or embryonic.

So far very little attention has been devoted to the history of religious beliefs during the colonial period. This is because, as indicated in the Introduction, we do not have enough evidence to reconstruct that history in detail. Naturally, in Niger as elsewhere Islam grew throughout the colonial period, especially the mystic or *sufi* Islam of the brotherhoods. The causes of this, which are in no way specific to Niger, are well enough known to need only brief mention here.[22] One was the attitude of the French, openly pro-Muslim in the early days,[23] but later more sceptical if not downright hostile, especially towards some of the *sufi* brotherhoods accused of being xenophobic.[24] In fact, whatever the official policy, the French had a tendency to favour and thus to facilitate the spread of Islam throughout the colonial period. To the French, Islam, as opposed to 'paganism' or 'animism', presented a codified and tangible reality they were familiar with and could grasp.[25] Another cause, stressed by Edward Alpers in particular for East Africa[26] and probably also valid for West Africa, is the enlargement of scale as a result of colonial conquest. A third cause was the attitude of the French auxiliaries and later of the *évolués*. These people, who were perceived by ordinary Nigeriens as being privileged by fate, were all Muslims. They had only contempt for paganism. Thus the 'old religion was progressively weakened through the shame of being despised'.[27] It could also be that the colonial conquest itself, by demonstrating the inefficiency and powerlessness of the local deities, dealt a severe blow to the prestige of traditional religious beliefs and thus paved the way for Islam.

The spread of Islam was perhaps not continuous; for instance, the liberation of the slaves in the West probably led to an animistic 'reaction', as did in all likelihood another and related phenomenon, the internal migration. It was probably also very slow. It seems that people *adhered* fairly quickly to Islam on the institutional level (in the sense that even pagans celebrated Muslim marriages),[28] but that *conversion* took much longer. In fact, the religious change occurred in two stages, the first stage being characterized by many different types of accommodation between the old and the new, although how and to what extent is not at all clear. It has been argued that Islam long remained not an exclusive religion, but what has been qualified as a 'religion supplémentaire',[29] 'un fétichisme supérieur',[30] only *one* of a number of 'divers systèmes religieux [qui] se partagent les croyances'[31] (Islam being for instance the religion of the after life).[32] But it could equally well be argued that the encounter between Islam and paganism gave rise to what was in reality a number of syncretic religions. It could also be argued that the new elements introduced by Islam *and* by the French conquest sparked off a process of reinterpretation of the very adaptable traditional religious beliefs, leading to a gradual absorption and even assimilation of these new elements. Thus the colonial period was characterized by extreme religious diversity. Let us look, for example, at the many so-called possession or mystery cults: the *bori* cult among the Hausa,[33] the *holey*[34] and *hauka*[35] cults in the West, to name but three. An appreciation of these cults depends upon the perspective one adopts. Seen from the point of view of traditional religious beliefs, they may be considered to represent a continuation or a more elaborate stage of these beliefs. Indeed, possession-dances and spirit-possession represent a well-known but nevertheless exceptional phenomenon among the pagans. Briefly, possession-dances are a means of establishing direct communications with the deities,[36] direct communication which now simply became permanent. However, these cults had a vastly expanded pantheon, with new spirits corresponding to the new occupational categories introduced by the French (Governor, *Commandant*, clerk etc.) making their appearance. Spirits which are without doubt of Muslim inspiration also appeared.[37] It would seem, therefore, that there is a certain syncretic dimension to these cults. On the other hand, the fact that the *bori* cult recruited its adherents mainly from women, that is among a category whose status stood to suffer a sharp deterioration under Islam, seems to imply that at least this particular (and in fact very widespread) cult represented a certain reaction against Islam.

These cults helped the people to comprehend their new situation. They also provided uprooted individuals with a substitute for the fast disintegrating kinship-community (hence their esoteric and sect-like character). But quite a few cults were markedly pathological in the sense that they featured distortions of social behaviour, and as such provided their adherents with the possibility of escaping for a short while their fate, to forget poverty and humiliation. It may be argued, therefore, that the spread of these cults perhaps bears witness to an incapacity to deal with the earthquakes of society. In fact, mystery cults are a universal phenomenon which, as in Niger, are characteristic of societies in crisis and/or in the process of social change.

According to Jean Rouch, the Zerma/Songhay of the West depict the encounter with Islam in terms of a battle between two groups of deities, on the one hand the 'masters of the land and of the water', i.e. the old fertility deities, and on the other deities which Jean Rouch has identified as the first Muslim clerics who settled in the region.[38] However, if the fertility deities lost out, they continued nevertheless to be worshipped; the fertility rites were perhaps the most resilient element of the indigenous religious beliefs. These rites apparently ceased to be communal and instead were confined exclusively to the priest-chiefs who tended increasingly to group together in so-called 'secret societies', often of an esoteric character; societies which people

117

5

The 'great silence': the classic period of colonial rule, 1922–45

It is hardly profound to argue that the years after 1922 constituted the classic or quintessential period, or the golden age of colonial rule in French West Africa. While it may be asserted that the type of colonial system set up by the so-called Vichy regime in 1940 constitutes an exception in the annals of French rule in West Africa, it can be argued that the difference between the pre- and post-1940 years was not one of kind, but of degree, in the sense that the authoritarian, arbitrary, and in many ways absurd regime which the Africans experienced for a while after 1940 represented merely a refinement, a more rigorous application of an already existing system.

The period of conquest and consolidation having come to an end by approximately 1922, the French became mainly preoccupied with purely practical administrative matters. Among these were: how to make the local administration function; how to forestall migrations; how to recruit soldiers, and especially how to secure adequate supplies of labour; how to deal with the 'new' villages; how to treat the chiefs; and last, but not least, how to persuade people to pay taxes. This pragmatic down-to-earth attitude may have been more pronounced in Niger than in most other territories in French West Africa, first, because of the perpetual shortage of personnel, and second, because few senior officials remained long enough in Niger to acquire the experience necessary for formulating long-term policies.

Although the administration in Niger was perpetually understaffed, the ratio of administrators to the total population seems to have been twice as high in Niger as in Nigeria.[1] However, such a comparison is not very relevant, since it can be argued that the British counterpart to the *Commandant de cercle* was not the District Officer, but the local emir and the Native Authority. In other words the frightening array of trivial matters that the French administrators had to attend to were left to indigenous political authorities in Nigeria. The French predilection for bureaucratic red-tape resulted in an inelastic and ill-adapted administration, whose local representatives found themselves in perpetual conflict between the way they were supposed to administer their districts according to official regulations and decrees, and the way local conditions often forced them to carry out their duties. However, elasticity increased as the 'indigenous chieftaincy-model' referred to in the preceding chapter gained ground.

By 1922 at the latest, it had been realized that Niger possessed few if any resources that could be tapped. Hence not a single kilometre of tarred all-season road, let alone railway, was built between 1922 and 1944. And no efforts whatsoever were made to encourage river transportation. In other sectors the record of the French achievement is equally bleak. Almost no money was spent on social services, and the veterinary service, only established in 1927, remained nearly non-existent.[2] In education, the number of pupils at all schools increased from 674 in 1921–2 to 2,872 in 1934, before dwindling sharply.[3] (These figures exclude those Nigeriens – Songhay and Fulani from the West – who had the opportunity to attend schools of the Catholic missions in Upper Volta.) The rate of literacy in Niger thus remained (and still is) among the very lowest in Africa.[4] In fact, only the children of French administrators and their indigenous mistresses were well cared for in the *Foyer des métis* established in Zinder in 1922.[5] The motives which prompted the French to build schools were purely practical, to provide the administration with candidates who could fill the score of minor posts. It is in this respect symptomatic that the American Protestant mission in Tibiri, which the French eyed with suspicion, was forced to close down its school on the grounds that it did not conform to official French regulations by dispensing teaching in Hausa instead of in French.[6]

These considerations raise the question of the position and role of the so-called *évolués*, i.e. the Africans who had been educated in French schools or who possessed a certain knowledge of the French language and matters French. It should be noted, first, that the educational opportunities open to the Nigeriens were limited indeed. The most they could hope for was the diploma of the famous *Ecole Normale* William Ponty (at Gorée, later Sébikotane, in distant Senegal), established in 1913, a diploma which did not even correspond to the French *baccalauréat*.[7] As *sujets* they were barred from attending the *Lycée* Faidherbe, established in 1920,[8] the only fully fledged secondary school in French West Africa, and again in Senegal.

In addition to the number of pupils cited above, a grand total of ninety-one Nigeriens successfully completed primary school between 1921 and 1929;[9] the first Nigerien who attended Ponty was admitted in 1923,[10] and it was only in 1931 that the *Ecole Primaire Supérieure* in Niamey was established.[11] There were only 631 African functionaries comprising all categories and grades in 1940,[12] the majority being non-Nigerien. We do not know how many Nigeriens graduated each year from Ponty, from the *Ecole Normale* in Katibougou and the *Ecole Normale Rurale* in Dabou, Ivory Coast (both federal schools which had been established in 1934 and 1938 respectively),[13] but there can hardly have been more than two to five a year. Nigerien *évolués* were very few indeed at the end of the 1930s, a few hundred at the most. Of these *évolués* by far the most numerous seem to have been

Zerma/Songhay.[14] The French administration thus had to continue to rely heavily upon Sudanese, Dahomean and Senegalese functionaries.

Schachter-Morgenthau has argued that the *évolués* tended to replace the chiefs as intermediaries as early as the inter-war years.[15] If so, it does not necessarily follow that they were looked upon by their kinsmen as authentic representatives. But the *évolués*, familiar with and used to French ways, the mentality and the language of the French, were useful to the local community. Thus illiterate African peasants often found it in their interest to enlist the support of an *évolué* in their relations with the administration. Some *évolués* were obviously able to take advantage of their 'usefulness', and to enjoy considerable influence and power, but by and large, although the *évolués* were looked upon with awe, they were *also* looked upon with fear and especially with suspicion. They suffered from their ambiguous and delicate position as outcasts, as individuals who belonged in the final analysis neither to the world of the Africans nor to that of the French. The paradox is that the *évolués* who represented in many ways the logical result, the ultimate consequence so to speak, of colonial rule, were for precisely that reason loathed and despised by the French, who preferred the 'uncorrupted' peasants, only superficially if at all influenced by European civilization. Nevertheless, the *évolués* never wavered in their attachment to and affection for France. To them the administrators in Africa were simply not 'true' Frenchmen, not like the metropolitan French, and not at all like their venerated former masters, the handful of primary school teachers in Niamey and at Ponty, who belonged to that famed school of Third Republic *instituteurs* to whom the word 'République' was still synonymous with *liberté, égalité, fraternité*, the ideals of 1789.[16]

Here we may continue the discussion on evolutionary trends started in preceding chapters. Although these made considerable impact after 1922, they are difficult to study in any detail. Internal colonization seems to have affected the whole of the sedentary south, and in certain regions reached such proportions that a number of traditional villages are reported to have disappeared altogether.[17] As usual, internal migration was more or less actively opposed by the French, especially in the West.[18] But at the same time the French unconsciously encouraged migration through their fiscal policy, which consisted in imposing heavier taxes in densely populated regions, presumed to be more prosperous, than in outlying and relatively sparsely populated regions, which became tax-havens.[19] The second trend briefly to be dealt with here is the migration of the pastoral Fulani. Up to the 1930s the general direction was northwards, but during that decade there was a general shift eastwards, a wholesale Fulani 'invasion' of the Far East according to official reports.[20]

The period after 1922 was fairly static. Apart from the famine of 1931 in the West and the beginnings of the Second World War, there were few outstanding events around which we may construct a coherent narrative. The history of Niger between 1922 and 1945 is principally made up of often subtle economic, social, religious and psychological changes, some of which have already been alluded to. Unfortunately, owing to the nature of the evidence, most of these changes remain difficult to chart. What *can* be charted, and in detail, are the economic fluctuations of the 1922–40 period. An overview of Niger's inter-war economy shows stagnation following the war, relatively rapid growth in the late 1920s, collapse between 1929 and 1932–3, and then faltering recovery. But these trends were in no way specific to Niger and can probably be observed nearly everywhere in Africa.[21]

FROM FEAST TO FAMINE, 1922–31

Governor Brévié and his policies
The history of Niger in the 1920s is in many ways a repetition of the post-1908 period. In both cases Niger slowly recovered after a series of disruptions. And in both cases this was due, first, to successive years of adequate rainfall; second, to the economic expansion in Northern Nigeria and on the Gold Coast; and finally, and perhaps most important, to the non-interference of the colonial administration.

The French policy in this period is associated with the name of Jules Brévié, a high-ranking official in Dakar who in 1922 was sent to Niger as that colony's first civilian governor to clear up the mess left behind by the military. (The military, however, remained in command of the *cercle* of Tahoua–Madaoua until 1927 and of that of Agades until after the Second World War.) Brévié, titular governor of Niger for seven years, is one of the very few French officials to have given serious thought to certain aspects of colonial rule. In his famous book *Islamisme contre 'Naturisme' au Soudan français*,[22] Brévié argued in favour of a reversal of the administration's hitherto pro-Muslim policy. This attempt to turn the clock back, to rehabilitate, as it were, the old religions, had few practical consequences. It is interesting, nevertheless, to note that Brévié, although he clothed his arguments in the paternalistic and colonialist jargon befitting a man in his position, displayed in his book an astonishing degree of insight into the old religions. In fact, many recent scholarly views are prefigured here, though packaged rather awkwardly.

Brévié's views with regard to the chiefs, on the other hand, were to have a more profound impact. Brévié advocated a sort of neo-traditionalist policy aimed at integrating the chiefs more closely with the administrative structure, while at the same time safeguarding the true nature of the chiefly institutions. It was particularly important, according to Brévié, never to lose sight of the fact that the chiefs were, and should be regarded as, the authentic representatives of their respective peoples. Brévié, the only Governor of Niger to have gone on from that position to a brilliant career,[23] is generally credited with having given a certain indirect touch to the administration during his tenure as Governor-General of French West Africa (1930–6).[24] This was in fact the policy of many of the Governors-General during the inter-war years, a period which brought a general bolstering of the chiefs.[25] As we shall see, Brévié first tried to implement his ideas while in Niger, and they led in the final analysis to the rise of an administrative system which functioned in accordance with what I have defined earlier as the 'indigenous chieftainship model'. However, first we must look at other aspects of his policy.

Brévié realized quickly that the peoples of Niger were in sore need of peace, good government and prosperity. He put an end to the requisitioning of food-stuffs and pack animals; he abolished all taxes on the markets while at the same time encouraging the exportation of hides and skins;[26] he saw to it that the recruitment of soldiers did not exceed a few hundred recruits a year;[27] and he kept very strict control of the application of the punitive measures known as the *indigénat*.[28] This was followed up by a Federation-wide decree which, in addition to the chiefs and the former servicemen, exempted from the *indigénat* yet new categories of *sujets*: the functionaries, the traders and all literate 'natives', including their families.[29] In order to prevent a repetition of the 1913–15 famine Brévié tried to establish a rudimentary system of village reserve granaries, and launched a modest anti-locust programme.[30] Taxes remained at a fairly moderate level,[31] and there was no question of re-erecting the customs barrier.

Finally, Brévié provided Niger with a reasonably stable administration. This is symbolized by the names of Horace Croccichia, Henry Fleury and de Loppinot, the *Commandants* of Niamey, Zinder and Tahoua respectively. (Croccichia later became Governor of the Ivory Coast.) Mention may also be made in this context of Brévié's very able young protégé, Jean Toby, successively *chef de subdivision* at Dogondoutchi, *Commandant* of Tillabery and Brévié's *chef de cabinet*. Toby was later to serve as Governor of Niger for a record-breaking twelve years.

Economic recovery

After the customs barrier had been abolished, economic growth in Northern Nigeria again began to affect the Centre and the East. First, the cultivation of groundnuts for export spread across the border into the *cercles* of Maradi and Zinder, and the *subdivision* of Magaria in particular. Exports began as early as 1924,[32] really getting under way around 1928.[33] According to J. D. Collins this was due primarily to the arrival of expatriate buyers, both Syro-Lebanese and French.[34] In 1929 Niger produced some 27,000 tons of groundnuts.[35] Second, the expanding market in Northern Nigeria again encouraged Nigeriens to export cattle and, more surprisingly, millet to the south. The cattle came mostly from the Tahoua–Konni–Madaoua region,[36] and the millet, like the groundnuts, from the *subdivision* of Magaria.[37] In addition, many Nigerien Hausa now found work in Northern Nigeria in the dry season.[38] The Tuareg, the *bugaje* in particular, also profited from this commercial expansion. Camels remained for the time being the preferred mode of transport in those regions situated beyond reach of the railway. Accordingly, the camel prices rose sharply.[39]

Astonishingly, in less than ten years after the Great Famine the people of the East and the Centre were able to export cattle, groundnuts and even millet southwards. This is another indication of the Hausa's (and the *bugaje*'s) readiness and ability to adapt themselves to the prevailing market conditions and also their willingness to innovate. Yet another indication of this is the fact that the Hausa adopted a new type of hoe for farming during the 1920s. This hoe, although far more efficient, was much harder to use than the previous type (called *iler*). However, its adoption, together with the general evolution towards a more intensive agriculture, led to increased yields.[40] These changes, and also the vast increase in farmland due to internal migration, and of course adequate rainfall explain why the Hausa were now able to produce a surplus for export.

Whereas the Hausa innovated at home, the Zerma/Songhay, who, characteristically, never adopted the new hoe, hired themselves out in ever increasing numbers as labourers abroad, principally on the Gold Coast. This, of course, was in accordance with a recurring pattern throughout the history of colonial Niger. But both the Hausa and the Zerma/Songhay benefited from the deterioration of the exchange rate of the franc, which lost half its value compared with sterling between 1921 and 1925,[41] although this may have been partly offset by the very steep rise in prices in Niger.[42]

There are several indications that the 1920s was a period of recovery, even one of modest prosperity. For instance, according to official figures, the population increased from around one million in 1922 to more than one and a half million nine years later.[43] This was in spite of two severe epidemics of meningitis and typhus which killed more than one-tenth of the population between 1923 and 1927.[44] Although official figures are by definition unreliable and although part of the increase was due to the transfer of a few regions from Upper Volta to Niger, these figures seem reasonably plausible. After all, we know from other sources that many refugees, including a fair number of Tuareg, returned from Northern Nigeria during the 1920s.[45] Another indication is provided by the figures for trade. The value of exports soared from around 5 to 45 million francs between 1922 and 1929, and the value of imports from 8 to 27 million.[46] Niger thus had in 1929 a high trade surplus. Yet another indication was the *azalaï*. Around four thousand camels took part in 1922–3[47] and more than ten thousand six years later.[48] It may also be that the Tuareg of Niger benefited from the revival of trade with Algeria, although this trade seems to have been in the hands of the Kel Ahaggar,[49] with whom the Nigerien Tuareg clashed frequently over pastures.[50] With regard to the North, it should also be noted that during the 1920s the French tried with some success to encourage communities of *bugaje* to clear land and to settle down as agriculturalists in some of the valleys of Aïr.[51]

The French attitude towards the various ethnic groups and the chiefs
There is evidence during the 1920s of a shift of emphasis in the attitude of the French towards the various ethnic groups and regions of Niger. Although the point should not be pushed too far, it seems as if the French decided to turn their backs on the East and the North to some extent, and to focus their attention on the West and on the Zerma/Songhay, whom the French probably considered to be more malleable than the 'traditionalist' Hausa; 'traditionalist', that is, outside the economic field. The Hausa were also 'suspect' in the eyes of the French because of their Northern Nigerian, i.e. British, 'connection'. This shift of emphasis is in a way symbolized by the transfer of the capital from Zinder to Niamey in 1927, officially because of the shortage of drinking water in Zinder which did indeed create a real problem.[52] The transfer of the capital was part of a major administrative shake-up which also brought about the incorporation of the Songhay and Fulani *subdivisions* of Tera and Say, hitherto part of Upper Volta, into Niger.[53] Finally, in 1932 the *cercles* of Fada N'Gurma and Dori became part of Niger as a consequence of the dismembering of Upper Volta.[54] The result of all these changes was to reduce the numerical superiority of the Hausa slightly and to make the colony more 'western' oriented.

In accordance with the ideas he had expressed earlier, Brévié abolished a number of petty chiefdoms, mainly in the West, while bolstering the position of those chiefs who remained. In 1924 alone eighteen cantons were obliterated,[55] but at the same time Brévié saw to it that these chiefs were more closely controlled than before through the creation (in 1924) of two new *cercles*, those of Tillabery and Dosso, both carved out of the over-sized *cercle* of Niamey. (In the Centre the *subdivision* of Konni became a *cercle* the same year.)[56] In Dosso the French reorganized the *commandement indigène* for the benefit of Saidou Moussa, the former lieutenant of the French army who – contrary to tradition but by the will of the French – succeeded his father as *zermakoy* in 1924. Saidou, 'le type accompli du chef indigène',[57] was made chief of a province comprising not only the traditional realm of the *zermakoy*, but also Kiota, Sokorbe, Falwell and Sambera.[58] Thus the French had in fact reestablished the pre-1913 organization. In Dogondoutchi the *sarkin* Arewa was also elevated to the rank of province-chief, and Arzika Gao, another *ancien combattant*, named heir apparent in 1927. He eventually succeeded his father Tassao Gao in 1931.[59]

There is no need to examine here in any greater detail the reorganization of the *chefferie* in the West during the 1920s. The pattern and the consequences are clear: first (as already noted), a general bolstering of the position of the chiefs, including quite a steep increase in their allowances.[60] Second, a tendency to readjust administrative entities, the cantons, in accordance with the pre-colonial pattern – the exception being the province of Dosso. Third, a tendency to choose able and competent chiefs, that is individuals who had acquired a certain familiarity with things French and who belonged to the ruling dynasty, or one of the ruling dynasties, without necessarily being high up on the traditional list of succession.

The situation which developed in the East was markedly different from that prevailing in the West. Indeed, it is difficult to see any logic behind a number of somewhat awkward French decisions regarding the *chefferie* in this region. The most extreme case is Maradi, where the French cut off the southern third of the canton. This southern third, Madarumfa, became a canton of its own under the former *sarkin* Fulani of the *subdivision centrale*, Moussa, a son of *k'aura* Assao.[61] But there was more to come. Forced to suppress the new canton due to widespread unrest, the French then went on in 1924 to appoint Moussa chief of a province consisting of the cantons of Maradi (including Madarumfa), Gobir and Kornaka. *K'aura* Assao's short-lived upstart 'realm' had thus been revived. Another round of civil unrest, this time accompanied by mass migration southwards, followed before the French finally came to their senses and abolished the new province in 1926.[62] Moussa, now reduced to his initial position as *sarkin* Fulani, fled to Northern Nigeria in 1929 with a small fortune, the result of the many exactions and abuses (to use the official French terms) he had committed during his successive appointments, the extent of which the French only then realized.[63] The Moussa episode is important in two respects: it constituted the last absurdity committed by the French in the field of chiefly appointments, and demonstrated yet again that no purpose was served by appointing as chief an individual who had no traditional claim to such a position.[64]

Further east, the French deposed the *sarkin* Katsina or 'sultan' of Tessaoua, Barmou, in 1927, together with several of his subordinate canton chiefs, and suppressed the sultanate. Thus ended the only important pre-colonial entity, which had been maintained as one entity by the French after the conquest. This major shake-up was a consequence of the many extortions the French accused Barmou and his lieutenants of having committed.[65] But it was also the consequence of a rather strange and isolated event, the attack on the French post of Tessaoua on 5 June 1927. According to the French, the attack, which cost the lives of one European and two African policemen, was perpetuated by a small band of Mahdists from Northern Nigeria, with the tacit approval of the local chiefs, including the 'sultan'.[66] It is difficult to make any sense of this. However, the point is that the attack had repercussions outside the region of Tessaoua. In Damergu, for instance, the sedentary kanuriphone agriculturalists, fearing that the events in Tessaoua preluded another Tuareg revolt, flocked to the more important villages for protection.[67] Their fear was not altogether unfounded since at least the Kel Gress are reported to have been in 'un état d'effervescence' – to use the official jargon of the day – after 5 June.[68] Finally, in Kurfey, Arewa and adjacent regions, an animistic 'sect' exploited the incident with considerable success, as we shall see.

Returning to the West and the renewed French interest in that region, we must note that this interest is clearly perceptible in the economic field as well. The desire to end labour migration led the French to encourage the young Zerma/Songhay to take up groundnut cultivation at home instead of expatriating themselves for many months each year.[69] The French tried to encourage 'pioneers' to settle down in the so-called *cuvettes* or small naturally irrigated basins along the river valley. The idea was to turn these *cuvettes* into pilot agricultural zones with massive government support. After an extensive study had been carried out in 1927, a project was agreed upon, and work started in the early 1930s.[70] These French initiatives met with conspicuously little success. Although the natural conditions are favourable for groundnuts in many regions of the West, much more favourable, in fact, in the *subdivision* of Gaya than in any part of the Centre or the East, the majority of the Zerma/Songhay took no interest in groundnuts. Perhaps this was due in the last analysis to the lack of adequate transport. Instead the seasonal migration to the Gold Coast reached new heights.[71]

Increased French demands and new difficulties after 1925
As in the post-1908 period, so in the period after 1922 the French were quick to 'catch up' with the economic expansion, and absorbed during the second half of the 1920s an increasing proportion of the surplus generated by this expansion. For instance, between 1925 and 1930 taxes increased substantially, as evidenced by the quadrupling of the budget during that period.[72] The inhabitants of the *cercle* of Tahoua paid a total of 2,224,000 francs in taxes in 1929, compared with 487,000 only three years earlier.[73] And in the *cercles* of Dosso and Tillabery taxes more than trebled between 1924 and 1930[74]. Not only did the per capita tax soar (in Dosso from 1.25 in 1918 to 7 francs in 1928–9),[75] but new items became taxable, notably the small stock of the sedentary population.[76] However, as indicated earlier, this was a period of inflation. We should therefore measure the increased taxation against a price deflator in order to evaluate the real growth in levels of taxation, but our evidence does not permit such an evaluation, and since the actual increase varied substantially from *cercle* to *cercle* (it was generally higher in Hausaland than in the West), all that can be said is that according to the scattered figures available, it would seem that the tax burden at the very least doubled during the second half of the 1920s. At any rate, by 1929 it had become clear to the *chef de subdivision* of Tanout, among others, that the Africans could not be expected to support any further increases.[77]

It was not only through higher taxes that increased French activity in the late 1920s made its impact. Thousands of man-days of compulsory labour were mobilized to provide the administration with offices and accommodation in the new capital. These construction works led, incidentally, to widespread requisitions of timber, and thus contributed to continuing deforestation. The main contingent of the labour force was sent to Dahomey, where the French had decided to extend the Cotonou–Save railway to Parakou. That the railway was projected ultimately to reach Niamey may explain the French interest in the West after about 1925–7. In any case, since the Save railway, as it became known, would benefit Niger, and the West in particular, the French felt justified in recruiting successive, large groups of labourers, especially from among the Zerma/Songhay. The question was how this could be done, for the provisions defining forced labour barred the French from employing the Nigeriens outside their home cantons. They got round this difficulty by 'asking' the chiefs to provide them with a regular supply of 'volunteers' both for the Save railway and for the construction works in Niamey.[78] Needless to say, these labourers were not, as one administrator put it, volunteers 'in the strict sense of that word'.[79] The multiple abuses this system generated, based as it was on the 'goodwill' of the chiefs, can easily be imagined.

In 1928 the French tried for the first time since the war to apply fully and throughout Niger the decree regarding compulsory military service.[80] And some time around 1930, they began to requisition food-stuffs again.

Prelude to disaster

The irony is that – once more following the post-1908 pattern – by the time the French began to 'catch up' with the moderate prosperity of the 1920s, signs of more difficult days ahead both locally and world-wide were already evident. In 1926 most of the Sahelo-Sudanese belt, including Western Niger, was hit by drought.[81] Niamey had only 433 mm of rainfall, as opposed to 776 mm two years earlier.[82] We know for certain that the drought led to famine in a few limited areas of the West.[83] Three years later the international economic crisis made its impact felt locally. The price of groundnuts suffered a 25 per cent drop between 1928 and 1930,[84] before collapsing altogether, along with most other prices.[85] In addition, the Zerma/Songhay found it increasingly difficult, and after a while impossible, to obtain work on the Gold Coast.[86] Naturally, these economic difficulties did not in any way induce the French to lower the tax rates.

At the very height of the economic crisis the people of the West were hit by possibly the greatest tragedy in their history, the famine of 1931. But before investigating this disaster in detail, it is necessary to turn our attention to religion and related matters.

RELIGIOUS AND PSYCHOLOGICAL EVOLUTION, 1922–46

The hauka movement

During the dry season of 1925 a Sudie 'priestess', Chibo, organized for the first time a number of unusual and spectacular religious manifestations among the pagan Gubawa of the village of Toudou Anza in northern Arewa.

These manifestations involved in particular dances during which the participants became possessed by unusual spirits, spirits intimately linked with the colonial phenomenon, since they went under such names as 'Governor', '*Commandant de cercle*' and 'captain'. Thus possessed, the participants became invulnerable, swallowing cinders, flogging each other with torches and so on.[87] As Chibo and her adherents displayed an attitude of marked hostility towards the *sarkin* Arewa, the French intervened and inflicted by virtue of the *indigénat* some hundred so-called 'disciplinary penalties'.[88] However, this did not stop the 'sect', as it now looked to be, from spreading to the predominantly Mawri regions of the south and east of the *subdivision* of Dogondoutchi,[89] and to the Filingue region, where the Sudie responded enthusiastically. By February 1927 all the villages of Kurfey had been 'contaminated'.[90] Following the pattern of events in Arewa, the spread of the 'sect' among the Sudie was accompanied by political agitation – a refusal to obey the chiefs and to pay taxes or to carry out forced labour[91] – and by French intervention. The administrator sent from Niamey, officially to take the census of the canton of Kurfey, found himself in an impossible situation, faced as he was with widespread, determined and effective passive resistance. He apparently behaved in a most tactless and clumsy manner, so much so that he was disavowed by his superiors. The penalties and punishments inflicted were repealed, and compensation paid to some of the victims[92] – an unheard-of measure in the annals of colonial rule.

The misadventure of the French envoy contributed considerably to strengthen the position and to enlarge the following of the 'sect'. So did two other important events: the death of the old and authoritarian *sarkin* Filingue, Gado Namalaya, on 3 March,[93] and the attack on the post of Tessaoua on 5 June referred to above. Gado Namalaya left behind him a political vacuum which the French had difficulties in filling. They finally opted for one of his sons, Chekou Seyni, who – whatever his merits – had far less prestige than his father. Chibo and her adherents, who had supported the candidature of a former warrant officer of the French army, Mainassara, refused to recognize Chekou Seyni as *chef de canton*.[94] The attack on the post of Tessaoua, and especially the fact that the participants were never captured by the French, provoked 'une fâcheuse impression en brousse',[95] and led, one may conjecture, to the impression that the 'force' or 'luck' of the French was declining.

In fact, after June 1927 the French and Chekou Seyni were no longer faced with a turbulent and somewhat exotic 'sect', but with a vast politico-religious movement, comprising probably a majority of the Sudie, refusing to pay taxes or to carry out forced labour, and completely ignoring the traditional chiefs. This was open rebellion as far as the French were concerned.[96] For the *hauka* or *baboule* movement, as it became known, constituted a new society. (*Hauka* signifies 'folly', *baboule* 'spirits of the fire'.)[97] As such it was perceived by the French as a danger, and especially since the movement seemed in the process of spreading to the Zerma of the neighbouring canton of Tondikanda and to the former slaves of the Tuareg-dominated cantons of Tagazar and Imanan.[98]

The severe repression which followed led to the imprisonment of several hundred of Chibo's followers, and to the deportation of the leaders including Chibo herself to Upper Volta and the Ivory Coast. (Chibo returned home some nine years later.)[99] In Imanan the Tuareg had to be disarmed.[100]

This, then, was the *hauka* or *baboule* movement, the first oppositional movement of a religious character in Niger. Although the movement as such collapsed in the late 1920s, a few strongholds survived, principally Chibo's home village of Chical, together with that of Lorma, which steadfastly refused to recognize the authority of the *sarkin* Filingue, and which the French had to administer directly.[101] (Chical had a long-standing record of opposition to Gado Namalaya, dating back to at least 1906.)[102] Furthermore, the *hauka* and the *baboule* spirits came eventually to be worshipped all over the West, although in a more diluted form when they were integrated into the pantheon of the Zerma/Songhay. Among the seasonal labourers in the Gold Coast this worship led to the rise of a markedly pathological cult.[103] But Chibo and her followers were certainly successful in one respect: as a direct consequence of the events of 1925–7, Filingue again became a *subdivision*.[104] The permanent presence of a French administrator in Filingue stripped the *sarki* of his previously nearly unlimited power and inaugurated an era of liberal rule. Indeed, it seems very likely the French, in order to prevent any further trouble, went out of their way to administer the new *subdivision* in a most enlightened and exemplary manner. Only able and competent administrators and functionaries, whether French or African, were posted to Filingue.[105]

One explanation which comes to mind for the *hauka* movement in Kurfey is that it represented a reaction against the changes and transformations operated by the French and Gado Namalaya on the local political level; especially the elevation of the latter to the rank of an authentic sovereign over a traditionally egalitarian and acephalous society. Gado, of course, turned out to be a particularly authoritarian sovereign who ruled his canton with an iron hand.[106] It is no coincidence, therefore, that the *hauka* movement arose to prominence between 1925 and 1927, at the time of Gado Namalaya's illness and death, when he was rapidly losing his 'force'. In Arewa the situation was slightly different. But here too the traditional political system had been modified by the French, who chose to bolster the authority of the *sarkin* Arewa and to ignore that of the *saranuyia* of Lougou and the other priest-chiefs of the Gube. And here too the *sarki* – Tassao Gao – began to grow old, and he was eventually to die in 1931.

It could also be argued that the *hauka* movement represented the most advanced and elaborate attempt to comprehend the colonial phenomenon within the framework of traditional religious beliefs, and above all to re-define these beliefs in the light of the new situation imposed by the French. It is possible to speculate that Chibo and her followers aimed at 'capturing' the 'force' or 'luck' of the French, by making contact with the supranatural powers which had endowed the French with their extraordinary 'force' (in some cases even making contact with the French themselves. At least two *Commandants* of the *cercle* of Niamey were elevated to the 'dignity' of deities: Victor Salaman, *Commandant* during the very first years of colonial rule, and Horace Croccichia, the *Commandant* responsible for the repression in 1927–8.)[107] In my view the *hauka* believed they had achieved this, notably through the possession dances, and so came to look upon themselves as the equals of the French. Hence their refusal to obey the chiefs. If this is so, the *hauka* movement was a potentially revolutionary movement, but as such it failed. The French, by dismantling the movement, proved that Chibo was mistaken. The *hauka* movement was the only movement we know of from Niger which aimed consciously at restructuring society in the light of the colonial experience and local traditions.

If the *hauka* movement did represent, among other things, a serious attempt to reform paganism, then it may also be looked upon as the apogee of a sort of animistic reaction in the West. The stages of this reaction were the freeing of the slaves, the internal migration, Governor Brévié's anti-Muslim policy, and finally the *hauka* movement. However, since the movement failed, it would seem convenient and logical to postulate a decisive breakthrough of Islam in the 1930s. This is not to say that the decade witnessed mass conversion to Islam, but that paganism from now on regularly lost ground to a slowly but steadily encroaching Muslim religion. However, it is significant that the second, and last, oppositional movement of a religious character in Niger was a *Muslim* religious movement, Hamallism. Niger is of course peripheral to the main events in the history of Hamallism, and it was only after 1940, and especially after 1946, that the sect made its impact felt in Niger (principally in the West). It is nevertheless appropriate to devote some attention to Hamallism here.

Hamallism

Hamallism – after the name of its founder, Shaykh Hamāhu'llāh b. Muhammad b. Umar (1886–1943),[108] commonly called Hamallah in the literature – originated among the Moorish population in the region of Nioro-du-Sahel in French Sudan. Hamallah was originally a cleric of the Tijaniya brotherhood, the most recent but also the most rapidly expanding of the two main Muslim brotherhoods in West Africa (the other being the Qādiriyya).[109] But he soon emerged as the leader of what has been described as a non-conformist, dissident, if not altogether schismatic branch of the Tijaniya.[110] The origin of the schism was a triviality, the number of times to cite before prayer the litany of the *tarikh*.[111] But behind this triviality there were real enough dissensions, and not only of a religious character. Indeed, whereas the previously militant Tijaniya had come more or less to support the established colonial order, Shaykh Hamallah preached a strongly individualistic doctrine, opposed to all forms of authority.[112] This doctrine spread rapidly among the servile strata of the population, leading to violent clashes in the Nioro region in 1924 and the Kaede region in 1930.[113] By virtue of the *indigénat*, Hamallah was exiled for ten years to the Ivory Coast. During his exile he resorted to the so-called 'abridged prayer' which is characteristic among Muslims at periods of crisis or danger and which usually precedes a holy war.[114] His followers also began to cite the litany of the *tarikh* and to pray in a most spectacular manner, 'with bodily inclinations culminating in nervous crisis'.[115] This was *la prière hurlée*, as the French came to call it,[116] not very dissimilar, one is tempted to argue, from possession dances.

Hamallah returned home in 1936. Four years later the fall of France led to a new outbreak of violence in the Nioro region: a violence which caused between three and four hundred casualties. The French response was quick and devastating. A total of thirty-three persons were executed, and a considerable number exiled, including Hamallah himself who was sent to France, where he died.[117]

Hamallism had spread to the western part of Niger around 1935, following, it seems, the ancient trade route via Dori to Tera and the river valley.[118] However, by 1937 the Governor still considered the number of Hamallists to be insignificant.[119] But from then on, and in spite of active French counter-propaganda,[120] the expansion was rapid, especially after the riots in Nioro in 1940, and the massacring of six Frenchmen in a café in Bobo-Dioulasso by a reputedly Hamallist band in 1941.[121] Many Hamallistic clerics from Niger were exiled in 1941, only to return in 1946 when the *indigénat* was abolished.[122] There is little doubt that the Hamallists in Western Niger as elsewhere recruited their adherents among the former slaves.[123] There is also little doubt that Hamallism contributed to the politicization of many parts of the West, and thus paved the way for the first political party in Niger after 1946, the *Parti Progressiste Nigérien* (PPN). Indeed, the strongholds of Hamallism (and also of the *hauka* movement) became PPN bastions after 1946. Furthermore, after 1950 both the PPN and Hamallism declined, the latter to the profit of yet another, but more orthodox branch of the Tijaniya, the Nyassist 'sect' whose instigator was Ibrahim Nyasse, a renowned cleric from Senegal.[124]

It is of course highly significant that both oppositional movements treated above were in the main confined to the West. No similar movements are detectable in the rest of Niger. The rather introspective, institutionalized and inoffensive *bori* cult of Hausaland proper, although it too featured possession dances, cannot possibly be classified in the same category as the *hauka* movement or Hamallism.

FROM FAMINE TO WAR, 1931–40

The famine in the West

The famine of 1931 in the West was a partly man-made, partly natural disaster. There were frequent invasions of locusts, affecting mainly the West, although they made their impact felt in many other parts of Niger as well, even regions as far east as Goure.[125] In 1930 there were particularly large-scale and widespread ravages, which unfortunately coincided with a very irregular distribution of rainfall, especially in the West.[126] Also, the fact that many of the able-bodied men of the West were absent, still working at that time on the Gold Coast, in Niamey, on the Save railway or fulfilling their military obligations, meant that many acres of farmland were left unattended. These factors taken together explain the appallingly bad harvest in the West at the end of the rainy season of 1930. Bush-administrators and chiefs sent messages and reports to Niamey outlining the disastrous situation which many Nigeriens would find themselves in at the end of the dry season of 1931. But the officials responsible, both in Niamey and in certain regional capitals, Dosso especially, seem to have judged the situation differently, and did nothing. Worse, they authorized a relatively large-scale requisitioning of millet – probably more than 500 tons – for the benefit of the functionaries.[127]

There can in fact be little doubt that the French administration, was to a large extent responsible for the famine and especially for its effects. This was the conclusion reached by the inspector sent out from Dakar in 1932, Bernard Sol, to investigate the situation.[128] Of course it could be argued that Sol's 'mission' constituted an attempt by the Federal authorities to exculpate themselves by putting the blame on the administrators on the spot, just as the latter tried to blame the chiefs.[129] On the other hand, Sol's reports contain too devastating a criticism and reveal too many glaring examples of malpractices and mismanagement for this argument to carry any real weight. A particularly tragi-comical example mentioned by Sol concerns the *Commandant* of Tillabery, who in 1930 squeezed out of the people under his jurisdiction a 'voluntary contribution' of some 30,000 francs for the benefit of the victims of a natural catastrophe in southern France – C'est de la folie pure', Sol concluded.

Although the famine apparently erupted in April 1931, it was not until two months later that the authorities in Niamey became aware of the situation.[130] Furthermore, the plight of the Nigeriens failed to stir them into action. According to the evidence available, Sol was correct in arguing that the administration could easily have acquired between 150 and 200 tons of grain from outside the West.[131] Had these quantities been distributed for seed to the agriculturalists of the West, Sol argued, then the harvest of 1931 might have been improved. As it happened, only some thirty-three tons were distributed. Since, in addition, drought struck in 1931,[132] the stage was set for a particularly deficient harvest, nearly non-existent in the *subdivision centrale* of Dosso[133] and in certain parts of the *cercle* of Tillabery.[134] In the *subdivision centrale* of Niamey the harvest amounted to 71 kg per head, far below the 140 kg mark considered to be the absolute minimum by the French.[135] Although the evidence is patchy and indirect, it seems as if the French authorities launched a relief programme after this second catastrophic harvest. Food and seed grains were distributed throughout the West, with the result that the harvest of 1932 turned out to be excellent.[136] But by then the damage had been done.

This is not the place to describe the naked misery which befell the West in 1931–2. Rather, we must try to ascertain the extent and impact of the disaster, and to investigate the consequences. According to Sol some 26,000 people died as a direct consequence of the famine. The highest figure was for the *subdivision centrale* of Dosso with a death-toll of 9,300. In addition some 12,500 people fled this region which, before the famine struck, contained according to official estimates about 81,000 inhabitants. In the *subdivision centrale* of Niamey, also very severely affected, 4,500 people died and another 4,500 fled, out of a total population of 100,000.

Although these figures do convey some impression of the magnitude of the disaster, they are of course unreliable in the extreme, as the French themselves for a change acknowledged. For instance, the *Commandant* of Niamey stated bluntly and frankly that he was unable to provide even approximate estimates.[137] The figures were often based on pure guesswork, a case in point being the figures for the *cercle* of Tillabery. We know for certain that between 1930 and 1933 no French official set foot in that region of the *cercle* most prone to drought, the Zermaganda.[138] Consequently the figures for the *cercle* as a whole must be looked upon as highly unreliable. With regard to the numbers of refugees specifically, it is nowhere stated whether they refer only to the first instantaneous mass migration triggered off by the acute food shortage, or whether these figures also include the second mass migration. This second exodus occurred some time later, occasioned by the administration's refusal to reduce taxes. Since taxes were imposed and paid communally, a reduction in the number of inhabitants of a given village in between censuses was not accompanied by a corresponding reduction in the sum the village had to pay. This was the case in 1913–15 and again in 1931–2. It left many of the survivors with the choice of paying higher taxes or migrating.[139] In fact, although the population of the West was sharply reduced, the miracle is that there were any people left in Western Niger at the end of 1932.

A close examination of the official figures, unreliable as they are, reveals an interesting pattern, and a pattern which is too clear-cut to be purely coincidental. This is that the regions most severely affected in 1931–2 were just those regions where the Zerma/Songhay, and particularly the former, constituted the main bulk of the population. *Subdivisions* such as Dogon-doutchi (predominantly Mawri), Filingue (inhabited mainly by Tuareg and Sudie) and Say (predominantly Fulani) seem to have fared much better. The explanation which comes immediately to mind is geographical, i.e. the fact that the Zerma in particular occupy some of the most arid and infertile parts of the West. But the geographical factor, albeit of considerable importance, does not provide a totally satisfactory explanation. A close examination of the figures we possess concerning individual cantons reveals the same pattern, the figures for the Zerma cantons within a given *subdivision* always revealing worse losses than those of neighbouring cantons, regardless of geographical conditions.[140] Certainly, the Tuareg/*bella* and the Fulani were better prepared than the Zerma/Songhay to face the crisis thanks to their cattle; of which they, as indeed all the inhabitants of the West, lost a very substantial proportion.[141] But this explanation will not do for the Mawri and the Sudie who were, like the Zerma/Songhay, mainly agriculturalists. Of course the explanation may simply be that more Zerma/Songhay than Mawri or Sudie were away on the Gold Coast. However, the demand for labour on the Gold Coast had dwindled sharply after the onset of the world economic crisis. Could it be then, that historical traditions – the aristocratic warrior ideal and its corollary, a certain distaste for manual labour (at least at home) – made the Zerma/Songhay particularly vulnerable in 1931? We do not know whether among the Zerma/Songhay the former slaves fared better than their former masters.

Conditions in the Centre, the East and the Far East
As indicated earlier, regions outside the West were also affected by locusts, but to what extent is difficult to ascertain. The Centre and the Far East suffered from what can be described as an acute and severe, but not catastrophic, shortage of food-stuffs in 1931.[142] But by and large the famine seems to have been confined to the West. Indeed, it may even be that the Hausa of the East, at least, were still able to produce a surplus of millet and other food-stuffs during the early 1930s and that their problem was that they could no longer, due to the depression in Northern Nigeria, find any buyers.[143] Certainly the administration was not interested. Being left with a substantially reduced income,[144] but forced to pay the same taxes as before (taxes which were, the point is worth recalling, much higher in the East than in the West), the Hausa had no choice but to break into their capital, in other words to sell their cattle.[145] As a consequence cattle prices experienced a very sharp drop.[146]

On top of all this came new demands for labour, for the 1930s were the pioneering years in the history of aviation in French West Africa. A number of survey flights toured the Federation, for which landing strips had to be built. And as Charles Le Coeur, an eyewitness, acidly remarked, 'l'administration supérieure [avait] donné l'ordre de payer les travailleurs mais n'[avait] pas accordé des crédits, si bien que les terrains [furent] faits, mais par des prestataires'.[147] In Zinder alone some ten thousand workers were needed, and thanks to the 'positive attitude' of the *sarkin* Damagaram, Barma Mustapha, the recruitment of this sizeable labour force went 'smoothly'.[148] How the forcibly recruited workers were treated in the 1930s is described by M. Vilmin, the chief of the *subdivision* of Madaoua, who stated bluntly that 'les bêtes en France sont mieux traités que ces êtres humains [les prestataires]'.[149]

Vilmin was not alone among the bush-administrators in being uncomfortably aware of the miserable state of the colony in the early 1930s. Many of them voiced their concern in official reports. The *Commandant* in Maradi warned in 1933 that 'si le taux de l'impôt continuait à n'être plus en rapport avec les moyens financiers des contribuables, des exodes importantes pourraient se produire'.[150] In fact, small and medium-scale exoduses were a common feature even of daily life throughout Niger during these years.[151] De Loppinot in Tahoua was even more outspoken than his colleague in Maradi, and stated that 'nous avons en partie ruiné le pays'.[152] What was the logic behind a system, he asked, which extorted exorbitant taxes from the Africans, taxes for which they received conspicuously little, if anything, in return, and which did not provide them with any opportunity to earn the cash necessary since 'tout se fait par prestation en fait sinon en droit'?[153]

The French change of Policy

There is a striking difference between the attitude of the French in 1913–15 and in 1931–2. Whereas in 1913–15 the sufferings of the Nigeriens passed by more or less unnoticed, in 1932 the French administration came under strong attack from no less an institution than the *Ligue Française pour la Défense des Droits de l'Homme et du Citoyen*.[154] News of the situation in Western Niger and in particular of the malpractices, real or alleged, committed by the French officials, made their way to Paris and very nearly provoked a scandal. Although Brévié apparently convinced the Minister of Colonies that the allegations put forward were unfounded,[155] he nevertheless admonished his top men on the spot severely,[156] and finally sacked nearly all of them.[157] More important, the famine led to a very marked shift of emphasis in the French policy. After 1931 the main preoccupation – some would even say obsession – of the administration was to prevent a repetition of what had happened in 1931–2. To this effect the system of millet granaries established by Brévié, but which had proved thoroughly inefficient in 1931 and earlier,[158] was remodelled. Under the new system granaries were to be established in each village (instead of in each canton) under the control and supervision of the French (instead of the canton chiefs). Finally, the administration, and not the chiefs, was to decide upon the quantity of millet each family head would have to store away.[159] Unfortunately the French decided to introduce the system as early as 1932 and to order the farmers to store quantities which represented in certain cases upwards of 50 per cent of that year's harvest. This provoked a storm of protest among the bush-administrators. De Loppinot was even mandated by his fellow *Commandants* to voice their concern in Niamey. His main argument, that the federal authorities in Dakar were not primarily concerned with the plight of the Nigeriens, but sought simply to make certain that any future famine could not be blamed on the French administration, failed to move the new Governor. Instead de Loppinot was told that inspectors were to tour the *cercles* to make certain that the instructions had been executed.[160]

Other measures decided upon by the French included the extension of the system of the *Sociétés Indigènes de Prévoyance* (see chapter 3), yet another programme designed to combat the locust plagues, and an intensive propaganda campaign in favour of root-crops, the argument being that these crops were immune to locusts (but not to termites).[161] Finally the French issued a decree establishing the principle of decennial proscription of land in the absence of any title deeds.[162] This decree was designed to check the continuing process of accumulation and capitalization of land in the West, a process which may have been stimulated by the famine. However, it does not appear to have had any effect.

Although the French in general maintained the pre-1931 tax level, they were of course unable to collect all the taxes. Frequently the bush-administrators looked the other way when villages could not pay.[163] The drastic reduction in the Africans' contribution to the public purse compelled the French to limit their activities. For instance the administration had to cut back on the already small sums spent on education and social services. The number of pupils dropped from 2,399 in 1935, already a scandalously low figure, to 1,892 in 1938. And in the purely administrative field the *Commandants* and *chefs de subdivision* were told to stay at home, and to undertake as few tours and as few censuses as possible. Those censuses that *were* undertaken led to a most welcome readjustment downwards of the population figures and the figures for cattle.[164] This fitted with the policy of Governors Bourgine (1933–5) and Court (Secretary-General 1933–5, Governor 1935–8). This policy, reminiscent of Brévié's, aimed at establishing an administration which was not overofficious or overfussy.[165] In particular Court tried to dissuade the bush-administrators from applying the *indigénat* altogether.[166] This was in harmony with the official policy of the Governor-General which had resulted in a decree exempting women from most of the stipulations of the *indigénat*.[167]

However, the main problem facing Bourgine and Court was how to provide a lasting, sound economic basis for colonial rule. Since at the metropolitan and federal levels a system of price supports for groundnuts had just been established, it was obvious what this economic basis would have to be. The administration in Niger decided after 1933 upon a policy designed to encourage the development of the cash-crop sector of the economy. What they actually did, apart from providing price supports, was to issue a number of measures destined to protect the interests of the producers, that is, to regulate the groundnut trade severely. Transactions were only permitted at a certain number of authorized markets during certain periods, and under the supervision of French officials. Furthermore, the administration operated a sort of unofficial financial information service; it tried to keep the farmers informed about the general situation, and specifically about prices in Kano.[168] This was in order to prevent speculation and to circumscribe the position of the intermediaries, who now included the newly established local branches of the major expatriate trading firms such as the SCOA, the CNF and the CFAO.[169] Finally, in

1936 and 1938 respectively the administration negotiated agreements with the Dahomean (or Benin-Niger) and Nigerian railways, which in the latter case guaranteed Niger an annual transit quota of forty thousand tons. By virtue of the former agreement, the French could offer the farmers of the West lower freight-rates to the coast than those in the East.[170] But to little avail. The Zerma/Songhay were uninterested in groundnuts, and the West remained a labour-supplying region. Some of my informants have argued that the French also made use of coercive measures in order to promote the cultivation of groundnuts, but there is no trace of such measures in the written record. This does not mean that such measures never existed, but if they did, they cannot have been very far-reaching, and were probably withdrawn very quickly. For groundnut cultivation was a field in which the interests of subjects and rulers converged.

Bourgine and especially Court were fortunate in that the improving international economic situation and the weather were on their side. Groundnut prices, which had reached a record low in 1933, doubled during the following year, and continued to rise relatively sharply until 1937–8. The incentives provoked an almost instant cash-crop boom in the *subdivision* of Magaria and adjacent regions. In 1934, 18,000 tons of decorticated ground-nuts were exported from Niger, and a record high of 45,000 tons was reached in 1935–6 (not to be surpassed until 1948–9).[171] Other export commodities such as gum, skins and hides also experienced a boom.[172] As a consequence of this upward trend, many of the refugees returned north, a trend the French actively encouraged by granting tax exemptions.[173]

New crisis, 1937–40

The moderate prosperity after 1933 gave way in 1937 to yet another economic crisis. The price of groundnuts dropped,[174] the franc was devalued (a measure which led to a steep rise in prices), the tax burden increased substantially, drought struck *and* the federal authorities in Dakar decided to reestablish the customs barrier.[175] Although the administration managed to avoid another famine thanks to an all-out effort,[176] it could not prevent the impact of the customs barrier being felt almost overnight. The *Commandant* in Zinder lamented as early as December 1937 that 'on a brisé net le courant d'échange qui s'était établi'.[177]

Four customs posts had already been established in October–November 1937,[178] and another seven were added in the early months of 1938.[179] The frontier-guards who manned these posts – most of them former servicemen – are reputed to have executed instructions and applied regulations in a most zealous manner, as in 1915–18. The result was that 'les contraventions, amendes et confiscations . . . effray[èrent] positivement le commerce'.[180] The markets along the border declined almost instantly and commercial activity moved south of the border.[181]

The drought of 1937 heralded another cycle of bad years. The harvests seem to have been deficient throughout Niger in both 1939 and 1940, producing half as much as in 1935.[182] In addition, the country was ravaged by two epidemics, one of typhus, which we unfortunately know very little about,[183] the other of meningitis, which claimed some four thousand lives according to the official figures.[184]

A STRANGE INTERLUDE: 1940–5

The establishment of the Vichy regime and its policy

It is now generally acknowledged that the government of Marshal Pétain which came to power in France in June 1940 after the Battle of France had been lost, and which signed the armistice with Germany, operated an authoritarian, conservative, even semi-fascist 'restoration'.[185] That this was so is amply borne out by the evidence from Niger.

Whereas French West Africa, including Niger, remained after 1940 obedient to Vichy France, the neighbouring colony, Chad, chose to secede and rallied to General de Gaulle and his Free French. De Gaulle, technically a rebel general, tried but failed to seize control of French West Africa in 1940.[186]

After 1940, Vichy-controlled Niger found itself bordering on no fewer than three colonies which in the eyes of Vichy belonged to hostile powers: Italian Libya, Gaullist Chad and British Nigeria. This meant, first, that Niger was the most vulnerable and exposed of the colonies, and, second, that it became of prime strategical importance to Vichy. Hence the appointment for the first time after 1922 of a military Governor, Brigadier-General Falvy, quickly dubbed von Falvy for his alleged pro-German sentiments.[187]

Federation-wide, Governor-General Boisson's policy was to refuse all collaboration with the Germans and the Italians, as well as with the British and the Gaullists, while at the same time supplying metropolitan France and North Africa inexpensively with whatever commodities the Africans could deliver, and strengthening the local armed forces which were increased from 15,000 *tirailleurs* to 80,000 by as early as 1941–2.[188] In Niger, this policy, as interpreted and put into practice by Governor Falvy, proved disastrous. The measures decided upon by Falvy were manifold and diverse. Since he considered Nigeria to be enemy territory, he closed the border and stationed sizeable military detachments including so-called (locally levied) partisan units in the frontier zone. These detachments, which spent their time patrolling and digging trenches along the border, were responsible for a number of malpractices which led to more exoduses.[189] Falvy's anglophobia even induced him to issue an order to the effect that all Britons who crossed the border in uniform were to be considered as prisoners-of-war.[190] More important, Falvy sent 'secret agents' into Nigeria to 'spy',[191] and *agents provocateurs* into Chad to incite the Africans to revolt against the local Gaullist authorities.[192] The Gaullists and the British retaliated, according to Falvy, by encouraging the Tubu of Tibesti to launch raids into

Niger, and by mounting an intense anti-Vichy propaganda.[193] This propaganda 's'avérait dangereuse pour le moral de l'élément européen', as Falvy had to admit.[194]

The economic reorientation and its consequences

Falvy, to whom Niger's interests were of no consequence, aimed at establishing a siege-type and entirely state-controlled economy geared principally towards the provisioning of North Africa and France. The system was simple enough: to ban all trade with Nigeria,[195] to retain by force the labour which usually migrated to the Gold Coast during the dry season (a measure which did not stop many adventurous Zerma/Songhay from getting through anyway);[196] to try and produce locally goods that had previously been imported; to persuade or force the Nigeriens to increase their production as much as possible; and to appropriate the produce of the Nigeriens directly through requisitions, or indirectly through a steep increase in taxes (around 60 per cent between 1939 and 1942/3) which forced the people of Niger to sell their 'surplus' to the administration at prices fixed arbitrarily by that same administration. These prices were of course well below the prices in Nigeria or the prices on the open market in Niger, which was from a narrow legal point of view a black market.[197] The commodities thus obtained were exported to North Africa via Agades. In order to facilitate this new northbound traffic the French set about constructing a road in the middle of the desert between Agades and Tamanrasset. Naturally, this road was built entirely by forced labour.[198]

With regard to groundnuts, the French created so-called obligatory *champs administratifs*, grouped together and therefore easy to control, where the local farmers were supposed to till and harvest under the watchful eye of the French.[199] In order to increase yields the French pressed the Nigeriens to adopt the plough,[200] an instrument notoriously unsuited for the soils of Niger. Since Niger no longer imported textiles, the cultivation of cotton was made compulsory and two centres of weaving were established in Tessaoua and Zinder.[201] In addition to groundnuts, pack animals, meat, clarified butter, millet etc. the French also needed a number of natural products which the Nigeriens were sent out in the bush to gather: castor oil, tannin, timber, charcoal, straw and so on.[202]

Naturally the official figures 'concernant les quantités de mil récoltées . . . étaient exagérément forcés', as the French admitted after the war.[203] Since, furthermore, the stepping up of the French demands coincided, as usual, with a period of unfavourable climatic conditions and a plague of locusts,[204] the result was that the peasants, after having satisfied the demands of the administration, were probably left with insufficient quantities of food-stuffs for themselves. We know that several regions experienced periods of an acute shortage of food-stuffs bordering on famine during the war years; the *cercles* of Niamey, Tillabery and N'Guigmi in 1940,[205] Dosso–Loga in 1941,[206] the *cercle* of Goure in 1941–2,[207] the *cercle* of Zinder in 1942[208] and the *cercle* of Maradi in 1942–3.[209] It was only in 1943–4, after the Gaullist take-over, that the harvest proved satisfactory.[210]

Figures concerning livestock were probably also inflated. For instance in 1942 the *Commandant* of Maradi protested vehemently against the fact that his *cercle* was ordered to deliver 400 head of cattle *per month*. He argued that even half that number was more than enough and slightly beyond the capacities of his *cercle*.[211]

The position of the chiefs

Falvy's system relied heavily if not exclusively on coercion. The French tightened control over their *sujets* by abolishing the previous exemptions from the *indigénat*,[212] and by making much more frequent and vigorous use of its stipulations.[213] As for forced labour, which for the first time affected the nomads,[214] its extent was such that even many chiefs of the West protested strongly.[215] This is remarkable on two accounts, first, because the chiefs of the West had in the past benefited from the abuses this practice engendered, and second, because of the very uncomfortable position the chiefs found themselves in after 1940. The chiefs were now, as always in times of excessive French demands, caught squarely in the middle. Since Falvy could not do without the chiefs, he did everything he could to bolster their position,[216] but at the same time he had no choice but to compel them to enforce the most repulsive aspects of his policy. The chiefs, once more forced to assume the role of front men for French policy, thus became the object of widespread public discontent. Of course any chief who did not display an evident, insistent and uncompromising pro-French (that is pro-Vichy) attitude faced not only deposition but also possible exile. The result was a pernicious climate of intrigues and denunciations which played into the hands of local ambitious pretenders who were quick to grasp and exploit the new opportunities suddenly available to them. In those days even the most partisan of denunciations could spell disaster for the incumbent chief. The *cas célèbre* here is that of Arzika Gao, *sarkin* Arewa of Matankari since 1931. Arzika was accused, by among others his close relative Soumana Gao, of maintaining close contacts with kinsmen on the other side of the border. This accusation led to Arzika's deposition and exile, and to the appointment of Soumana as his successor. But although the French quickly realized that the accusation was unfounded, they preferred to let Arzika linger on in exile in Timbuctu.[217] The other *sarkin* Arewa (of Takassaba), Marafa Garba, was also deposed and exiled in 1941 for having, according to the French, hidden and protected British subjects, hampered the action of the 'partisans', failed to inform the French about the situation in Nigeria, and finally having failed to stop some of his subjects from joining the British Army.[218] (Marafa's successor Adamu only lasted for two years before he too was deposed.)[219] Other chiefs who suffered a similar fate for roughly the same motives were the *sarki* of Magaria and the *sarkin* Myrriah in 1941, the *amiru* of Torodi in 1942, and Cherif Mochtar of N'Guigmi and Mahaman Katiallami of Kawar in 1943.[220]

The Vichy 'ideology'

The absurdity of a situation in which one of the world's poorest people (the Nigeriens) was to provide one of the richest (the French) with all sorts of commodities at the lowest possible price is of course evident to anyone who investigates the 1940–5 period today. This is only so with the wisdom of hindsight. It was much less evident at the time, when exploitation of the colonies was taken for granted. The French also assumed, as their predecessors had in 1914–18, that the Nigeriens felt concern for the fate of France, and were willing to suffer and even to die for *la mèe-patrie*. 'Nous sommes en guerre, chaque homme doit travailler pour deux',[221] was the message. In fact, the representatives of Vichy in Niger (as elsewhere in West Africa) displayed a somewhat hysterical 'superpatriotic' attitude, not exempt from a considerable degree of paternalism often bordering on racism.[222] A typical example comes from a letter the *chef de subdivision* of Magaria 'persuaded' the local chiefs to send to Pétain and which runs as follows: 'Nous les chefs ... te saluons, toi le Maréchal Pétain, notre chef à tous ... nous sommes tes fils ... tu es notre Père et notre grand-Père ... Nous et nos gens resterons toujours à ta disposition et à celle de la France que nous aimons'.[223] Another and equally revealing example, one that deserves to be quoted extensively, comes from a circular emanating from the Ministry of Colonies and concerning the schools (it has been translated from telegram-style French into intelligible French):

> Je vous prie d'ordonner que le drapeau national soit hissé chaque jour dans tous les établissements ... d'enseignement ... Il s'agit d'entretenir dans l'âme de la jeunesse le sentiment de la patrie et l'amour de la France ... Tous les lundis matin, l'ensemble des élèves remis en carré, assistera à l'envoi des couleurs, par le meilleur élève. Au moment de l'envoi, le chef de l'établissement prononcera le mot FRANCE et les élèves, tête nue, le repeterons en coeur. Les autres jours de la semaine les couleurs seront envoyées devant une seule classe qui tournera par roulement ... Les couleurs seront amenés tous les soirs ... par le meilleur élève de la classe de jour ... La première cérémonie sera suivie dans chaque classe par une instruction se rapportant à la France et à son empire et par un commentaire sur la devise de l'Etat français: Travail, Famille, Patrie![224]

With the defeat of 1940, 'le mythe de l'infaillibilité des Français s'écroula d'un seul coup',[225] according to Jean Rouch. However, according to him the defeat was not attributed by the Africans to a loss of 'force', but rather to a diminishing control of it; to the fact that the French had allowed an 'old woman' – Pétain – to usurp power temporarily.[226] The implication is that the Nigeriens became Gaullists at a time when French officialdom in West Africa was still firmly behind Pétain. This is in many ways an attractive theory, and one which fits well into a line of argument which has been developed in earlier chapters. But it is of course highly conjectural. Perhaps only a handful of Nigeriens perceived clearly the distinction between Gaullists and Pétainists. In any case, the fact that the rural masses 'ne comprenaient guère les raisons de la tension anglo-française'[227] is hardly surprising. They were not the only ones. Did the attempt by the French to revive the traditional hostility between the societies of Niger and the Sokoto Caliphate[228] meet with the same incomprehension?

The Gaullist take-over

The Gaullists seized control of North and West Africa in June 1943. This was a consequence of the allied landing on the coast of North Africa on 8 November 1942.[229] In Niger the Gaullist take-over did not lead to any change in personnel. Governor Jean Toby, the seasoned bush-administrator who had succeeded Falvy late in 1942, was kept on. Nevertheless, it soon became apparent that a new era had begun. The ban on trade with Nigeria was lifted; some of the victims of Vichy were liberated and paid damages for the injustice they had endured; the unpopular *champs administratifs* were abolished; and the French attitude was purged of the hysterical patriotism and paternalism of the Vichy years.[230] However, although the evidence is extremely scarce, it does not appear that the lot of the Nigeriens improved in any significant way. The Gaullists, like their predecessors, were in sore need of supplies, and thought in terms of their own needs rather than in terms of what the country could supply. Thus after June 1943 no less than before, the French made extensive use of forced labour, and they continued to requisition huge quantities of millet, groundnuts, cotton and so on.[231] Neither did the Gaullists shrink away from removing chiefs who failed to meet their demands (the most famous case being that of the *sarkin* Katsina of Maradi, Dan Kollodo, in 1944).[232] They also increased the tax burden very substantially through a so-called *contribution exceptionnelle de querre*, at the rate of one to three francs per head and 10 per cent of the taxes on cattle.[233] A further addition in 1946 was the local road tax (*taxe vicinale*) to the tune of three to nine francs per head.[234] Finally the Gaullists undertook an extensive recruitment of *tirailleurs*, of which unfortunately no details are known.

CONCLUSION

The preceding account of the history of Niger between 1922 and 1945 has been primarily an account of French policy and French aims. This is inevitable, given that during this period the initiative lay nearly exclusively with the French. It was – and this is the first conclusion that can be drawn – a time when the African voice remained silent or barely audible outside the field of religion. More than that, it was a period during which the African voice could not have been heard had it existed. For, as Georges Balandier notes, the administration '[visait] à la mise en place d'un appareil dépolitisé'.[235] It was in the nature of classic colonial rule to sterilize all political activity, to silence the African voice. This the French achieved between 1922 and 1945. It does not follow, however, that the Nigeriens exercised no influence upon the general evolution of their country during the inter-war years. The *hauka* movement, the internal migration, the relative success of groundnut cultivation in Hausaland as well as its failure in the West, among other factors prove the contrary.

The second conclusion is that after 1922 history to a large extent repeated itself. In the period after 1922, as in the period after 1908, the country recovered and enjoyed for a while a modest prosperity, thanks to the international economic situation, favourable climatic conditions and above all the *laissez-faire* attitude of the French. And in both periods drought, whether combined with locusts or not, the repercussions of the wars in Europe *and* the stepping up of French activities had catastrophic consequences. Of course, in times of crisis the French were forced to rely heavily upon the chiefs. Thus both in 1914–18 and after 1931, and also in 1940–3, the chiefs found themselves caught squarely in the middle. The recurring crises of the colonial period demonstrated the narrow limits of so-called direct rule which only functioned satisfactorily – if at all – in times of recovery and prosperity.

There were also differences between these periods. Whereas a major revolt and widespread unrest constituted both one of the causes and one of the consequences of the difficulties experienced during the 1910s, it is significant that, with the exception of the *hauka* movement, nothing of the sort occurred in the 1930s or the 1940s. Furthermore, it was between 1940 and 1943, very late in the day, that the Nigeriens experienced the harshest rule of their history. Under the Vichy regime the Nigeriens were for the first time effectively reduced to a state not unlike slavery as the French organized the systematic plundering and looting of their country and its meagre resources.

The third and related conclusion is that the colonial administration must be ranked as one of the major scourges of Niger, along with drought and locusts. To adopt for a moment McNeillian terminology,[236] both macro- and microparasitism progressed during the inter-war years (the latter probably as a consequence of the general weakening of the population and the more intense intercourse between regions and ethnic groups). Yet – and here we are once again up against the fundamental ambiguity characteristic of the colonial period – although the French can be placed in the category of predatory macroparasites, it should be noted that with the exception of the few years under Vichy, the French no longer pursued an exploitative policy in Niger. Nor did the local administrators in any way facilitate the task of the expatriate traders. If anything, the former heartily despised the latter. No administrator ever made a fortune in Black Africa (indeed, it is far from certain that France made a profit out of its African colonies). What then induced the French to adopt measures whose effects were manifestly disastrous? The answer has already been given in the Introduction and can be summarized as follows: first, the necessity to make the administration function, that is to establish a firm economic basis for colonial rule; and second, the ignorance and incompetence of the administrators, the implication being that they lacked the will and the wisdom to foresee the consequences of their own action. The French were a 'luxury' which Niger could not afford.

The fourth conclusion is that the inter-war years revealed the true non-evolutionary or non-historical and therefore sterile and self-destructive nature of colonial rule. Jacques Berque and John Iliffe have argued that the colonial period can be divided into two phases which merged dialectically between the two world wars at the moment when colonial society both took its most complete form and bore within itself its own negation.[237] The non-evolutionary nature of colonial rule can be explained as follows. Since the 'backwardness' of Africa constituted the major justification for colonial rule, it was not in the interest of the Europeans to promote and encourage any sort of development profitable to the Africans. Such a development would inevitably contribute to establish socio-economic conditions incompatible with colonial rule, or at least with colonial rule in its classic form. What action *was* undertaken was motivated by the necessity to enable the Africans to pay taxes – once again, by the necessity to make the administration function. Thus, as Hubert Deschamps has noted, there was no clearly defined administrative policy prior to 1940; the French had no purpose, no aim.[238] It is as if, having conquered most of West Africa and established themselves as the rulers of that region, the French paused, not knowing what to do next. Certainly, theoretical notions such as assimilation and association did not survive the encounter with reality.[239] It is significant that they are virtually never alluded to in the French records from Niger. And they had no place in the daily life of the average bush-administrator, which was, so Robert Delavignette tells us, essentially busy, burdensome and trivial.[240] Delavignette served as a bush-administrator in Niger in his early years, and speaks from experience.

Thus we see a number of striking parallels between the French policy in 1914–18 and that in 1940–3. But what was acceptable in 1914–18 was no longer so in the early 1940s. In fact, the Vichy regime, by pushing the classic colonial system to its logical extreme so late in the day, had in a sense done the Africans a favour, that of thoroughly discrediting the system. Thus, the Vichy regime ultimately generated its own negation. Reforms had become necessary for two reasons, the one practical, the other sentimental. The first was that only reforms could defuse the powder-keg many believed French Africa had now become, without imperilling the French position; the second, that de Gaulle, the new leader of France, owed a debt to the Africans. Without Africa and the African *tirailleurs*, de Gaulle would perhaps have remained a historical curiosity. Thanks in part to the Africans, he had emerged as a figure of historical significance.

The principles of a new colonial policy were first articulated at the famous Brazzaville conference in 1944. This conference proposed a shift of emphasis and of responsibility. The French now acknowledged that they were under a moral obligation to assist their colonies, and that it was time for France to apply effectively some of the principles of 1789 and later revolutions in the colonies as well.[241] French colonial rule thus embarked upon an evolutionary process, a process in many ways incompatible with its very nature. As a consequence the nature and impact of colonial rule, and above all the nature of the interaction between the French and the Nigeriens, changed radically after 1944.

It fell to the constituent assemblies in charge of elaborating the constitution of the new Fourth Republic to implement the Brazzaville programme.

6

Towards a new order, 1945–60

The shaping of the constitution of the Fourth French Republic proved laborious. The first step was taken on 21 October 1945 with the election of a Constituent National Assembly. This election was a novelty, or rather an anomaly, in French legal history, in the sense that not only citizens but also (a severely restricted number of) *sujets* were entitled to vote. Ten deputies representing French West Africa were seated in the Assembly, five elected by the few citizens resident in the Federation, the other five by African *sujets*.[1] Among the five, Fily Dabo Sissoko represented both French Sudan and Niger. (The other four were Léopold Sédar Senghor, Félix Houphouët-Boigny, Yacine Diallo and S. M. Apithy. Lamine Guèye represented the citizens of Senegal.) The very liberal constitutional draft adopted by the Assembly having been rejected in the referendum of 5 May 1946 (in which only the citizens had the right to vote), a second Constituent National Assembly was elected on 2 June 1946. All five representatives of the West African *sujets* recovered their seats.[2] The citizens of France approved of the new constitutional draft, less liberal from the African point of view than the preceding one, in the referendum of 13 October 1946, and thus put an end to the period of transition. The Fourth Republic had been born.

The Constitution of 1946 abolished, so to speak, the colonial empire by placing the former colonies – renamed Overseas Territories (*Territoires d'Outre-Mer*) – inside the unitary structure of the republic. From a strict constitutional point of view, the French republic, together with a certain number of Overseas Territories and the so-called Associate States of Indo-China and North Africa, constituted the French Union. But French West Africa had in reality been integrated into the republic. As a consequence the Africans were no longer *sujets*, but citizens, with (not quite) the same rights and duties as the people of metropolitan France. All measures incompatible with French citizenry, such as forced labour and the *indigénat*, were abolished. As citizens, the Africans were called upon to take part in the shaping of their own future, that is to elect representatives to the Parliament in Paris – with its three component chambers, the all-important National Assembly or Chamber of Deputies, the Council of the Republic or Senate, and the Assembly of the French Union. Within this system there were, from a theoretical point of view, no legal or institutional obstacles barring, say, a literate Nigerien from becoming *Commandant de cercle*, Governor, or even President of the Republic.[3] There are many comments to be made here. The first is that the system of 1946 was at the same time absurd and generous. Absurd, in the sense that the Africans were not and probably had no desire to become French, official declarations to the contrary notwithstanding. Generous nevertheless, since it abolished (nearly) all legal distinctions between colonizers and colonized, at a time when France was by no means forced to adopt such an extreme 'solution'. The second comment is that the system of 1946 was the logical consequence of the revolutionary tradition, including the Jacobin principle of *la République une et indivisible*. A somewhat unkind comment, however, would be that the system or – perhaps more appropriately – the 'Revolution' of 1946 constituted an elegant solution to a particularly thorny problem: how to put an end to classic colonial rule, distasteful by now to most Frenchmen, without at the same time letting go of the empire; and a solution which had the advantage of blurring the real issues at stake while at the same time fulfilling the aspirations of the *évolués*, who emerged as the major beneficiaries of the 'Revolution' of 1946. They were indeed the only Africans in a position to reap all the benefits of the new situation, in that only they possessed the necessary 'tools' to compete within the system: literacy and fluency in French, and also a certain, although theoretical, familiarity with the way the new system was supposed to function. Only the *évolués* possessed the necessary requirements laid down by the law to stand for election to Parliament or to the lesser assemblies in Dakar and the various territorial capitals. Thus the new 'rules of the game' imposed the *évolués* on Africa as its leaders, to the detriment of for instance the 'traditional' elite, the chiefs. However, by recognizing the *évolués* as the only authentic interlocutors, the metropolitan French committed the error of simplifying to a dangerous extent the very complex African reality. The French on the spot were more lucid and aware of the (at times) limited influence of the local *évolués*. Hence frequent conflicts arose between the decision-makers in Paris and the bush-administrators. But one can hardly blame the metropolitan French for having been 'prisoners' of their own notions and concepts, that is for having chosen as interlocutors the only Africans with whom a dialogue was possible, from a linguistic, cultural, and especially a conceptual point of view.

Thus 1946 saw a resounding victory for a tiny, and in many ways corporate, group. The *évolués* had at last achieved what they cherished most, equality. But since it was only a theoretical equality, their natural inclination was to press for more, or real, equality. Animated by a *soif de l'égalité*, they pressed for an ever wider application of the principles enunciated in the constitution of 1946. The gulf separating these principles from day-to-day reality was indeed sometimes large. True, the distinction between 'citizens' and *sujets* had been abolished. But the French had invented another distinction, that between citizens who observed French civil laws and citizens who observed Muslim or local customary civil law. The latter were called *citoyens de statut personnel*. The former, the tiny European minority resident in Africa together with the handful of Africans who had acquired citizen status before 1946, were, as members of the so-called first electoral college, to elect on average one-third of the members of the territorial assemblies or *Conseils Généraux*. And as the representatives in the *Grand Conseil* in Dakar as well as in two of the metropolitan parliamentary assemblies (the Senate and the Assembly of the French Union) were elected indirectly by each *Conseil Général*, it follows that the Europeans in Africa acquired a political impact out of all proportion to their numerical strength. Worse still, only a limited number of Africans were admitted to the so-called second electoral college composed of *citoyens de statut personnel*. The size of the purely African electorate remained modest, the criteria for the vote being individual identity or importance in the society. This was indeed a far cry from the republican principle of one man one vote.[4]

Africa was also grossly under-represented in the National Assembly. Niger was granted only one seat in 1946, and two in 1948 (both directly elected by citizens regardless of civil status), whereas its population entitled it to about twenty. More fundamentally, although Africans now took part in the decision-making process at the highest level, this was not the case on the local level, where much remained unchanged. 'On [veut] toujours bâtir la maison en commencant par le toit', as Houphouët-Boigny and Hamani Diori put it.[5] Both the *Grand Conseil* in Dakar and the *Conseil Général* in Niamey had only limited powers. And in the *cercles* and *subdivisions* the administrators remained as before *les vrais chefs de l'Empire*, still relatively safe from political interference. The position of the chiefs became even more ambiguous than it had been during the period of classic colonial rule. Their prestige could no longer, or so it seemed, be compared with that of the *évolués*. But the latter found themselves in the awkward position of being able to exercise far more influence upon the general course of French policy-making than upon the state of affairs in their home cantons. A policy designed to implement the principles of 1946 thus had strong justification. But the *évolués* were not content to press for formal equality. They also wanted parity with the metropolitan French in matters economic, financial and social; the same salaries, same holidays, same social legislation, same educational opportunities etc. – in short, genuine equality as well as formal equality. We must, to be fair, note here that the old principle of colonial financial self-sufficiency was discharged in favour of state-planning and state expenditure on a huge scale, through the famous *Fonds d'Investissement pour le Développement Economique et Social* (FIDES).[6] But although the French public purse contributed substantially to this fund, the sums spent were finally negligible compared with the needs. To implement fully the generous principles enunciated in the Constitution of 1946 (i.e. total integration and assimilation) would cost money, a lot of money; more money than the French could afford or were prepared to spend. Such a course of action was also bound to pose very serious political problems. Indeed, given the numerical strength of the Africans, it would inevitably place the black politicians in a position of considerable, if not in certain cases determinant, political influence, an unacceptable eventuality to most Frenchmen. Having thus described the inherent contradictions – the ambiguity – of the system established in 1946, we could perhaps conclude that the only colonial system acceptable to the French from a financial and practical point of view was that of the pre-1940 period, the one system that was unacceptable from an ideological point of view. In the case of the post-1946 system, exactly the reverse is true. The gap between finance and ideology proved impossible to bridge.

It was only when the French realized the extremes which the system of 1946 could lead to, and the African politicians realized that the French were not prepared to implement to their utter logical conclusion the principles of 1946, that a new notion appeared on the horizon, that of independence.

After 1946 the colonies turned Overseas Territories were no longer ruled by administrative decrees, but by laws; governed, that is, in the last instance not by the President of the Republic but by Parliament. The role of the Minister of Overseas France was ideally to execute the will of Parliament. To this effect he disposed of a civil service, i.e. the corps of administrators, whose members were supposed to assume the role of neutral onlookers in the political struggle in Africa. But neither the *évolués* nor the administrators respected the new rules of the game, and the two were set on a collision course after 1946. In the absence of elected local bodies (with the exception of the largely powerless territorial *Conseil Général*), the administrators continued to exercise more or less the same functions as before 1940, and could thus hardly avoid taking decisions of a political nature. But there was also another and more fundamental reason why the institutional framework established by the Constitution of 1946 *could* not function according to the spirit of that Constitution. Aristide Zolberg provides us with the first clue to this problem when he writes that 'if we conceive the [presumably pre-colonial] African societies as sets of values, norms and structures, it is evident that they survived to a significant extent everywhere',[7] that is within the new institutional framework. Professor Miège touches upon the same point when he speculates that it might be possible to trace the nature of political influence in Africa back to a 'tendance monarchique ou charismatique liée aux cultures traditionelles'.[8] The implication here is that the political system was governed by two sets of values and structures, the one deriving from the pre-colonial, indigenous and 'traditional' system, the other deriving from the imported, or rather imposed, European political system.[9] In other words, since a political-institutional framework supposes and corresponds to an underlying political culture (defined as a certain number of concepts, norms, ideas, ideals, values, notions, etc.), this framework can only function satisfactorily if the underlying political culture is shared by a vast majority of the people. But in West Africa in 1946 the French imposed an institutional framework which did not correspond to the extant political culture. The result was a hybrid or ambiguous system, in which the 'traditional' African concepts, norms, ideas, ideals, values and notions had to accommodate themselves to a new institutional framework familiar (theoretically) only to the *évolués*.

We know very little about the traditional culture of the Nigeriens. We can do no more, therefore, than to advance a few hypotheses concerning certain aspects of it. I am nevertheless of the opinion that a notion already frequently mentioned, that of 'force' or 'luck' (and the analogous Muslim notion of *baraka*) is of importance to our purpose. It can be argued that the reforms introduced in 1946, and especially the fact that the French now had to share power with the *évolués*, were interpreted by the Africans as proof of the deterioration of the 'force/luck' of the French. But since the notion of 'force/luck' seems to be that the available amount is finite, the 'force/luck' lost by the French could be, and was, recuperated by another group, in this case the *évolués*. The *Commandant* of Niamey, Ignace Colombani, said much the same when he minuted that 'la masse, elle, cherche de nouveaux maîtres'.[10] (Colombani was told by the chief of Karma 'que je n'étais plus le chef, que ... la terre ne m'appartenait plus, qu'elle était à Fily Dabo Sissoko',[11] i.e. the first member of the National Assembly in Paris representing Sudan and Niger.) The notions mentioned above obviously exclude any distinction between a legislative and an executive branch of government or between spheres reserved to politicians and civil servants respectively. It may be tentatively concluded, then, that the years after 1946 saw a struggle between the administrators and the *évolués*, in which the latter sought – through the local branch of the inter-African *Rassemblement Démocratique Africain* (RDA), the *Parti Progressiste Nigérien* (PPN) – to *supplant* the French administration. The issue at stake was perfectly clear: were the *évolués* or the administrators to remain, or to take over as, the legitimate rulers of Niger? The struggle was all the more bitter, since on the one hand the *évolués* had the (justified) impression that the administrators were not prepared to respect the spirit of the Constitution of 1946, and since, on the other hand, the administrators felt to a certain extent betrayed by the decision-makers in Paris, who in their mind had reserved for a handful of rudimentarily educated Africans a position out of all proportion to their abilities and real influence. How could *they*, responsible administrators, share power with a band of 'rhetoriciens sans rhetorique, architects sans plans, sociologues primaires, artisans sans art' (Colombani again)[12] or 'semi-intellectuels aigris, cherchant des places, que nous avons suffisamment mal formés pour en faire des ennemis' (according to another administrator).[13] This is not to deny that there were on both sides able, competent, unbiased and unselfish men and women whose main preoccupation was to improve the conditions of the Africans. But they found themselves bogged down in a struggle, the nature of which we have tried to define above.

POLITICS, 1945–52

The spirit of 1946

The consequences of the reforms of 1946 (the 1789 of French black Africa as they have been called)[14] were instantly perceptible to the Nigeriens. It hardly escaped the attention even of the most ignorant and miserable of peasants that he could no longer be forced to work for, or to deliver supplies to, the French against his will, that the local *Commandant* could no longer throw him in prison without trial, that he could complain to the new judge in Niamey if he fell victim to extortions committed by the village or even the canton chief. One is thus tempted to conclude that he perceived the reforms of 1946 as a liberation, but I feel that this point should not be pressed too hard. What seems certain, however, is that many Nigeriens considered the French to have lost their 'force'. Indeed, a *Commandant* who could no longer give orders, or punish, but who had to rely exclusively upon persuasion, in other words a *Commandant* whom everyone could try to best, did not command much respect. As a consequence, the French found themselves not only more and more isolated but also confronted with a more oppositional, or at least much less subservient, mood than before,[15] in the West at any rate. For if it is true, as one administrator remarked, that the Hausa 'obéissent à ceux, quels qu'ils soient, qui leur donnent l'impression de commander . . . les plus forts',[16] and that they by temperament respected law and order,[17] then the new state of affairs in 1946 was perhaps looked upon as a mixed blessing, in the sense that the country was now ruled by chiefs (i.e. the French) who no longer had the favour of the supernatural powers, as demonstrated by the fact that their very position no longer went unchallenged, a positively dangerous situation. But this is partly speculation.

The global impact of the reforms of 1946 was, we may safely presume, stronger on the societies of the West than on the other societies of Niger. The reasons for this have been developed throughout the preceding chapters, and can briefly be summarized as follows: the societies of the West were at the time of the arrival of the French in a state of disintegration which the action of the French only contributed in accelerating. Furthermore, by strengthening the position of the chiefs, and by endorsing their definition of landed property (*droit foncier*), the French were in part responsible for the permanent social crisis and the land problem which characterized the West after the 1910s. If we consider also that the West had suffered severely from certain aspects of classic colonial rule, forced labour in particular, while at the same time reaping considerable benefits from the presence of the French (who recruited most of their auxiliaries in the West), one can conclude that the West was permeable to European influence, that the people of the West had more cause to complain than, say, the Hausa, *and* that they were more politicized than the other peoples of Niger. Given this situation, the reforms of 1946, functioning as a sort of catalyst and contributing to the exacerbation of local antagonisms generated by the evolution of the preceding decades, had the effect of plunging the West into a state of near-riot. Thus after 1946 the West witnessed a new outbreak of the Hamallist movement (particularly significant in the Fulani cantons, such as Lamorde, of the right bank of the Niger),[18] and of the pagan or semi-pagan mystery cults; millet granaries were plundered;[19] the French suddenly found themselves submerged by land disputes and complaints;[20] the customary taxes paid to the chiefs fell into disuse[21] (along with so-called communal labour for the benefit of the chiefs);[22] the internal colonization soared, now that there was nothing the French could do to stop people from settling down wherever they chose;[23] the seasonal migration to the coastal territories also soared, involving during the early post-war years as many as 50 per cent of the total male population of certain cantons.[24] It was not only the French who found their position threatened, but also the canton and village chiefs, and even the family heads and elders. The number of divorces reached unprecedented heights, while the very nucleus of the society, the extended family, seemed to be on the threshold of disintegration.[25] This troubled atmosphere had been preceded by, and was in part the consequence of, the introduction of European-style politics. Although only a few Nigeriens had the right to vote, they were called upon to exercise that right five times in the span of fourteen months: twice to elect the representative of French Sudan and Niger to the successive Constituent Assemblies, once to elect the first Nigerien deputy to the first Assembly of the Fourth Republic – on 10 November 1946 – and twice – on 15 December 1946 and 5 January 1947 – to elect the members of the first territorial assembly, or *Conseil Général* of Niger.[26] In the middle of it all, two political events of considerable importance occurred; the creation of Niger's first political party, the *Parti Progressiste Nigérien*, on 17 June 1946;[27] and the Bamako congress, from 19 to 21 October 1946, which laid the foundation of the first inter-territorial African political party, the *Rassemblement Démocratique Africain* (RDA).[28]

The nature of post-1946 politics
The following pages devote considerable attention to politics, mainly party politics and elections. This needs to be justified, for it can be objected to on the grounds that 'modern' or European-style politics did not make much sense to the average Nigerien. For instance, voting participation remained exceptionally low throughout the colonial period, and especially after the introduction of universal suffrage in 1956 (less than 30 per cent in the referendum of 1958).[29] But although the rural masses of Niger participated very little in 'modern' politics, that is within the alien institutional framework imposed by the French in 1946, it does not necessarily follow that they were unaware of the outcome of the political struggle, namely whose

influence (or 'force') was paramount or predominant at any time. But a further objection is that since the administrators were barred constitutionally from competing within the new institutional framework, surely their influence, standing or 'force' cannot be measured in terms of votes? But the point here is that everyone knew which candidates were supported by the French and which were not, and which were for and which against the local administrator. Among the candidates supported by the French, we find a considerable number of chiefs and noblemen, people who belonged to the 'traditional' society. That they, as well as the French, should deem it necessary to indulge in politics has been deplored and even condemned by many authors. But could a chief afford to remain aloof from politics if that aloofness meant that his opponent would be elected and derive considerable prestige from his mandate? Besides, whatever definition one chooses to apply to the *chefferie*, that definition can hardly afford to overlook the political dimension of a chief's functions. In fact, it was in the interest of the *évolués* for chiefs and nobles to enter the political arena. Nothing could be more damaging to the prestige of the local chiefs than an electoral defeat at the hands of a commoner. Administrative interference, however, presents us with a more difficult problem. There is no excuse here, *if*, that is, we expect the French administration in Africa to function according to the norms and values prevalent in metropolitan France. But given the way the administration *did* function, in fact the only way it *could* function in Niger; given furthermore the indigenous and traditional political culture, and considering the prestige enjoyed among the Africans by their elected representatives, the bush-administration could not afford *not* to intervene in politics. This they did, and this is what was expected of them by the Nigeriens.

The creation of the Parti Progressiste Nigérien and the first elections

A convenient starting-point here is the creation of the *Parti Progressiste Nigérien* in June 1946. There are differing versions as to who took the initiative, but the most likely one stresses the importance of Issoufou Saidou, who was to become the party's first president. Issoufou Saidou represented the (at that time) very rare combination of being both an *évolué and* a nobleman (he was in fact a son of the late Saidou *zermakoy*). His relations with the French were also excellent, too good for the taste of many. Issoufou Saidou was in those days the unofficial leader of a small band of young *évolués* nearly all in their twenties, who all knew each other intimately, who were nearly all Zerma or Songhay, but unlike Issoufou were either commoners or of servile origin. With the exception of Issoufou, who had attended a fully fledged French *lycée*, they were graduates either of William Ponty in Dakar, or of the less prestigious *Ecole Normale* of Katibougou. Inexperienced, they seem to have been 'helped' along the road by a personality who possibly played an important although discreet role in 1946, the fascinating figure of Francis Borrey, a French doctor, but a self-styled *nègre blanc*. Borrey probably hoped to convert the considerable esteem he had built up as an extremely conscientious doctor into political capital, which would enable him to use Niger as a base for forays into French politics.[30]

Although a political party was a novelty in those days, and the evidence at our disposal is extremely patchy, it seems nevertheless that the PPN, perhaps as a symbol of a new era, was received with sympathy throughout Niger. Even the chiefs and a bewildered French administration, whose titular head, Jean Toby, was on leave of absence, adopted a friendly attitude.[31]

The first problem facing the PPN was what attitude to adopt towards the inter-territorial party which the Bamako conference had taken the initiative in establishing. Although a delegation from the PPN attended the conference, opinion within the party was divided. Issoufou Saidou, officially a member of the French socialist party (the *Section Française de l'Internationale Ouvrière* – SFIO), was tempted to follow the lead of the more prominent African SFIO leaders, such as Léopold Sédar-Senghor, Lamine Guèye and Fily Dabo Sissoko, who had proclaimed their intention of remaining aloof from Félix Houphouët-Boigny's RDA. But apart from Issoufou's personal position, there was another and fairly significant reason for the hesitations of the PPN. Indeed, many party members were afraid that an inter-territorial party would pay very limited attention to such a peripheral and insignificant colony as Niger. They suffered in a sense from an inferiority complex *vis-à-vis* the richer and more developed coastal territories and their already well-known leaders.[32] But before the final decision was taken in this matter, another event had seriously shaken the cohesion within the party: the designation of the candidate for the election of the first Nigerien deputy on 10 November 1946. The most obvious candidate was the party president, Issoufou Saidou. But among the prominent party members, there were misgivings over both Issoufou and the other declared candidate, Dr Borrey; the latter because he was after all a European, the former because he was of noble birth, *and* because he maintained too close contacts with the administration (which, rumour had it, paid his debts). In fact, neither men belonged to the small group which emerged fairly quickly as the dominant one within the party, and which consisted mainly, as we have noted, of a certain number of Ponty-educated 'westerners' of common or servile origin (but, it is worth noting, no former servicemen. Indeed the political contribution of the *anciens combattants* turned out to be surprisingly small.) And this group had a candidate of its own, Hamani Diori; a thirty-year-old Zerma who had got himself favourably noticed as a hard-working and able primary school teacher and headmaster. But the main reason why Diori stood out was the fact that he alone among the *évolués* (excluding Issoufou Saidou) had personal experience of France from his time as a colloquial assistant at the *Ecole Coloniale* in Paris before the war. Diori was in short selected as a candidate mainly because he possessed the geographical and linguistic 'know-how' deemed necessary for a representative in the French National Assembly. Since the Nigerien deputy was above all considered as a representative of Niger, one might even say as the territory's *ambassador* in Paris, he had to possess the tools required for that position.[33]

Issoufou Saidou and Dr Borrey, somewhat embittered by the refusal of the PPN to nominate them, decided to run nevertheless. Including Djibrilla Maiga, the unofficial RDA candidate, and Rouland Gougis, a veterinarian from the West Indies, there was thus a total of five candidates, two foreigners and three 'westerners', but no Hausa, Kanuri, Fulani or Tuareg. With the exception of the *Commandant* of Zinder (who 'advised' the Sultan to campaign in favour of Dr Borrey),[34] no administrative interference nor any violence was reported. There were in fact riots in Zinder on 28 and 29 October 1946, during which four people were killed and twenty-eight wounded, but they seem to have had little if anything to do with the election, and rather much to do with the latent and persistent antagonism between *tirailleurs* and mainly Dahomean clerks.[35]

Of the 57,276 electors, some 25,809 cast valid votes. Hamani Diori emerged as the winner, with 8,250 votes, a thousand more votes than Dr Borrey and three thousand more than Issoufou Saidou.[36]

The next step in the political process was the election of the first *Conseil Général* in December 1946 and January 1947, an important event, not because the *Conseil* wielded much power, but because it would be called upon to designate the Nigerien representatives to the *Conseil de la République* (or Senate), in Paris, the Assembly of the French Union in Versailles and the *Grand Conseil* of French West Africa in Dakar. Unfortunately (and surprisingly), no figures exist concerning this election; only a list of the twenty second-college (African) representatives, and the ten first-college (European) representatives.[37] But this list does yield some interesting information. Among the twenty Africans elected, the majority can be classified as belonging to the 'nobility', including six incumbent province or canton chiefs. Most were local figures. Indeed, the absence of all but four or five of those who had already or who were to become prominent in politics in Niger leads one to suspect that Hamani Diori was correct when he argued in Paris that Governor Toby had been able to secure the election of a certain number of docile 'supporters' of his.[38] In particular, Toby interpreted the conditions of eligibility very widely, thus enabling a number of nearly illiterate *notables* to run.[39] Curiously enough the French did not introduce the metropolitan proportional electoral system, but the Anglo-Saxon 'winner-takes-all' system, unfair in the extreme, especially since each constituency disposed of several seats. This system has been described as 'the surest way to kill the idea of democracy in a plural [African] society. For if the minorities are to accept [the political system], they must be adequately represented.'[40]

The alliance of the PPN/RDA with the French communists and its consequences

If the political dividing lines were somewhat obscure in 1946, it did not take long before they became clear enough for everyone to see. In May 1947, when the RDA was formally established,[41] the PPN became its local branch in Niger. By then the RDA parliamentarians in Paris had already joined the communist groups (but *not* the Communist Party, or *Parti Communiste Français* – PCF) of the various assemblies. This alliance can be explained, first, by the PCF's marked anti-colonial policy, second, by the fact that the communist parliamentarians were simply the only ones who took care of and guided the first fumbling steps of their inexperienced African colleagues, and third, because the PCF was represented within the government, and could thus promote the interests of the Africans.[42] But the communists were excluded from the government by Prime Minister Paul Ramadier as early as in May 1947, and considered after that date as a threat to the very existence of the Fourth Republic.[43] Hence, the 'crushing' of the allies of the PCF, i.e. the RDA, became almost a patriotic duty for the administrators in Africa – the ideal excuse, in short – and they set about doing it all the more willingly because of certain grudges they now had against the RDA and its various territorial branches such as the PPN in Niger.

The PPN adopted a policy characterized by an extreme hostility towards the chiefs and the administration; but never against France or the French as such. The aim of this policy, which consisted in denouncing and exploiting systematically alleged and/or genuine abuses, extortions and injustices, muckraking as it would have been called elsewhere, was to demolish the authority and prestige of the local administrators and chiefs. One of the most lucid French observers in Niger, Ignace Colombani, summarized the situation as follows:

> lorsque au hasard de leur action; ils [the PPN members] mettent en avant un argument vrai, une faute commise, une cause juste, cela arrive . . . ils l'enrobent dans le mensonge . . . Je sais que nous avons commis des erreurs. Mais je suis sûr que, n'en eussions nous pas commis une seule, le problème demeurait entier, car l'erreur que l'on relève n'est qu'un prétexte . . . Ce ne sont pas les coupables qui sont visés, mais l'autorité française.[44]

His superior, Governor Toby, expressed himself more bluntly when he stated in a public speech in 1950, that the PPN/RDA members 'ont choisi de se perdre dans des mouvements de rebellion sous le signe de la trahison et de l'imposture', and that they waged 'une action criminelle [qui] obéit à une stratégie politique étrangère'.[45] This harsh reaction of the French is to a certain extent understandable, for there is no doubt that the PPN/RDA members made use at times of questionable means and methods.

But one suspects nevertheless that the violent reaction of the French was more psychological than political. Accustomed to consider themselves the undisputed masters of the country, they understandably had some difficulties in adjusting to the new realities of the post-1946 era. They were not prepared to be patient, to adopt a conciliatory attitude towards the *évolués*, but expected instead the latter to behave as perfect gentlemen, to 'play the game' as it were, a game they were supposed to have learnt overnight, with courtesy and deference. It did not occur to the French that they were asking for the impossible. Indeed, a brutal change from an authoritarian and oppressive regime to a more democratic and liberal one is generally known to lead to excesses, especially when – as was the case in Niger – the institutional framework imposed did not correspond to the local political culture. One could argue furthermore that the *évolués* applied the only effective political pressure available to them: 'to precipitate crisis and show that the system could not be allowed to work'.[46] That being said, however, the PPN/RDA fell victims to what John Lonsdale has qualified as the 'central paradox of any national movement', namely that 'nationalist leaders must appeal for mass support . . . an appeal [which] brings into central focus those rivalries of tribe, language and culture . . . hitherto . . . contained within the respective localities'.[47] Thus the reforms of 1946 and action of the PPN/RDA exacerbated a considerable number of local conflicts, in the West in particular: between Hamallists and orthodox Muslims, between pretenders and incumbent chiefs, between land-owners and tenants, between the Fulani and Zerma/Songhay, between former slaves and former masters and so on. The consequence was a permanent climate of agitation and unrest, which caused considerable difficulties to the French.

If it is possible to draw any conclusion from all this, it is that the mutual incomprehension which characterized the relationship between the PPN/RDA members and the French was detrimental to both groups, and above all to Niger. Each group displayed a rigid and excessive hostility towards the other. It was not necessary for a seasoned administrator to proclaim that the PPN/RDA tried to establish a 'véritable dictature appuyée sur la menace et le chantage'.[48] Nor was it necessary for the PPN/RDA members to try and make people believe that party cards were miraculous *gris-gris*.[49] To attack systematically *all* the chiefs, as the PPN/RDA did, made little sense. But it was equally absurd for the French to defend even those chiefs who were indefensible, such as the *sarkin* Damagaram, Barma Mustapha, the chief of Dungass and a number of their peers, who – the French were forced to acknowledge later – had carried out extortions of a criminal nature.[50] It is altogether a sad story, in which it is difficult not to put more blame on the French administrators than on the *évolués*. For the latter at least had good excuses: they were young, inexperienced, had been inadequately trained and schooled, *and* were uprooted individuals, at ease neither in the European nor in the traditional African society.[51]

The attitude and reaction of the Toby administration

The important point here is, however, that the PPN/RDA hardly possessed the means to implement its policy. The tiny group of *évolués* which constituted the inner core of the PPN/RDA was in the last analysis no match for such a towering figure as Governor Jean Toby. Toby belonged to that rare breed of post-war governors who had started at the bottom, as a bush-administrator, which he had remained at heart. Even rarer in the annals of colonial history, Toby, as we have seen, had served as a bush-administrator for a number of years in the very same colony of which he was later appointed Governor. But most astonishing of all, Toby was the only colonial Governor to survive both the fall of Vichy in 1944 and the departure of de Gaulle in 1946. He served as Governor of Niger for nearly twelve years (1942–52 and 1953–4), an all-time record in French Africa. It is not an exaggeration to argue that Niger became for all practical purposes Toby's private domain; one is tempted to say, his realm or empire. Toby, tall, strongly built, and full of vitality, not only looked and behaved like a chief in the African sense of that word, he *was* the supreme chief (even the sacred king?) of Niger, and as such virtually independent of the Governor-General in Dakar. Strange and awe-inspiring stories were told about him throughout the country.[52] Whether Toby provided Niger with good government is open to dispute. But he certainly headed an efficient and smooth-working administration if ever there was one in French West Africa; an itinerant administration staffed with a number of seasoned bush-administrators, confirmed bachelors like their chief, all completely at ease in the tortuous labyrinths of African politics, all extremely well-informed about local affairs. The administration under Toby was an almost perfect example of an administration functioning according to what we have called 'the indigenous chieftaincy model', with all its advantages and drawbacks. Among the latter, the most significant was an almost total lack of interest in economic matters.[53] It may be argued therefore that the Toby administration constituted in the final analysis an anachronism, better suited to meet the needs of the inter-war period than of the new epoch inaugurated by the reforms of 1946.

If the administration had been taken completely by surprise in 1946, it was mainly because of Toby's prolonged leave of absence. But once the head of the administration was back, the French were quick to react. No spectacular measures were decided upon. Rather, Toby defined a certain line of action which was to prove highly successful, at least in Hausaland. First and foremost, he stressed the importance of maintaining close and sustained contact with the countryside, through frequent tours – on horse or camel-back – and censuses.[54]

Second, Toby encouraged (one could almost say forced) each *Commandant* and *chef de subdivision* to study his district and its problems in depth, in short to take his job seriously. This was possible for the first time in Niger's history, simply because the administration under Toby enjoyed a hitherto unknown stability. Never content with superficial or rudimentary explanations, Toby watched the activities of each bush-administrator very closely and very carefully. The result is still visible today in the shape of a considerable number of voluminous annual reports, quite remarkable documents which more often than not present the researcher with a nearly complete anatomy of the relevant district. The contrast with the reports we possess for the pre-war period is truly astonishing. As for the chiefs, they were associated very closely with the activity of the administrator, not only in order to strengthen their position, but also, and perhaps primarily, in order to educate them, to make them aware of their rights and duties (and the limits of their power) under the new system.[55] An important contribution to the strengthening of the chiefs' position was the steep increase in their salaries. The scale, which ranged from 3,600 to 72,000 francs in 1946, was three years later raised to 40,000–286,000 francs CFA (see below). A further increase of 50 per cent on average occurred in 1951. In addition the chiefs were entitled to considerable sums in allowances, bonuses, commissions and premiums; especially the village-chiefs, who for the first time disposed of revenues in proportion with the duties they performed.[56]

Among other concrete measures decided upon by the French, three deserve to be mentioned here because they contributed towards the quieting of widespread public discontent. The first was the establishment of individual tax-rolls, which meant that no one could henceforth be called upon to pay taxes for someone else. The second was the abolition of the village granaries, which were replaced by granaries for each ward, and later by family granaries.[57] The third consisted of recognizing at long last the autonomy of all the new villages which had sprung up as a consequence of the internal colonization (forty-four in the region of Tanout alone).[58] In fact, the French went further and now proceeded to organize and to establish orderly conditions in regions which had been populated and settled over the last twenty to thirty years, such as the region of Dakoro, where the French created three new cantons in 1947–8, and which became a *subdivision* in 1948,[59] or the region south-west of Tahoua where the cantons of Bambey and Kalfou were established.[60]

Vis-à-vis the PPN/RDA, Toby adopted an extreme attitude of non-collaboration. He simply chose to ignore the party, while seeing to it that none of the claims put forward by the PPN/RDA leadership were examined, let alone met. They apparently got nowhere. On the other hand, it may be surmised that the smooth efficiency of the Toby administration owed a lot to the opposition of the PPN/RDA. By keeping a watchful eye on administrators and chiefs alike, the party did Niger and the Nigeriens a great service in the sense that it forced the French to abide by the rules of the game. Nevertheless the PPN/RDA leadership undermined its own position through a number of impressive political blunders. For if they were correct in concluding that nothing could be achieved as long as Toby remained governor, it was of little avail to petition Governor-General Béchard and Minister of Overseas France, Paul Coste-Floret, to sack Toby, when they visited Niamey in January and May 1948 respectively; especially not when the motion to this effect was accompanied by rather puerile attempts to discredit Toby in the eyes of his superiors. This action probably had the opposite of the desired effect: according to unsubstantiated rumours, Coste-Floret *was* thinking of replacing Toby, but changed his mind during or immediately after his visit. Toby retaliated by transferring the PPN/RDA politicians who belonged to the federal civil service (*le cadre fédéral*) to other territories, and those who belonged to the local civil service to regions far away from their political strongholds.[61]

The emergence and nature of UNIS

Before these measures had become effective, another event was to have a disastrous effect upon the position of the PPN/RDA: the election of a second deputy on 27 June 1948. The party leaders, conscious of the party's lack of appeal in the East, and aware of the growing tension, even within the party, between 'westerners' and 'easterners', thought it essential to choose a candidate from the East and/or a Hausa (especially since the first deputy, Hamani Diori, was a Zerma). There are conflicting versions as to who this candidate was to be. But the two most likely names were Mahaman Georges Condat and Adamou Mayaki. Both had adequate training: Condat was a Ponty graduate, and Mayaki had been to Katibougou. But Adamou Mayaki, although a hausaphone, was not from the East, but from Filingue. He had another serious drawback in the eyes of the PPN/RDA leaders, that of being the son of the late Gado Namalaya, *sarkin* Filingue. Condat on the other hand was an authentic 'easterner'. But he was very young, only twenty-four, and he was not a Hausa, but a half-caste, son of a former French administrator and his temporary Fulani 'wife'. Besides, there were strong misgivings as to Condat's personality. One administrator described him cruelly as a non-existent politician. Faced with what was considered a field of inadequate 'eastern' and/or Hausa candidates, the party finally decided to nominate its Secretary-General, Djibo Bakary; a choice which deeply antagonized chiefs and 'easterners'. Djibo was not only another young (born 1921) Ponty-educated Zerma of low birth, he was also a *cousin* of Hamani Diori, *and* leader of the most radical wing within the party.[62] (That Djibo had spent most of his childhood and early youth in Tahoua, a Hausa town, did not make much difference in this respect.)

Many 'easterners' seceded from the PPN/RDA and planned to set up a party of their own, which was to be named the *Parti Indépendant du Niger-Est*. It was then, and only then, that Toby intervened. The split within the PPN/RDA provided the administration with a golden opportunity to divide and rule. But we may also argue that Toby deemed it necessary to avoid an open confrontation between the West and the rest of the country; to prevent the new party becoming a purely *regional* one. He therefore made contacts with politicians who, like Condat, had seen their ambitions thwarted by the PPN/RDA establishment: Dr Borrey, and especially Issoufou Saidou. Toby used the split within the PPN/RDA, by moulding disgruntled party members, well-known politicians outside the party, and above all the chiefs into a national party, the *Union Nigérienne des Indépendants et Sympathisants* (UNIS).[63]

The new party was officially established on 4 June 1948, only twenty-three days before the election. The candidate of UNIS, Condat, obtained 15,219 votes and easily defeated Djibo Bakary who obtained only 5,375 votes. A

161

regional breakdown of these results shows that whereas Condat gained 71 per cent of the votes in the territory as a whole, his score in Hausaland was 79 per cent. His highest score came however in the Zerma *cercle* of Dosso – Issoufou Saidou's own backyard – where he took a suspiciously high 96 per cent. Djibo on the other hand took 50 per cent of the vote in the three most urbanized *subdivisions*, Niamey, Maradi and Zinder, and close to 70 per cent in the only *subdivision* comprising a non-traditional town, Niamey. He also won a majority in the 'western' *subdivisions* of Say and Filingue.[64] This voting pattern is interesting to note, for it was to remain fairly stable throughout the colonial period.

That the administration and the chiefs supported Condat is without doubt.[65] That UNIS belongs to that category of parties which has been described as *partis administratifs* or 'patron' parties – both rather perjorative terms – is equally without doubt. But to conclude that UNIS was not a representative party or that it was less representative than the PPN/RDA is questionable. The defeat of the PPN/RDA corresponds in fact to a certain logic. For if the party's programme was admirably suited to the realities in the West, it was much less suited to the realities of other regions of Niger, where colonial rule had not proved disruptive to the same extent as in the West. Besides, the fact that the Hausa paid on the average more taxes than the Zerma/Songhay, while the latter reaped most of the benefits of colonial rule and especially of the new regime in 1946, hardly escaped the attention of the former. And finally, since the PPN/RDA had obtained nothing after 1946, i.e. since its 'force' or *baraka* was declining, then it was only natural and logical from a certain point of view that the party should be defeated.

The classic distinctions between mass and patron (or cadre) parties[66] is now considered to be outmoded (among other reasons because even many mass parties tended to 'function in a largely vacuous fashion', that is as a patron party within the mass party).[67] But it never applied to Niger in the first place; one is hard put to describe the PPN/RDA as a mass party whatever definition one chooses to give to that term. The PPN/RDA was the party of the *évolués* and of the West; UNIS the party of the chiefs and the East. Perhaps we can also apply the term 'modern' (or 'Europeanized') to the PPN, 'traditional' (or 'neo-traditionalist') to UNIS, in that the latter, much more than the former, represented not only the traditional element in society, but also traditional or more precisely indigenous norms, values and notions; in short, the pre-existing political culture, which it tried to adapt to the new institutional framework.[68] Election day became for instance a day of public celebration, during which chiefs and subjects exchanged gifts, while the latter renewed their allegiance to the former by voting for the 'right' party.[69]

The decline of the PPN/RDA and new reforms
The election of June 1948 marked only the beginning of the decline of the PPN/RDA. The defeat of Djibo Bakary was followed shortly afterwards by the elimination of Djibrilla Maiga from the Senate where he was replaced by

Oumar Ba of UNIS;[70] by the legislative election of 1951 in which Hamani Diori lost his seat as deputy; and by the even more disastrous territorial election of 1952 in which all the PPN/RDA candidates were eliminated. After 1953 not a single seat in any of the territorial, federal or metropolitan parliamentary assemblies was held by the PPN/RDA. But it was already clear by 1948 that the French had recovered from the shock of 1946, and that the attempt of the PPN/RDA to challenge their position had failed. At the federal and metropolitan levels, the result of the activity of the RDA was equally dismal. For the party 'had forfeited its bargaining potential by giving unconditional support to the one party [i.e. the PCF] which all other politicians were determined to keep out of office'.[71] Nevertheless, the African deputies, whether members of the RDA, the SFIO, or the new emerging inter-parliamentary group known as the *Indépendants d'Outre-Mer* (IOM), indeed all African *évolués*, won a resounding corporate victory when the *deuxième loi Lamine-Guèye* was voted in 1950. This law established the principle of parity of wages, allowances and fringe benefits between metropolitan and African civil servants and functionaries[72] (a principle which was to have a crippling effect upon the budgets of the independent West African states after 1960). Such a step was logical enough considering the spirit of the Constitution of 1946. But apart from the fact that the federal and territorial budgets had now to grapple with comparatively high wage bills, the *deuxième loi Lamine-Guèye* contributed to the very substantial rise in the standards of living of the *évolués* and to the widening of the gap which separated their material position from that of the average peasant; especially in Niger, where – as opposed to the Ivory Coast and Senegal – no indigenous middle-class composed of planters and truck-owners existed. To the rural masses, the *évolués* probably looked more and more like a small privileged class, perhaps even an aristocracy, with which they had few if any affinities. It has thus been demonstrated that the passport to wealth and standing in society was European-style education, clerical work and above all political influence, rather than entrepreneurship.

The *deuxième loi Lamine-Guèye* was followed by the law of 8 August 1950 which extended the principle of equality of the pensions of the former servicemen, but in this case it was a much-needed measure. Indeed, former African servicemen lived miserably, depending to a great extent upon alms from the administration.[73] The problem specific to Africa was that a considerable number of former servicemen were not entitled to any pension at all, simply because they could not produce the necessary certificates and official documents which a pusillanimous administration, determined not to treat the Africans differently from their metropolitan comrades, required. Matters seem to have improved considerably even in this respect after 1950. The problem of the former servicemen cannot be discussed without mentioning the role of Hamani Diori. His vigorous and persistent action on their behalf in the National Assembly helped to pave the way for the law of 8 August 1950.[74]

The turning-point of 1950–1

The disappointing result of the action of the RDA on the political level, combined with the incidents in the Ivory Coast in early 1950 (which prompted Toby to ban all PPN/RDA meetings in Niger, a ban later ruled unconstitutional by the French *Conseil d'Etat*),[75] and perhaps the very tangible consequence of the *deuxième loi Lamine-Guèye*, led many of the RDA leaders to question the wisdom of a political alliance with the Communist Party and of a hostile policy towards the French administration. The events in the Ivory Coast in 1950, for instance, which got out of hand,[76] perhaps made the RDA leadership realize that the policy pursued so far had merely exacerbated local micro-antagonisms, always latent in such an extremely heterogeneous society as that of the Ivory Coast, while serving no practical political purpose. Perhaps more could be achieved through collaboration than through confrontation.[77] This political reappraisal prompted the RDA parliamentarians to put an end to the alliance with the Communist Party in the fall of 1950. Instead, in 1951 they affiliated themselves to the small pivotal group of the *Union Démocratique et Social de la Résistance* (UDSR), headed by René Pleven, who was also the Prime Minister, and François Mitterand, the Minister of Overseas France. Thus the RDA became a *parti administratif*. The left-wingers within the RDA, such as Gabriel d'Arboussier on the federal level and Djibo Bakaray in Niger, who disapproved of the new political orientation, either left or were excluded from the party.[78]

The change, however, came too late to save Hamani Diori's seat in the National Assembly. In the legislative elections of 17 June 1951, the UNIS ticket, composed of Condat and Zodi Ikhia (a Kel Gress Tuareg who had distinguished himself as headmaster of the first nomadic school of the Madaoua region),[79] won an overwhelming victory and carried both seats. But although the election provoked a storm of protest among the RDA deputies led by M. Konate of Sudan, and came very close to being annulled,[80] Condat and Zodi both joined the same parliamentary group as the RDA deputies. (Zodi, however, switched to the IOM in 1952.)[81] One year later, in the election for the renewal of the *Conseil Général*, now renamed the Territorial Assembly, and at a time when liberal-minded Governor Roland Casimir, who ordered his administrators to observe a strict neutrality,[82] had taken over from Toby (who succeeded his successor one year later), UNIS won thirty-four out of the thirty-five second-college seats, the last seat going to an independent candidate from N'Guigmi.[83]

All fifteen first-college seats went to the Gaullist *Rassemblement du Peuple Français*. Although we have no detailed results for this election, it does seem that the PPN/RDA fared better in the polls than the distribution of seats seems to imply. Indeed, the party took over 40 per cent of the votes in two of its western strongholds: 43 per cent in the *subdivision* of Dogondoutchi (and 30 per cent in the *cercle* of Dosso as a whole), and 42 per cent in the *subdivision centrale* of Niamey.[84] It was thus the electoral system which barred the party from obtaining seats in the Territorial Assembly. Nevertheless, after 1948 the PPN/RDA was virtually non-existent east of Dogondoutchi, and had become a regional party.

ECONOMIC AND SOCIAL EVOLUTION, 1945–60

Economic consequences of the reforms of 1946

In the face of an impressive number of traps and pitfalls, the non-specialist, such as myself, who has to devote some attention to the economic and social evolution after 1945 feels tempted to hide behind R. O. Collins's remark, that 'development to one [author] is exploitation to another, as each cavalier gerrymanders the meagre statistics to support fact and fancy'.[85] One could of course add that 'the economy of French West Africa [after 1945] expanded at a rate unmatched in its earlier history',[86] and that the period from 1945 to 1960 was one of economic expansion and returning prosperity.[87] But economic expansion or growth, reflected in improved production statistics, is not necessarily synonymous with economic *development*, i.e. improved standards of living. With regard to R. O. Collins's remark, the unfortunate point is that the statistics available for this period are far from meagre, but present us instead with an abundance, if not a profusion, of figures which if anything complicates the task of the historian. The reliability of these figures is obviously open to doubt, but their very profusion is a point which deserves attention in its own right, since it indicates a profound shift in the emphasis of French activity in West Africa towards economic matters.

The post-war years saw the real beginnings of state expenditure and development planning. Corresponding with the political reforms of 1946 there was an economic 'New Deal'. Such activity meant a new level of government penetration of society, in the sense that it accentuated the colonial state's natural interventionist tendency. Government became increasingly managerial and impersonal. The old-time, *Commandant*, that jack-of-all-trades, was on his way out, replaced progressively by a new type of colonial official, the statistician, the economist, the expert in development planning. Unfortunately, this emphasis on economics led to a very complex institutional set-up. The economy of Niger became more and more embroiled with that of the Federation and of France and less and less autonomous. In this, the trend which can be observed in the economic field is quite the opposite of that which can be observed in the political one. The budgets of Niger, the Federation and even of France were interrelated so that there was 'no clear-cut demarcation between them either as to the sources of their revenues or to the objectives or their expenditure'.[88] If this complexity presents the present-day historian with a headache, it also confused utterly the elected African representatives, especially since they were under the (justified) impression that the important decisions affecting the economies of their home territories were not only taken outside Africa, but were also to a considerable extent outside their control. No one really had a clear-cut overall picture of the economic and financial situation. Hence economic and financial matters never became political issues; worse still the whole set-up encouraged an attitude of irresponsibility and carelessness in these matters among the African parliamentarians.[89]

Enough has been said to conclude that the crude, unpretentious model developed earlier for the study of the economic evolution of Niger up to 1945 is of little value for the post-1945 period. That model was based on the assumption that Niger constituted up to 1937/8, and from an economic point of view, an appendix to Nigeria. People crossed the border to sell their surpluses, thus obtaining the necessary cash to pay their taxes. Hence the exchange rate between the French franc and sterling, together with the tax rates, was of importance to our model. So were prices on the world market, the activities of the French, and, last but not least, climatic oscillations. For the period after 1945 we have, however, to deal with a much more complex and intricate situation in which a number of additional factors must be taken into consideration. For example, the customs barrier was maintained after 1945, and the tariffs which applied were impressive enough. But after the withdrawal of the border garrisons, it became relatively easy to cross the frontier, especially for the local *dyulas* (or retail traders). What was from an official point of view smuggling developed considerably over the years, and presented a threat to the position of the expatriate firms.[90] In 1956 the *dyulas* were able to offer to the consumers the most common varieties of cloths at prices ranging from 495 to 592 francs CFA, that is 80 to 120 francs CFA below prices offered by the French firms.[91] The expatriate firms also met severe competition from North African traders, who tended after 1952 to monopolize the local commerce in the Tahoua, Agades and Tanout regions, where they undersold the expatriate firms at the rate of 20 to 30 per cent.[92] One suspects that the French administration tried its best to stop the widespread smuggling across the Nigerien border. But the local *Commandants*, aware of the potentially damaging effect of the customs barrier, and not always favourably disposed towards the expatriate firms, to say the least,[93] did exactly the opposite; not only did they look the other way, but occasionally they virtually encouraged the Africans to take advantage of the lax supervision of the frontier.[94] A good example is provided by the exportation southward of cattle, especially from the Konni–Adar–Gobir Tudu region, which recovered quickly after 1944, and which was apparently never interfered with by the French.[95]

This does not mean that the customs barrier was for all practical purposes non-existent after 1946, or that Niger became once more an appendix of Nigeria in economic matters. Nor should it be concluded from what has been said so far that the expatriate firms were slowly squeezed out of the market; although they lost ground in the local retail trade, they still controlled *le grand commerce*, that is trade with Europe, mainly France. It was in fact in the interest of the African producers to sell some of their products, especially groundnuts, in Niger itself, where prices were, at least during the 1950s, higher than in Nigeria. Then, an increasing amount of imported merchandise was after 1945 destined for the administration, merchandise for which customs duties had to be paid. From 1945 we thus have, on the one hand, an official, legal trade, and on the other an important illicit, but semi-officially encouraged trade.

As if this were not enough, in the monetary field we have to grapple with three currencies, plus very steep inflation in France. The law of 23 November established a semi-autonomous African currency, the franc CFA (*Colonies Françaises d'Afrique*, later *Communauté Financière Africaine*), worth 1.70 metropolitan francs.[96] The metropolitan franc was devalued a number of times, in 1945, 1948 and 1949, but not at the same rates as the franc CFA. By 1949–50, which marked the beginning of a certain monetary stability, the franc CFA had been definitively pegged to the French franc at the rate of 2 French francs for each franc CFA. But by then the value of the franc was only one-tenth of its value in 1939 (the franc CFA one-fifth). As for the official exchange rate between French francs and sterling, in 1949–50 it was 480 French francs (or 240 francs CFA) to the pound, compared to 170.59 francs in 1938.[97] But here too matters are complicated by the existence of a local, black-market exchange rate much more unfavourable to the franc than the official ones.[98] It is of course hazardous to try and ascertain the consequences of the establishment of the CFA franc. But one is under the inadequately substantiated impression that the French exporters did not always take the exchange rate (two francs to each franc CFA) into account when they fixed their sales prices in Africa. If this is so, the establishment of the CFA franc was in part responsible for the high costs and price level which predominated in French West Africa during the late 1940s and the 1950s. The other main factor responsible here seems to have been the high rate of inflation in France. Indeed, by 1949, the price-index (base 1938 = 100) had reached 1,817. Although inflation slowed down after 1949, the rate was still 8.4 per cent per annum during the period from 1949 to 1954,[99] much too high a rate in those pre-stagflation times. As a consequence, French goods were not always competitive on the world market. But due to the system of imperial preferences, the overseas territories were under the obligation to trade principally with France, and so to buy goods at prices often far above those prevailing in foreign markets.[100]

The figures and considerations advanced above serve mainly to under-line the difficulties in studying the economic and social evolution of Niger after 1945. If we add that in spite of the profusion of figures, the more significant statistics concerning, say, the local purchasing power, standards of living, price-levels and so on are – for very obvious reasons – not available, then the conclusion must be that we can do no more in the following pages than to present an imperfect and in many ways unsatisfactory picture of the economic and social evolution in Niger during the last years of colonial rule.

Climatic oscillations and staple and cash-crop production
The period after 1945 (to about 1968) was on the whole one of favourable climatic conditions,[101] with plentiful rainfall. This is reflected in the fact that the millet harvests seem to have been, on average, satisfactory during the second half of the 1940s and throughout the 1950s. The only exceptions were the years 1949 and 1953–4. In 1949 drought struck and millet production dropped, according to official figures, by 34 per cent.[102] Although the region worst hit seems to have been as usual the West, people all over Niger had to sell their cattle at low prices.[103] However, no famine, localized or otherwise, was reported. Then, after a mediocre harvest in 1950, both 1951 and 1952 seem to have been fairly good years.[104] The harvest of 1953 or 1954 (the sources are not agreed, strangely enough, on the precise date) was apparently deficient throughout Niger, but especially so in the West. This may have been due, not to drought, but to excessive rainfall.[105] The word 'apparently' is used here purposely, for the situation became a matter of political controversy and was thus blurred. The administration in Niamey organized a relief programme, and the Federal authorities in Dakar granted special subsidies. But whether this was politically motivated, or whether it really corresponded with a necessity, is not altogether clear, although the latter hypothesis seems by far the most plausible.[106] Whatever the situation in 1953–4, Governor Jean Ramadier, a member of the SFIO who took over after Toby, felt justified in suppressing the obligatory millet granaries throughout Niger in 1955, a suppression the PPN/RDA had campaigned in favour of ever since 1946. Not that Ramadier was unaware of the necessity to dispose of reserves in case of drought. But he argued in substance that a new method would have to be devised (it never was) since the granaries, because of their unpopularity, were never adequately filled up and had thus proved – as demonstrated in 1953–4 – inefficient. Furthermore, with the improvement in transport, it was no longer necessary to maintain a system based on the principle of self-sufficiency.[107] Because of the relative abundance of the harvests during the following years, the wisdom of Ramadier's decision was not put to the test.

The favourable climatic conditions go a long way in explaining the unprecedented expansion in the cash-crop sector of the economy after 1945. In 1944–5 about 9,000 tons of (decorticated) groundnuts were marketed. After the return to free marketing during the 1945–6 season[108] and the end of the programme of obligatory groundnut production in 1946,[109] the figure of 45,500 tons, a new record, was reached in 1948–9[110] (the previous record dated from 1935–6). A fairly severe slump between 1949 and 1951/2 was due of course to the drought of 1949, but an unprecedented level of 63,000 tons was reached in 1953–4.[111] But this was only a beginning, since the figures for the period after 1955 oscillated between 70,000 and 90,000 tons a year,[112] that is on the average 10 to 15 per cent of the total commercialized production of groundnuts in French West Africa.[113] As before, more than 90 per cent of the Nigerien production came from the Centre and especially the East, principally the *subdivision* of Magaria which alone produced between about one-third and half of the commercial crop in Niger.[114] In value the exportation of groundnuts represented 483 million francs CFA in 1949, 1,419 million in 1953, probably more than 3,000 million in 1956–7 (and 'only' 6,000 million in 1966–7 in spite of the fact that production had more than doubled compared with 1956–7.[115] After 1966–7 the production declined steadily.) Throughout the period groundnuts accounted for about 90 per cent of the total value of 'legal' exports.[116] The price per kilo actually paid to the producer rose sharply from 1.20–1.80 francs in 1944, to 7–8 francs CFA in 1946, and to 20–27 francs in 1955–6.[117] After 1956 prices rose very slowly if at all (and actually decreased in the 1960s).[118] A superficial calculation would seem to indicate that these prices largely kept pace with the rate of inflation in France up to about 1950 and then tended to lag behind, especially after independence.

The steep increase in production after 1952 was undoubtedly due in part to French initiative and intervention. The measures introduced included outright price supports (from 1954 onwards), subsidies destined to cut transportation costs, regulations governing the operations of the markets (in 1955) and more generally speaking the whole marketing process.[119] These measures principally benefited the ordinary producers.

The Opération Hirondelle
In 1954, after it had been realized that the Nigerian railways could not, due to endemic strikes in particular, be relied upon to carry the whole of Niger's exports, the French in the shape of the Director of Economic Affairs, G. Besse, took a most spectacular initiative, launching what was to become known as the *Opération Hirondelle*. This *Opération* consisted in taking what the Nigerian railways could not handle by trucks to Parakou in Northern Dahomey and then by rail to the port of Cotonou. The necessary funds were provided by the producers, and the territorial and Federal budgets, and paid into a *Caisse de stabilisation et de transport* which could guarantee uniform prices to the producers throughout Niger, regardless of the mode of transport and the distance from Parakou. The *Opération*, which became an annual event, proved highly successful and especially profitable. In fact the *Opération Hirondelle* avoided the strangling of the cash-crop sector of the Nigerien economy, refloated the previously unprofitable Benin–Niger railway, enabled the French to save appreciable sums of foreign currency and lorry-drivers and owners (few of whom were Nigeriens) to make considerable profits, and finally put Niger in a bargaining position *vis-à-vis* the Nigerian railways. However, in spite of all this and although the per kilo levy (*prélèvement*), operated at the expense of the producers, may be qualified as negligible, the bill for the whole *Opération* was footed in the last analysis by the Hausa peasants. They thus subsidized indirectly both the Benin–Niger railway and more generally the West, a region which benefited considerably from the new transportation facilities; facilities which did not however,

contrary to what the French had anticipated, induce the peasants of the West to cultivate groundnuts.[120]

The development programmes and the economic policy of the Toby administration

We now turn to another important source of revenue, the FIDES or development fund and associated programmes. It is difficult to ascertain their importance and impact after 1946; in fact we do not even know how much money was actually spent in Niger. The most reliable figure seems to be about 4,000 million francs CFA for the period 1947 to 1957. (This figure includes not only sums invested by the FIDES, but also by the less important FERDES, or rural equipment fund, together with sums granted by the federal authorities.)[121] The sum of 4,000 million francs CFA must be compared with that of 105,000 million francs CFA which represents the money spent by FIDES in French West Africa during the same period;[122] and with the figure of 1,800 francs CFA which represents, according to Professor Berg, the per capita investment in Niger during the period under investigation and which was five times less than in Senegal and between three to four times less than in the Ivory Coast.[123] (As a comparison the private sector had in 1957 alone a turnover of 8,070 million francs CFA and an officially declared gain of 377 million.)[124] The uneven distribution over time of the funds granted and actually spent is interesting to note. In the case of FIDES, Niger had by 1952 spent some 555 million francs CFA, that is roughly half the amount originally granted for that period, or about 1.6 per cent of the money spent in French West Africa.[125] It was only after the final departure of Governor Toby in 1954 that Niger's share increased substantially, *and* that the money actually granted was spent. If Governor Toby was hardly a spendthrift, he presented a number of solid arguments to justify his position. Given the structure of the Nigerien economy, Toby reasoned, the country could only absorb a very limited amount of investments. For it was all very well to build airports, schools, hospitals, roads, etc., in short to provide Niger with an embryonic infrastructure, which was in fact the aim of the FIDES and the corresponding development plan. But the problem was whether Niger would be able to meet the maintenance costs, and to pay for the necessary staff.[126] A cursory glance at the budget of Niger after 1954 gives credit to Toby's viewpoint, since it shows that external funds represented approximately between 30 and 40 per cent of the expenditures, whereas the share of the *budget d'équipement* (or development budget) amounted to roughly 10 per cent and even less of the total volume of the budget.[127] Thus most of the external funds granted to Niger were simply used to meet the costs of maintenance and to support the already existing administrative and institutional framework. Given that Niger's share of the various development funds established after 1945 was much less than that of the other territories of the Federation (Upper Volta excluded), it would be interesting to try and evaluate how much money Niger actually paid *into* the

Federal budget, principally in customs duties. Here the startling conclusion seems to be that the latter sum exceeds the former.[128] But it would be unfair to stretch this point too far. We are on very thin ice here, among other reasons because this conclusion does not take into account the fact that a number of services were paid for directly from the Federal and metropolitan budgets. What can be safely concluded is that the official development plans between 1947 and 1957 contributed to widen the gap between the richer coastal territories and the inland territories such as Niger, and also the gap between the towns and the countryside.[129] The second plan (1952–7) tried to reduce this imbalance, but apparently with little success. Nevertheless, sums earmarked for rural development enabled the French in Niger to launch a vast programme of well sinking after 1952.[130]

Even if Governor Toby had spent more than he did, it is probable that Niger would still have been unable to absorb a more significant portion of the public funds granted up to 1951–2. There were simply no firms which could undertake the necessary work, first because the contracts offered by the authorities in Niamey were not important enough, and second, because Niger, partially as a consequence of the very low wages offered, had an insufficient labour force.[131] But after 1951, when the administration established three *Centres de Formation Professionnelle accélérée* in Maradi, Zinder and Niamey,[132] and when it became apparent that the Nigeriens were less and less reluctant to be engaged as workers, the situation improved markedly.[133]

The emergence of new socio-economic groups

Since credits granted through FIDES and other funds were in the last analysis paid out to expatriate firms (thus representing an investment in the French metropolitan economy *also*), it followed that the number of Europeans resident in Niger increased considerably after the war. There were only 650 Europeans in Niger in 1946, but 1,487 in 1951 and an astonishing 3,040 in 1956.[134] Many of the new arrivals can be classified as adventurers and *petits blancs* occupying modest functions in the private sector, and much more prejudiced towards the Africans than the administrators or the army officers.[135]

The most significant consequence of the public works undertaken in Niger after the war was, however, the emergence of an urban proletariat which had very little in common with the *évolués*. Naturally, in a country where by 1955 the most important town (Niamey) counted some 15,000 inhabitants (which is, after all, double its population ten years earlier), the second town (Zinder) 13,000 and the third (Maradi) 10,000,[136] this new social class was not very important from a numerical point of view (probably less than one per cent of the total population of Niger). But it was to play a significant although short-lived role in politics in Niger, thanks to two remarkable trade unionists and politicians, Djibo Bakary and Mamani Abdoulaye.

On the surface, Djibo Bakary seems an improbable trade-union leader. He

171

was after all a Ponty graduate, and as such an *évolué*. But unlike his fellow graduates from the Ponty, who by now were so well off that they could organize parties in the finest colonial style, complete with dinner-jackets and evening gowns,[137] Djibo's attitude towards the new emerging working class was not a condescending one. Instead he resigned his position as a teacher (or was sacked according to another version of the story) to become a gardener, while devoting most of his time to the plight of the workers in Niamey.[138] One of Djibo's first actions was to create an efficient *Société Coopérative ouvrière de consommation*, which nearly all the workers in Niamey joined.[139] Djibo very early caught the eyes of the leaders of the main trade union in France, the communist-oriented *Confédération Générale du Travail* (CGT), which provided him with a seat on the *Conseil Economique et Social* in Paris,[140] a sort of consultative assembly.

In Zinder, Mamani Abdoulaye, a modest employee of one of the trading firms, pursued activities similar to that of Djibo Bakary in Niamey, but with less success, at least initially. For in Zinder, the modern trade union movement found a tough rival in the neo-traditionalist *Association Professionnelle à caractère coutumier de Zinder*, which the Sultan controlled.[141]

Action in favour of the new urban proletariat, which had been completely neglected by Governor Toby and his administration, was much needed. Indeed, the first labour inspector, appointed in 1952, could only conclude that the wages paid in Niger were the lowest in French West Africa and completely out of pace with the cost of living.[142] (A 25 per cent pay increase in 1951[143] had made little, if any, difference.) But after the application of the overseas *Code du travail* in 1953, which granted the African trade unions the same rights as the trade unions in France, Djibo Bakary and Mamani Abdoulaye were able to organize in July–August of that year a number of successful strikes which resulted in important wage increases both in 1953 and in 1954.[144] (The salary of the lowest paid labourers represented in 1955–6 three times the salary of 1949.)[145] These strikes marked the rise to prominence of Djibo Bakary's trade union movement, the communist-affiliated *Union des Syndicats Confédéralistes du Niger* (USCN), which the vast majority of labourers and workers now joined.[146] The French were, however, able to thwart a timid but nevertheless revolutionary attempt to organize the rural masses, by interpreting the trade union laws in a very restrictive sense.[147]

Ecological problems
Some reservations about the somewhat optimistic picture of the economy of Niger between 1945 and 1959 presented so far have already been made, particularly concerning groundnut prices. Others need to be added here. The first concerns the sharp increase in the acreage reserved for groundnut cultivation in the Centre and especially the East, which doubled between 1951 and 1960.[148] This was achieved partially at the expense of the subsistence sector.[149] It led, for the first time in the history of the Centre and

especially the East, to a shortage of land; a shortage which provoked a chain reaction that was to have far-reaching consequences. The first to be hit were (one is tempted to say, as usual) the Fulani nomads, already adversely affected by the creation of a forestry service and the launching of a programme of forest protection which had the effect of reducing considerably the amount of available pastures.[150] The Fulani and their herds were now forced to move further and further eastwards and especially northwards; into the outer northern edges of the Sahel and even into the southern fringes of the desert. It could be argued that the Fulani were merely responding to the incentives given by the programme of well sinking launched by the French. However, this programme was destined to aid the impoverished Tuareg and not the Fulani, who were able partly to evict the former from the northern Sahel and the southern edge of the Sahara; and finally that precisely because of the existence of these wells it was no longer necessary to keep the cattle constantly on the move in search of water, it led to such a heavy and permanent concentration of sizeable herds in certain areas that it threatened the local and very delicate ecological balance.[151] (The full effects of these ominous trends were to be felt much later, during the drought of the 1970s.)

Both the Fulani and the Tuareg saw their economic position deteriorate as a consequence of the poor performance of cattle prices compared with those of millet.[152] In addition, the Tuareg – especially the *imajeghen* and the *ineslemen* of the Kel Dinnik – lost many of their (domestic) captives during these years as a direct result of 'anti-slavery' campaigns waged by Djibo Bakary and other (black) politicians.[153] However, this dismal picture does not apply to the *ighawellan* or *bugaje* of the south. These people, whose ties with the rest of the Tuareg 'community' had become more and more tenuous, and who were slowly being integrated into the Hausa world, had developed rather an original and certainly prosperous agro-pastoral economy.[154] Nor does this picture apply without qualifications to the semi-sedentarized Kel Gress.

The shortage of land in the south, including apparently the West, induced (as has been noted in the Introduction) many agriculturalists to move into regions hitherto considered unfit for cultivation on a permanent basis; that is regions situated for the most part north of the isohyet of 500 mm. Warnings about the dangers represented by this extension northwards of cultivated land and more generally about what was seen as an inconsiderate expansion of the cash-crop sector were relatively frequent in official reports during the 1950s, especially in those emanating from administrators posted in the Centre and the East.[155] But apart from a decree in 1954 establishing a northern limit of cultivation – a decree which it proved difficult in the extreme to enforce[156] – the 'technocrats' who took over after Toby and his bush-administrators of the old school in the early 1950s do not seem to have heeded these warnings. Instead they went out of their way, as we have seen, to encourage the peasants to grow groundnuts.

The incidence of inflation and taxes

The second reservation about the economy of Niger is that after about 1953–4 cost inflation and an appreciable tax yield to the colonial administration ate away local purchasing power. First there were customs duties and various other indirect taxes which represented in 1952–3 about 10 per cent of the price of a ton of decorticated groundnuts at the port of embarkation. (Transportation costs represented 21 per cent, profits, insurance etc. 22 per cent and the price actually paid to the producer 43 per cent, as opposed to 64 per cent in Senegal.)[157] More important, however, was direct taxation. Between 1946 and 1951 the scale of the poll-tax rates increased from 10–40 francs to 40–280 francs. As usual, the rates rose more quickly in Hausaland than in the West. The highest rates in the West and the East respectively were 35 and 40 francs in 1946, and 165 and 280 francs in 1951. (The cattle and small-stock taxes increased in the same proportions.)[158] To calculate the tax level after 1951 is slightly more complicated because of the introduction of a more sophisticated system of taxation, but, according to official estimates, the tax burden (excluding indirect taxes) rose quite sharply after 1951 (and after 1956 more quickly than the price of groundnuts).[159] The nation-wide average was 635 francs per head in 1954–5, higher than in any other territory of the Federation. The corresponding figures for the Ivory Coast were 545 francs, for French Sudan 461 francs, and for Upper Volta 353 francs.[160] A comparison with Northern Nigeria is unfortunately impossible. However, according to the *chef de subdivision* of Magaria his 'subjects' paid in 1953 five to six times more taxes than their kinsmen south of the border.[161] If we compare these figures with estimates for the Gross National Product per head during the 1956–60 period, we find that the ranking list is nearly the reverse of that for the tax burden, with Niger in seventh position.[162]

Although the figures advanced above are only fragmentary, there can be no doubt as to the long-term trend they represent, a trend that becomes even clearer if we widen our period of investigation and take into account studies covering the late 1950s and the 1960s.[163] On the one hand the price of groundnuts, after an initially sharp rise, stabilized in the 1950s and began to slide in the 1960s; tax rates on the other hand rose continuously, even after 1960, leaving the Hausa of the Centre and especially of the East with an exceptionally heavy tax burden, possibly by far the heaviest in French-speaking Africa. Given this situation, the agriculturalists of Hausaland had no choice but to cultivate and sell ever *increasing* quantities of groundnuts in order to maintain their standard of living. The effect of taxation on seasonal migration to the Gold Coast and the Ivory Coast from the West, a migration for which figures have been given earlier, is much more difficult to evaluate, but should not be overestimated. Seasonal migration had become a way of life for many Zerma or Songhay.

Niger's positive balance of trade throughout the 1950s (especially in 1955 when the value of exports represented *double* the value of exports)[164] could be taken as an indication of the levy imposed on the revenues of the

Nigeriens. However, matters are complicated by the fact that whereas prices on imported goods were higher in Niger than in Nigeria, exactly the reverse is true for the groundnut prices.[165] This implies, first, that it was in the interest of the Nigeriens to export 'legally' but to import 'illegally'; and secondly, that large quantities of groundnuts from Nigeria found their way into Niger. However, the figures presented by J. D. Collins make it clear that the cross-border groundnut flow was by no means one way, and that it was only during the 1955–6 and 1957–8 buying seasons that appreciable quantities of groundnuts from Nigeria were sold in Niger, an estimated 10,000 tons in 1955–6, the peak year,[166] i,e. only slightly more than 10 per cent of the total volume purchased that season. Finally, any evaluation of the figures concerning Niger's external trade must take into account the fact that cattle continued to be exported illegally.

The problem of structural underdevelopment

Thus the authorities in charge in Niger, both before and after independence, pursued a policy which resulted in making the Nigerien economy dependent upon a single primary commodity. To be fair, attempts *were* made to try and diversify the economy, for instance, the introduction of cotton in 1956 in the Centre proved quite successful.[167] Furthermore, Governor Ramadier had a second look at the by now notorious naturally irrigated basins of the Niger river valley. But once it was realized that the development scheme devised in the 1930s had come to nothing, not just because of official neglect but also because the peasants of the West simply had no experience of irrigated cultivation, whatever plans existed were apparently abandoned.[168] Another attempt, profitable and successful to a degree, was to encourage the exportation of goat-skins from the Maradi region to Europe, where they were able to compete with the better-known goat-skin variety from Sokoto.[169] It was followed by a general expansion in the exportation of hides and skins.[170] Finally, some of the credit for the establishment of Niger's second (small) groundnut oil mill (at Matameye in 1954) must go to the administration.[171] However, all this amounted to very little in the long run, and neither cotton nor skins nor hides were of much importance compared with groundnuts. Above all, the administration seems to have neglected the subsistence sector completely.

Why then this emphasis on groundnuts and especially why the heavy tax burden? The answer, in my opinion, is to be found in the fact that the process of decolonization had been set in motion by the early 1950s. The French were (by virtue, one could argue, of the myth of the 'White man's burden') under a moral obligation to provide Niger with what I would call the prerequisites of a modern state, a state machinery according to the European model. This meant equipping Niger with a (modest) infrastructure of institutions and services; a parliament, a government, a civil service etc. It also entailed the building of roads, airports, hospitals, schools and the like. We have in short a policy of 'modernization' designed to implement as fully

175

as possible the principles implicit in the FIDES programme. This required funding, and since the funds granted by the FIDES proved inadequate, the immediate source of new revenue was perceived to be the expansion of groundnut exports. The caution advocated by Governor Toby having thus been brushed aside, the end result is neatly illustrated by the budgets between 1958 and 1961. External funds represented one-third of revenue in 1958, a huge 57 per cent in 1959 and slightly less than 50 per cent in 1961. The rest originated for the most part, directly or indirectly, from the commercialization of groundnuts at (and the point is worth repeating) prices subsidized by the French. Geographically one *subdivision* (*cercle* after 1956), that of Magaria, provided close to 50 per cent of the revenue not originating from external funds. As far as expenditure is concerned the *budget de fonctionnement*, designed to cover operating and maintenance costs, continued to absorb some 90 per cent of the total volume of the budget.[172]

We may now conclude that the administration after 1954, in sharp contrast to the administration under Governor Toby, was not particularly concerned with laying the foundations of a balanced although modest economy. It was a spendthrift administration which sacrificed the future for the present and the basic for the spectacular; an administration which thus contributed to accentuate the fragility and disequilibrium of the Nigerien economy, and so to accelerate the process of structural underdevelopment. Furthermore, as the study of the budget indicates, the very burden of a modern state machinery, however modest, became so heavy that it seemed to rule out any possibilities of real economic development. The price of modernization and independence, on the terms dictated by the French *and* the *évolués*, was so high that the average Nigerien could barely afford it, if at all. If we consider the politicians and the *évolués* as a corporate group, the least we can say is that, after the transfer of the reins of power between 1957 and 1960, they did not try to reverse the policy inaugurated by the French. Indeed, it was in their interest to maintain this policy since it guaranteed their standard of living. This they certainly did. For instance between 1958 and 1961 the civil service multiplied rapidly and salaries rose steeply both in absolute and relative terms.[173] As J. Delpy has remarked, the budget became 'exclusivement un instrument de distribution de pouvoir d'achat'.[174]

Some considerations regarding the state of the educational service may serve as an additional illustration of some of the points made above. There were some 1,629 pupils in the schools of Niger in 1942, 3,355 in 1946, 7,703 nine years later[175] and 28,020 in 1961,[176] apparently a most spectacular progress. But if we compare this with the population – close to three million in 1961 according to official estimates[177] – we arrive at a ridiculously low percentage, possibly the lowest in French Africa.[178] Even more distressing is the fact that in the mid-1950s many school-leavers were already unable to find work.[179]

The fact that the final stage of the process of decolonization took place during a period of very favourable climatic conditions locally (in sharp contrast with the period of colonial conquest at the turn of the century), and also a period of rapid economic growth in the world at large, probably had the effect of concealing some of the potentially damaging effects of the economic policy summarized above. No one asked in 1960 what would happen if, or rather when, drought struck again (as it did after 1968, and especially between 1972–4[180] in conformity with J. Tilho's prediction in 1928);[181] if the French should decide one day to discontinue the programme of subsidizing groundnut prices (as they did in 1967);[182] if the price of groundnut oil on the world market should drop drastically (as it did in the 1970s); and if Ghana should decide to close its borders to seasonal labourers (as it did under the Busia administration). All these factors came together during the early 1970s. The result was a disaster of some magnitude known as the Great West African Drought and Famine of 1972–4. (Naturally, in 1972–4 as in 1913–15 and in 1931–2, 'there was an incredible lack of a sense of urgency to start with', personal tax was not suspended, and tax collection remained much better organized than relief.)[183]

Concluding remarks

If in 1980 the future of Niger looks reasonably bright, it is because of revenues from a new and unexpected source; a source that has quadrupled in value since the steep rise in oil prices after 1973. I am referring to the uranium mine at Arlit in Aïr from which in 1978 the Government of Niger collected an estimated 12 billion francs CFA in royalties.[184] It remains to be seen, however, how far the consequences of the Harrisburg incident will affect the external trade of Niger. But the future of Niger lies in its subsoil, rich in minerals and probably also in oil.[185]

If the French had not imposed such heavy taxes, would there have been genuine economic development? This is hardly plausible, given the economic mentality, behaviour and attitude of the Hausa. It is no longer fashionable to argue that the 'attitudes and institutions [of the rural population] hinder the emergence of the necessary entrepreneurial behaviour required to take advantage of the new opportunities created by the expansion of the export sector'.[186] Nevertheless, works by C. Raynaut, G. Nicolas and others[187] make it clear that whatever money the Hausa earned from selling groundnuts was not invested in productive undertakings. Instead it mainly contributed to the ostentatious sector of the economy. This is hardly surprising considering the resilience (even in the economic sphere) of 'traditional' values, still predominant in the 1950s, within Hausa society. Hence the economic system continued to be based not on the principle of accumulation, but on the principle of permanent redistribution of wealth. But what would have happened to these 'traditional' values had the radical Sawaba party led by Djibo Bakary (see below) been in a position to continue its action after 1958–9?

The fact that it was precisely that ethnic group least 'contaminated' by 'modernity' that monopolized the cash-crop sector is a paradox which remains to be properly investigated.

POLITICS, 1953–60

The reorientation of French policy
With the appointment of Bernard Cornut-Gentille as Governor-General of French West Africa in 1951, and of Robert Buron as Minister of Overseas France in the Mendès-France Government in 1954; and with the final departure of Governor Toby from Niger in the same year, and his replacement by the socialist Governor Jean Ramadier in early 1955, the political situation changed radically, on the metropolitan, Federal and on the local level. These moves marked a reorientation of official French policy, equivalent in a sense to the one operated by the RDA in 1950–1. A period of appeasement was inaugurated. The French were now intent on dealing with so-called *interlocuteurs valables*, that is with politicians who could be regarded as genuine representatives of the African masses, as opposed to – in the mind of Buron – those politicians (such as Georges Condat and Zodi Ikhia in Niger) who owed their election to administrative interference.[188] This new French policy coincided in Niger with the period when the economic expansion began to make its impact felt, when economic considerations replaced politics as the major concern of the French administration. In this sense the departure of Toby in 1954 marked the end of a period in the history of Niger; the end also of a system and concept of colonial administration which had become obsolete. The various functions of the hitherto polyvalent *Commandant* were taken over one after the other by the various technical services, whose numerical as well as absolute importance increased every day, and whose local agents had a tendency to ignore the administrators.[189] In fact, even the old-time *Commandant*, who behaved as if he were the supreme chief of his *cercle*, had become obsolete. He was replaced progressively by a new brand of administrators, frequently married, and more interested in facts and figures than in local intrigues. To these men, the chiefs and the politicians of UNIS represented more or less relics of the past. It was inevitable that they should turn to the only group which possessed the necessary know-how, the necessary 'tools' to grapple with the intricate problems of economic development and of running a modern administration: the *évolués*.[190] But the problem was that the politicians of the PPN/RDA now looked more like a privileged caste than like the authentic representatives of the Nigerien masses. Besides, their influence was negligible east of Dogondoutchi. In this situation Governor Ramadier tried to operate a general political reorientation and realignment which favoured in the last analysis a new political party which had sprung out of the nascent trade union movement and which cannot be satisfactorily categorized as either 'modern' or 'traditionalist'. In the process the French disentangled

themselves from the 'indigenous chieftaincy model'. By doing so, they lost some of that permanent and intimate contact with the local society which had characterized the administration under Toby. Then, and only then, could the process of *mental* decolonization be set in motion.

The loi-cadre and other reforms

The period after 1953 was also one of important changes or reforms on the institutional level. Since the reforms of 1946 had granted the Africans seats in the parliamentary assemblies in Paris, it was logical that this second round of reforms should concern itself primarily with local institutions. The first of the reforms, adopted by Parliament in 1955,[191] created twenty-six *communes de plein exercise* in French West Africa, but only one in Niger: Niamey. (Niamey and Zinder had become *communes de moyen exercise* in 1954, that is *communes* with a partly elected, partly appointed municipal council presided over by a mayor-administrator.) The second and by far the most important reform was the famous *loi-cadre* of 1956, presented by Gaston Defferre, the Minister of Overseas France in the predominantly Socialist government of Guy Mollet. (Paul Ramadier, father of Governor Jean Ramadier, was Minister of Finance.) In substance, the *loi-cadre* accelerated the process of devolution by granting internal autonomy to the territories of French West Africa. An executive or government was established in each territory in May 1957, headed in theory by the Governor in his capacity as *Président du Conseil des Ministres*, but in fact by the African chief minister who was *Vice-Président*. If each territorial government in theory held power by delegation of the local Governor, it was in reality responsible to the Territorial Assembly. Nevertheless, the Governor 'could refer to the French government for annulment within three months both decisions of the Assembly he believed exceeded the law and decisions of the Council of Government he believed illegal, exceeded the law, endangered security, national defence, public order or public liberties'.[192] The technical and administrative services were split into two, the French state services responsible to and financed by the French government (and controlled locally by the Governor), and the territorial services responsible to and financed by the territorial governments.[193] Though the French retained considerable power, and in particular the power of control, even after May 1957, and only the Parliament in Paris could vote laws, it remains, nevertheless, that after May 1957 the French were for the first time effectively sharing power in Niger itself with a Nigerien executive elected by the Territorial Assembly, in turn elected by the people of Niger – *all* the people, since the *loi-cadre* introduced universal suffrage and abolished the two-college system.

Party politics and elections

The rupture between the RDA and the PCF in 1950–1, the new French policy perceptible from 1951 onwards and especially evident both locally and Federation-wide after 1954, the institutional reforms of 1955 and 1956, together with the economic expansion after 1952 and its consequences, profoundly affected both party politics and politics more generally in Niger during the 1950s. The overwhelming victories of UNIS in 1951 and 1952 were a prelude to the decline of the party. The French were after all not prepared to exchange one dominant party for another. And they also feared that the chiefs might take undue advantage of these victories, of their now (apparently) all-powerful position, to indulge in malpractices. In short, after having contributed considerably to strengthen the position of the chiefs, and having eliminated the PPN/RDA, the French wondered whether they had gone too far, and whether it was time to reverse the trend. Now that the position of the chiefs had recovered from the very low ebb of 1946–7, it was perhaps time to make them understand that winning at the polls was not enough; positive action was now required of them and they had to justify the electoral successes by letting local intrigues lie and instead taking the lead in Africa's evolutionary process. And finally, since the PPN/RDA now looked increasingly like a 'respectable' party, it could provide – so the French reasoned – UNIS and the country with a constructive, useful and even necessary opposition.[194] Thus Governor Toby appointed two PPN/RDA politicians as members of the six-man strong municipal commission of Niamey which, together with Zinder, became a *commune mixte* in 1954.[195] Hamani Diori, the former deputy, was appointed headmaster of the most important primary school of the capital, where he could devote his spare time to reorganizing the PPN. Finally, most of the party's members who had been transferred to other territories in 1948 were now allowed to return home.[196] Another manifestation of the same spirit was to appoint the elected representatives of each *cercle* to the local *Conseils des Notables*. Simultaneously, the role of these councils, which had hitherto been to ratify administrative decisions, was changed. Henceforth they looked more and more like deliberative local assemblies, with important decisions to take, concerning in particular the redistribution of the *taxe du cercle* (local tax) instituted in 1951. There was a conscious attempt at decentralization, particularly marked after 1955 when six *subdivisions* were erected in *cercles* and each *cercle* granted financial autonomy.[197]

The reconciliatory mood of the French after 1952 encouraged some of the UNIS politicians, led by Georges Condat, to try and effect a rapprochement with the PPN/RDA.[198] Other party leaders, Zodi Ikhia and Dr Borrey, wanted UNIS to become the local section of the new inter-territorial party in the making, the *Indépendants d'Outre-Mer* (IOM), hitherto simply a parliamentary group. But due to opposition from Condat and especially from the Secretary-General of the party, Adamou Mayaki, no official Nigerien delegation was sent to the constituent congress held in Bobo-Dioulasso in February 1953.[199] This internal division led to two successive party splits. First, Condat and his supporters left to form the *Union Progressiste Nigérienne* (UPN).[200] Then in December 1955 the majority of party members deserted the UNIS and established the *Bloc Nigérien d'Action*

(BNA), leaving Zodi Ikhia (and Dr Borrey) with little more than a rump UNIS, which eventually became the Nigerien section of the IOM.[201] The refusal of the majority within UNIS to join the IOM was motivated by the same fear which haunted a number of PPN members in 1946, namely that an inter-territorial party was bound to pay only scant attention to the specific problems of peripheral Niger. This has been called the Nigerien particularism, characterized by a certain distrust of the other territories, and also of the non-Nigerien members of the party, such as Dr Borrey.[202]

But the main event on the political front in 1954 (apart from the final departure of Toby) was the foundation of the *Union Démocratique Nigérienne* (UDN), led by Djibo Bakary and Mamani Abdoulaye. The UDN constituted in a sense the political wing of the trade union movement. But the leaders of the party considered themselves above all as the heirs of the RDA, the genuine RDA, the combative RDA of the 1940s, not the sedate and respectable version of the post-1951 era.[203] As such, the UDN was anathema to the French administration. Had the clock been turned back again? It looked that way. For Governor Toby deemed it necessary to warn his administrators against the menace represented by this new ally of the communists.[204] And the *Commandant* of Tahoua wrote that 'Djibo Bakary doit être tenu pour un agitateur fanatique, habile et dangereux. L'implantation de son parti doit être combattue ... discrètement ... mais avec la plus grande détermination.'[205] But Djibo Bakary had learned his lesson well, and had drawn the necessary conclusions from the failure of the PPN/RDA in the late 1940s. To begin with, many prominent party leaders, especially the members of the local sections, were petty employees, *dyulas*, clerics, workers, craftsmen, etc., and as such much more difficult for the administration to tackle than the functionaries of the PPN/RDA.[206] Compared with the PPN/RDA, UDN was also much more decentralized, in the sense that local sections enjoyed a considerable degree of autonomy. It also made serious efforts to build up genuine mass support, *and* to encourage mass participation within the party. A French observer could write as early as December 1955 that the UDN was by far the most dynamic and the most methodical of the political parties in Niger; in fact the only structured and organized party. He added that UDN seemed to be gaining recruits in the countryside at an alarming pace.[207] This was, it seems, thanks to the numerous semi-urbanized members of the party, who maintained close contacts with their home villages. Through these channels Djibo's political message was conveyed to the rural masses, and conveyed in such a discreet way that the French did not even notice till election day.[208] The UDN also tried with considerable success to penetrate traditional movements, such as the *samariats* (or youth leagues), the *sanaas* (traditional guilds), and the women's (i.e. 'free women's') organizations.[209] Finally, Djibo was – thanks to his links with the international communist trade union movement – able to offer many of his petty-employee lieutenants fabulous trips abroad to such far off places as Sofia, Moscow and Peking.[210]

The rise of Djibo Bakary and the MSA

The first demonstration of the new party's strength was provided by the legislative election of January 1956. This election was also the first to be held after the adoption by the Parliament in Paris of a new electoral law, which had substantially increased the suffrage and so constituted a test to all parties concerned. It has also been claimed that it was the first election in French West Africa without administrative interference. This is only partially true in the case of Niger; although none of the party lists presented was actively supported by the French, they opposed vigorously the UDN ticket composed of Djibo Bakary and Mamani Abdoulaye.[211] Out of the 698,000 Nigeriens entitled to vote – a tremendous increase – some 305,985 effectively cast votes. A joint BNA/UPN ticket composed of Georges Condat, that chameleon of Nigerien politics (who, after having flirted with the PPN in 1953, had now allied himself with the BNA), and Issoufou Saidou came in first with 125,000 votes.[212] It was thus demonstrated that the traditionalists could manage without administrative support, and that the BNA was no longer, as a party member had complained earlier, 'la chose d'une tierce personne'.[213] However, the re-emerging PPN/RDA with 82,437 votes (52,000 in the West alone) had every reason to be satisfied with the result, especially since Hamani Diori recovered the seat in the National 'Assembly which he had lost to Zodi Ikhia five years earlier. But the big surprise was the UDN, which finished third with an astonishing 74,000 votes. Most astonishing of all, it was in the Centre and the East, the most tradition-bound regions of Niger, that the UDN realized its most impressive votes, more than 50 per cent in the *cercle* of Zinder, hitherto the private domain of the most prestigious of all the traditional chiefs of Niger, the *sarkin* Damagaram. The prospect of some of the very bastions of traditionalism in Niger going communist scared even the leftist administration of Governor Ramadier. As for the rump UNIS, which had presented Zodi Ikhia, and that eternal loser, Dr Borrey, it finished a dismal fourth with only 24,000 votes.

Faced with this threat from the UDN, the other parties – probably encouraged by Governor Ramadier (and his successor and fellow-socialist Paul Bordier) – were seriously considering a merger. The UPN of Condat was dissolved and its members joined the BNA, but negotiations between the BNA and the PPN/RDA broke down a few days before the first municipal elections to be held in Niger (on 18 November 1956). Instead the two parties presented separate lists in both Niamey and Zinder. In Niamey the PPN/RDA won thirteen seats, the UDN ten and the BNA four. But in Zinder the UDN emerged as the most important party with eleven seats, compared with nine for the BNA and four for the PPN/RDA, while a local list took the three remaining seats.[214] Then, on 19 November, the day after the election, the UDN and BNA leaders suddenly announced their intention to unite and to create a new party, the *Mouvement Socialiste Africain* (MSA), which duly materialized a few days later with Issoufou Saidou as President and Djibo Bakary as Secretary-General. It was specified that the new party would maintain close ties with the metropolitan SFIO. As the new party held the majority of the seats in the municipal council of Niamey, Djibo Bakary was elected mayor.[215]

This most spectacular reversal of alliances clearly calls for some explanation. On the surface, the merger looks absurd, and perhaps it was in the last analysis. To argue, however, as did the PPN/RDA politicians (and as did Chaffard in his book),[216] that it could only be explained in terms of administrative interference and pressure would seem too far-fetched. This is not to deny that Governor Ramadier played an important role, and that he hoped to convert as many Nigerien politicians as he could to socialism.[217] He seems indeed to have made offers both to the PPN/RDA and to the UDN. But although the RDA supported the socialist government of Guy Mollet, it was not in favour of any close ties with the SFIO, and remained affiliated to the UDSR, which was also represented in the Mollet government. Its Nigerien section seems nevertheless to have benefited from discreet but efficient administrative support.[218] ('Nul n'ignore au Niger comment . . . Ramadier a pu . . . redonner vie à l'agonisante section nigérienne du RDA', according to Djibo Bakary.)[219] As for Djibo, a firm believer in the necessity of establishing a federal executive, he had perhaps realized that he would remain relatively isolated on the federal level as long as he was the only prominent politician of French West Africa to maintain close ties with the PCF. Given moreover the policy of the UDN and the line of action the party had chosen, given the socio-economic conditions in Niger, and especially the hostility of the administration, not to mention the still powerful position of the chiefs in Hausaland in particular, Djibo could hope to attain a prominent position in Niger, but never a predominant one. But the ambitious Djibo, who was probably already thinking in federal terms, could not hope to make his impact felt on the federal scene if he did not control his own backyard. In short, he needed allies. So did the BNA, whose leaders were no longer in favour with the French and feared that they might be squeezed between the UDN and the PPN. But they still held the balance of power, and thus found themselves in a very profitable bargaining position. By joining the MSA, they could control Djibo from the inside and force him to moderate his policy, especially towards the traditional chiefs. Above all, they had made certain that they would not be left out in the cold when the first Nigerien executive was to be established. That being said, however, the MSA represented a fragile and unholy alliance between politicians with very different opinions. It did not make much difference in this respect that Issoufou Saidou, the *chef de file* of the traditionalists, was an old SFIO member.

The establishment of the Nigerien MSA was only the first step towards the creation of an inter-territorial socialist party, which materialized at the congress of Conakry in January 1957. Lamine Guèye was elected President, and Djibo Bakary Deputy Secretary-General of the Federal MSA.[220] But Djibo's position within the party was stronger than this appointment seems to indicate, for he controlled the only local section which had any hope of winning the forth-coming and all-important territorial election.

Towards autonomy

The only surprise in the election of 31 March 1957 was the relatively strong showing of the PPN/RDA, which captured an unexpected nineteen seats in the new Territorial Assembly. But the MSA won handily enough with forty-one seats. The figures are given in the table,[221] which shows the totally dominant position of the MSA in Hausaland, the most populous but also the traditionally least politicized region of Niger; and the relatively good performance of the PPN/RDA in its traditional stronghold, the West. Another point which deserves attention is the strong showing of local independent candidates in Kanuriland and in the North, in other words the Nigerien periphery; and the very low electoral participation in the North. That nomads are not very assiduous voters is well enough known, but this low participation can also be explained in terms of Tuareg hostility towards both territory-wide and all-black parties.[222] The Tuareg eyed the *loi-cadre* and the future government of Niger with suspicion.[223] Instead they pinned their hopes on the newly established *Organisation Commune des Régions Sahariennes* (OCRS) and the planned Department of the Sahara which was to exercise a vague and ill-defined authority over the whole of French Sahara.[224]

In conformity with the election result, Djibo Bakary was appointed *Vice-Président du Conseil des Ministres* or *de facto* Prime Minister. He formed an MSA government which assumed office on 21 May 1957.[225] It is interesting to note that of the eleven ministers, only four were natives of Niger. The others came from French Sudan, Senegal and Guinea; two were French.[226]

Results of the election of 31 March 1957 (in percentages)

	Electoral participation	MSA	PPN RDA	Others	
North[a]	13.0	46.7	21.8	21.8	38.8[b]
Far East	24.8	54.0	31.0	14.0	(but 57.9[b] in the *cercle* of N'Guigmi)
East	35.6	81.6	16.8	1.6[b]	
Centre[c]	22.9	83.4	10.7	5.9[b]	
West	26.0	37.3	60.5	2.2[d]	

a. Excluding the nomadic *subdivision* of Tahoua.
b. Local lists.
c. Including the nomadic *subdivision* of Tahoua.
d. *Convention Africaine* (ex-UNIS).

The referendum of 1958, the fall of Djibo Bakary, and independence

Djibo Bakary fell from power after only eighteen months, a victim of his own misjudgment, and more fundamentally, a victim of his own radical ideas which were out of tune with the socio-economic realities of Niger. The direct cause was his decision to opt for a 'no' vote in the referendum of September 1958. At stake in the referendum was the new French constitution (de Gaulle's constitution), enacting the Fifth Republic. In Africa, however, voting for or against this constitution also implied something else, namely whether the Africans accepted the elevation of their territories as self-governing but not independent republics, members of a French-style Commonwealth called *La Communauté*, or whether they preferred immediate independence. It was understood that a negative vote would be followed by quick and complete French retreat.

In the light of Djibo's federalist commitment,[227] and considering Niger's geopolitical position, his decision is difficult to comprehend. It meant going it alone, severing all ties with the rest of French West Africa (i.e. with the home territories of many of Djibo's lieutenants). Had he not recently been elected Secretary-General of the federation-wide *Parti du Regroupment Africain*, an enlarged MSA? More important, how would he be able to manage without the subsidies from Dakar? The official explanation is, first, that Djibo considered the French all-or-nothing attitude tantamount to blackmail and therefore an insult to the African dignity, and second that he wanted complete independence not in order to secede, but in order to negotiate with France on *equal* terms the entry into the *Communauté*.[228] This explanation is void of any sense of political reality and therefore highly implausible. It is more likely that Djibo's decision was taken in desperation, a last attempt to cling to a power that was fast eroding.[229] Djibo was at the head of a heteroclite and circumstantial coalition which was bound to disintegrate sooner or later, and which was already showing signs of severe strain. The near success of the attempt by Adamou Mayaki to persuade a number of prominent party members to secede and to establish a party of their own,[230] and the revocation or suspension by Djibo of a total of twenty chiefs, among them the *alfaize* and the *sarkin* Katsina of Maradi,[231] were two such signs. Djibo needed the full command of the whole state machinery and, therefore, independence, in order to eliminate first the PPN/RDA opposition and second the BNA wing within the Sawaba party, as the MSA was now known. ('Sawaba' is a *Hausa* word meaning 'freedom', and also – perhaps more significantly in the light of what has been said earlier about the mentality and attitude of the Hausa – 'quietness' or 'tranquillity'.)[232] Djibo found himself confronted by a formidable alliance composed of many former BNA members led by Issoufou Saidou, the PPN/RDA, the chiefs, many prominent non-Nigerien politicans (such as Félix Houphouët-Boigny of the Ivory Coast who provided the 'yes' side with funds)[233] *and* the French. There is no doubt that the French, and in particular the new Governor (now entitled High-Commissioner) Don Jean Colombani, campaigned vigorously in favour of 'yes'. De Gaulle was apparently willing to tolerate the secession of Sekou Touré's Guinea, but the secession of *two* territories would involve too heavy a loss of prestige. Besides, the French were perhaps not prepared to tolerate a left-wing Niger serving as a base for the Algerian rebels. On the other hand, there is little if any evidence to suggest that the French (with the exception of the military in Agades) indulged in malpractices or fraudulent transactions. There *is* however evidence to show that Djibo and his companions did.[234]

In the end, only 36 per cent of the voters cared to take part in the referendum – the lowest percentage in the whole of French West Africa – and 76 per cent of the votes cast were 'yes', 24 'no'.[235] It is tempting to argue that this result was in tune with the prevalent political configuration of Niger, and in particular that the percentage of the 'no' vote corresponded roughly to the electoral strength of the UDN wing within the Sawaba party.

The referendum was followed by a series of rather murky transactions which led to the resignation both of the Sawaba cabinet and of thirty-two members (a majority) of the Territorial Assembly; and to the convening of a general election.[236] Governor Colombani ordered – in writing – the administrators to observe a rigorous neutrality before and during the elections.[237] There is little doubt that this order went largely unheeded. Many a *Commandant de cercle* was eager for revenge. Nevertheless, although the country was in an excitable mood, no shot was fired, nobody was killed, no riots were reported and very little detectable fraud was denounced in this, the last election worthy of that name in the history of Niger. The expurgated Sawaba carried the *cercles* of Tessaoua and Zinder, winning a total of eleven seats. In Zinder the Sawaba, headed by Mamani Abdoulaye, defeated a list headed by no less a political figure than Hamani Diori. But in Maradi, Djibo – still mayor of Niamey – was beaten by his old foe Adamou Mayaki. The coalition composed of the PPN and of those politicians who had seceded from the Sawaba party won a total of forty-eight seats. The remaining seat was carried by an independent candidate in the *cercle* of N'Guigmi, where both national parties fared badly as usual.[238] In spite of his electoral defeat, Hamani Diori became Prime Minister of the autonomous Republic of Niger on 18 December.

The irony is that the PPN leaders carried out exactly the same policy that Djibo Bakary and his companions had intended (we presume) to pursue in case of a 'no' majority: they monopolized power for themselves. This happened in several stages. First, the elections in Tessaoua and Zinder were invalidated by the Assembly in the spring of 1959 and the vacant seats were simply given instead to the lists defeated in 1958. Then the Sawaba party was outlawed, and Djibo Bakary went into exile, from whence he returned only after the coup in 1974. The third stage was the full independence of Niger proclaimed on 3 August 1960. Independence came not as a result of local claims, but rather as a result of external events which left Hamani Diori with little choice but to follow the lead of the Federation of Mali and the Ivory

Coast. The French were only too happy to comply. With independence and with the PPN in command of all the key positions in the state machinery, Hamani Diori was able first to 'persuade' all the leading non-PPN politicians into joining the party, and second, after a suitable interval, to eliminate them from the scene.[239] Niger had fallen victim to the 'sub-imperialism' of the Zerma/Songhay and the nascent political awakening of the Hausa had been cut short. In a sense the Diori government pursued exactly the same policy as the French after 1922, that of trying to sterilize all political activity, to silence the voice of the average Nigerien.

The subsequent story of how the attempted military coup in 1963 failed; how the exiled Sawaba stalwarts tried and failed to incite the Nigerien masses to revolt against their new masters; how the PPN establishment was finally toppled by a successful military coup in 1974, has been told – at least partially – elsewhere.[240]

CONCLUSION

The 'revolution' of 1946 came as something imposed from outside and above, a sort of artificial earthquake, rather than as the slide of long loosened land.[241] It took the Nigeriens by surprise. This is not to say that they preferred the classic colonial system of earlier days; far from it. It suggests however that the process of decolonization as defined and imposed by the French may perhaps not have been perceived by the average Nigerien as very meaningful. Nigerien nationalism, to the extent that it existed at all, was imitative nationalism, and as such it affected only a small circle of initiated. There is in any case no trace of anything resembling a genuine nationalist mass movement in Niger. Indeed, the independence of Niger (and of many other African countries?) came not as a result of the struggle of its people, but as a result of a long series of external events: the Second World War, the war of Indochina, the independence of India, of Ghana, the Algerian rebellion, the return to power of de Gaulle, to name but a few. It was perhaps a consequence of the French determination not to risk a repetition of the war in Indochina or the Algerian rebellion. The word 'independence' itself is something of a misnomer, since what actually happened in 1960 was that the French exchanged a formal empire for an informal one. As for the men who took over the reins of government from 1957 onwards, one would like to know to what extent (if any) they commanded the respect and devotion of their fellow citizens, to what extent they articulated the grievances of the people of Niger? Were they perceived as the authentic leaders? These questions, however fundamental, must remain unanswered. But it should be pointed out that the inheritance they sought to assume was European rather than African. Above all, the *évolués* wanted to promote their own corporate interests. The *évolués*, none of whom had ever, to the best of my knowledge, been imprisoned for political motives, and who had never had to fight an uphill struggle in the face of heavy odds, were the chosen few, selected by the French to assume the role of *interlocuteurs valables*. As such they may be considered as the successors of the French whose policies they continued. It may even be argued that whatever legitimacy they could claim, they owed to the fact that they had been invested, so to speak, by the French.

After 1946 the administrative superstructure expanded enormously (although of course it remained microscopic compared with that of the industrial nations). In 1970 18,500 persons or nearly 55 per cent of all wage earners were employed in the public sector.[242] This phenomenon is, as we have seen, closely linked with the process of decolonization. It led to the rise of what I believe can be called a new and dominant social class, even in the Marxist sense of that expression; an urban bureaucracy.

Since the distinction between the political and administrative-bureaucratic sphere has been completely obliterated, all holders of so-called political offices must be included in this class. It is a class which ruthlessly exploits the rural masses it proclaims to serve; rural masses that are defenceless for the simple reason that the exploiters are legally and institutionally the elected representatives of these same masses. Perhaps the emergence of this (from the point of view of the Hausa, Kanuri and Tuareg) partly foreign, urban, exploitative, parasitic and all-powerful bureaucracy should be ranked as the second major structural change (the first being cash-crop farming) brought about by French rule.

Seen in retrospect, the period between 1946 and 1960 appears in many ways as a 'golden age' in the history of Niger. Rainfall was by and large adequate, the international economic situation was relatively favourable, and the Nigeriens enjoyed a degree of freedom and liberty which, although appallingly imperfect, was far from negligible. In these and other fields the 1946–60 period compares very favourably indeed with both the preceding and succeeding periods. It is to be hoped that the royalties from the uranium mines will soon invalidate this statement.

7

Conclusion

This book has presented a tentative reconstruction of the history of Niger between 1850 and 1960. I have in a sense aimed at writing what the French call *une histoire totale* (although I am painfully aware of the somewhat presumptuous connotations the expression carries). It is a complex and ambiguous story with no heroes and almost no villains. The approach has been descriptive and analytical as well as also sociological, rather than theoretical and ideological (or quantitative). Such an approach implies a low level of generalization, and does not therefore arrive at any grand conclusions. Nevertheless, it may be useful here to list some of the points made, and more generally to offer a chronological and thematic summary.

I have called the period between 1850 and 1908 'the revolutionary years', although the changes referred to trace their origins right back to 1591 in the case of the West and to 1804 in the case of Hausaland. During this period, a number of groups and societies experienced one brand or another (including the Tuareg brand) of foreign domination. Others, especially in Damagaram, experienced increasingly harsh rule. But still others, probably a majority, fought bravely against neighbouring expansionist powers and a host of alien adventurers and invaders, the last wave being the French.

With the exception of the North-East, the military conquest of Niger had been virtually completed – at least on paper – by 1908. However, the establishment of colonial rule may best be conceived of as a process rather than an event; a process whose final stage in Niger was the acquiescence of the people to French rule. It may be that this had already been achieved in the West by 1906 (and if so it was as a result of putting down the Zerma/Songhay revolts). But in the rest of Niger it took much longer, and occurred only after the trials of the 1908–22 period, which included the Great Famine of 1913–15, the recruitment drives, the Tuareg revolts, and more generally the repercussions of the war in Europe. They exhausted both the Africans and the French. The latter in particular failed to restructure society as they had intended. They failed to a considerable degree – though not totally. By crushing the Tuareg, by clipping the wings of the Hausa *sarauta* and by strengthening the position of the Zerma/Songhay aristocracy, the French had made allies in the West, while at the same time making certain that the Tuareg no longer represented a threat and that Hausa society no longer had any leadership capable of opposing the new masters of Niger. In fact, even before 1908 the demise of trans-Saharan trade had sapped the economic foundations of many of the Tuareg confederacies and of the most powerful of the Hausa polities, Damagaram.

By and large, however, the military failed. The civilian administrators who, in 1922, took over a colony in chaos were no more successful in the long run. They were short of means and had no clearly defined policy. Above all they found themselves prisoners of the static and therefore sterile nature of classic colonial rule. At times their actions, especially the attempt to secure a viable economic base for colonial rule, proved as detrimental to the Nigeriens as the actions of their military predecessors. However, cash-crop farming spread relatively rapidly among the Hausa and the *bugaje*, many of whom had long been accustomed to producing for a wider market. But the West became, much to the dismay of the French, a labour-exporting region. Here the pattern of the pre-colonial era survived to a degree, since many Zerma/Songhay wandered far in search of fortune and glory even in the nineteenth century.

If the French were unsuccessful in restructuring society, the same can be said of the Africans, as the *hauka* and Hamallist movements, which both failed in the end and which at no stage had a substantial following, bear witness.

The excesses of classic colonial rule under the Vichy government generated their own negation – the liberal and extremely complex system of 1946. This system was evolutionary and as such incompatible in the long run with the very nature of colonial rule. The paradox is that the French were the first to realize this. After 1946 the African voice could again be heard. However, it was channelled through institutions controlled by a group of people, the *évolués*, whose organic link with the Nigerien masses was far from evident. As a consequence, a harmonious evolution in accordance with the Nigeriens' own premises would seem to be out of the question. Structurally speaking, such an evolution was impossible, considering the cultural-conceptual gap separating the French and the *évolués* from the Nigerien peasantry. Perhaps this is the main ambiguity, also the main misunderstanding, of the colonial system and the colonial period. The post-1946 era witnessed the emergence of a new socio-economic group, an exploitative urban bureaucracy, and thus the emergence of a new structural configuration.

If independence, in the form of the system of 1960, is considered by some as a sort of new synthesis, it nevertheless remains true that the new system was as riven as the old with internal contradictions. The men who came to power in 1960 did their best to silence the voice of the Nigerien peasantry, and in so doing they turned the clock back to the era of classic colonial rule. Furthermore, from economic, climatic and other related points of view, the 1946–60 period was one of relative prosperity and therefore also of optimism. This optimism had the unfortunate consequence of concealing the basic structural weaknesses of Niger, but the combined effects of locusts, drought, an incompetent administration, a world-wide economic crisis and ecological imbalance once again brought disaster.

The ambiguity and complexity of the colonial period has already been noted extensively. We must now consider the interrelation between the various ethnic groups of Niger. The first important point here is that the Tuareg, the former masters of many regions of Niger, never recovered from the marginal position which they had been reduced to by, at the very latest, 1922, and which was, if anything, more marginal after 1946. The evolution of Zerma/Songhay society proved paradoxical in the extreme. On the one hand, the action of the French strengthened the political power and the economic position of the local nobility, but at the price of a climate of permanent tension, which the reforms of 1946 did much to exacerbate. During the first decades of the colonial period the former slaves were turned into a landless rural proletariat. However, for just this reason the former slaves (but also many other Zerma/Songhay) became increasingly receptive to French ways, and were able, therefore, to exploit effectively the opportunities offered by the colonial administration. Thus the system of 1946, which favoured those who had assimilated the values and norms of the French, saw the rise to prominence of the Zerma/Songhay, while at the same time operating among the Zerma/Songhay a social reversal to the benefit of people originally of modest social conditions. These people came to constitute the majority of the new urban bureaucracy referred to above. It is highly significant, of course, that even the military leaders who took over in 1974 were in the main Zerma/Songhay.

The Hausa of Niger, who had defended their traditional values against the Torodbe-Fulani rulers of the Hausa heartland, continued to do the same against the French, although no longer through armed conflict. From the French point of view the Hausa proved to be not very amenable. However, in the end the Hausa were severely penalized for their 'aloofness'. There were in 1946 relatively few Hausa *évolués*, and therefore few Hausa who could take part in the competition for influence and power within the post-1946 system. Thus the Hausa, although they contributed very substantially to the public purse, and although they constitute by far the most numerous ethnic group in Niger, came (together with the Fulani, the Tuareg, the Kanuri and others) to be dominated politically by the Zerma/Songhay.

A further theme is the changing nature and impact of colonial rule, together with the interaction between the French and the Nigeriens. After an initial phase of aloofness, from 1908 onwards the French tried to establish a sort of direct rule, part of their general increase of activity. However, the difficulties of the 1910s forced the French increasingly to rely on the chiefs. Although in general terms the 1922–45 period witnessed a *retour en grâce* of the *chefferie*, it seems safe to argue that the French made extensive use of the chiefs in times of crisis and whenever they were faced with a difficult situation (witness the Vichy years) and less so in times of prosperity. But since 1922 the Nigeriens seem to have acquiesced to colonial rule (by virtue of the concepts of 'force', 'luck' and *baraka*), and French administrators after that date became increasingly incorporated into the local social landscape and progressively assumed a stature in many ways comparable to that of the indigenous chiefs. The 'indigenous chieftaincy-model', as we have called it, flourished during the inter-war years, reaching its most complete form after 1945 under the governorship of Jean Toby. The irony is that by then the reforms of 1946 and especially the new emphasis on economic development had rendered this type of administration obsolete. After about 1952 the old-time administrators were progressively replaced by a new type of administrator, more interested in development planning and other such technical matters than in local intrigues. Since, moreover, many of these administrators were married, the relationship between the French and the indigenes became less and less intimate and informal and more and more impersonal and bureaucratic.

It can hardly be argued that the 'new' administrators were more successful than their predecessors of the Toby school. By 1960 the French had resolved none of the basic problems of Niger, while in fact creating new ones. Seen from this perspective, the global impact of sixty years of colonial rule was slight, and figures concerning the process of modernization confirm this.

Finally we must assess the scope of religious, social and economic change. Several such changes have been noted: the end of trans-Saharan trade, the freeing of the slaves, the adoption of the Zerma/Songhay (but not by the Hausa) of European concepts of land tenure, the growing importance of cash-crop farming and the spread of a new type of hoe in Hausaland (but not in the West); the migration of the Fulani nomads northward and later eastward; the conversion of the West into a labour-exporting region; the slow rise of Islam (and the corresponding and even slower de-sacralization of society); the internal migration and the corresponding changes in settlement patterns; the rise of an urban bureaucracy; the emergence during the very last years of the colonial period of a form of structural underdevelopment. But the basic question remains: to what extent are we confronted with structural changes? Even more fundamental: did colonial rule first dismantle and then restructure society? I cannot give a firm answer to these questions, although I feel that few of the changes mentioned above ought to be classified as structural. This is not only because the evidence is patchy, but also because Niger is a far less clear-cut case than, for instance, Zimbabwe or South Africa, or for that matter America during the first centuries of Spanish rule, the most clear-cut example for the historian of colonialism. The European conquest of the Central Sudan did not put an end to one particular evolutionary trend, did not destroy (as in America[1]) one particular type of local society, nor can the period of colonial rule be seen or understood in isolation from the preceding and succeeding periods. It constituted a moment in history, an important moment, a *temps fort* as the French would say, but one whose impact and uniqueness it is all too easy to exaggerate.

Notes and abbreviations

The following abbreviations are used in the notes and bibliography.

14 MI	Microfilms of the Archives du Gouvernement Général de l'AOF in the Archives Nationales. Dépôt des Archives d'Outre-Mer, Aix-en-Provence. (Originals in the Archives Nationales du Sénégal, Dakar.)
AA	*African Affairs*
AEH/AEHR	*African Economic History/Review*]
Afr.fr.	*(Bulletin du Comité de l') Afrique Française*
Aix	Archives du Gouvernement Général de l'Afrique Equatoriale Française in the Archives Nationales. Dépôt des Archives d'Outre-Mer, Aix-en-Provence
ALS	*African Language Studies*
ANN	Archives Nationales du Niger
AOF	Afrique Occidentale Française
AP	Archives of the Préfecture of . . .
APA	(Bureau des) Affaires Politiques et Administratives
APSR	*American Political Science Review*
ASP	Archives of the Sous-Préfecture of . . .
Ass.French Union	Debates in the Assembly of the French Union, reproduced in the *Journal Officiel de la Rép. Française. Débats parlementaires* (Assemblée de l'Union Française)
BCEAO	Banque Centrale des Etats de l'Afrique de l'Ouest
BCEHSAOF	*Bulletin du Comité d'études historiques et scientifiques de l'Afrique Occidentale Française* (continued as BIFAN)
BIFAN	*Bulletin de l'Institut Française/Fondamental de l'Afrique noire* (continuation of BCEHSAOF)
BNA	Bloc Nigérien d'Action
BSOAS	*Bulletin of the School of Oriental and African Studies*
C. de . . .	Cercle de . . .
CEA	*Cahiers d'Etudes Africaines*
CGD	Commissariat Général du Développement, Centre de Documentation (Niamey)
CHEAM	Centre des Hautes Etudes Administratives sur l'Afrique et l'Asie Musulmanes (Paris)
CIS	*Cahiers Internationaux de Sociologie*
CJAS	*Canadian Journal of African Studies*

Abbreviations

CN	Colonie du Niger
CNRS	Centre National de la Recherche Scientifique (France)
CNRSH	Centre Nigérien de Recherches en Sciences Humaines (presently IRSH, Institut de Recherches en Sciences Humaines)
CO	Colonial Office
COM	*Cahiers d'Outre-Mer*
Dakar	Archives du Gouvernement Général de l'AOF, nouvelles séries, in the Archives Nationales du Sénégal, Dakar
EPS	Ecole Primarie Supérieure
FIDES	Fonds d'Investissement pour le Développement Economique et Social
FO	Foreign Office
Gov. Gal.	Gouvernement Général/Gouverneur Général
GJ	*The Geographical Journal*
HA	*History in Africa*
IJAHS	*International Journal of African Historical Studies*
INSEE	Institut National de la Statistique et des Etudes Economiques
IOM	Indépendants d'Outre-Mer
JA	See *JSA*
JAH	*Journal of African History*
JAS	*Journal of African Studies*
JHSN	*Journal of the Historical Society of Nigeria*
JMAS	*Journal of Modern African Studies*
JO	*Journal Officiel*
JSA (later *JA*)	*Journal de la Société des Africanistes/Journal des Africanistes*
MSA	Mouvement Socialiste Africain
NA	*Notes Africaines*
Nat.Assembly	Debates in the French National Assembly, reproduced in the *Journal Officiel de la République Française. Débats parlementaires* (Assemblée Nationale)
NDV	*Notes et Documents Voltaïques*
ORSTOM	Office de la Recherche Scientifique et Technique d'Outre-Mer
PCF	Parti Communiste Français
Ponty	Ecole Normale William-Ponty
PPN	Parti Progressiste Nigérien
PRO	Public Record Office
R/Rapp.pol./ann. /d'ens./trim.	Rapport politique/annuel/d'ensemble/trimestriel
RA	*Revue Africaine*
RCD	*Renseignements Coloniaux et Documents* (supplement to *Afr.fr.*)
RDA	Rassemblement Démocratique Africain
RF	République Française
RFHOM	*Révue Française d'Histoire d'Outre-Mer*
RH	Rhodes House, Oxford
RJPUF/RJPOM	*Révue Juridique et Politique de l'Union Française/de l'Outre-Mer*
ROMM	*Revue de l'Occident Musulman et de la Méditerranée*
RTC	*Revue des Troupes Coloniales*
SCOA	Société Commerciale de l'Ouest Africain
SD/SDC	Subdivision/Subdivision centrale
Senate	Debates in the French Senate (officially the Conseil de la République between 1947 and 1959), reproduced in the *Journal Officiel de la République Française. Débats parlementaires* (Conseil de la République)

194

SFIO	Section Française de l'Internationale Ouvrière
SIP	Société Indigène de Prévoyance
SM	*Synthèse Mensuelle*
SOM	Archives Nationales, Section Outre-Mer, Paris
SOM-AP	SOM–Archives privées
SOM-NS	SOM–Nouvelles séries
THSG	*Transactions of the Historical Society of the Gold Coast/Ghana*
TIRS	*Travaux de l'Institut de Recherches Sahariennes*
TM	Territoire Militaire
TN/T.du Niger	Territoire du Niger
TOM	Territoire(s) d'Outre-Mer
UDN	Union Démocratique Nigérienne
UDSR	Union Démocratique et Sociale de la Résistance
UNIS	Union Nigérienne des Indépendants et Sympathisants
UPN	Union Progressiste Nigérienne
Vincennes	Ministère des Armées. Etat-Major de l'Armée de Terre. Service Historique, Section Outre-Mer, Vincennes

Introduction

1 *Etude démographique du Niger*, vol. II (Ministère de la Coopération/INSEE, 1963), 5.

2 François Lancrenon, 'La République du Niger', *Notes et Etudes Documentaires* (La Documentation française), nos. 3994–5, 12 June 1973, p. 8; François Lancrenon & Pierre Donaint, *Le Niger* (1972), 57; *United Nations Statistical Yearbook for 1977* (vol. XXIX) gives the figure of 4,727,000 for the population of Niger.

3 Edmond Séré de Rivières, *Histoire du Niger* (1965), 232.

4 *Ibid.*, 237.

5 Heinrich Barth, *Travels and Discoveries in North and Central Africa*, vol. III (1965, originally published 1857–8), 171; C. K. Meek, 'The Niger and the classics: the history of a name', *JAH*, I, 1 (1960), 1–17; Lancrenon & Donaint (1972), 5.

6 For further details, see the following works (upon which this paragraph is based): Lancrenon & Donaint (1972), 6–44; Pierre Donaint, *Le Niger. Cours de géographie* (Niamey, Ministère de l'Education Nationale, 1965); R. J. Harrison-Church, *West Africa. A Study of the Environment and of Man's Use of it* (1969), 263–71; A. Seck & A. Mondjannagni, *L'Afrique occidentale* (1967); J. Cochémé & R. Franquin, *A Study of the Semiarid Areas South of the Sahara in West Africa* (Rome, FAO/UNESCO/WHO – Interagency project on agroclimatology, 1967); Alain Beauvilain, *Les Peul du Dallol Bosso* (Niamey, 1977).

7 Sharon Nicholson, 'The methodology of historical climate reconstruction and its application to Africa', *JAH*, XX, 1 (1979), 31–49.

8 Here I have borrowed from John Iliffe. See his *A Modern History of Tanganyika* (1979), 1. This outstanding work unfortunately appeared too late to serve as a model for my own. I have, however, taken the liberty of borrowing a number of formulations from Iliffe and a host of other scholars.

9 South Africa and East Africa have fared much better of course. In addition to Iliffe's book, mention should be made of the august multi-volume Oxford Histories of East and South Africa.

10 Elizabeth Isichei, 'The quest for social reform in the context of traditional religion: a neglected theme of West African history', *AA*, LXXVII, 309 (1978), 463–78.

11 Many of the documents in the local archives of Niger have been damaged and so are difficult to decipher. It is hoped that the newly established Service des Archives will be successful in

its efforts to rescue this material. For further details, see my 'Archival research in Niger – Some practical hints', *African Research & Documentation*, 16/17 (1978a), 26–7.

12 Three altogether for the colonial period proper. They are: Pierre Gentil, *Confins libyens, lac Tchad, fleuve Niger* (1948); Dugald Campbell, *On the Trail of the Veiled Tuareg* (1928); Angus Buchanan, *Out of the World. North of Nigeria* (1921).

13 The sources for early medieval European and especially northern European history are a case in point. In my view these sources reflect very imperfectly the degree of resilience of pre-Christian religious beliefs. I have tried to substantiate this point in an article called 'Earth-priests, "priest-chiefs" and sacred kings in Ancient Norway, Iceland and West Africa. A comparative essay', *Scandinavian Journal of History*, IV, 1 (1979), 47–74.

14 'The history of the masses has always posed problems for the historian; the masses, characteristically, do not write about themselves ... and those who observe 'hem as contemporaries necessarily do so from a perspective that is bound to conceal many of the realities of social life.' Sidney W. Mintz, 'History and anthropology: a brief reprise', in Stanley L. Engerman & Eugene D. Genovese (eds.), *Race and Slavery in the Western Hemisphere: Quantitative Studies* (Princeton, 1975), 477–94 (484).

15 The historian of the inland regions of colonial West Africa has fewer reliable and diverse sources than has for instance a colleague working on nineteenth-century coastal regions, who can draw upon material from many different quarters. On the African side there are the oral traditions, writings by 'westernized' Africans, and also – in some regions – a few Arabic manuscripts. On the European side there are consular and other official reports and despatches, together with the writings of a host of visiting traders, travellers, adventurers, and missionaries who often tried to record all they saw. (See, for instance, the impressive list of sources in Ivor Wilks, *Asante in the Nineteenth Century: The Structure and Evolution of a political order*, 1975.) In the case of Niger, on the other hand, the historian is forced to rely heavily, nearly exclusively in fact, on one type of source, the records of the colonial administration.

1. Peoples and societies of Niger: early history to 1850

1 This point has already been forcefully argued by Derrick J. Thom in his 'The Niger–Nigeria borderlands: a politico-geographical analysis of boundary influence upon the Hausa' (PhD thesis, Michigan State University, East Lansing, 1970), 85–121. For a very different viewpoint, see J. C. Anene, *The International Boundaries of Nigeria, 1885–1960* (1970), 285ff.

2 Yves Urvoy, 'Histoire des Oulliminden de l'est', *BCEHSAOF*, XVI, 1 (1933), 66–98.

3 See Jean Dresch, 'Notes de géographie humaine sur l'Aïr', *Annales de Géographie*, LXVIII, 367 (1959), 257–62. It is significant that Yveline Poncet has not even bothered to include Aïr in her *Cartes ethno-démographiques du Niger* (Niamey, 1973).

4 Based on Dresch (1959); Raymond Mauny, *Tableau géographique de l'Ouest Africain au Moyen Age d'après les sources écrites, la tradition et l'archéologie* (Dakar, 1961), 137–45; J. E. G. Sutton, 'Towards a less orthodox history of Hausaland', *JAH*, XX, 2 (1979), 179–201; and the many works of Suzanne Bernus and associates, especially her 'Recherches sur les centres urbains d'Agadèz et d'In Gall', *ROMM*, 11 (1972), 51–6. This section has also benefited from a lecture of hers delivered at the Institut de Recherches Méditerranéennes of Aix-en-Provence on 26 April 1980.

5 Could it be that they constituted in a sense the 'missing link' between the Songhay and the other Nilo-Saharan speakers much further east?

6 A. D. H. Bivar & P. L. Shinnie, 'Old Kanuri capitals', in J. D. Fage & R. Oliver (eds.), *Papers in African Prehistory* (1970), 289–302.

7 This paragraph is largely a summary of the relevant pages in F. Fuglestad, 'A reconsidera-

tion of Hausa history before the jihad', *JAH*, XIX, 3 (1978b), 319–39. See also H. J. Fisher, 'The Eastern Maghrib and the Central Sudan', in R. Oliver (ed.), *The Cambridge History of Africa*, vol. III (1977), 232–330; and by the same author, 'The Central Sahara and Sudan', in R. Gray (ed.), *The Cambridge History of Africa*, vol. IV (1975), 58–141; Abdullahi Smith, 'The early states of the Central Sudan', in J. F. Ade Ajayi & M. Crowder (eds.), *History of West Africa*, vol. I (second edn 1976), 152–95; J. O. Hunwick, 'Songhay, Bornu and Hausaland in the sixteenth century', *ibid.*, 264–301; Yves Urvoy, 'L'autorité du chef de famille, du chef de village et du prince chez les Hausa du Nord-Ouest', *BIFAN*, XXXIX, 1 (1977), 202–21 (written in 1934).

8 See his 'Territorial cults in the history of Central Africa', *JAH*, XIV, 4 (1973), 581–97.

9 For references, see Fuglestad (1978b), 320–3.

10 For references to, and a discussion of, the Bayajida legend, see W. K. R. Hallam, 'The Bayajida legend in Hausa folklore', *JAH*, VII, 1 (1966), 47–60; H. R. Palmer, *Sudanese Memories. Being Mainly Translations of a Number of Arabic Manuscripts relating to the Central and Western Sudan* (1928/1967), 133; R. S. Rattray, *Hausa Folklore, Customs and Proverbs* (1913), 2ff; Guy Nicolas, *Dynamique sociale et appréhension du monde au sein d'une société hausa* (1975), 62–4; Sutton (1979), 195–9.

11 Reproduced in Palmer (1928/1967), 97–131. According to M. Hiskett, the *Kano Chronicle* 'represents a very old oral tradition . . . which can be shown by external evidence to be remarkably truthful'. See his 'The historical background to the naturalization of Arabic loan-words in Hausa', *ALS*, VI (1965), 18–26 (18).

12 According to M. G. Smith, 'Barbushe exercised ritual jurisdiction and leadership in concert with other lineage heads.' See his 'The beginnings of Hausa society, A.D. 1000–1500', in J. Vansina, R. Mauny & L. V. Thomas (eds.), *The Historian in Tropical Africa* (1964a), 339–57 (342).

13 M. Hiskett, 'The Song of Bagauda: A Hausa king-list and homily in verse', part 2, *BSOAS*, XXVIII, 1 (1965), 112–35 (113–14).

14 Fuglestad (1978b), 327.

15 On the history of Arewa and the Mawri, see Marc-Henri Piault, *Histoire Mawri* (1970); Capt. Landeroin, 'Du Tchad au Niger. Notice historique', in Ministère des Colonies, *Documents scientifiques de la mission Tilho, 1906–1909*, vol. I (1911), 309–537 & 538–52.

16 *Ibid.*; H. D. Gunn, *Pagan Peoples of the Central Area of Northern Nigeria* (1956), 18, 24–6, 42–4, 62; C. K. Meek, *The Northern Tribes of Nigeria* (1925/1971), vol. I, 245–6, & vol. II, 18–30; *id.*, *Tribal Studies in Northern Nigeria*, vol. II (1931), 11 & 111; Henri Raulin, 'Un aspect historique des rapports de l'animisme et de l'Islam au Niger', *JSA*, XXXII, fasc. II (1962), 249–74; H. Leroux, 'Animisme et Islam dans la subdivision de Maradi', *BIFAN*, X (1948), 595–693; Guy Nicolas, 'Fondements magico-religieux du pouvoir politique au sein de la Principauté Hausa du Gobir', *JSA*, XXXIX, fasc. II (1969), 199–231.

17 In addition to the works cited in the preceding note, see Nicolas (1975), 55; Marc-Henri Piault, 'Captifs du pouvoir et pouvoir des captifs', in Claude Meillassoux (ed.), *L'Esclavage en Afrique précoloniale* (1975), 321–50.

18 I have relied upon the French translation by C. Defrémery and R. Sanguinetti, first published in 1854 and reprinted in 1968, pp. 436–45.

19 See in particular, Suzanne Bernus & Pierre Gouletquer, 'Du cuivre au sel. Recherches ethno-archéologiques sur la région d'Azelich (campagne 1973–1975)', *JSA*, XLVI (1976), 7–68.

20 Copper metallurgy at Azelik, Ibn Battuta's Takedda, has a very long history, dating in all likelihood from the first millennium B.C. See D. Calvocoressi & N. David, 'A new survey of radiocarbon and thermoluminescence dates from West Africa', *JAH*, XX, 1 (1979), 1–29. Another oasis further south, Marandet, was probably also an ancient centre of metallurgy. See Suzanne Bernus & Pierre Gouletquer, 'Azelik et l'Empire Songhay. (Etat de la question

de Takedda)', in *Fondation SCOA pour la recherche scientifique en Afrique noire. Troisième colloque international de Niamey, 30 nov.-6 déc. 1977*; Henri Lhote, 'Recherches sur Takedda, ville décrite par le voyageur arabe Ibn Battouta et située en Aïr', *BIFAN*, XXXIV, 3 (1972), 429–70 (esp. 488–55); R. Castro, 'Examen de creusets de Marandet (Niger)', *ibid.*, XXXVI, 4 (1974), 667–75.

21 René Bucaille, 'Une probable monnaie sahélienne de la période des grands empires', *NA*, 51 (1976), 74–7; H. T. Norris, *The Tuaregs. The Islamic Legacy and its Diffusion in the Sahel* (Warminster, 1975), 36.

22 *Ibid.*; Lhote (1972); P. L. P. Gouletquer & D. Kleinmann, 'Structure sociale et commerce du sel dans l'économie touarègue', *ROMM*, 21 (1976), 131–9.

23 In addition to works already cited, see Jean Devisse, 'Routes de commerce et échanges en Afrique Occidentale en relation avec la Méditerranée. Un essai sur le commerce africain médiéval du XIe au XVIe siècle', part II, *Revue d'Histoire Economique et Sociale*, L, 3 (1972), 357–97 (esp. 381–5).

24 On the Wangara communities in Songhaland, see Paul Lovejoy, 'The role of the Wangara in the economic transformation of the Central Sudan in the fifteenth and sixteenth centuries', *JAH*, XIX, 2 (1978a), 173–93.

25 Fuglestad (1978b), 328–36.

26 J. O. Hunwick, 'The dynastic chronologies of the Central Sudan in the sixteenth century: some reinterpretations', *Kano Studies* (new series), 1 (1973), 35–56 (esp. 42–3).

27 F. de F. Daniel, 'The regalia of Katsina, Northern Provinces, Nigeria', *JAS*, XXXI (1932), 80–3.

28 Fuglestad (1978b), 329–30. It should be noted that Hausaland was not the only region of the Central Sudan where traders originally of foreign extraction intervened directly in politics, even to the point of seizing power. For an interesting parallel, see Dierk Lange, 'Progrès de l'Islam et changement politique au Kãnem du XIe au XIIIe siècle: un essai d'interprétation', *JAH*, XIX, 4 (1978), 495–513.

29 Fuglestad (1978b), 327.

30 See for instance, Nicolas (1969); M. G. Smith, *Government in Zazzau* (1960); Polly Hill, *Rural Hausa. A Village and a setting* (1972), esp. 175–8.

31 This is not to say that slavery remained exclusively an urban phenomenon. However, it seems that urban, in fact 'state' slavery represented in many parts of the Sudan an institution rather different from that of rural slavery. Rural slaves were eventually incorporated into the core social units, but urban slaves, by virtue of the fact that they did not belong to any kindred and as such were theoretically at the mercy of their masters, proved useful to many a ruler. This was especially so for administrative-bureaucratic and military purposes. Needless to say, life for these 'state' slaves seems to have been precarious, in the sense that theirs was a high-risk, high-gain occupation. See Roberta Ann Dunbar, 'Slavery and the evolution of nineteenth-century Damagaram (Zinder, Niger)', in Suzanne Miers & Igor Kopytoff (eds.), *Slavery in Africa, Historical and Anthropological Perspectives* (Madison, 1977), 155–77; Piault (1975); J. P. Olivier de Sardan, 'Captifs ruraux et esclaves impériaux du Songhay', in Claude Meillassoux (ed.), *L'Esclavage en Afrique précoloniale* (1975), 99–134; H. J. & A. G. B. Fisher, *Slavery and Muslim Society in Africa. The Institution in Saharan and Sudanic Africa and the Trans-Saharan Trade* (New York, 1972), 154–70.

32 Louis Brenner, *The Shehus of Kukawa. A History of the Al-Kanemi Dynasty of Bornu* (1973), 23. The myth that the Songhay empire once controlled Hausaland has now been laid to rest by Humphrey J. Fisher. See his 'Leo Africanus and the Songhay conquest of Hausaland', *IJAHS*, XI, 1 (1978), 86–112. It is probable that Hausaland was earlier subjected to the Jukun empire. See C. K. Meek, *A Sudanese Kingdom. An Ethnographical Study of the Jukun-Speaking Peoples of Nigeria* (1931); Yves Person, 'Dauma et Danhome',

JAH, XV, 4 (1974), 547–61; H. R. Palmer, 'Notes on the Korôrofawa and Jukun', *JAS*, XI (1921), 401–15.

33 On the Fulani jihad and the history of the Sokoto Caliphate, see H. A. S. Johnston, *The Fulani Empire of Sokoto* (1967); Murray Last, *The Sokoto Caliphate* (1967); M. Hiskett, *The Sword of Truth. The Life and Times of the Shehu Usuman dan Fodio* (1973); J. P. Smaldone, *Warfare in the Sokoto Caliphate. Historical and Sociological Perspectives* (1977).

34 B. G. Martin, *Muslim Brotherhoods in Nineteenth-Century Africa* (1976), 15.

35 J. R. Willis, 'The Torodbe clerisy: a social view', *JAH*, XIX, 2 (1978), 195–212 (211).

36 Richard W. Hull, 'The development of administration in Katsina emirate, Northern Nigeria, 1887–1944' (PhD thesis, Columbia University, New York, 1968), 23–4.

37 Hiskett (1973), 22–3 and 63.

38 Last (1967), lxvii and 24; Séré de Rivières (1965), 168–70.

39 On the history of this region, see P. David, *Maradi. L'Ancien état et l'ancienne ville des origines aux inondations de 1945* (Paris/Niamey, 1964); Jean Périé, 'Histoire politique et administrative de la subdivision de Maradi', Maradi, 1938 (AP Maradi); G. Nicolas, H. Doumesche & M. dan Mouché, *Etude socio-économique de deux villages Hausa* (Paris/Niamey, 1968); Leroux (1948).

40 Alhaji Hassan & Mallam Shuaibu Na'ibi, *A Chronicle of Abuja* (Lagos, 1962).

41 Yves Urvoy, *Histoire des populations du Soudan Central (Colonie du Niger)* (1936), 281.

42 Nicolas (1975), 57.

43 *Ibid.*, 56–7; Nicolas (1969). The *sarkin* Kano-in-exile was less fortunate and soon faded into oblivion. See Derrick J. Thom, 'The city of Maradi: French influence upon a Hausa urban center', *Journal of Geography*, LXX, 8 (1971), 472–82 (474).

44 By Smaldone (1977), 56, and Johnston (1967), 130, respectively.

45 See Barth (1965), vol. I, 476; Smaldone (1977), 56–68; Hull (1968), 33–8; Johnston (1967), 130–50; R. A. Adeleye, *Power and Diplomacy in Northern Nigeria, 1804–1906. The Sokoto Caliphate and its Enemies* (1971), esp. 52–65.

46 On the history of Borno, see Brenner (1973); Yves Urvoy, *Histoire de l'Empire du Bornou* (1949); R. Cohen, *The Kanuri of Bornu* (New York, 1967).

47 On the Tubu, i.e. the Teda, the Daza and the Azza, see Jean Chapelle, *Nomades noirs du Sahara* (1957); Cathérine Baroin, *Les Marques de bétail chez les Daza et les Azza du Niger* (Niamey, 1977b).

48 Are the Budduma 'relics' of Sutton's 'aquatic civilization'? See J. E. G. Sutton, 'The aquatic civilization of Middle Africa', *JAH*, XV, 4 (1974), 527–46.

49 Term coined by P. E. Lovejoy & S. Baier, 'The desert-side economy of the Central Sudan', *IJAHS*, VIII, 4 (1975), 551–81.

50 B. G. Martin, 'Kanem, Bornu and the Fazzān: notes on the political history of a trade route', *JAH*, X, 1 (1969), 15–27; Urvoy (1949), 12.

51 P. E. Lovejoy, 'The Borno salt industry', *IJAHS*, XI, 4 (1978b), 629–68; Knut S. Vikør, 'The oasis of salt. The history of Kawar, a Saharan centre of salt production' (MA thesis, University of Bergen, 1979).

52 Nicholson (1979), 47. The drought was felt throughout the Sahel and the Sudan. See for instance, P. D. Curtin, *Economic Change in Precolonial Africa. Senegambia in the Era of the Slave Trade* (Madison, 1975), 110–11.

53 Lovejoy (1978b), 660–1; Brenner (1973), 24–5.

54 In fact this route also bypassed Borno, since its main southern terminus seems to have been Wadai, at least after the middle of the nineteenth century. See Dennis D. Cordell, 'Eastern Libya, Wadai and the Sanūsīya: a Tarīqa and a trade route', *JAH*, XVIII, 1 (1977), 1–36.

55 Captain Grandin, 'Notes sur l'industrie et le commerce du sel au Kawar et en Agram', *BIFAN*, XIII, 2 (1951), 488–533.

56 R. Cohen & L. Brenner, 'Bornu in the nineteenth century', in J. F. Ade Ajayi & M. Crowder (eds.), *History of West Africa*, vol. II (1974), 93–128.

57 General Daumas & A. de Chancel, *Le Grand Désert. Itinéraire d'une caravane du Sahara au pays des nègres, royaume de Haoussa* (1875), 229–33; Barth (1965), vol. III, 81 and 117; E. W. Bovill, *The Golden Trade of the Moors* (1961), 238–9.

58 Dunbar (1977), 158.

59 P Lovejoy & Baier (1975), 554.

60 Inspired by Jeremy Swift, 'Disaster and a Sahelian nomad economy', in D. Dalby & R. J. Harrison-Church (eds.), *Drought in Africa* (1973), 71–8.

61 Unless otherwise stated, the section on the Tuareg is based on Francis Rodd (Lord Rennell of Rodd), *People of the Veil* (1926); Bovill (1961); Johannes Nicolaisen, *Ecology and Culture of the Pastoral Tuareg* (Copenhagen, 1963); L. C. Briggs, *Tribes of the Sahara* (Cambridge, Mass., 1960). Although the Tuareg also call themselves Kel Tagelmoust or 'People of the Veil', this definition does not include the 'non-free' and the 'freed slaves'. On the veil, see Rodd (1926); J. H. Keenan, 'The Tuareg veil', *ROMM*, 17 (1974), 107–18; J. Nicolaisen, 'Slaegt og samfund hos Tuaregerne', in K. Birket-Smith (ed.), *Menneskets mangfoldighet* (Copenhagen, 1957), 110–25.

62 Note that the institution of *ar'holla* does not exist among the Kel Dinnik and that there are no *imghad* among the Kel Gress. See, E. Bernus, 'L'Evolution des relations de dépendance depuis la période pré-coloniale jusqu'à nos jours chez les Iullemmeden Kel Dinnik', *ROMM*, 21 (1976), 85–99 (88); Pierre Bonte, 'Esclavage et relations de dépendance chez les Touareg Kel Gress', in Claude Meillassoux (ed.), *L'Esclavage en Afrique précoloniale* (1975a), 49–76 (esp. 60).

63 See in addition to the works cited above, R. F. Murphy, 'Social structure of the Southeastern Tuareg' (paper presented at the Burg-Wartenstein symposium on pastoral nomadism, 15–26 July 1964, Wenner-Gren Foundation for Anthropological Research).

64 Paragraph based on Bernus (1976); Bonte (1975a); Stephen Baier & Paul Lovejoy, 'The Tuareg of the Central Sudan: gradations in servility at the desert edge (Niger and Nigeria)', in Suzanne Miers & Igor Kopytoff (eds.), *Slavery in Africa. Historical and Anthropological Perspectives* (Madison, 1977), 391–411; Edmond & Suzanne Bernus, 'L'Evolution de la condition servile chez les Touaregs sahéliens', in Claude Meillassoux (ed.), *L'Esclavage en Afrique précoloniale* (1975), 27–47; J. Clauzel, 'Les Hiérarchies sociales en pays Touareg', *TIRS*, XXI, 1 (1962), 120–75; H. Guillaume, 'Les Liens de dépendance à l'époque précoloniale chez les Touaregs de l'Immaneñ (Niger)', *ROMM*, 21 (1976), 111–29; P. Bonte, 'Structure de classe et structures sociales chez les Kel Gress', *ibid.*, 141–62; Edmond Bernus, 'Les Composantes géographiques et sociales des types d'élevage en milieu touareg', in T. Monod (ed.), *Pastoralism in Tropical Africa. Studies Presented and Discussed at the XIIth International African Seminar, Niamey, December 1972* (1975), 229–44 (esp. 234).

65 Baier & Lovejoy (1977), 396.

66 'Notice sur les tribus de l'Anastafidet des Kel Oui', MSS. Agades, 1939 (ANN).

67 Norris (1975), 35ff.

68 Edmond Bernus, 'Les Touareg du Sahel nigérien', *COM*, 73 (1966), 5–34 (esp. 17); Lieut. Prautois, 'Le pays d'In Gall, Tadress et Irazer', MSS. Agades, Oct. 1952 (ANN). On this region, including the oases west of Aïr, see also Edmond & Suzanne Bernus, *Du sel et des dattes. Introduction à l'étude de la communauté d'In Gall et de Tegidda-n-tesemt* (Niamey, 1972).

69 Perhaps as a result of the research project presently under way directed by Mrs Suzanne Bernus.

70 G. Féral, 'Monographie du cercle d'Agadez', Agades, 14 October 1955, ch. 4, pp. 4–5 (ANN).

71 Suzanne Bernus (ed. and commented upon by), *Henri Barth chez les Touaregs de l'Aïr. Extraits du Journal de Barth dans l'Aïr, juillet–decembre 1850* (Niamey, 1971), 178.

72 G. Féral, 'Monographie du cercle d'Agadez', ch. 4, p. 11.

73 Rodd (1926), 273–97; Johannes Nicolaisen, 'Essai sur la religion et la magie touaregues', *Folk.Dansk Etnografist Tidsskrift*, III (1961), 113–62; F. Foureau, *Documents scientifiques de la mission saharienne, mission Foureau-Lamy*, vol. II (1905), 852; Campbell (1928), 194, 254, 261. The fact that certain Tuareg clerics, such as Jibril bin 'Umar al-Aqdasi, who deeply influenced Usuman dan Fodio, have attained position of fame, is not in itself sufficient to invalidate this supposition. On Jibril, see Hiskett (1973), 8, 23, 40–1, 109, 126–7, 130–3.

74 S. Bernus (1972), 53.

75 Colonel Méchet, 'Rapport de tournée', Zinder, 15 September 1918 (14 MI 864).

76 Suzanne Bernus, 'Stratégie matrimoniale et conservation du pouvoir dans l'Aïr et chez les Iullemmeden', *ROMM*, 21 (1976), 101–10 (109).

77 G. Féral, 'Monographie du cercle d'Agadez', ch. 4, p. 9.

78 Based on S. Bernus (1976).

79 Unless otherwise stated, this section is based on Nicole Echard, *L'Expérience du passé: histoire de la société paysanne Hausa de l'Ader* (Niamey, 1975); *id.*, 'L'Habitat traditionnel dans l'Ader', *L'Homme*, VII, 3 (1967), 48–77; *id.*, 'Histoire et phénomènes religieux chez les Asna de l'Ader', in CNRS, *Systèmes de pensée en Afrique noire* (1975), 63–77; Pierre Bonte & Nicole Echard, 'Histoire et histoires: conception du passé chez les Hausa et les Twareg Kel Gress de l'Ader', *CEA*, XVI, 1–2 (1976), 237–96; Djibo Hamani, *Contribution à l'étude de l'histoire des états hausa: l'Ader précolonial (République du Niger)* (Niamey, 1975); Major Bétrix, 'Histoire résumée du cercle de Tahoua', 1908 (AP Tahoua).

80 On the history of the Kel Gress, see Lieutenant Renaud, 'Etude sur l'évolution des Kel Gress vers la sédentarisation', *BCEHSAOF*, V, 2 (1922), 252–62; Pierre Bonte, 'Production et échanges chez les Touareg Kel Gress du Niger' (thesis, Institut d'Ethnologie, Paris, 1971); and other works by the same author cited above and below.

81 On the history of the Kel Dinnik, see Urvoy (1933); F. Nicolas, *Tamesna: Les Ioullemmeden de l'est ou Touareg 'Kel Dinnik'* (1950); Agg-Alăwjelj Ghubăyd, *Histoire des Kel Denneg*, edited and published by Karl-G. Prasse (Copenhagen, 1975).

82 Norris (1975), 145; Bonte & Echard (1976), 281.

83 Among the works cited above, see especially Norris (1975), 145–9; Major Bétrix, 'Histoire résumée du cercle de Tahoua'.

84 On the history of Damergu see Yves Riou, 'Les Touaregs dans le cercle de Tanout', MSS. 1944 (ANN); J. Richardson, *Narrative of a Mission to Central Africa Performed in the years 1850–51 under the orders and at the Expense of Her Majesty's Government*, vol. II (1853), 162–78; Foureau (1905), 853–905; S. Baier, 'Trans-Saharan trade and the Sahel: Damergu, 1870–1930', *JAH*, XVIII, 1 (1977), 37–60.

85 Unless otherwise stated, the section on the West is based on the relevant chapters in Urvoy (1936); Séré de Rivières (1965); Jean Rouch, *Les Songhay* (1954), and by the same author, *Contribution à l'histoire des Songhay* (Dakar, 1953a).

86 Séré de Rivières (1965), 40–5; Poncet (1973).

87 On this paragraph, see in addition to the works cited above, Colonel Abadie, *La Colonie du Niger* (1927), esp. 111; Jean Rouch, 'Rites de pluie chez les Songhay', *BIFAN*, XV, 4 (1953b), 1654–89; Michal Tymowski, *Le Développement et la régression chez les peuples de la Boucle du Niger à l'époque précoloniale* (Warsaw, 1974), 14–15; J. O. Hunwick, 'Religion and state in the Songhay empire 1464–1591', in I. M. Lewis (ed.), *Islam in Tropical Africa* (1966), 296–317; Jean Rouch, 'Les Sorkawa, pêcheurs itinérants du Moyen Niger', *Africa*, XX, 1 (1950), 5–25; Henri Raulin, *Techniques et bases socio-économiques des sociétés rurales*

nigériennes (Paris/Niamey, n.d.). See also the interesting remarks in Lancrenon & Donaint (1972), 72.

88 The term 'free Songhay' as used by Rouch (1953a, 217) has been criticized by P. F. de Moraes Farias. See his 'Review article: Great States revisited', *JAH*, XV, 3 (1974), 479–88 (483). The term originated in fact with H. Barth (1965), vol. III, 524.

89 According to J. P. Olivier de Sardan, 'Personnalité et structures sociales (à propos des Songhay)', in G. Dieterlen (ed.), *La Notion de personne en Afrique Noire* (Colloques Internationaux du CNRS no. 544, 1973a), 421–45 (424). See also by the same author, 'Esclavage d'échange et captivité familiale chez les Songhay-Zerma', *JSA*, XLIII, fasc. I (1973b), 151–67.

90 See M. Perron, 'Le pays Dendi', *BCEHSAOF*, VII, 1 (1924), 51–83; Chief subdiv. of Gaya to *Commandant*-Dosso, Gaya, 15 September 1950 (ASP Gaya).

91 Chatelain, 'L'Exode des Djerma de l'Andiarou vers le Dallol Bosso, le Djigui et le Fakara', *BCEHSAOF*, IV, 2 (1921), 273–9.

92 Jean Périé & Michel Sellier, 'Histoire des populations du cercle de Dosso', *BIFAN*, XII, 4 (1950), 1015–74 (1026); Fatoumata-Agnès Diarra, *Les Femmes africaines en devenir. La femme zarma entre la tradition et la modernité* (1971), 35. *Koy*, as in *koy-ize* or *labukoy*, means noble or chief.

93 Mahamane Karimou, *Tradition orale et histoire. Les Mawri zarmaphones des origines à 1898* (Niamey, 1977), 3–10.

94 Séré de Rivières (1965), 95–6.

95 See J. P. Olivier de Sardan, *Les Voleurs d'hommes. Notes sur l'histoire des Kurtey* (Paris/Niamey, 1969a); *id.*, *Système des relations économiques et sociales chez les Wogo (Niger)* (1969b). See also Nicolas Leca, 'Monographie du cercle de Tillabery', 1941, 6; Edmond Séré de Rivières, 'Note sur le régime des terres et quelques coutumes dans le canton du Kourtey', Tillabery, 1 December 1943 (both ASP Tillabery).

96 Yves Person, 'Du Soudan nigérien à la côte atlantique', in Hubert Deschamps (ed.), *Histoire générale de l'Afrique noire, de Madagascar et des archipels*, vol. II (1971), 85–122 (91); J. P. Olivier de Sardan (ed. & trans.), *Quand nos pères étaient captifs. Récits paysans du Niger* (1976); R. Malfettes, 'Rapport de tournée de recensement, canton du Kourteye, 6.6 au 8.11.1953', 3–4 (ASP Tillabery).

97 Guillaume (1976), and by the same author, *Les Nomades interrompus. Introduction à l'étude du canton twareg de l'Imanan* (Niamey, 1974).

98 On the history of the Sudie I have relied upon Nicole Echard, 'Histoire du peuplement. Les traditions orales d'un village Sudye, Shat (Filingué, République du Niger)', *JSA*, XXXIX, fasc. I (1969), 57–77; Léopold Kaziendé, 'Une épisode de l'histoire de Filingué. Procès-Verbal d'une conservation avec Chékou Mayaki', MSS. Niamey, 1937 (consulted by courtesy of the author); and on several interviews with Adamou Mayaki.

99 According to Boubou Hama, *Contribution à la connaissance de l'histoire des Peuls* (Paris/Niamey, 1968), 326.

100 Barth (1965), vol. III, 172.

101 Séré de Rivières (1965), 94. See also Beauvilain (1977); Périé & Sellier (1950), 1037–41.

2. The revolutionary years, 1850–1908

1 Séré de Rivières (1965), 98–9; Cros, 'R. de tournée de recensement, canton de l'Anzourou', Tillabery, 20 July 1947 (ANN).

2 Olivier de Sardan (1969b), 25 & 43.

3 Yehoshua Rash, 'Un établissment colonial sans histoires. Les premières années françaises au Niger, 1897–1906' (thesis, Paris, 1972a), 104.

4 R. Malfettes, 'R. de tournée de recensement, canton du Kourteye, 6.6 au 8.11.1953', 3–4 (ASP Tillabery).

5 Emile Baillard, 'Cartes économiques des pays français du Niger' (*c.* 1899), reproduced in *Cartes Historiques de l'Afrique occidentale* (Société des Africanistes, 1969). Barth was struck some forty-four years earlier by the miserable state of affairs in Say and noted that the town depended heavily upon Sinder and the Sorko fishermen for its supplies (1965, vol. III, 172–8, 534).

6 *Ibid.*, vol. III, 180 3; P. L. Monteil, *De Saint-Louis à Tripoli par le lac Tchad. Voyage au travers du Soudan et du Sahara accompli pendant les années 1890–91–92* (n.d.), 185–7.

7 'Dossier signalétique des chefs de Ouro-Gueladio', n.d. (ASP Say); A. Hampaté Ba & J. Daget, *L'Empire peul du Macina* (Dakar, 1955/Paris, 1962); W. A. Brown, 'The caliphate of Hamdallahi' (PhD thesis, University of Wisconsin, Madison, 1969); Marion Johnson, 'The economic foundations of an Islamic theocracy – the case of Masina', *JAH*, XVII, 4 (1976a), 481–95.

8 'Lettre du capitaine Betheder, commandant le poste de Say, à M. le Chef de Bataillon, commandant la région Est et Macina', Say, 11. June 1897 (14 MI 855).

9 The best accounts of the wars against the Fulani (and the Tuareg) are found in Urvoy (1936), 101–10; Johnston (1967), 187–95; Muhammad Bello Alkali, 'A Hausa community in crisis: Kebbi in the nineteenth century' (MA dissertation, Ahmadu Bello University, Zaria, 1969), 240.

10 Pierre Ménard, 'Rapp. sur la chefferie du canton de Tibiri', Tibiri, 24 April 1953 (ASP Dogondoutchi).

11 *Ibid.*

12 Rouch (1953a).

13 Raulin (n.d.), 6.

14 Séré de Rivières (1965), 95 & 100; *Commandant*-Dosso to Gov., Dosso, 22 March 1943; P. Urfer, 'Rapp. de tournée, canton de Loga', Dosso, 20 April 1947 (both ANN).

15 Rouch (1953a), 218.

16 Nehemia Levtzion, *Muslims and Chiefs in West Africa. A Study of Islam in the Middle Volta Basin in the Pre-Colonial Period* (Oxford, 1968), 139–60; J. J. Holden, 'The Zabarima conquest of north-west Ghana', *THSG*, VIII (1965), 60–86.

17 Périé & Sellier (1950), 1028–51; Rash (1972a), 165.

18 'Capitaine Angeli, adjoint au Résident de Say, commandant le poste de Dosso, à M. le Général, Lieut. Gouv. du Soudan français', Dosso, 14 June 1899 (14 MI 1855).

19 He had virtually no power according to Monteil (1895), 198.

20 Raulin (n.d.), 96–9.

21 This was at the expense of Algeria where trade failed to recover after the French conquest and the revolts of the 1850s. See C. W. Newbury, 'North-African and Western Sudan trade in the nineteenth century', *JAH*, VII, 2 (1966), 233–46; H. Lhote, 'Le Cycle caravanier des Touaregs de l'Ahaggar et la saline d'Amadror. Leurs rapports avec les centres commerciaux du Soudan', *BIFAN*, XXXI, 4 (1969), 1014–27 (esp. 1016–17).

22 Ettore Rossi, *Storia de Tripoli e della Tripolitania dalla conquista araba al 1911* (Rome, 1968), 297–312 (I have been unable to consult K. Folayan's *Tripoli during the reign of Yussuf Pasha Qaramanli* (Ife, 1979)).

23 *Ibid.*, 304–5.

24 *Ibid.*, 317–18.

25 Jean-Louis Miège, 'La Libye et le commerce transsaharian au XIXe siècle', *ROMM*, 19 (1975), 135–68 (esp. 144–5); C. H. Dickson, 'Account of Ghadames', *J. Royal Geogr. Society*, XXX (1860), 260; Commandant Gadel, 'Notes sur Bilma et les oasis environnantes', *Revue Coloniale*, VII (1907), 361–86 (375). This is slightly at variance with the findings of Ralph Austen who argues that the 'nineteenth century witnessed the highest

annual rate for slave trading in the history of trans-Saharan commerce' (p. 59). However, Austen's figures may be interpreted to show a very sharp decline in the slave trade across the Sahara during the second half of the century, and that this trade was much more significant in the eastern and western parts of the Sahara than in the centre. See his 'The trans-Saharan slave trade: a tentative census', in Henry A. Gemery & Jan S. Hogendorn (eds.), *The Uncommon Market. Essays in the Economic History of the Atlantic Slave Trade* (New York, 1979), 23–76.

26 Newbury (1966); Miège (1975); Marion Johnson, 'Calico caravans: the Tripoli–Kano trade after 1880', *JAH*, XVII, 1 (1976b), 95–117; Stephen Baier, 'African merchants in the colonial period. A history of commerce in Damagaram (Central Niger), 1880–1960' (PhD thesis, University of Wisconsin, Madison, 1974).

27 Newbury (1966); Miège (1975).

28 Baier (1974). See also Miège (1975); Cordell (1977).

29 A. G. Hopkins, *An Economic History of West Africa* (1973), 131.

30 Baier (1974), 13 & 57–8; *id.* (1977); Miège (1975), 146–8. The ivory, however, seems to have crossed by the Central Sudan. Most of it apparently came from Adamawa and adjacent regions. See C. H. Robinson, *Hausaland or Fifteen Hundred Miles through the Central Sudan* (1896), 122; Marion Johnson, 'By ship or by camel: the struggle for the Cameroons ivory trade', *JAH*, XIX, 4 (1978), 539–49.

31 Baier (1974), 13.

32 By Baier (1977), 45–51.

33 Richardson (1853), vol. II, 203; Roberta Ann Dunbar, 'Damagaram (Zinder, Niger), 1812–1906: the history of a Central Sudanic kingdom' (PhD thesis, University of California at Los Angeles, 1970), 211–13.

34 See for instance, Dunbar (1977); Jan Hogendorn, 'The economics of slave use on two "plantations" in the Zaria emirate of the Sokoto Caliphate', *IJAHS*, X, 3 (1977), 369–83.

35 One consequence was that there developed among the Hausa a sharp difference between status and prestige. See M. G. Smith, 'The Hausa system of social status', *Africa*, XXIX, 3 (1959), 239–52 (251).

36 This is one of the main themes developed in Smaldone (1977). For further references see below.

37 Daumas & Chancel (1857), 202; Miège (1975), 139 & 149–50; M. Brulard, 'Aperçu sur le commerce caravanier Tripolitaine–Ghat–Niger vers la fin du XIXe siècle', *Bull. Liaison Saharienne*, 31 (1958), 202–15.

38 Johnson (1976b), 108–9. See also Miège (1975), 148.

39 Smaldone (1977), 99.

40 *Ibid.*, 105–7.

41 Erwin de Bary, *Le Dernier Rapport d'un Européen sur Ghat et les Touaregs de l'Aïr. Journal de voyage d'Erwin de Bary, 1876–77, traduit et annoté par Henri Schirmer* (1899), 89; Stephen Baier, 'Local transport in the economy of the Central Sudan, 1900–1930', paper presented to the Seminar on Economic History of the Central Savanna of Western Africa, Kano, 5–10 January 1976(a).

42 Richardson (1853), vol. II, 202. Such a theory is however at variance with some of the conclusions formulated by Hopkins (1973), 131.

43 See for instance, Stephen Baier, 'Economic history and development. Drought and the Sahelian economy', *AEH*, 1 (1976b), 1–16; and especially Sharon E. Nicholson, 'Climatic variations in the Sahel and other African regions during the past five centuries', *Journal of Arid Environments*, 1 (1978), 3–24 (11–14).

44 The quotation is from Robert Smith's review of Smaldone (1977) in *JAH*, XIX, 2 (1978), 285–7 (286).

45 M. G. Smith, 'Historical and cultural conditions of political corruption among the Hausa', *Comparative Studies in Society and History*, VI, 2 (1964b), 164–94 (174).
46 *Ibid.*, 174.
47 *Ibid.*, 180–1.
48 Hull (1968), 27.
49 Last (1967).
50 Smaldone (1977).
51 Hull (1968), 35–7.
52 E. A. Ayandele, 'Observations on some social and economic aspects of slavery in pre-colonial Northern Nigeria', *Nigerian Journal of Economic and Social Studies*, IX, 3 (1967), 329–38 (333).
53 Hull (1968), 48–9; Smaldone (1977), 130.
54 In addition to the works cited in note 44 above, see Paul E. Lovejoy, 'The characteristics of plantations in the nineteenth-century Sokoto Caliphate (Islamic West Africa)', *American Historical Review*, LXXXIV, 5 (1979), 1267–92; Hull (1968), 48–9; Smaldone (1977), 130.
55 Smaldone (1977), 149.
56 *Ibid.*, 128ff.
57 Hull (1968), 52.
58 Smaldone (1977), 93, 157 & 162.
59 Piault (1975), 333.
60 Ayandele (1967).
61 Hull (1968), 37 & 82.
62 Smith (1964b), 177.
63 See for instance, Mary Smith, *Baba of Karo. A Woman of the Muslim Hausa* (1965), 48–50; Richardson (1853), vol. II, 127–8; Hull (1968), 54–5.
64 See Saburi Biobaku & Muhammed al-Hajj, 'The Sudanese Mahdiyya and the Niger–Chad region', in I. M. Lewis (ed.), *Islam in Tropical Africa* (1966), 425–41 (esp. 435); Adeleye (1971), 94–109; A. M. Fika, 'The political and economic reorientation of Kano Emirate 1882–1940' (PhD thesis, University of London, 1973); Johnston (1967), 182–3 & 220–2; Smaldone (1977), 118.
65 M. G. Smith, 'A Hausa kingdom: Maradi under Dan Baskoré, 1857–75', in D. Forde & P. M. Kaberry (eds.), *West African Kingdoms in the Nineteenth Century* (1967), 93–123. See also Adeleye (1971), 66; Landeroin (1911), 463; R. W. Hull, 'The impact of the Fulani jihad on interstate relations in the Central Sudan Katsina emirate', in D. McCall & N. R. Bennett (eds.), *Aspects of West African Islam* (Boston, 1971), 87–100 (95–8); William Wallace, 'Notes on a journey through the Sokoto Emirate and Borgu in 1894', *GJ*, VIII, 3 (1896), 211–19; Smaldone (1977), 157.
66 Baier (1974), 6.
67 Damagaram thus provides us with a particularly neat illustration of the theory that in Africa – and elsewhere – long-distance trade often encouraged large-scale political organization.
68 Captain Gamory-Dubourdeau, 'Etude sur la création de cantons de sédentarisation dans le Cercle de Zinder et particulièrement dans la subdivision centrale', *BCEHSAOF*, VIII, 2 (1924), 239–58 (esp. 239–41); Dunbar (1970), 131.
69 Baier (1976b), 4.
70 On the Sossebaki empire see Landeroin (1911), 425–9; G. Brouin, 'Un îlot de vieille civilisation africaine. Le pays de Ouacha (Niger français)', *BCEHSAOF*, XXI, 4 (1938), 469–79.
71 Dunbar (1970), 124, 259–60; Séré de Rivières (1965), 134–5; Daumas & Chancel (1875), 201–12; Landeroin (1911), 445–61. For a very different version of the origins of

Damagaram, see Gustav Nachtigal, *Sahara and Sudan*, vol. II (translated with an introduction by A. G. B. & H. J. Fisher, in press), 267.

72 According to Johnston (1967), 197, Tanimune is said to have built up an armoury of some 6,000 rifles or muskets and 40 cannons and to have created units of slave musketeers under slave officials. See also Landeroin (1911), 444–6 & 524–5; Abadie (1927), 125–8; H. Gaden, 'Notice sur la résidence de Zinder', *RTC*, 2 (1903), 608–56 & 740–94 (esp. 756).

73 Landeroin (1911), 414–21; Brenner (1973), 122–3.

74 Nachtigal, vol. II, 267.

75 Brenner (1973), 122.

76 Adeleye (1971), 10.

77 Landeroin (1911), 446.

78 Victor Low, *Three Nigerian Emirates. A Study in Oral History* (Evanston, 1972), 201–2.

79 Roberta Ann Dunbar, 'Economic factors in the development of Damagaram (Zinder, Niger) in the nineteenth century', paper presented to the fourteenth annual meeting of the African Studies Association, Denver, Colorado, 3–6 November 1971; Richardson (1953), vol. II, 274.

80 *Ibid.*, vol. II, 223–71. See also the historical section in the 'Rapport annuel du cercle de Zinder pour 1959'; and G. Brouin, 'Rapp. pol. pour 1951, Cercle de Zinder', 3 February 1952, pp. 61–2 (both AP Zinder).

81 Agg-Alāwjelj Ghubāyd (1975), 62–82.

82 *Ibid.*, 86.

83 See Michel Museur, 'Un exemple spécifique d'économie caravanière: l'échange sel-mil', *JA*, XLVII, 2 (1977), 49–80; Foureau (1905), vol. II, 120–34 & 853; Agg-Alāwjelj Ghubāyd (1975), 120ff.

84 Smaldone (1977), 101.

85 See Barth (1965), vol. III, 73; Hans Vischer, *Across the Sahara from Tripoli to Bornu* (1910), 254, 275 & 280; Gadel (1907), 364–5; Lieut. Ayasse, 'Première reconnaissance N'Guigmi-Agadem-Bilma', *RTC*, 6 (1907), 553–82 (esp. 556).

86 Based on Bonte (1971); *id.*, 'Les Kel Gress', in Edmond & Suzanne Bernus (eds.), *Les Touareg* (in press).

87 See John E. Flint, *Sir George Goldie and the Making of Nigeria* (1960), 162–6; Boniface I. Obichere, *West African States and European Expansion. The Dahomey-Niger Hinterland* (New Haven/London, 1971), 128–30.

88 *Afr.fr.*, 2 (1909), 56–62.

89 Based on Monteil (1894); Yves de Tessières, 'Une épisode du partage de l'Afrique: la mission Monteil de 1890–1892', *RFHOM*, LIX, 3 (1972), 345–410; Obichere (1971), 141–2; Flint (1960), 218.

90 See G. J. Toutée, *Dahomé, Niger, Touareg. Récit de voyage* (1897); *Sur le Niger et au pays des Touareg. La mission Hourst* (1897); and the file SOM Dahomey III.

91 Rash (1972a), 60.

92 *Ibid.*, 1–8.

93 By J. D. Hargreaves, 'The European partition of West Africa', in J. F. Ade Ajayi & M. Crowder (eds.), *History of West Africa*, vol. II (1974), 402–23 (406).

94 On the conquest of the Western Sudan generally, see A. S. Kanya-Forstner, *The Conquest of the Western Sudan 1879–1899* (1969).

95 These and the following reflections on the aims and purposes of the French conquest of the Central Sudan have been inspired by the *Bulletin du Comité de l'Afrique française* (later *Afrique française*); the *JO-RF. Débats parlémentaires* between 1897 and 1900; and the following works: L. Gann & P. Guignan (eds.), *The History and Politics of Colonialism in Africa*, vol. I (1969); Yehoshus Rash, 'Des colonisateurs sans enthousiasme: les premières années françaises au Damergou' (thesis, Paris, 1970), published in *RFHOM*, LIX, 1–2

(1972b), 5–69 & 240–311; Edouard Blanc, 'Les Routes de l'Afrique septentrionale au Soudan', *Bull. Soc. de Géographie de Paris*, 7th series, 11 (1890), 169–216; and finally by Captain Moll's report, 'La Situation politique de la région de Zinder', 1 January 1901, reproduced in *Afr.fr.*, 1–2 (1902), 44–8 & 88–90.

96 T. W. Roberts, 'Railway imperialism and French advances toward Lake Chad 1890–1900' (PhD thesis, University of Cambridge, 1972), 378–9.

97 See R. S. O'Fahey & J. L. Spaulding, *Kingdoms of the Sudan* (1974), 115 & 179–86; P. M. Holt, 'Egypt and the Nile valley', in John E. Flint (ed.), *The Cambridge History of Africa*, vol. V (1976), 13–50 (esp. 43–5).

98 On the Sanūsīya, see E. E. Evans-Pritchard, *The Sanusi of Cyrenaica* (Oxford, 1949/1954); Martin (1976), 99ff.

99 Dunbar (1970), 109.

100 Baier (1974), 31.

101 Foureau (1905), vol. II, 852. This was probably the case as well with the Tubu of Kawar and Tibesti. See Lieut. Guérin, 'Réconnaissance des traces qui mènent au beau Kaouar', Bilma, 1954 (ANN).

102 Cordell (1977).

103 Johnston (1967), 201.

104 On the story of Rābīh in Borno and on Rābīh generally, see Brenner (1973), 125–8; Urvoy (1949), 126–8; R. A. Adeleye, 'Rābīh b. Fadlāllah and the diplomacy of European imperial invasion in the Central Sudan, 1893–1902', *JHSN*, V, 3 (1970), 399–418; Emile Gentil, *La Chute de l'Empire de Rabeh* (1902).

105 Urvoy (1949), 127.

106 This point is particularly stressed by D. J. Muffett, 'Nigeria-Sokoto Caliphate', in M. Crowder (ed.), *West African Resistance. The Military Response to Colonial Occupation* (1971), 269–99 (293).

107 Biobaku & al-Hajj (1966), 434.

108 Germaine Poux-Cransac, 'Tage Rabebe, chansons de Rabah', *JSA*, VII, fasc. II (1937), 173–87; H. F. Backwell (ed.), *The Occupation of Hausaland. Being a Translation of Arabic Letters found in the House of the Wazir of Sokoto, Bokari, in 1903* (Lagos, 1927), 60–1.

109 Dunbar (1970), 74–5.

110 Fika (1973), 134–6; C. G. B. Gidley, 'Mantanfas – a study in oral tradition', *ALS*, VI (1965), 32–51. On Ahmadu's policy generally, see also Landeroin (1911), 450–2; Urvoy (1949), 127.

111 On Mallam Yaro, see André Salifou, 'Mallam Yaroh, un grand négociant du Soudan Central à la fin du XIXe siècle', *JSA*, XLII, fasc. I (1972), 7–27.

112 Dunbar (1970), 74–80; Rash (1972b).

113 Dunbar (1970), 109.

114 Based on P. David, *La Geste du grand K'aura Assao* (Paris/Niamey, n.d.); J. Périé, 'Histoire politique et administrative de la Subdivision de Maradi', Maradi, 1938 (AP Maradi).

115 Hull (1968), 64–6.

116 B. O. Oloruntimehin, *The Segu Tukulor Empire* (1972), esp. 293–323.

117 Based on Bendaoud Mademba, 'La Dernière étape d'un conquérant. Odyssée des dernières années du sultan Ahmadou de Ségou, racontée par son cousin et compagnon d'infortune Mohammadou Hassimou Tall', *BCEHSAOF*, IV (1921), 473–80; Michel Sellier, 'Note sur le peuplement et l'histoire du cercle de Niamey', 1951 (ASP Say); Périé & Sellier (1950), 1057; Rash (1972a), 172; Séré de Rivières (1965), 96.

118 Smaldone (1977), 120.

119 On the Destenave column I have relied upon *L'Occupation et l'organisation de la Boucle du Niger. Création de la région Est et Macina. Résumé des opérations par M. le Chef de Bataillon Destenave*, official report published by the Comité de l'Afrique française, n.d.

120 'Résidence de Dori. Bull. pol.', 1 February 1898 (14 MI 1047).

121 'Dossier signalétique, chefs indigènes, subdiv. de Say' (ASP Say).

122 'Lettre du capitaine Betheder', Say, 11 June 1897; 'Résidence de Say, Rapp. pol. Août 1898' (14 MI 855).

123 'Résidence de Say, Rapp. pol. février 1898' (14 MI 855).

124 'Rés. Dori. Bull. pol.', 1 February 1898.

125 Roberts (1972), 311; Minister of Foreign Affairs to Min. of Colonies, Paris, 17 April 1897 (SOM Afr., IV, 36). On the Cazémajou mission generally, see Capt. Cazémajou, 'Du Niger vers le lac Tchad. Journal de route', *Afr.fr.*, 2–3, 5–10 (1900); Commandant Chailley, *Les Grandes Missions françaises en Afrique occidentale* (Dakar, 1953), 70.

126 Roberts (1972), 305–6.

127 See the file FO 2/118 (PRO).

128 Roberts (1972), 305.

129 *Ibid.*, 315.

130 A.T., 'Le Pays Zerma', *RCD*, 1 (1901), 28–30.

131 Muriel Mathieu, 'La Mission Afrique centrale' (thesis, University of Toulouse-Le-Mirail, 1975), 116–18.

132 Based on Lieut. Gov. Sudan to Gov. Gal., Kayes, 17 February 1898 (14 MI 1060); Min. of Colonies to Gov. Gal., Paris, 3 December 1898; 'Résidence de Dori. Rapp. pol. pour février', 1 March 1899 (both 14 MI 1047).

133 See in particular, 'Résidence de Say. Rapp. pol. août 1897' (14 MI 885).

134 Unless otherwise stated, the following pages are based on Finn Fuglestad, 'A propos de travaux récents sur la misson Voulet-Chanoine', *RFHOM*, LXVII, 1–2 (1980), 73–87.

135 On the Foureau–Lamy expedition, see Foureau (1905), vol. II; and by the same author, *D'Alger au Congo par le lac Tchad. Misson saharienne Foureau–Lamy* (1902); Charles Guilleux, *Journal de route d'un caporal de tirailleurs de la mission saharienne (Mission Foureau–Lamy), 1898–1900* (Belfort, 1904); General Reibell, *L'Epopée saharienne. Carnet de route de la mission saharienne Foureau–Lamy (1898–1900)* (1931).

136 Gentil (1902).

137 'Projet d'instruction pour le chef de la mission du Tchad', n.d.; Min. Colonies to Min. Foreign Affairs, Paris, 11 July 1897 (both SOM Afr., III, 37).

138 On the Marchand mission, see Marc Michel, *La Mission Marchand 1895–1899* (Paris/The Hague, 1972).

139 Charles Michel, *Mission de Bonchamps. A la rencontre de la mission Marchand à travers l'Ethiopie* (1900).

140 In addition to the works cited above (including General Chanoine (ed.?), *Documents pour servir à l'histoire de l'Afrique Occidentale Française de 1895 à 1899* (n.d.), 15 & 161), see General Joalland, *Le Drame de Dankori. (Mission Voulet–Chanoine, mission Joalland–Meynier)* (1930, but written in 1905), 10–11.

141 Kanya-Forstner (1969), 274; and the debate in the 'Chambre des Députés' on 23 November 1900 (*JO-RF. Débats parlementaires. Chambre des Députés*, 1900, 2269).

142 On the Convention of 1898 and its consequences, see Hargreaves (1974), 419–20; Henri Brunschwig, *Le Partage de l'Afrique noire* (1971), 139–41; R. E. Robinson & J. Gallagher, 'The partition of Africa', *New Cambridge Modern History*, vol. XI (1962), 593–640 (629–31); E. Rouard de Card, *Traités de délimitation concernant l'Afrique française* (1910), 225–31; Flint (1960), 293–4.

143 Madeleine Rebérioux, *La République radicale? 1898–1914* (vol. XI of *Nouvelle Histoire de la France contemporaine*) (1975), 151.

144 Min. of Foreign Affairs to Min. Colonies, Paris, 13 & 25 July 1898 (SOM Afr. III, 37). See also Mathieu (1975), 60–2.

145 G. Trouillot (Min. of Colonies), 'Instructions confidentielles', Paris, 27 July 1898 (14 MI 672).
146 According to Robinson & Gallagher (1962), 631.
147 The following pages constitute a summary of Mathieu (1975) and Fuglestad (1980). See also Jacques-Francis Rolland, *Le Grand Capitaine* (1976).
148 G. Goldie, 'Memorandum on telegram received to-day from Nigeria', London (Surrey House), 21 March 1899 (CO 446/5); Michael M. Horowitz, 'Ba Karim: an account of Rabeh's wars', *African Historical Studies*, vol. III (1970), 391–402 (394); Edmond Bernus, 'Drought in Niger Republic', *Savanna*, II, 2 (1973), 129–32 (130); Arouna Hamidou Sidikou, *Sédentarité et mobilité entre Niger et Zgaret* (Niamey, 1974), 22; Beauvilain (1977), 18; Lugard to Secr. State Colonies, 9 March & 31 August 1904 (CO 446/38 & 40).
149 Mathieu (1975), Fuglestad (1980).
150 Acting Gov. (Vimard) to Gov. Gal., 7 October 1899 (SOM Afr. III, 38).
151 A. Guillain in the 'Chambre des Députés', 23 November 1900 (*JO-RF.*, 2273).
152 Rebérioux (1975), 28.
153 See for instance the speech by P. Vigné d'Octon in the 'Chambre des Députés' on 23 November 1900 (*JO-RF.*, 2261–3).
154 *Ibid.*, 160–8; O. Meynier, *La Mission Joalland Meynier* (1947), 71–5.
155 Dunbar (1970), 84–7.
156 Meynier (1947), 74–6.
157 Capt. Métois in *Afr.fr.*, 6 (1901), 203–4; Salifou (1972).
158 Foureau (1902), 291.
159 Guilleux (1904), 132, 159–60 & 166.
160 According to T. S. Jago (HM Consul in Tripoli) to Foreign Office, Tripoli, 15 August & 16 September 1899 (CO 446/5).
161 'Rapp. du Sergeant Bouthet, commandant le poste de Zinder, sur l'établissement de ce poste et sur les événements qui y sont survenus depuis le 3 octobre 1899', Zinder, 27 November 1899 (Vincennes, Niger VII).
162 Mathieu (1975), 200–7.
163 Reibell (1931), 239; Moll (1902), 47.
164 Kousseri is situated on the modern Cameroon–Chad border.
165 Pierre Gentil, *La Conquête du Tchad (1894–1916)* (roneotyped, Vincennes, 1971), 116–33; Adeleye (1971), 413.
166 Lugard to Secr. State-Colonies, 12 April 1901 (CO 446/15).
167 Johnston (1967), 237.
168 See for instance, Lieut. Col. Péroz, 'Instructions à M. le Commandant Gouraud, commandant la colonne du Djerma', Say, 20 December 1900 (ANN).
169 *JO-AOF*, no. 249, 26 July 1900, 313.
170 Séré de Rivières (1965), 234–5.
171 *Ibid.*, 205.
172 Capt. Granderye (Resident Say) to 'Commandant Supérieur', Say, 27 February 1900; 'Commandant Supérieur (Col. Combes)', to Resident Say, St Louis, 2 March 1900 (both 14 MI 293); 'Commandant Nord-Est au Lieut. Gouv. à Kayes', n.d. [1899], (SOM Soudan IV, 8); Rash (1972a), 80; P. Urfer, 'R. tournée, canton de Loga', Dosso, 20 April 1947.
173 Léopold Kaziendé, 'Un épisode de l'histoire de Filingué. Procès-Verbal d'une conversation avec Chékou Mayaki', MSS. Niamey, 1937 (consulted by courtesy of the author).
174 Capt. Angeli to Lieut. Gov. Sudan, Dosso, 14 June 1899 (14 MI 855).
175 Périé & Sellier (1950).
176 Unless otherwise stated, the following is based on 'Occupation et organisation de la contrée Niger–Tchad en Territoire Militaire. Rapport de fin de campagne du Lieut. Colonel Péroz 1900–1', Sorbo-Haoussa, 8 January 1902 (SOM Tchad I, 1).

177 Dunbar (1970), 98 & 102–3; Gentil (1971), 133–5.
178 See for instance Péroz to Lugard, Porto-Novo, 4 November 1900 (CO 446/14).
179 In addition to 'Occupation et organisation de la contrée Niger–Tchad', 81–5, see report by Péroz, Zinder, 24 April 1901 (ANN); 'Le Lieut. Col. du Génie, Chef du Bureau Militaire, à M. le Directeur des Affaires Africaines au Ministère des Colonies', Paris, 27 January 1902 (SOM Tchad I, 2bis); *Afr.fr.*, 2 (1903), 47.
180 'Région Ouest à Commandant, 3e territ.', 13 May 1901; Lieut. Col. Noël, 'Rapp. sur la situation pol. du 3e territ. mil., 3e trim. 1902', Niamey, 12 November 1902 (both ANN).
181 P. Cambon (French Ambassador in London) to Minister of Foreign Affairs, London, 12 March & 1 May 1902 (SOM Tchad I, 2bis).
182 Destenave (n.d.), 86.
183 See for instance two reports by Major Gouraud, 4 October 1901 & 28 June 1902 (ANN & SOM Tchad I, 2bis); Lugard to Secr. State-Colonies, 2 January 1902 (CO 446/30); Noël, 'R. sit., 3e trim. 1902'; Lieut. Gov. Upper-Sen. Niger to Gov. Gal., 26 March 1906 (14 MI 294).
184 *Ibid.*; Sellier, 'Note sur le peuplement . . . du cercle de Niamey'; Rash (1972a), 284; and the reports and works cited in note 148.
185 Report by Noël cited in Gov. Gal. to Minister, 13 March 1904 (SOM Tchad I, 2bis).
186 Noël, 'R. sit. 3e trim. 1902'.
187 *Ibid.*; TM Niger, 'Rapp. d'ensemble annuel' (signed Gouraud), 12 December 1902 (ANN).
188 Destenave (n.d.), 28.
189 *Ibid.*, 29.
190 Lugard to Secr. State-Colonies, 2 & 26 October, 13 December 1900 (CO 446/11); same to same, 27 February 1901 (CO 446/14).
191 Paragraph based on Bonte (1971), 38–62.
192 *Ibid.*, 363–9 (reports by Major Gouraud). See also *Commandant* Niger to Gov. Gal., Say, 7 August 1901 (SOM Tchad I, 1bis).
193 Major Gaden, 'Notice sur la résidence de Zinder-Tchad', n.d., 33 (SOM Soudan IV, 9); Captain Bloch, 'Rapp. annuel, poste de Zinder', 1903, part 8, ch. 2 (SOM AOF XVI, 11); Reibell (1931), 246; Rash (1972b), 57.
194 'Rapp. sur la situation géographique et politique du Kanem et du Dagana', Fort-Lamy, 2 December 1901 (SOM Tchad I, 3); 'Journal de marche du Bataillon de tirailleurs sénégalais no. 3, 1902–29' (referred to henceforth as 'J. de marche . . .'), 2–3 (Vincennes, Niger I); Gaden (1903), 34; Gentil (1971), 126–7.
195 Report by Lieut. Col. Gouraud, 9 August 1905 (Aix 4(4)D-9); Jean Ferrandi, *Le Centre-Africain Français* (1930), 7–9.
196 'Télégramme-lettre du gouv. du Tchad au gouv. du Niger', Fort-Lamy, 30 January 1916 (ANN).
197 See for instance reports by Lieut. Mangin, 10 & 11 August 1902 (ANN); 'Rapp. 3e territ. mil. janvier à juillet 1903' (signed Merlin) (SOM Tchad I, 2bis); Bloch, 'R. ann., Zinder', 1903; 'J. de marche . . .', 4–12.
198 Lugard to Secr. State-Colonies, Zungeru, 29 January 1903 (CO 446/30).
199 Séré de Rivières (1965), 235.
200 Based on TM Niger, 'R. d'ens. annuel', 12 December 1902; 'Rapp. 3e territ. mil. janvier à juillet 1903'; Gov. Gal. to Minister, Dakar, 29 January 1904 (SOM Tchad I, 2bis); Capt. Lefebvre, 'Rapp. sur la question de l'Azbin', Zinder, 1 April 1904 (Vincennes, Niger III).
201 Lhote (1969).
202 'J. de marche . . .', 12; C. Jean, *Les Touareg du Sud-Est-l'Aïr. Leur rôle dans la politique saharienne* (1909), 71–8.
203 Adeleye (1971), 278–82.

204 *Afr.fr.*, 2 (1909), 58–9; Brunschwig (1971), 141–6.
205 Major Dardignac to Gov., 18 April 1907; Major Bétrix to Gov., Zinder, 21 June 1907; Capt. Laforgue to Commandant, Region of Niamey, Tahoua, 30 March 1908 (all ANN).
206 'J. de marche . . .', 15–17.
207 Lieut. Gov. Upper-Sen. Niger (W. Ponty) to Gov. Gal., Kayes, 22 June 1906 (14 MI 293); Major Gadel, 'Rapp. sur la tournée de pacification effectuée dans l'Aïr du 27.8. au 25.11.1905' (SOM Afr. IV, 70ter).
208 'Monographie du poste militaire d'Agades', Agades, June 1942 (Vincennes, Niger VII).
209 'Rapp. en Conseil de Gouvernement. Organisation du Territoire Militaire du Niger' (signed E. Roume), Gorée, 26 December 1904 (ANN).
210 Périé & Sellier (1950), 1063–74.
211 P. Urfer, 'R. tournée, canton de Loga'; Sellier, 'Note sur le peuplement . . . du cercle de Niamey', 49.
212 *Ibid.*, 52.
213 Paragraph based on L. Kaziendé, 'Une épisode de l'histoire de Filingée'; and oral sources.
214 Although Gouraud for one was not entirely duped. See Gouraud to Gov., Sorbo, 2 October 1901 (ANN).
215 Sellier, 'Note sur le peuplement . . . du cercle de Niamey', 59 & 87.
216 Gamory-Dubourdeau (1924).
217 Gov. Gal. to Minister, 29 January 1904 (SOM Tchad I, 2bis); Sellier, 'Note sur le peuplement . . . du cercle de Niamey', 58; Olivier de Sardan (1973b); Commandant Rivet, *Notice illustrée sur le Territoire Militaire du Niger et le Bataillon de Tirailleurs de Zinder* (1912), 158–60.
218 *JO-AOF*, 6 January 1906, 17–18.
219 Circulaire W. Ponty, 25 June 1906, reproduced in *JO du Haut-Sénégal Niger*, I, 3 (1 September 1906), 35–6.
220 Based on Olivier de Sardan (1973a, 1973b, 1975, 1976).
221 Based on Raulin (n.d.), 80–91; and by the same author, 'Travail et régimes fonciers au Niger', *Cahiers de l'ISEA*, 5th series, 9 (1965), 119–39.
222 *Commandant*-Niamey (Major Froment) to Gov., 22 January 1906 (ANN); Denise Bouche, *Les Villages de liberté en Afrique noire française, 1887–1910* (Paris/The Hague, 1968), 265–6; Capt. Salaman to Region of Niamey, Niamey, 28 May 1906 (ANN).
223 According to J. Robin, 'Note sur les premières populations de la région de Dosso (Niger)', *BIFAN*, I, 2–3 (1939), 401–4.
224 See for instance, Destenave (n.d.), 157.
225 Rouch (1953a), 236.
226 Sellier, 'Note sur le peuplement . . . du cercle de Niamey', 59.
227 Périé & Sellier (1950), 1064; *Afr.fr.*, 2 (1903), 125; Gov. Gal. to Minister, 29 January 1904 (SOM Tchad I, 2bis); Lieut. Col. Noël, 'Rapp. sur la sit. pol. du 3e territ. militaire en août 1903', 2 October 1903 (SOM AOF XVI, 13).
228 Périé & Sellier (1950), 1064–5; Séré de Rivières (1965), 220.
229 Lieut. Gov. Upper-Sen. Niger to Gov. Gal., 26 March 1906 (14 MI 294); 'Compte-rendu succinct des faits et opérations militaires intéressant la politique générale' (signed Lamolle), 31 January 1906 (ANN).
230 *Commandant-cercle* Djerma (Capt. Löfler) to Region of Niamey, 2 February 1906 (ANN); Lieut. Gov. Upper-Sen. Niger to Gov. Gal., 26 March 1906 (14 MI 294).
231 Sellier, 'Note sur le peuplement . . . du cercle de Niamey', 64.
232 Karimou (1977), 157–8.
233 Based in particular on the various 'Dossiers signalétiques de chefs indigènes' in the archives of Magaria, Tessaoua and Zinder; and on the 'Monographie du Cercle de Gouré', 1941, 4–5 (ANN).

234 Major Gadel to Gov., Gougoufera, 23 January 1906; Gov. Gal. to Lieut. Gov. Upper-Sen. Niger, Gorée, 1 February 1906 (both 14 MI 592).

235 Rash (1972b); and the 'Dossiers signalétiques de chefs indigènes' (AP Tahoua and ASP Magaria).

236 See for instance, Chief of the Subdiv. of Tessaoua to *Commandant*-Maradi, 13 November 1928 (AP Maradi); Bonte (1971).

237 Gouraud to *Commandant supérieur*, Paris, 14 January 1904 (ANN); and report by the same, dated 9 August 1905 (Aix 4(4)D-9).

238 Report by Lieut. Jigandon, 5 February 1901 (ANN).

239 Colonial Office, *Annual Reports, Northern Nigeria 1900–1911* (report no. 406 for 1902), 101.

240 Lieut. Col. Noël, 'Rapp. sit. pol. 3e territ. mil. au cours du 3e trim. 1903', 4 November 1903 (SOM AOF XVI, 13).

241 H. Gouraud, *Zinder-Tchad. Souvenirs d'un africain* (1944), 93.

242 *Ibid.*, 93–4.

243 Gaden to his father, Zinder, 9 May, 25 May, 9 June, 23 August 1902 (SOM Gaden papers, AP 15); and report by Gouraud, 20 October 1902 (SOM Tchad I, 2bis).

244 Gouraud (1944), 94.

245 Capt. Lefebvre, 'Rapp. concernant le mouvement d'effervescence qui se manifeste à Zinder depuis quelques jours', Zinder, 1904 (AP Zinder).

246 Most of them were liberated in 1908, with the exception of Ahmadu II, who had to wait until 1917. Decree of the Gov. Gal., 22 June 1907 (14 MI 857); Lieut. Gov. Ivory Coast to Gov. Gal., Bingerville, 30 June 1917 (14 MI 1077).

247 Based on Dunbar (1970), 114–15; André Salifou, 'La Conjuration manquée du sultan de Zinder (Niger), 1906', *Afrika Zamani*, 3 (1974), 69–103.

248 The main source of information here is once more the various 'Dossiers signalétiques des chefs indigènes'.

249 'J. de marche . . .', 25–6.

250 Capt. Lagaillarde, 'Rapp. sur les faits reprochés au chef de province Bellama', Zinder, 9 February 1921 (AP Zinder).

251 'Région de Zinder. Rapp. pol. pour avril 1906', Zinder, 30 May 1906 (AP Zinder).

252 Reports by Capt. V. Salaman, 26 April & 3 December 1906; and by Major Dardignac, 6 June 1906 (all ANN).

253 Sellier, 'Note sur le peuplement . . . du cercle de Niamey', 69.

254 The main source of information is *Northern Nigeria. Correspondence relating to Sokoto, Hadeija and the Munshi Country. Presented to both Houses of Parliament by Command of His Majesty, August 1907* (HMSO, 1906, Cd. 3620).

255 I. Nicolson, *The Administration of Nigeria 1900–1960. Men, Methods, and Myths* (Oxford, 1969), 143.

256 Lugard to Secr. State, Zungeru, 21 February 1906 (RH Brit. Emp. s. 62).

257 *Northern Nigeria. Correspondence*, 42–3.

258 Major Burdon to High-Commissioner, 28 February 1906 (RH Afr. s. 547); Intelligence report (signed Lugard), Zungeru, 22 June 1906 (CO 446/54); Lugard to Secr. State, 28 February 1906 (RH Brit. Emp. s. 62); F. P. Gall, *Gazetteer of Bauchi province* (1920, reprinted 1972), 11.

259 'Extreme loyalty of all Emirs most striking', Lugard to Secr. State, 28 February 1906 (CO 446/52). See also Burdon to High-Commissioner, 15 February 1906, and to the officers commanding reinforcements, 18 February 1906 (RH Afr. s. 547).

260 Lugard to Secr. State, 9 May 1906 (RH Brit. Emp. s. 62).

261 Burdon to High-Commissioner, 12 March 1906 (RH Afr. s. 952).

262 Letter from H. S. Goldsmith to Mrs Goldsmith, n.d. [February 1906?], (RH Brit. Emp. s. 62).

263 The Resident, Sokoto Province, to M. le Capitaine Laforgue, Commanding the *cercle* of Tahoua, Sokoto, 13 March 1906 (RH Afr. s. 547).

264 Burdon to High-Commissioner, 12 March 1906 (RH Afr. s. 952). A. H. M. Kirk-Greene talks of 'the extreme ugliness of the scale of the atrocities'. See his 'Introduction' (p. v) to J. Burdon, *Northern Nigeria. Historical Notes on Certain Emirates and Tribes* (n.d.). See also the allegations of the various members of the Church Missionary Society (RH Brit. Emp. s. 62). H. S. Goldsmith (in a letter to Mrs Goldsmith (RH Brit. Emp. s. 62) notes that 'All Satiru men that got away are being caught by the Sokoto army, brought in, tried and killed in the market-place, their bodies left there for a day or two.'

265 Lugard to Secr. State, 21 February 1906 (RH Brit. Emp. s. 62). See also *Northern Nigeria. Correspondence*, 38–44.

266 Fika (1973), 218.

267 *Northern Nigeria. Correspondence*, 31.

268 See for instance, Major Gadel to Gov., Zinder, 17 April 1906 (14 MI 592); Min. of Colonies to Gov. Gal., Paris, 29 July 1906 (14 MI 856).

269 *Northern Nigeria. Correspondence*, 16.

270 According to Abel Olorunfemi Anjorin, 'The British occupation and the development of Northern Nigeria, 1897–1914' (PhD thesis, University of London, 1965), 113–37.

271 See for instance, *Northern Nigeria. Correspondence*, 15–21. My analysis is at variance with that offered by R. A. Adeleye. See his 'Mahdist triumph and British revenge in Northern Nigeria; Satiru 1906', *JHSN*, VI, 2 (1972), 193–214.

272 Fika (1973), 214.

273 Min. of Colonies to Gov. Gal., 29 July 1906 (14 MI 856).

274 Lieut. Gov. Upper-Sen. Niger (W. Ponty) to Gov. Gal., Kayes, 3 April 1907 (14 MI 295).

275 Min. of Colonies (G. Leygues) to Gov. Gal., 24 April & 30 April 1906 (14 MI 856); *Le Temps* (daily newspaper, Paris), 10 July 1906; letter of G. Leygues in *Le Figaro* (daily newspaper, Paris), 17 January 1923.

276 Min. of Colonies to Gov. Gal., Paris, 12 April 1907 (14 MI 858).

277 Lieut. Gov. Upper-Sen. Niger to Gov. Gal., 22 June 1906 (14 MI 293), 4–7; Gov. Gal. to Min. of Colonies, Gorée, 14 March 1907 (14 MI 298).

278 See for instance, Major Mouret, 'Rapp. sur la politique générale pendant le mois de mars 1908', Zinder, 28 June 1908 (AP Zinder); Director of Political and Administrative Affairs (J. Brévié) to the Director of Finances, Dakar, 13 December 1920 (14 MI 864).

279 Report by Capt. Laforgue (*Commandant*-Tahoua), 3 January 1908 (ANN); Lugard to Secr. State, 21 February 1906 (RH Brit. Emp. s. 62); Jean Tilho, 'Variations et disparition possible du Tchad', *Annales de Géographie*, 37 (15 May 1928), 238–60 (242).

280 'J. de marche . . .', 30–1; Major Bétrix to Gov., Zinder, 21 April 1907 (ANN); Major Bétrix, 'Rapp. sur la situation pol. de l'Azbin en mars-avril-mai 1907, et propositions la concernant', Zinder, 8 June 1907 (AP Tahoua).

281 Major Mouret to Gov., Zinder, 9 August 1908 (ANN); Lieut. Halphen to the Captain-in-Chief of the Tidikelt company, Iferouane, 30 October 1907 (14 MI 607); Lieut. Théral, 'Rapp. sur la tournée de police chez les Ikaskazen', Agades, 29 November 1907; Report by Major Bétrix, Tahoua, 19 December 1907 (both 14 MI 296); Rivet (1912), 161–2.

3. The decisive years, 1908–22

1 *Commandant*-Zinder (Major Mouret) to Gov., Zinder, 27 April 1908 (ANN); Gov. (Lieut. Col. Hocquart) to Gov. Gal., Zinder, 20 April 1912 (14 MI 859).

2 Gov. Gal. to Gov., Dakar, 26 November 1909 (14 MI 859); Gov. Gal. to Minister of

Colonies, Dakar, 22 December 1909 (14 MI 858); Gov. Upper Sen. Niger to Gov. Gal., 4 December 1909 (14 MI 298). The ensuing Franco-Turkish tension led to a minor incident at Yat in 1910. See Rivet (1912), 167–9; Gov. Gal., 'Lettre au Cabinet et Directeurs des Services Militaires', Dakar, 22 October 1910 (14 MI 859).

3 Lieut. Dromard, 'Rapp. à M. le Chef de Bataillon, commandant la région de Bilma, au sujet du combat livré au nord d'Agadem le 7 Janvier 1908', Bilma, 30 January 1908 (14 MI 295).

4 TM Niger, Annual Political Report for 1909 (signed Venel), Zinder, 31 December 1909, 23–4 (ANN).

5 'Rapp. du Lieut. Ripert, commandant la section montée de la 3e compagnie . . . sur le combat de Karam', N'Guigmi, 3 June 1910 (ANN); Gov. (Lieut. Col. Scal) to the General-in-Chief, French West Africa, Niamey, 18 June 1910 (14 MI 298); 'Journal de marche du Bataillon de tirailleurs sénégalais no. 3, 1902–29', 58 (Vincennes, Niger I).

6 Gov. (Scal) to the Gen.-in-Chief, Niamey, 27 July 1910 (14 MI 296); 'J. de marche . . .', 53 *passim.*

7 Scal, 'Rapport . . . sur les tournées de police nécessitées par l'arrivée d'un rezzou dans le cercle de Zinder en août 1911', Zinder, 19 October 1911 (14 MI 591).

8 Lieut. Col. Venel, 'Rapp. portant projet de réorganisation du Territ. Mil. du Niger', 25 October 1919 (ANN).

9 General Goullet, 'Note résumant les mesures prises . . . à la suite de l'attaque d'Agadès', Dakar, 13 January 1917 (14 MI 303).

10 TM Niger, Annual Report for 1908 (signed Venel), 26 (ANN).

11 P. Bonte, 'L'Organisation économique des Touareg Kel Gress', in R. Creswell (ed.), *Elements d'Ethnologie*, vol. I (1975b), 166–215 (208).

12 *Annuaire du Gouvernement Général de l'AOF, 1917–21*, 1030.

13 Gov. Gal. (W. Ponty), 'Instructions pour M. le Col. Hocquart', n.d. [1911?] (14 MI 859).

14 *Annuaire-GG-AOF, 1917–18*, 1019–23.

15 Based on *Annuaire-GG-AOF, 1915–16*, 571–4.

16 Decree by the Gov. Gal., 25 November 1912 (14 MI 1574).

17 *Annuaire-GG-AOF, 1915–16*, 94. See also Rivet (1912), 173.

18 Johnson (1976b). According to a French source 10,000 camels were engaged in the trans-Saharan trade via Zinder and Agades in 1875, against only 400 in 1911–12. See Lieut. Col. Hocquart to Gov. Gal., Zinder, 20 April 1912 (14 MI 859), 1–2.

19 T. de Maugras, 'Rapp. sur le mouvement caravanier entre le T. du Niger, les oasis sahariennes et la Tripolitaine', Zinder 1913, annexe I (14 MI 607).

20 Based on Bonte (1971), 215; J. Périé, 'Carnet monographique du cercle de Bilma', 1941, ch. 1, p. 27 (ANN).

21 J. Hogendorn, 'The origins of the groundnut trade in Northern Nigeria', in C. K. Eicher & Carl Liedholm (eds.), *Growth and development of the Nigerian economy* (East Lansing, 1970), 30–51.

22 *Ibid.*; Baier (1977), 37; (1976a).

23 Gov. to Gov. Gal., 25 September 1913 & 7 March 1914 (14 MI 607).

24 *Ibid.*; Gov. (Venel), 'Note circulaire à tous cercles et secteurs', Zinder, 28 September 1914 (14 MI 1286).

25 'Rapp. sur les pertes en chameaux subies par les Kel Gress pendant le transport du ravitaillement du Tchad', Guidam Bado, 9 August 1908; Acting *Commandant*, Region of Niamey, to Gov., 27 August 1908; TM Niger Political Report for August 1911 (all ANN).

26 TM Niger Political Report for third trimester of 1912, Zinder, 30 October 1912 (Dakar 2G12–18); Quarterly Report, March 1913. Northern Division, Kano Province, 15 April 1913 (RH Afr. s. 230); Commandant Mercier, 'La Mission de ravitaillement du Tchad par Kano (janvier 1912–décembre 1913)', *RCD*, 7 (1914), 261–82.

27 TM Niger Annual Report for 1913, IV, 6–7 (14 MI 860).
28 *Commandant*-Niamey to Gov., 6 September 1915 (ANN).
29 'Circulaire sur l'impôt', Madaoua, 13 September 1916, 3 (AP Tahoua); *Commandant*-Niamey to Commissioner, 19 January 1917 (AP Niamey).
30 Guy Nicolas, 'Circulation des biens et échanges monétaires au sud du Niger', *Cahiers de l'ISEA*, 5th series, 4 (1962a), 49–62 (55).
31 'Circulaire sur l'impôt', 13 September 1916.
32 Based on figures from TM Niger, 'Rapport d'ensemble for 1914' (signed Venel), Zinder, 20 March 1915, 11 (Dakar 2G14–11); *Outre-Mer 1958. Tableau économique et social des Etats et Territoires d'Outre-Mer* (Paris, Service des Statistiques d'Outre-Mer, 1959), 79; Marc Michel, 'Le Recrutement des tirailleurs en AOF pendant la Première Guerre Mondiale. Essai de bilan statistique', *RFHOM*, LX, 4 (1973), 644–60 (657).
33 According to the 'Rapport sur le recensement des Peuls et Bouzous de la subdivision de Tessaoua', Tessaoua, 29 April 1939 (ASP Tessaoua).
34 *Annual Report, Northern Nigeria, 1904*, 33 (printed in Colonial Office, *Annual Reports, Northern Nigeria 1900–1911*).
35 According to the British. See June Quarterly Report 1913, Northern Division, Kano Province, 23 July 1913, Appendix D, 38 (RH Afr. s. 230).
36 'Circulaire sur les chefs indigènes', Madaoua, 19 July 1916, 1–3 (AP Tahoua).
37 A summary of the variable French approach in this matter is found in G. Brouin, 'Rapport de tournée', Tahoua, 18 May 1943 (AP Tahoua). See also Bonte (1971).
38 Capt. Piétri, 'Notes sur les Touareg Oulliminden du cercle de Tahoua', Tahoua, 21 February 1923, 10 (AP Tahoua); Bonte (1971), 317; Edmond Bernus, 'Espace géographique et champs sociaux chez les Touareg Illabakan (République du Niger)', *Etudes rurales*, 37–9 (1970), 46–64.
39 J. Périé, 'Histoire politique et administrative de la subdivision de Maradi', Maradi, 1938 (AP Maradi), 32.
40 Based on the various 'Dossiers signalétiques des chefs indigènes', and on Séré de Rivières (1965), 215–58.
41 In the words of one administrator: 'jusqu'en 1922 on s'est imposé, on a sabré'. See C. de Maradi, 'R. pol. pour 1932', 8–9 (AP Maradi).
42 See *inter alia* David (1964), 128; Gov. (Venel) to Gov. Gal., Zinder, 26 December 1914 (14 MI 860); TM Niger, 'R. pol. du 4e trimestre 1921' (signed Ruef), Zinder, 11 January 1922, 3 (Dakar 2G21–14); *Commandant*-Dosso to Gov., Dosso, 6 May 1924 (ANN); Périé, 'Histoire ... de la subdivision de Maradi', 23–6; 'Dossiers signalétiques des chefs indigènes'.
43 Gamory-Dubourdeau (1924), 242.
44 He seems however to have been accepted as chief by the Songhay, in any case remaining at the head of the canton to his death in 1951. See Acting Gov. (J. Durand-Viel), 'C. Niger Révue des événements du 4e trim. 1951', 6–7 (AP Zinder).
45 Jean Périé, 'Notes historiques sur la région de Maradi (Niger)', *BIFAN*, I, 2–3 (1939), 377–400 (379).
46 Gov. (Venel) to Gov. Gal., 23 June 1914 (14 MI 861); Gov. (Mèchet), 'Liste des juridictions indigènes du TM du Niger. Leur composition', Zinder, 20 February 1919 (14 MI 1243).
47 Gov. (Venel) to Gov. Gal., Zinder, 26 June 1914 (14 MI 861); David (1964), 131; Périé, 'Histoire ... de la Subdivision de Maradi', 27.
48 Capt. Ferrière, 'Rapp. au sujet des faits ayant motivé l'envoi du nommé Tchikama, chef de province de Zinder, devant le tribunal du cercle de Zinder, et du jugement l'ayant condamné à trois ans de prison', 1914 (14 MI 860).
49 David (1964), 119–21; oral sources.
50 Capt. Ferrière to Commissioner, Zinder, 1 March 1916 (AP Zinder).

51 *Commandant*-Zinder (H. Fleury) to Gov., Zinder, 24 August 1922; Capt. Lagaillarde, 'Rapp. sur les faits reprochés . . . Bellama', 9 December 1921 (both AP Zinder).

52 Francis Agbodeka, 'Sir Gordon Guggisberg's contribution to the development of the Gold Coast, 1919–27', *THSG*, XIII, 1 (1972), 51–64.

53 Based on Jean Rouch, *Migrations au Ghana, 1953–55* (Société des Africanistes, 1956), esp. 25–7; Olivier de Sardan (1969a), 9–10.

54 TM Niger Annual Report for 1913, 30 August 1914, esp. 32 (Dakar 2G13–16).

55 Marguerite Dupire, 'Situation de la femme dans une société pastorale (Peul woDaBe, nomades du Niger)', in Denise Paulme (ed.), *Femmes d'Afrique noire* (Paris/The Hague, 1960), 51–92 (70).

56 Rivet (1912), 178; *Afr.fr.*, 9 (1922), 429–30.

57 Buchanan (1921), 77.

58 This is the opinion of J. Périé, himself an administrator in Niger. See his 'Histoire . . . de la Subdivision de Maradi', 22.

59 *Commandant*-Goure (Ceccaldi) to Gov., Goure, 25 March 1945 (APR Niamey). See also Baier (1974), 85–6.

60 Here I have paraphrased John Iliffe.

61 M. Vilmin, Annual Report for 1950, SD-Dakoro, 1 January 1951 (AP Maradi).

62 E. Séré de Rivières, 'Le Zermaganda', December 1942, 11–12.

63 Bonte (1971), 511; Bonte & Echard (1976), 289.

64 Jacques Serre, 'Monographie géographique du canton de Bambeye' (thesis, Aix-en-Provence, 1950), 46.

65 Evans-Pritchard (1949/1954), 114–17.

66 Obissier (Chef du cabinet militaire), 'Note pour M. le Chef du Service des Affaires Civiles', Dakar, 30 January 1913 (14 MI 860).

67 The occupation of Tibesti did in fact lead to some tension with Italy, especially after the end of the war, when Italian claims *were* forthcoming. See Min. of Foreign Affairs to Min. of Colonies, Paris, 1 December 1917 (14 MI 610); Gov. Gal. to Minister, Dakar, 30 August 1919 (14 MI 860).

68 Min. of Colonies (A. Lebrun) to Gov. Gal., Paris, 5 March 1914; Gov. Gal. to Min., Dakar, 13 March 1914 (both 14 MI 860).

69 Brig. General Pineau, 'Troupes du Groupe de l'AOF. Ordre Général no. 46', Dakar, 2 August 1915; TM Niger, 'Bull. renseignements juin-août 1914' (both Vincennes, Niger III). On the military operations in Tibesti, see Aix 4(4)D-12.

70 Governor (Venel) to *Commandants* of Zinder, Agades and Madaoua, Zinder, 28 August 1916 (Vincennes, Niger III); Capt. Fonferrier, 'Etudes historiques sur le mouvement caravanier dans le cercle d'Agades', 1920 (ANN), published in the *BCEHSAOF*, VI (1923), 202–15.

71 Governor (Venel) to *Commandants* of Zinder, Agades and Madaoua, Zinder, 11 August 1916 (Vincennes, Niger III).

72 TM Niger, 'R. pol. du 4e trim. 1915', Zinder, 11 February 1916 (14 MI 104); Fonferrier (1923), 3.

73 Acting Gov. Gal. to Minister, Dakar, 30 September 1916; Gov. (Mourin) to Gov. Gal., Zinder, 9 August 1916 (both 14 MI 304); TM Niger, 'R. pol. du 4e trim. 1915'.

74 See note 279 to chapter 2 above.

75 Kano, Annual Report for the year ending 31 December 1909, by Resident C. L. Temple (RH Afr. s. 230).

76 A. T. Grove, 'A note on the remarkably low rainfall of the Sudan zone in 1913', *Savanna*, II, 2 (1973), 133–8; E. Bernus & G. Savonnet, 'Les Problèmes de la Sécheresse dans l'Afrique de l'Ouest', *Présence Africaine*, 88 (1973), 113–38.

77 Nigeria, Report on the Blue Book 1914, 22 (CO 657/1).

78 Marcel Roche, 'Note sur la sécheresse actuelle en Afrique de l'Ouest' in D. Dalby & R. J. Harrison-Church (eds.), *Drought in Africa* (1973), 53–61.
79 Beauvilain (1977), 64.
80 TM Niger, Annual Report for 1913, 30 August 1914, 32 (Dakar 2G13–16).
81 André Salifou, 'Les Français, Firhoun et les Kounta', *JSA*, XLIII, fasc. II (1973a), 175–96 (189).
82 Beauvilain (1977), 64.
83 Périé, 'Histoire ... de la subdivision de Maradi', 24.
84 J. Brévié, 'Circulaire no. 32', Zinder, 26 July 1922 (Dakar 11G26).
85 Capt. Ferrière, 'Instructions aux commandants de secteurs', Zinder, 6 March 1915 (ANN).
86 Lugard to Secr. State, 1 July 1914 (CO 583/16).
87 *Ibid.*; Nigeria, Report on the Blue Book 1914, 11 (CO 657/1).
88 A. C. Hastings, *Nigerian Days* (1925), 111.
89 Baier (1974), 81.
90 TM Niger, Annual Report for 1914 (signed Venel), Zinder, 20 March 1915 (Dakar 2G14–11).
91 *Commandant*-Zinder (Capt. Ferrière) to Gov., Myrriah, 5 April 1915 (ANN).
92 Périé, 'Histoire ... de la subdivision de Maradi', 24.
93 Unpublished paper by S. Baier, cited in Lovejoy & Baier (1975), 576.
94 TM Niger, Annual Report for 1914, 1.
95 By 1917 taxes were 1,380,000 francs and had thus not reached the pre-1914 level, a fact which points to the long-lasting effects of the famine. Tables in *Budget local du Niger*, 1917, 28–9.
96 See various documents in the file 14 MI 1286, esp. 'Note circulaire à tous cercles et secteurs', Zinder, 28 September 1914.
97 Governor (Mourin) to Gov. Gal., Zinder, 9 August 1916 (14 MI 304); Gentil (1971), 237.
98 Périé, 'Carnet monographique du cercle de Bilma', ch. 1, 27.
99 A. Richer, *Les Oullimindens* (1925), 258–9; Salifou (1973a), 189.
100 Gov. (Venel) to Gov., Upper-Senegal and Niger, 30 January 1914 (ANN).
101 *Commandant*-Timbuctu (Major Cauvin) to *Commandant*-Niamey, 12 April 1915 (ANN).
102 Lieut.-Guérin, 'Reconnaissance des traces qui mènent au beau Kaouar', Bilma, 1954, ch. 3 (ANN); Capt. H. Petragnani, 'Turcs et Senoussistes au Fezzan pendant la grande guerre: histoire d'une révolution ignorée', *RCD*, 11 (1925), 508–26; G. Féral, 'Monographie du cercle d'Agadez', Agades, 14 October 1955 (ANN); O. Meynier & Lehuraux, 'La Guerre sainte des Senoussya dans l'Afrique française', *RA*, LXXXIII, 2–3–4 (1939), 227–75 & 323–57; Jeremy Keenan, *The Tuareg. People of the Ahaggar* (New York, 1977), 86–90.
103 TM Niger, 'R. pol. du 4e trim. 1915', Zinder, 11 November 1915 (14 MI 304).
104 Acting Gov. Gal. (G. Angoulvant) to Minister, Dakar, 6 September 1916 (14 MI 1282).
105 TM Niger, 'R. pol. 3e trim. 1916', Zinder, 1 October 1916, p. 5 (ANN); Acting Gov. (de Jonquières) to Gov. Gal., Zinder, 26 December 1916 (14 MI 306).
106 Jean Hébert, 'Révoltes en Haute Volta de 1914 à 1918', *NDV*, III, 4 (1970), 3–54; Luc Garcia, 'Les Mouvements de résistance au Dahomey (1914–1917)', *CEA*, X, 1 (1970), 144–78; Michael Crowder, 'The 1916–17 revolt against the French in Dahomeyan Borgu', *JHSN*, VIII, 1 (1975), 99–116.
107 J. Osuntokun, 'Disaffection and revolts in Nigeria during the First World War, 1914–1918', *CJAS*, V, 2 (1971), 171–92; Michael Crowder, 'The 1914–18 European war and West Africa', in J. F. Ade Ajayi & M. Crowder (eds.), *History of West Africa*, vol. II (1974), 484–513 (508–9).
108 Acting Lieut. Gov. Northern Provinces (H. S. Goldsmith) to Gov. Gal. Nigeria, 16 July 1915 (CO 583/36).
109 Gov. to Gov. Gal., Zinder, 28 October 1916 (14 MI 304).

110 Meynier & Lehuraux (1939), 324; Gov. (Mourin) to Gov. Gal., Zinder, 8 February 1916 (14 MI 304); Michel Sellier, 'Note sur le peuplement et l'histoire du cercle de Niamey', 1951 (ASP Say), 76; Hébert (1970).

111 TM Niger, 'R. pol. du 4e trim. 1915'; Sellier, 'Note sur le peuplement . . . du cercle de Niamey', 76–7; Gov. (Mourin) to Gov. Gal., Zinder, 24 May 1916 (14 MI 304).

112 TM Niger, 'R. pol. du 4e trim. 1915'.

113 See for instance, Capt. Sadoux, 'Rapp. sur les opérations de recrutement, Cercle du Madaoua', Madaoua, 8 September 1918 (14 MI 371).

114 TM Niger, 'R. pol. du 4e trim. 1915'.

115 'Bulletin de renseignements politiques, subdivision de Dogondoutchi', January 1931, 2 (ASP Dogondoutchi).

116 Pierre Bonardi, *La République du Niger. Naissance d'un état* (1960), 43; Gov. to Gov. Gal., Zinder, 15 January 1916, 2 (14 MI 361).

117 Olivier de Sardan (1973b).

118 Félix de Kersaint-Gilly, 'Essai sur l'évolution de l'esclavage en Afrique Occidentale Française', *BCEHSAOF*, IX, 3 (1924), 469–78 (474).

119 Capt. Sadoux, 'Rapp. sur les opérations de recrutement', 1–2.

120 TM Niger, 'R. pol. du 4e trim. 1915', and '2e trim. 1916', Zinder, 1 July 1916 (ANN); Gov. Gal. to Minister, 16 April 1916 (SOM-NS c. 591 d. 18).

121 Gov. to Gov. Gal., 26 March 1918 (14 MI 371).

122 Gov. (Mourin) to Gov. Gal., 22 March 1916 (14 MI 361).

123 Deduced from Michel (1973), 657.

124 *Ibid.*; Crowder (1974), 497.

125 Gov. (Mourin) to Gov. Gal., 22 March 1916 (14 MI 361).

126 TM Niger, 'R. pol. du 2e trim. 1916', Zinder, 1 July 1916, 3–4 (ANN).

127 Based on Salifou (1973a), 190–3.

128 Séré de Rivières (1965), 225.

129 *Ibid.*, 231.

130 Gov. to Gov. Gal., Zinder, 28 October 1916 (14 MI 304).

131 Gov. (Mourin) to Gov. Gal., Zinder, 30 August 1916 (14 MI 304).

132 *Ibid.*; Acting Gov. Gal. to Minister, Dakar, 30 September 1916 (14 MI 304).

133 Minister to Gov. Gal., Paris, 1 November 1916 (14 MI 304).

134 Acting Gov. to Gov. Gal., 26 December 1916 (14 MI 306).

135 Yves Riou, 'La Révolte de Kaocen et le siège d'Agadès', roneotyped manuscript, Niamey, 1968, 21 (in my possession).

136 Gov. (Mourin) to Gov. Gal., Zinder, 28 October 1916 (14 MI 304).

137 See various documents in the file 14 MI 304, and Riou (1968), 20–1.

138 Service des Affaires Civiles (to Minister), 'Rapport sur le siège et la délivrance d'Agadès', Dakar, 18 May 1917, 4–8; Capt. Sabatié, 'Rapp. . . . sur le siège du poste (d'Agadès), du 13.12.1916 au 3.3.1917', Agades, 10 March 1917, 1–3 (both Vincennes, Niger V).

139 Service Aff. Civiles, 'Rapport . . .', 18 May 1917.

140 According to letters found in Agades after the end of the siege (*ibid.*).

141 According to a proclamation by Kaocen in October 1916 (14 MI 863 and CO 583/57). See also General P. Mangeot, 'Le Siège d'Agadès raconté par un prisonnier de Kaossen', *RCD*, 8 (1930), 479–82; *Le Temps*, 20 July 1917.

142 Périé, 'Carnet monographique du cercle de Bilma', ch. 2, 14; Féral, 'Monographie du cercle d'Agadez', ch. 3, 6; Gov. (Mourin) to General-in-Chief Zinder, 18 January 1917 (14 MI 303); General Goullet, 'Note résumant les mesures prises', 13 January 1917.

143 Féral, 'Monographie du cercle d'Agadez', ch. 3, 6; André Salifou, *Kaoussan ou la révolte senoussiste* (Niamey, 1973b), 55–8; 'Note sur le Chef Senoussiste Kaocen ou Kaoussen', 30 December 1916 (Aix 4(4)D-16).

144 Périé, 'Carnet monographique du cercle de Bilma', ch. 2, 15.
145 Riou (1968), 25ff.
146 *Ibid.*, 25.
147 *Ibid.*, annexe III.
148 *Ibid.*, annexe II; Périé, 'Carnet monographique du cercle de Bilma', ch. 2, 15–16; Service Aff. Civiles, 'Rapport . . .', 18 May 1917, 14.
149 Lieut. Guérin, 'Réconnaissance des traces qui mènent au beau Kaouar', ch. 3, 2.
150 Service Aff. Civiles, 'Rapport . . .', 18 May 1917, 2–4; Gen. Goullet, 'Note résumant les mesures prises', 13 January 1917.
151 Lugard to Secr. State-Colonies (W. Long), 23 February 1917; Lieut. Col. F. Jenkins (Acting Commandant Nigeria Regiment) to Gov. Gal., Kaduna, 1 February 1917 (both CO 583/56); Gov. Gal., French West Africa, to Minister, Dakar, 8 January 1917 (14 MI 864).
152 *Ibid.*
153 Capt. J. Dare, Report on the Military Operations on the Northern Frontier from 1 February to 13 March 1917, Kaduna, 14 March 1917 (CO 583/56).
154 Report by Lieut. Col. Jenkins, Kaduna, 21 June 1917 (CO 583/58).
155 *Commandant*-Niamey (G. Mere) to Gov., 30 March 1917 (AP-Niamey); Renaud (1922), 252–62; Gamory-Dubourdeau (1924), 248–9.
156 Gov. to Gov. Gal., Zinder, 17 January 1917 (14 MI 305).
157 Riou (1968), 41–4.
158 Gov. to Gov. Gal., Zinder, 17 January 1917.
159 Lugard to Secr. State-Colonies, 23 February 1917; Acting Gov. (Laforque) to Gov. Gal., Zinder, 17 April 1917 (14 MI 864). According to Margery Perham, 'Lugard hated the whole business because he believed the French, when they regained control, would use terribly severe measures against [the Tuareg].' See her *Lugard. The Years of Authority 1898–1945*, vol. III (1960), 548. He was, of course, right. But then such an accurate evaluation of the situation is to be expected from a man with experience of post-revolt repression (re Satiru, 1906). On the Nigerian contribution generally, and on the situation in Nigeria itself, see J. Osuntokun, 'The response of the British colonial government in Nigeria to the Islamic insurgency in the French Sudan and Sahara during the First World War', *BIFAN*, XXXVI, 1 (1974), 14–24.
160 Lugard to Secr. State-Colonies, 9 March 1917 and other documents in CO 583/56.
161 Salifou (1973b); Riou (1968).
162 Gov. Gal. (Clozel) to Gen. Laperrine, Dakar, 16 February 1917 (14 MI 303).
163 Gov. (Lefebvre) to Gov. Gal., Zinder, 6 August 1920 (14 MI 610).
164 Salifou (1973b), 90–1.
165 F. Nicolas (1950), 93.
166 Acting Gov. (Laforgue) to General-in-Chief, Zinder, 11 March 1917 (14 MI 303); Salifou (1973b), 91–100.
167 *Ibid.*, 89–97.
168 Campbell (1928), 125.
169 In May 1917 alone, caravans arrived in Agades with 108 tons of millet requisitioned in the south. See Acting Gov. (Laforgue) to Gov. Gal., Zinder, 2 May 1917 (14 MI 305). And in June the French were already desperately short of camels. See same (de Jonquières) to same, 14 June 1917 (14 MI 305).
170 Salifou (1973b), 101–13.
171 Gamory-Dubourdeau (1924), 249.
172 Périé, 'Carnet monographique du cercle de Bilma', ch. 2, 16.
173 Acting Gov. (Laforgue) to Gov. Gal., Zinder, 28 February 1917 (14 MI 305).
174 Capt. Piétri, 'Notes sur les Touareg Oulliminden', 21 February 1923, 13.

175 F. Nicolas (1950), 95; Séré de Rivières (1965), 228–9.
176 E. Bernus (1966), 12. See also Agg-Alăwjelj Ghubăyd (1975), 156.
177 Bonte (1971), 41–2.
178 Nicolas (1950), 93.
179 Gov. Gal. (Van Vollenhoven) to General-in-Chief, Sahara, Dakar, 31 July 1917 (14 MI 307).
180 Gov. (Mourin) to Gov. Gal., Zinder, 19 September 1917 (14 MI 307).
181 Dresch (1959), 258–9.
182 'Rapp. du Col. Méchet sur la tournée effectuée par lui du 20.2. au 3.5.1919', 3 (14 MI 864); Naval Intelligence Division (Geogr. Handbook Series), *French West Africa*, vol. II (*The Colonies*) (1944), 377.
183 Gamory-Dubourdeau (1924), 249.
184 Gov. (Mourin) to Gov. Gal., Zinder, 17 December 1917 (14 MI 864); Lugard to Secr. of State-Colonies, 7 & 9 March, 25 July 1917 (CO 583/56 & 58); Acting Gov. Gal. (J. Carde) to Gov. Gal. of Nigeria, Dakar, 22 January 1918 (CO 583/65). It may be, however, that the French overestimated the number of animals in Northern Nigeria and that the shortage in transport animals was caused by the decimation of the camel herds during the Tibesti column and the revolts. See Lugard to Gov. Gal. of French West Africa, 22 February & 7 March 1918 (CO 583/65).
185 Petragnani (1925), 511–15.
186 Riou (1968), 94–5.
187 'SD. Tanout. R. pol. 4e trim. 1917', Tanout, 31 December 1917 (AP Zinder).
188 Fifty-two rebels were killed during *one* month alone, by *one* of the detachments. See Gov. Gal. (Angoulvant) to General-in-Chief, Sahara. Dakar, 10 March 1918 (14 MI 307).
189 Salifou (1973b), 137.
190 TM Niger, 'R. pol. du 2e trim. 1916', Zinder, 1 July 1916 (ANN); Nigeria, Report on the Blue Book 1915, 10 (CO 657/1); TM Niger, 'R. pol. du 3e trim. 1915' (signed Mourin), Zinder, 11 November 1915, 11 (SOM-NS c. 591 d. 18).
191 Tilho (1928), 240. This method is a valid one, as illustrated by Tilho's remarkably accurate prediction that the 1950s would be a decade of abundant rainfall; and his prediction, only a few years out, that the Central Sudan would suffer again from drought after 1975.
192 TM Niger, 'R. pol. du 2e trim. 1916', 4; Périé, 'Histoire de la subdivision de Maradi', 25.
193 TM Niger, 'R. pol. du 3e trim. 1916' (signed Capt. F. de Jonquières), Zinder, 1 October 1916, 1–2 (ANN).
194 Gov. (Méchet) to Gov. Gal., Zinder, 8 March 1918 (14 MI 371). See also note 169.
195 Acting Gov. Gal. (J. Carde) to Gov., Dakar, 11 January 1918 (14 MI 1287); Crowder (1974), 505–6.
196 Acting Gov. Gal. (J. Carde) to Governors of Mauritania and Niger Mil. Territory, and to the Lieut. Governors of Senegal and Upper-Sen. Niger, Dakar, 1 February 1918 (14 MI 371); Crowder (1974), 500–1.
197 Gov. Gal. . . . 1 February 1918 (14 MI 371); 'Rapport du Colonel Méchet sur les opérations de recrutement de l'année 1918', Zinder, 5 September 1918, 1 (14 MI 371).
198 Crowder (1974), 500–1.
199 Gov. Gal. (Angoulvant) to Commissioner, Dakar, 5 March 1918 (14 MI 371).
200 Gov. (Méchet) to Gov. Gal., Zinder, 8 March 1918 (14 MI 371).
201 Méchet, Zinder, 26 March 1918 (14 MI 371).
202 Gov. Gal. (Angoulvant) to Gov., Dakar, 30 March 1918; Gov. (Méchet) to Gov. Gal., Zinder, 5 April 1918; Gov. Gal. (Angoulvant) to Gov., Dakar, 8 April 1918 (all 14 MI 371).
203 Capt. Sadoux, 'Rapp. sur les opérations de recrutement'.
204 G. Mère, 'Rapp. sur le recrutement de 1918 dans le Cercle de Niamey', Niamey, 19 July 1918 (14 MI 371).

205 'Rapport du Col. Méchet', 5 September 1918; TM Niger, 'Bull. de renseignements', no. 79, 1 June 1918 & no. 80, 8 June 1918 (14 MI 864).
206 On this point, and on the problem of conscription generally in French West Africa, see Myron J. Echenberg, 'Paying the blood tax: military conscription in French West Africa, 1914–1929', *CJAS*, IX, 2 (1975), 171–92.
207 TM Niger, 'R. pol. du 1er trim. 1921', Zinder, 14 May 1921 (signed Ruef) (Dakar 2G21–14); TM Niger, 'R. pol. du 1er trim. 1922' (signed Ruef), Zinder, 5 April 1922 (Dakar 2G22–16).
208 Michel (1973), 647.
209 There were 1,421 recruits from the West, that is about 1 per cent of the total population of that region, as opposed to about 0.35 per cent for Niger as a whole. See Michel (1973), 658–9; Mère, 'Rapp. sur le recrutement . . . Niamey', 19 July 1918.
210 *Annuaire GG-AOF, 1917–21*, 1038; Thom (1970), 159.
211 TM Niger, 'R. pol. du 2e trim. 1920' (signed Ruef), Zinder, 19 August 1920 (Dakar 2G29–13).
212 Acting Gov. (Lefebvre) to the *Commandants*, Zinder, 20 August 1918 (ASP Magaria).
213 *Annuaire GG-AOF, 1917–21*, 93–4.
214 J. Soucadaux, 'Les Elites noires en AOF' (unpublished paper, CHEAM, 1941). J. Lombard in his *Autorités traditionnelles et pouvoir européen en Afrique noire. Le déclin d'une aristocratie sous le régime colonial* (1967) argues (124) that there was a general 'retour en grâce de la chefferie' throughout French West Africa after 1917. He could have added that in this matter the French simply made a virtue of necessity.
215 Based on Abdou Ibrahim, 'La Co-opération; un des facteurs fondamentaux du développement rural au Niger' (dissertation, Institut de Droit Rural et d'Economie Agricole, Paris, n.d.).
216 TM Niger, 'R. semestriels 2e & 3e semestres 1918' (signed Méchet), Zinder, 15 November 1918 & 1 February 1919 (SOM-NS c. 591 d. 18).
217 TM Niger, 'Bull. de renseignments no. 103', Zinder, 16 November 1918 (the date is evidently wrong) (14 MI 864).
218 TM Niger, 'R. pol. du 1er trim. 1921', 2.
219 TM Niger, 'R. pol. du 3e & 4e trimestres 1920' (signed Ruef), Zinder, 20 November 1920 & 29 January 1921 (Dakar 2G20–13).
220 Sellier, 'Note sur le peuplement . . . du cercle de Niamey', 84–9; Echard (1975), 225; Colony of Niger, 'Rapp. Agricole, 3e trim. 1922', 25 October 1922 (Dakar 2G22–16) and the reports cited in note 216 above.
221 J. Périé, 'Histoire . . . de la subdivision de Maradi', 30; Guy Nicolas & Guy Mainet, *La Vallée du Gulbi de Maradi* (Paris/Niamey, n.d.), 41; TM Niger, 'R. pol. du 2e trim. 1921' (signed Ruef), Zinder, 22 August 1921, 164 (Dakar 2G21–14).
222 TM Niger, 'R. sur la situation politique des régions dépendant des territoires sahariens' (signed Lieut. Col. Méchet), Zinder, 25 July 1919 (14 MI 610); Périé, 'Carnet monographique du cercle de Bilma', ch. 2, 17; TM Niger, 'R. pol. du 3e trim. 1919' (signed Lieut. Col. Lefebvre), 17 November 1919, 3–9 (SOM-NS, c. 591 d. 18); TM Niger, 'Rapports politiques 4e trim. 1920 & 1921' (both signed Ruef), 29 January 1921 & 11 January 1922 (SOM-NS c. 591 d. 18 and Dakar 2G21–14); Campbell (1928), 136–42.
223 Capt. Vitali, 'Rapp. sur le sultan Ibrahim', Agades, 23 September 1919 (14 MI 863); 'Rapp. du Lieut. Col. Lefebvre', Zinder, 29 November 1919 (14 MI 1077).
224 TM Niger, 'R. pol. du 3e trim. 1919', 17 November 1919, 16.
225 Capt. Vitali, 'Rapp. sur le sultan Ibrahim'.
226 Salifou (1973b), 146–7.
227 For a fuller treatment of the Tegama 'affair', see Finn Fuglestad, 'Révolte et mort de Tegama, sultan d'Agadès (1920)', *NA*, 152 (1976), 96–101.

228 'Rapport du Capitaine Vitali sur les motifs et raisons qui l'ont conduit à se recuser comme juge-président du tribunal du cercle d'Agades pour l'affaire Tégama', Agades, 17 April 1920. See also 'Rapport sur les actes commis au cours de la révolte de l'Aïr par Tegama (etc.)', Zinder, 19 January 1920 (both 14 MI 863).

229 'Rapp. Capt. Vitali', 17 April 1920; Dr Souchaud, 'Procès-verbal d'autopsie du cadavre de l'ex-sultan d'Agadès Tegama (etc.)', Agades, 30 April 1920 (14 MI 863); Gov. to Gov. Gal., Zinder, 19 April 1920 (14 MI 360); 'Rapp. d'enquête concernant les causes et circonstances de la mort de Tégama (etc.)', Zinder, 9 August 1920 (14 MI 863).

230 Salifou (1973b), 138–40; Capt. Piétri, 'Notes sur la Touareg Oulliminden', 21 February 1923, 13.

231 Fuglestad (1976); H. T. Norris and Jean-Louis Dufour are of the same opinion. See Norris (1975), 164; Jean-Louis Dufour, 'La Révolte touareg et le siège d'Agades (13 décembre 1916–3 mars 1917)', *Relations Internationales*, 3 (1975), 55–77 (57–8).

232 Norris (1975), 162–8.

233 *Ibid.*; F. Fuglestad, 'Révolte dans le desert. Les mouvements de révolte chez les nomades du Sahara Nigérien (1915–1931)' (dissertation, Aix-en-Provence, 1971); extracts published under the title 'Les Révoltes des Touareg du Niger (1916–17)', *CEA*, XIII, 1 (1973), 82–120.

234 Norris (1975), 162–3.

235 *Ibid.*, 171.

236 Urvoy (1933), 95–7.

237 It seems to me that Jean-Louis Dufour is arguing along the same lines when he states (1975, p. 76) that 'la révolte est un soulagement, un exutoire, un immense défoulement'.

238 Salifou (1973b), III.

239 Moussa had been strongly tempted to join the rebels but in the end he decided to side with the French. See Dufour (1975), 70; André Bourgeot, 'Les Echanges transsahariens, la Senusiya et les révoltes twareg de 1916–17', *CEA*, XVIII, 1–2 (1978), 159–85.

240 TM Niger, 'R. pol. du 3e trim. 1919'; 'Les Touaregs du Cercle de Tanout', monograph, 1944 (ANN); Norris (1975), 16; Gamory-Dubourdeau (1924), 244; Bonte (1971), 41–2, 317.

241 Evans-Pritchard (1949/1954), 143–52.

242 TM Niger, 'R. sur la situation . . . territoires sahariens' (Méchet); Gov. Gal. to Min. of Colonies, Dakar, 17 January & 30 August 1919 (14 MI 610 & 864); Campbell (1928), 128.

243 J. Périé, 'Carnet monographique du cercle de Bilma', ch. 2, 20–3; TM Niger, 'Bulletins de renseignements nos. 7, 11 & 12', Zinder, 7 July, 2 October & 5 November 1920 (all AP Zinder); TM Niger, 'R. pol. du 4e trim. 1920 (signed Ruef)', Zinder, 29 January 1921, 3–7 (Dakar 2G20–13); C. Niger, 'Bull. rens.', Zinder, 1 February 1923 (AP Zinder).

244 Based on Evans-Pritchard (1949/1954), 156–87; Jean-Louis Miège, *L'Impérialisme colonial italien de 1870 à nos jours* (1968), 179; Périé, 'Carnet monographique du cercle de Bilma'.

4. Summing up and looking ahead

1 Hull (1968), 164–6.

2 For a summary of the debate, see *Afr.fr.*, 5 (1929), 228. See also A. I. Asiwaju, 'Migrations as revolt: the example of the Ivory Coast and the Upper Volta before 1945', *JAH*, XVII, 4 (1976), 577–94.

3 Raulin (n.d.), 80–91; *id.* (1965), 134.

4 Cathérine Baroin, 'Effets de la colonisation sur la société traditionnelle Daza (République du Niger)', *JA*, XLVII, fasc. II (1977), 123–32 (125).

5 See in particular Robin Palmer & Neil Parsons (eds.), *The Roots of Rural Poverty in Central and Southern Africa* (1977); and also more generally the first chapters of Iliffe (1979).

6 See for instance G. Féral, 'Monographie du cercle d'Agadez', Agades, 14 October 1955, ch. 3, 18 (ANN).

7 Bonte (1971), 196–7.

8 Baier (1974), 121–8.

9 Edmond Bernus, 'Maladies humaines et animales chez les Touaregs sahéliens', *JSA*, XXXIX, fasc. I (1969), 111–37.

10 The remarkably low birth rate among the Kanuri in 1960, only 60 per cent of the Hausa birth rate, gives credit to this theory. See *Etude démographique du Niger*, vol. II (Ministère de la Coopération/INSEE, 1963), 23.

11 *Le Niger* (published by the Gouvernement Général de l'AOF, 1931), 14.

12 Among other reasons because 'toute culture (et histoire) nationale ... est prise de conscience', and as such a 'moyen de résistance': Jean Suret-Canale, *L'Afrique noire. L'Ere coloniale 1900–45* (1964), 460.

13 See for instance Bonte (1975a), 63–4; Bonte & Echard (1976), 272–3.

14 Smaldone (1977), 150–1.

15 Olivier de Sardan (1973a), and (1975), 116–17.

16 See for instance R. G. Jenkins, 'Some aspects of the evolution of the religious brotherhoods in north and north-west Africa, 1523–1900' (MA dissertation, University of Birmingham, 1969), 40; J. S. Trimingham, *Islam in West Africa* (1967), 236. It is difficult to follow Trimingham when he argues (p. 66) that 'the idea of *baraka* gained no essential hold upon Negro Islam'.

17 Pierre Alexandre, 'Le Problème des chefferies en Afrique noire française', *Notes et Etudes Documentaires* (La Documentation française), no. 2508 (10 February 1959), 8.

18 Oral sources.

19 According to the 'Monographie sommaire du Cercle de Niamey', 15 September 1921 (14 MI 696).

20 See for instance, E. Bernus (1975), 237–8; Murphy (1964).

21 *Le Niger* (1931), 40 & 74–6.

22 For a general discussion, see J.-C. Forelich, 'Essai sur les causes et méthodes de l'Islamisation de l'Afrique de l'Ouest du XIe au XXe siècle', in I. M. Lewis (ed.), *Islam in Tropical Africa* (1966), 160–71.

23 Donald Cruise O'Brien, 'Towards an "Islamic policy" in French West Africa, 1854–1914', *JAH*, VIII, 2 (1967), 303–16.

24 According to Pierre Alexandre, 'A West African Islamic movement: Hamallism in French West Africa', in R. I. Rotberg & Ali A. Mazrui (eds.), *Protest and Power in Black Africa* (1970), 497–512 (esp. 503).

25 See for instance, A. Gouilly, *L'Islam dans l'AOF* (1952), 254–5.

26 Edward Alpers, 'Towards a history of the expansion of Islam in East Africa: the matrilineal peoples of the southern interior', in T. O. Ranger & I. N. Kimambo (eds.), *The Historical Study of African Religions* (1972), 172–201.

27 Trimingham (1967), 35.

28 See for instance, *Coutumiers juridiques de l'AOF*, vol. III (1939), 310.

29 Jean Rouch, *La Religion et la magie Songhay* (1960b), 17.

30 Leroux (1948), 672.

31 Nicolas, Doumesche & Mouché (1968), 165.

32 Rouch (1954), 57–8.

33 See for instance, Michael Onwuejeogwu, 'The cult of the "Bori" spirits among the Hausa', in Mary Douglas & Phyllis M. Kaberry (eds.), *Man in Africa* (1969), 279–305; Jacqueline Monfouga-Nicolas, *Ambivalence et culte de possession. Contribution à l'étude du Bori hausa* (1972), and by the same author (writing under the name of Jacqueline Broustra-Monfouga), 'Approche ethno-psychiatrique du phénomène de possession. Le Bori de Konni (Niger)', *JSA*, XLIII, fasc. II (1973), 197–221.

34 Rouch (1954), 61–2; *id.*, *Essai sur la religion Songhay* (1960a), 29–48.

35 See chapter 5.
36 According to R. Horton, 'Stateless societies in the history of West Africa', in J. F. Ade Ajayi & M. Crowder (eds.), *History of West Africa*, vol. I (1971), 78–119.
37 In addition to the works cited in note 33 above, see Ludger Reuke, *Die Maguzawa in Nordnigeria. Ethnographische Darstellung und Analyse des beginnenden Religionswandels zum Katholizismus* (Bielefield, 1969), 59–60; Rouch (1953a), 238.
38 Rouch (1960b), 62–3.
39 Trimingham (1967), 38; Guy Nicolas, 'Une forme atténuée du "potlatch" en pays Hausa (République du Niger). Le "Dubu" ', *Cahiers de l'ISEA*, 5th series, 10 (1967), 151–214.
40 For a discussion, see Leroux (1948), 680; R. Verdier, 'Problèmes fonciers nigériens', *Penant*, 703–4 (1964), 587–93; Henri Raulin, *La Dynamique des techniques agraires en Afrique tropicale du nord* (1967), 23–6.

5. The 'great silence': the classic period of colonial rule, 1922–45

1 Gov. (J. Court), 'Circulaire no. 48, APA', Niamey, 30 July 1935 (ASP Birnin Konni).
2 *Le Niger* (1931), 40.
3 *Ibid.*, 76; Victor Roehrig, 'Evolution de l'enseignement au Niger, de ses débuts jusqu'en 1951', Niamey (Inspection Académique), 15 October 1951 (consulted by courtesy of the author).
4 For recent figures, see J. N. Paden, D. G. Morrison, R. C. Mitchell & H. M. Stevenson, *Black Africa. A Comparative Handbook* (New York, 1972), 62 & 70.
5 Michel Sellier, 'R. ann. pour 1954, Cercle de Maradi', Maradi, 8 February 1955 (AP Zinder).
6 C. de Maradi, 'R. pol. ann. pour 1933', Maradi, 6 January 1934, 41 (AP Maradi).
7 'The curriculum and diplomas of the schools [in French West Africa, including Ponty] were pegged considerably below their counterparts in France, making the diplomas useless as a basis for admission to French schools.' Peggy Sabatier, ' "Elite" education in French West Africa. The era of limits, 1903–1945', *IJAHS*, XI, 2 (1978), 247–66 (248). See also Bergo, 'L'Ecole William-Ponty', *Europe-France-Outre-Mer*, 368 (1960), 22–3.
8 Commandant Chailley, *Histoire de l'Afrique Occidentale Française* (1968), 422.
9 *Le Niger* (1931), 75.
10 Roehrig, 'Evolution de l'enseignement au Niger', 1.
11 *Ibid.*, 2.
12 *Budget local du Niger*, 1940, XXX–XXXII.
13 Chailley (1968), 422.
14 Oral sources.
15 Ruth Schachter-Morgenthau, *Political Parties in French-Speaking West Africa* (1967), 29.
16 These remarks are essentially speculative. They are based on interviews with a considerable number of graduates from the *Ecole Primaire Supérieure* and from Ponty; and on Boubou Hama, *Kotia-Nima*, vol. I (Niamey, 1968), 119–24. See also Rouch (1954), 58; Thomas Hodgkin & Ruth Schachter, 'French-speaking West Africa in transition', *International Conciliation*, 528 (1960), 373–436 (385); Guy de Lusignan, *L'Afrique noire depuis l'indépendence. L'évolution des états francophones* (1970), 50–7.
17 Serre (1950), 46; C. de Tillabery, 'Bull. de renseignements pol. 3e trim. 1931' (signed Dielenschneider), 30 September 1931 (ASP Tillabery); Gov. to *Commandant*-Dosso, Niamey, 30 November 1937 (ASP Gaya); SD-Madaoua, 'R. pol. pour 1941'; C. de Tanout, 'R. pol. pour 1931' (signed Loubert), 31 December 1931; J. Robin, 'Rapp. de tournée du canton de Sambéra', Dosso, 28 October 1938; 'Rapp. de tournée, canton de Keita',

Tahoua, 25 June 1932; 'R. de tournée', Goure, 4 February 1934; R. Jacob, 'R. de tournée de recensement du 9 au 14 December 1933', Tanout; 'R. de tournée du Commandant de cercle de Manga', Goure, 4 February 1934 (all ANN); 'Rapp. sur le recensement des Peuls et Bouzous de la SD de Tessaoua', Tessaoua, 29 April 1939, 4 (ASP Tessaoua).

18 Gov. to *Commandant*-Dosso, 30 November 1937 (ASP Gaya); C. de Tillabery, 'Bull. de renseignements', 30 September 1931; 'R. de tournée, canton de Courteye', Tillabery, 28 June 1933 (ASP Tillabery).

19 This was particularly the case of the Tarka valley. See for instance Mathey, 'R. trimestriel, 3e trim. 1934', Tanout, 30 September 1934 (ANN).

20 Loubert, 'Bull. rens. 3e trim. 1932, C. de Tanout'; 'R. de tournée du commandant de cercle', Goure, 10 December 1946 (both ANN).

21 Including Tanganyika. The preceding sentence has been taken directly from Iliffe (1979), 301.

22 J. Brévié, *Islamisme contre 'Naturisme' au Soudan français. Essai de psychologie coloniale* (1923).

23 But as a member of the Vichy government Brévié went on trial after France was liberated and was convicted of treason. See Robert Aron (with Georgette Elgey), *Histoire de Vichy, 1940–44* (1954), 749.

24 Michael Crowder, *West Africa under Colonial Rule* (Evanston, 1968), 189–90.

25 See for instance William B. Cohen, *Rulers of Empire: The French Colonial Service in Africa* (Stanford, 1971), 140.

26 'Rapport à Monsieur le Gouverneur Général en Conseil de Gouvernement. Séance du 3.12.1926' (SOM-NS Aff. pol. 167); 'Reponse du Lieut. Gov.' (to the report presented by the Inspector of Colonies), Niamey, 5 June 1929 (Dakar 11G26).

27 CN, 'R. pol. ann. 1926' (signed Brévié), 31 March 1927, 22ff (Dakar 2G26–18).

28 CN, 'R. pol. ann.', Zinder, 26 February 1925, 22 (Dakar 2G24–23).

29 *JO-AOF*, XXI (18 July 1925), 576.

30 CN, 'R. pol. 4e trim. 1922' (signed Brévié), 20 February 1923, 1–16 (Dakar 2G22–16); CN, 'R. pol. 1er trim. 1923', 22 May 1923, 17–18 (Dakar 2G23–24).

31 See for instance *Budget local du Niger*, 1921–5.

32 Yves Pehaut, 'L'Arachide au Niger', in *Bibliothèque de l'Institut d'Etudes Politiques de Bordeaux*, vol. I, *Etudes d'Economie Africaine* (1970), 9–103 (44).

33 Baier (1974), 224.

34 John Davidson Collins, 'Government and groundnut marketing in rural Hausa Niger: the 1930s to the 1970s in Magaria' (PhD thesis, Johns Hopkins University, Baltimore, 1974), 35–9.

35 Pehaut (1970), 44.

36 Pierre Bonte, *L'Elevage et le commerce du bétail dans l'Ader-Doutchi-Majya* (Paris/Niamey, n.d. [1967?]), 175.

37 See *Le Niger* (1931), 24 & 44–5; SD Magaria, 'R. écon., 4e trim. 1927', 31 December 1927 (AP Zinder).

38 'Reponse du Lieut. Gov.', 5 June 1929 (Dakar 11G26).

39 CN, 'R. ann. 1925' (signed Brévié), Zinder, 24 February 1926, 7 (Dakar 2G25–20); Baier (1976a), 12.

40 See Raulin (n.d.), 21–43.

41 Alfred Sauvy, *Histoire économique de la France entre les deux guerres*, vol. I (1965), 444.

42 'Procès-verbal de la réunion du Conseil des Notables de la SDC de Zinder du 27.4.1926' (AP Zinder).

43 *Annuaire-GG-AOF* (1922), 1015; Edmond Séré de Rivières, *Le Niger* (1951), 21.

44 Based on Colonel Abadie (1927), 350; Speech by Gov. Gal. J. Carde, December 1927 (printed), 16; *Commandant*-Zinder (H. Fleury) to the chiefs of the SD of Tanout and

Magaria, 17 February 1923 (AP Zinder); Laforest, 'R. de tournée, Maine-Soroa, 24 April 1924 (ANN).

45 CN, 'R. d'ensemble, 2e trim. 1923', Zinder, 20 July 1923, 1–3 (Dakar 2G23–24); CN, 'R. pol. ann.' (signed Jore), 25 January 1924, 1–2 (SOM-NS c. 591 d. 14); CN, 'R. pol. ann.', 31 March 1927, 15 (Dakar 2G26–18).

46 *Le Niger* (1931), 46.

47 CN, 'R. pol. 4e trim. 1922', 20 February 1923, 8 (Dakar 2G22–16); CN, 'R. pol. 1er trim. 1923', Zinder, 22 May 1923, 6 (Dakar 2G23–24).

48 Lieut. Riou, 'L'Azalay d'automne 1928', *RCD*, 5 (1929), 281–5.

49 CN, 'R. pol. ann. 1924', 26 February 1925, 3 (Dakar 2G24–23).

50 See for instance Séré de Rivières (1951), 70; de Loppinot, 'Rapp. de tournée', Tahoua, 2 December 1930 (AP Tahoua); Chimier, 'Rapp. du chef de la subdivision nomade', Tahoua, 25 November 1932 (ANN).

51 Commandant Rottier, 'La Vie agricole en Aïr (Sahara central)', *RCD*, 11 (1927), 408–15.

52 A. Rovagny, 'Villes d'Afrique: Niamey', *RCD*, 6 (1930), 329–37.

53 Séré de Rivières (1951), 40.

54 *Id.* (1965), 237.

55 See for instance CN, 'R. pol. ann. 1924', 26 February 1925, 14–15 (Dakar 2G24–23); Gov. (Brévié) to *Commandant*-Dosso, Zinder, 5 March 1926 (ANN); SD Dogondoutchi, 'R. pol. 3e trim. 1930', 10 November 1930 (ASP Dogondoutchi).

56 'Chef du bureau des APA au Lieut. Gouverneur', Zinder, 15 December 1923 (ANN).

57 According to CN, 'R. pol. ann. 1924', 26 February 1925, 5.

58 *Commandant*-Dosso to Gov., 18 February 1926 (ANN); J. Robin, 'Description de la Province de Dosso', *BIFAN*, IX, 1–4 (1947), 56–98 (67).

59 Babuty, 'R. pol. 1928, cercle de Dosso' (ANN); 'Dossier signalétique des chefs indigènes, SD Dogondoutchi' (ASP Dogondoutchi).

60 See for instance, CN, 'R. pol. ann. 1926', 31 March 1927, 28 (Dakar 2G26–18).

61 Chief, SD Maradi to *Commandant*-Tessaoua, 27 October 1923 (AP Maradi).

62 *Commandant*-Tessaoua (Calteau) to Chief, SD Maradi, 19 January & 13 February 1925 (AP Maradi): J. Périé, 'Histoire politique et administrative de la subdivision de Maradi', Maradi, 1938, 34–5 (AP Maradi); David (1964), 121.

63 *Commandant*-Maradi to Gov., 8 February 1929; same to same, 13 July 1938 (both AP Maradi).

64 One of the consequences was the suppression of the institution of *sarkin* Fulani in most parts of Niger. See SD Dogondoutchi, 'R. pol. 3e trim. 1930', 10 November 1930, 2 (ASP Dogondoutchi); Chief, SD Tessaoua (Mauger) to *Commandant*-Maradi, 13 November 1928 (AP Maradi); 'Cercle de Dosso. Bull. pol. 3e trim. 1933' (ANN); J. P. Pinaud, 'Rapp. d'ensemble sur le recensement des Peuhls de la SD de Magaria', 29 November 1946 (ASP Magaria).

65 CN, 'R. ann. 1925', 24 February 1926, 12 (Dakar 2G25–20).

66 Speech, J. Carde, 1927; Chief, SD Tessaoua, 13 November 1928 (AP Maradi); Gov. (Petre) to all *cercles*, Niamey, 30 March 1935 (AP Zinder).

67 'SD Tanout. R. pol. 1927' (AP Zinder).

68 CN, 'R. pol. ann. 1927' (signed Brévié), 15 May 1928, 5–6 (Dakar 2G27–12).

69 Pehaut (1970), 44.

70 Speech by Gov. Jean Ramadier in the Territorial Assembly of Niger, 29 March 1955 (printed), 8–9.

71 Rouch (1956), 27.

72 *Budget local du Niger*, 1925 & 1930.

73 De Loppinot, 'Rapp. de tournée de recensement, canton de Tamaske', Tahoua, 14 February 1933 (ANN).

74 Report by Bernard Sol, 7 August 1932 (Dakar 11G26); Babuty, 'R. pol. 1928, Dosso' (ANN).
75 *Ibid.*
76 Gov. to *Commandants*, Niamey, 6 March 1926 (ANN).
77 Esperet, 'R. pol. pour 1929, SD Tanout' (ANN).
78 Paragraph based on Babuty, 'R. pol. pour 1927, cercle de Dosso' (ANN); CN, 'R. pol. pour 1928 & 1929', 12 May 1929 & 10 April 1930 (Dakar 2G28–14 & 2G29–17); de Loppinot, 'Cercle de Tahoua: R. ann. pour 1930', 1 January 1931 (AP Tahoua).
79 SD Dogondoutchi, 'R. pol., 3e trim. 1930', 10 November 1930 (ASP Dogondoutchi).
80 CN, 'R. pol. 1928', 12 May 1929, 24 (Dakar 2G28–14).
81 Speech, J. Carde, 1927, 43.
82 S. Frolow, 'Note sur le climat de Niamey', *BCEHSAOF*, XIX, 1 (1936), 150–87 (167).
83 Babuty, 'R. pol. 1928, Dosso' (ANN). See also Beauvilain (1977), 18; 'Note, renseignements agricoles' (signed Brévié), Niamey, 11 March 1926 (Dakar 2G26–7).
84 Pehaut (1970), 45–7.
85 CN, 'Rapp. pol. ann. 1930' (signed Blacher), 2 April 1931, 13–14 (Dakar 2G30–11).
86 CN, 'Rapp. pol. ann. 1931', 4–5 (Dakar 2G31–8).
87 Chief, SD Dogondoutchi (J. Toby) to *Commandant*-Dosso, 30 November 1926 (ASP Dogondoutchi); *Commandant*-Niamey (H. Croccichia) to Gov., Niamey, 24 May 1927; Pierre Brachet, 'Monographie du canton de l'Imanan', Filingue, 28 February 1943 (both ASP Filingue); 'Rapp. sur la situation politique du canton du Kourfei', Niamey, 28 February 1927 (Vincennes, Niger VII).
88 Chief, SD Dogondoutchi to *Commandant*-Dosso, 30 November 1926 (ASP Dogondoutchi).
89 The ensuing agitation provoked another 'vigorous' French intervention (*ibid.*).
90 *Commandant*-Niamey to Gov., 24 May 1927 (ASP Filingue).
91 'Rapp. sur la situation . . . Kourfei', 28 February 1927 (Vincennes, Niger VII).
92 This is according to a report dating from as late as 1944: Scheurer, 'Rapp. de tournée de recensement, canton de Kourfeye', Filingue, 31 March 1944, 4 (ASP Filingue).
93 Letter from Adamou Mayaki to the author, 25 July 1973.
94 Brachet, 'Monographie du canton de l'Imanan', 13.
95 *Ibid.*, 14.
96 *Idem*; 'Rapp. sur la situation . . . Kourfei', 28 February 1927 (Vincennes, Niger VII); Rouch (1953a), 237–8.
97 R. C. Abraham, *Dictionary of the Hausa Language* (1968), 382; Rouch (1960a), 74.
98 CN, 'R. pol. ann. 1927' (signed Brévié), 15 May 1928 (Dakar 2G27–12).
99 E. Pelissier, 'R. pol. C. de Niamey pour 1936', 25 February 1937, 2 (AP Niamey).
100 CN, 'R. pol. ann. 1928' (signed Brévié), 12 May 1929, 6 (Dakar 2G28–14).
101 J. Mathey, 'R. pol. C. de Niamey pour 1935', 31 December 1935, 3 (AP Niamey).
102 Report by Capt. V. Salaman, 27 August 1906 (ANN).
103 At least this is the impression conveyed by some of Jean Rouch's films, especially his 'Les Maîtres fous' from 1956. See also Rouch (1954), 29–48; Monfouga-Nicolas (1972), 344–51; and finally Charles Pidoux, 'Les Cultes de possession', *La Vie Intellectuelle* (Dec. 1956), 42–60.
104 Brachet, 'Monographie du canton de l'Imanan', 14.
105 Oral sources.
106 See for instance, report by the Inspector of Administrative Affairs, Niamey, 22 March 1927 (Dakar 11G7).
107 'Rapp. sur la situation . . . Kourfei', 28 February 1927 (Vincennes, Niger VII); Rouch (1953a), 237–8; Diarra (1971), 114–15. For further details on the *hauka* movement, see F. Fuglestad, 'Les "Hauka": une interprétation historique', *CEA*, XV, 2 (1975a), 203–16.

108 Trimingham (1967), 99.
109 *Ibid.*, 97–100.
110 Alexandre (1970), 497.
111 Trimingham (1967), 99.
112 Michel Sellier, 'Le Hamallisme dans la politique locale africaine', Niamey, 15 May 1948, 2 (ASP Say); Alexandre (1970), 500–1.
113 Trimingham (1967), 99.
114 Sellier, 'Le Hamallisme dans la politique locale africaine', 3.
115 Trimingham (1967), 99.
116 Sellier, 'Le Hamallisme dans la politique locale africaine', 4.
117 Alexandre (1970), 505–6.
118 Acting Gov. (Petre) to all *cercles*, Niamey, 30 March 1935 (AP Zinder).
119 Gov. to *Commandant*-Dosso, Niamey, 30 November 1937 (ASP Gaya).
120 Gov. (J. Toby), 'Circulaire no. 339 APA', Niamey, 18 September 1942 (ASP Say).
121 Alexandre (1970), 506.
122 Gov. (J. Toby), 'Circulaire . . .', Niamey, 16 May 1947 (AP Zinder).
123 *Ibid.*; Texier, 'R. tournée de recensement, Tera', Tillabery, 9 January 1943 (ASP Tillabery); P. Lobry, 'R. de recensement', Say, 18 November 1951, 6–7; L. Regnault, 'R. de tournée, Gueladio', Say, 1953 (both ASP Say).
124 On the spread of Nyassism, see for instance, SD Boboye, 'R. ann. 1952', 15 January 1953, 8 (AP Niamey); 'Note concernant El Hadj Mahaman dan Ibrahim', Konni, 31 July 1960 (ASP Birnin Konni); C. de Goure, 'R. ann. 1953' (signed R. Winckler), Goure, 22 January 1954, 14–15 (AP Zinder).
125 CN, 'R. pol. ann. 1931', 1–2 (Dakar 2G31–8); 'Rapp. de tournée', Goure, 21 March 1931 (ANN); de Loppinot, 'R. ann. pour 1930', 1 January 1931, 11 (AP Tahoua).
126 *Ibid.*; E. Bernus (1973).
127 'Rapport fait par M. Bernard Sol, Inspecteur des Colonie, concernant la situation alimentaire du cercle de Niamey dans les années 1931–1932', n.d.; and reports by the same author regarding the situation in the *cercles* of Tillabery and Dosso, dated 7 & 10 August 1932 (Dakar 11G26).
128 Unless otherwise stated this section is based on the reports by Bernard Sol (Dakar 11G26). Sol's reports were also used by André Salifou. See his 'Quand l'histoire se répète: la famine de 1931 au Niger', *Environnement africain*, I, 2 (1975), 25–52.
129 CN, 'R. pol. de 1931' (Dakar 2G31–8); Blacher to the Director of the Cabinet, of the Minister of Colonies, Paris, 20 January 1933 (Dakar 11G40).
130 Gov. (Blacher) to Gov. Gal., 13 November 1931 (Dakar 11G26).
131 See for instance the telegrams dated 8 & 16 July 1931; Inspector of Administrative Affairs to Gov., Niamey, 1 July 1932; Gov. Gal. to Gov. Niger, 1 September 1932 (all Dakar 11G26). During the famine in the West 'certaines circonscriptions de l'est regorgaient de mil' according to CN, 'R. pol. ann. pour 1933', Niamey, 22 March 1934, 15 (Dakar 2G33–13).
132 'Rapp. écon. annuel. Cercle de Tillabery', 28 January 1932 (SOM-NS Aff. pol. c. 592 d. 2).
133 'Rapp. écon. annuel. Cercle de Dosso' (signed Teillet), 18 January 1932 (SOM-NS Aff. pol. c. 592 d. 2).
134 'Rapp. écon. annuel. Tillabery', 28 January 1932 (SOM-NS Aff. pol. c. 592 d. 2).
135 'Rapp. écon. annuel. C. de Niamey' (signed Duranteau), 18 February 1933, 2 (AP Niamey).
136 CN, 'R. pol. ann. pour 1932', 12 April 1933, 1–2 (Dakar 2G32–18).
137 *Commandant*-Niamey (Garnier) to Gov., 14 June 1932 (AP Niamey).
138 Hébert, 'Rapp. de tournée dans le Djermaganda', Tillabery, 2 December 1933 (AS Tillabery).
139 *Ibid.* See also CN, 'R. pol. ann. pour 1933', 22 March 1934, 7 (Dakar 2G33–13); Gov. Gal. to Gov. Niger, 20 September 1933 (Dakar 11G26).

140 'Circulaire à Messieurs les Administrateurs des Cercles de Niamey, Dosso et Tillabery', Niamey, 2 May 1932 (AP Niamey); Finn Fuglestad, 'La Grande Famine de 1931 dans l'Ouest nigérien: réflexions autour d'une catastrophe naturelle', *RFHOM*, LXI, 1 (1974), 18–33 (esp. 26–8).

141 'Rapp. écon. annuel. Niamey', 18 February 1933 (AP Niamey).

142 CN 'R. pol. ann. pour 1932', 12 April 1933, 14 (Dakar 2G32–18); CN, 'R. pol. ann. pour 1933', 22 March 1934, 7 (Dakar 2G33–13); Deputy-*Commandant* to *Commandant*, Goure, 7 April 1932 (ANN); G. Brouin, 'R. de tournée, SDC', Tahoua, 23 September 1944 (AP Tahoua).

143 CN, 'R. pol. ann. 1933', 22 March 1934, 6–7.

144 Gov. Gal. to Gov. Niger, 20 September 1933 (Dakar 11G26); Gov. Niger to Gov. Gal., 25 July 1933 (Dakar 11G26).

145 See for instance, de Loppinot, 'Rapp. de tournée', Tahoua, 16 November 1933 (ASP Madaoua).

146 Baier (1974), 124.

147 Charles le Coeur, *Mission au Tibesti (Carnets de route 1933–34)* (1969), 24–5.

148 J. Court, 'Décision no. 668 APA', Niamey, 5 July 1935 (AP Zinder).

149 M. Vilmin, 'R. de tournée', Madaoua, 31 October 1936 (ASP Madaoua).

150 C. de Maradi, 'R. ann. 1933', 6 (AP Maradi).

151 L. Faitg, 'R. tournée', Goure, Oct.–Nov. 1934 (ANN); C. de Dosso, 'R. ann. 1933' (ANN); *Commandant*-Tahoua (de Loppinot) to Gov., 21 October 1933 (ASP Madaoua).

152 De Loppinot, 'Rapp. de tournée', 16 November 1933.

153 *Id.*, 'Rapp. de tournée', 14 February 1933 (ANN).

154 Letters from the League dated 9 April and 29 September 1932 (SOM-NS c. 591 d. 2).

155 See the correspondence between the Min. of Colonies and the Gov. Gal. in SOM-NS c. 591 d. 2.

156 See for instance, Gov. Gal. to Gov., 1 September 1932 (Dakar 11G26).

157 André Thiellement, 'Menaces de famine au Niger', in Pierre Gentil (ed.), *Derniers chefs d'un Empire* (1972), 45–52. For the point of view of Blacher, the governor who was sacked, see Dakar 11G40.

158 Blacher to the *Directeur de Cabinet* of the Minister of Colonies, Paris, 20 January 1933 (Dakar 11G40).

159 See Abdou Ibrahim (n.d.). See also Leroy, 'Sécurité alimentaire au Niger' (unpubl. paper, CHEAM, 1949); *JO-Niger*, 1933, 78–9, and 20 January 1937, 23; Acting Gov. (J. Court), 'Circulaire', Niamey, 11 October 1935 (ASP Magaria).

160 Based on Thiellement (1972), 45–8.

161 See for instance, CN, 'R. pol. ann. pour 1933', 22 March 1934, 13–15 (Dakar 2G33–13); Cercle de Niamey, 'R. écon. pour 1937', 28 March 1938 (AP Niamey).

162 Verdier (1964), 589.

163 For concrete examples see for instance, C. de Maradi, 'R. pol. ann. 1933', Maradi, 6 January 1934, 12 & 50 (AP Maradi); 'R. pol. 3e trim. 1933', Tanout, 13 October 1933 (ANN).

164 CN, 'R. pol. ann. 1933', 22 March 1934, 5–6 (Dakar 2G33–13); CN, 'R. écon. trim.', Niamey, May 1938, 83 (Dakar 2G37–11).

165 See for instance, Gov. (Bourgine) to *Commandant*-Goure, 4 January 1934 (ANN).

166 C. de Maradi, 'R. pol. ann. 1933', Maradi, 6 January 1934, 47 (AP Maradi); Gov. to *Commandant*-Dosso, 30 November 1937 (ASP Gaya); SD Say, 'R. pol. 1er trim. 1938', 31 March 1938 (ASP Say).

167 According to a federal decree of 9 December 1936, reproduced in *JO-Niger*, 1 August 1941, 142.

168 CN, 'R. pol. d'ensemble pour 1934', 25 March 1935, 1–2 (Dakar 2G34–9); Collins (1974), 40–6.

169 *Ibid.*, 39–42. For an assessment of the long-term impact of these firms in French West Africa generally, see Cathérine Coquery-Vidrovitch, 'L'Impact des intérêts coloniaux: SCOA et CFAO dans l'Ouest Africain, 1910–1965', *JAH*, XVI, 4 (1975), 595–621.

170 Based on Pehaut (1970), 46–54. See also Guy Nicolas, 'Un village haoussa de la République du Niger: Tassao Haoussa', *COM*, 52 (1960), 421–50 (esp. 438–40); Gov. (J. Court) to *Commandant*-Zinder, Niamey, 12 August 1935 (AP Zinder); Latour, 'R. de tournée', Goure, 27 November 1938 (ANN).

171 *Annuaire statistique de l'Union Française. Outre-Mer, 1939–1949* (Service des Statistiques d'Outre-Mer/INSEE), 231; Pehaut (1970), 46–7.

172 CN, 'R. pol. pour 1936' (signed J. Court), 22 April 1936, 28 (Dakar 2G35–7).

173 See for instance, CN, 'R. pol. pour 1935' (signed J. Court), 22 April 1936, 28 (Dakar 2G35–7); Gov. to *Commandant*-Maradi, Niamey, 18 November 1937 (AP Maradi).

174 CN, 'R. pol. pour 1937', 5 (Dakar 2G37–6).

175 *Ibid.*, 17; Alfred Sauvy, *Histoire économique de la France entre les deux guerres*, vol. II (1967), 202–24 & 488.

176 CN, 'R. écon. trim.', May 1938, 1–12 (Dakar 2G37–11); CN, 'R. pol. pour 1937', 8 (Dakar 2G37–6).

177 G. Brouin, 'SDC Zinder. R. d'ens. pour 1937', 31 December 1937, 12 (AP Zinder).

178 *JO-Niger*, 20 October 1937, 404.

179 *Ibid.*, 20 January 1938, 2.

180 C. de Zinder, 'Enquête sur le commerce extérieur de l'AOF', Zinder, 19 July 1940 (AP Zinder).

181 *Ibid.*; *Commandant*-Goure to Gov., Goure, 25 March 1945 (ANN).

182 'R. de tournée', Goure, 31 March 1939 (ANN); 'Exécution des prescriptions du télégramme officiel du 24.3.1942', Zinder, n.d. (ASP Magaria).

183 *JO-Niger*, 1938, 227–30, 324 & 342.

184 Dr Tchelle & Dr Chamorin, 'La Méningite cérébro-spinale au Niger', roneotyped report, Niamey (World Health Organization, n.d.); *JO-Niger*, 1938, 106 & 176, 1939, 34–7.

185 Jean-Pierre Azéma, *De Munich à la Libération, 1938–1944*, vol. XIV of the *Nouvelle Histoire de la France contemporaine* (1979).

186 Charles de Gaulle, *Mémoires de guerre*, vol. I (1954), 95–110.

187 Oral sources.

188 H. Deschamps, J. Ganiage & O. Guitard, *L'Afrique au XXe siècle* (1966), 323; Gentil (1948), 12.

189 Based on CN, 'R. pol. pour 1941' (signed Falvy), 20 April 1942 (SOM-NS c. 591 d. 7); Duchiron, 'R. de sortie de poste', Gaya, 1 August 1942 (ASP Gaya); 'Compte-rendu de tournée', Dosso, 13 August 1941 & 23 February 1942 (ANN); *Chef de subdivision*-Magaria (J. Pinaud) to *Commandant*-Zinder, Magaria, 3 December 1945; H. Leroux, 'R. de la tournée de recensement effectuée du 27 janvier au 2 mars 1946, subd. de Magaria' (both ASP Magaria).

190 'Note de service du Gouverneur', Niamey, 23 February 1942 (ASP Gaya).

191 Bourcart, 'R. de tournée', Dosso, 6 September 1941 (ANN).

192 Lieut. Michel Lesourd to Gov., N'Guigmi, 18 March 1941 (ANN).

193 Gov. (Falvy) to all *Commandants*, 21 January 1941; Gov. (Falvy), 'Bulletin no. 1 de renseignements intérieurs', 25 January 1941 (both ASP Dogondoutchi); CN, 'R. pol. pour 1941', 20 April 1942 (SOM-NS c. 591 d. 7).

194 CN, 'R. pol. pour 1940' (signed Falvy), Niamey, 15 April 1941, 52 (Dakar 2G40–5).

195 CN, 'R. écon. annuel, 1940', Niamey, 12 April 1941 (Dakar 2G40–38); *JO-Niger*, 1 February & 1 May 1941, 34 & 100; 1 January 1942, 19–20.

196 Latour, 'R. de tournée', Dosso, 26 October 1942 (ANN); Rouch (1956), 28.

197 Based on CN, 'R. écon. annuel, 1940', 12 April 1941 (Dakar 2G40–38); 'Procès-verbal du Conseil des notables de la subdiv. centrale de Zinder du 2.6.1941' (AP Zinder); *JO-Niger*, 1 November 1942, 132; 'Journal du poste de Dogondoutchi du 1.1.1935 au 31.12.1947', entry for 15 April 1942 (ASP Dogondoutchi).

198 Oral sources.

199 The evidence here is indirect, namely that these 'champs' were abolished in 1944. See J. Escher, 'R. de tournée, Magaria', 22 April 1944 (ASP Magaria).

200 'Circulaire, Gouverneur', 14 April 1941 (Dakar, 11G–26).

201 'P-v. Conseil notables, subd. centrale, Zinder', 1 July 1940 & 6 September 1941 (AP Zinder).

202 'J. poste . . . Dogondoutchi', entries for 5 February & 14 March 1942 (ASP Dogondoutchi); Gov. (J. Rapenne) to all *cercles* and *subdivisions*, Niamey, 9 August 1940 (ASP Tessaoua); 'Compte-rendu de tournée',·Dosso, 23 February 1942 (ANN).

203 C. de Niamey, 'R. pol. 1945' (signed I. Colombani), 5 February 1946, 1 (AP Niamey). Ignace Colombani was administrator in Niger throughout the war years.

204 Pehaut (1970), 19.

205 CN, 'R. écon. annuel, 1940', 12 April 1941, 3 (Dakar 2G40–38); Yves Riou, 'R. de tournée', N'Guigmi, 20 December 1941 (ANN).

206 According to a later report. See P. Urfer, 'Rapp. de tournée, canton de Loga', Dosso, 20 April 1947 (ANN).

207 Lemaitre, 'R. de tournée du canton de Gouré', 5 January 1945 (ANN).

208 'Chronique de la mission catholique de Zinder' (handwritten document consulted by courtesy of the parish priest of Zinder).

209 C. de Maradi, 'R. semestriel d'ensemble, 2e sem. 1942', 25 January 1943; J. Paumelle, 'R. sur le recensement du canton du Gobir', Maradi, 9 October 1945 (both AP Maradi).

210 According to the 'Chronique de la mission catholique de Zinder'.

211 C. de Maradi, 'R. sem. d'ens., 2e sem. 1942' (AP Maradi).

212 *JO-Niger*, 1 August 1941, 142.

213 CN, 'R. pol. pour 1940', 15 April 1941, 38 (Dakar 2G40–5); CN, 'R. pol. pour 1941', 20 April 1942, 43 (SOM-NS c. 591 d. 7).

214 *Contributions, taxes et redevances* . . ., 1941, 9.

215 Philippe, 'R. d'une tournée dans le Dargol', Tillabery, 30 August 1942 (ASP Tillabery); CN, 'R. pol. pour 1940', 15 April 1941, 6–9.

216 Gov. (Falvy), 'Bull. no. 1 de renseignements intérieurs'.

217 'J. poste . . . Dogondoutchi', entries for 30 July, 14 & 29 August 1941 (ASP Dogondoutchi); *Commandant*-Dosso to Gov., Dosso, 26 July 1941 (ASP Dogondoutchi).

218 'R. sur les agissements de Marafa Garba, chef du canton de Takassaba', Dogondoutchi, 16 September 1941; *Commandant*-Dosso to Gov., Dosso, 21 September 1941 (both ASP Dogondoutchi).

219 *Chef de subdivision* Dogondoutchi (G. Bideau) to *Commandant*-Dosso, 2 February 1943 (ASP Dogondoutchi).

220 'P-v. d'interrogation du chef de canton de Magaria', Zinder, 7 January 1941 (ASP Magaria); *JO-Niger*, 1 October 1942, 121, 1 August 1943, 51 & 1 July 1943, 43.

221 Claude Michel, 'Compte-rendu de tournée', Dosso, 20 March 1940 (ANN).

222 See for instance, Edward Mortimer, *France and the Africans, 1944–60. A Political History* (1969), 45.

223 'P-v. de la réunion du conseil des notables de la subdiv. de Magaria', 15 July 1941 (ASP Magaria).

224 High-Commissioner (P. Boisson) to all Governors, Dakar, 10 February 1941 (ASP Tessaoua).

225 Rouch (1956), 28.
226 *Ibid.* 29–30; *id.* (1953a), 238.
227 SD Madaoua, 'R. pol. annuel, 1941' (ASP Madaoua).
228 Bourcart, 'R. de tournée', Dosso, 6 September 1941 (ANN).
229 Chailley (1968), 439–40.
230 Based on Gov. to *Commandant*-Zinder, Niamey, 5 December 1943 (ASP Magaria); Gov. to *chef de subdivision* Filingue, 17 August 1945 (ASP Filingue); *JO-Niger*, 1 September 1945, 116; Escher, 'R. de tournée, Magaria', 22 April 1944 (ASP Magaria).
231 'R. tournée du Commandant de cercle de Tillabery dans le canton du Dargol', 27 September 1943 (ASP Tillabery); Gov. (J. Toby) to *Commandant*-Niamey, 22 February 1944; C. de Niamey, 'R. écon. 1944' (signed L. Ortoli), 3 February 1945, 6–7; C. de Niamey, 'R. pol. 1945', 5 February 1946 (all AP Niamey).
232 *Commandant*-Maradi (Rigal) to Gov., 12 & 21 June 1944 (AP Maradi).
233 *JO-Niger*, 1 January 1944, 5.
234 *Ibid.*, 1 January 1945, 6.
235 Georges Balandier, 'Les Mythes politiques de colonisation et de décolonisation en Afrique', *CIS*, XXXIII (1962), 85–96 (86–7).
236 See William McNeill, *Plagues and Peoples* (1976/1979).
237 Iliffe (1979), 4.
238 Hubert Deschamps, 'Et maintenant, Lord Lugard?', *Africa*, XXXIII, 4 (1963), 293–306 (299).
239 '... theories like assimilation and association ... were at best marginal to the issues which preoccupied the rulers of the Empire. At the worst they were no more than little-understood myths.' B. Olatunji Oloruntimehin, 'Theories and realities in the administration of colonial French West Africa from 1890 to the first world war', *JHSN*, VI, 3 (1972), 289–312 (290).
240 R. Delavignette, *Freedom and Authority in French West Africa* (1950), 11–19.
241 Based on Schachter-Morgenthau (1967), 37–41; and on D. Bruce Marshall, 'Free France in Africa: Gaullism and colonialism', in Prosser Gifford & W. Roger Louis (eds.), *France and Britain in Africa. Imperial Rivalry and Colonial Rule* (New Haven & London, 1971), 713–48.

6. Towards a new order, 1945–60

1 Jacques Fauvet, *La Quatrième République* (1959), 45–6; Schachter-Morgenthau (1967), 40. Many of the ideas expressed here have already appeared in my 'UNIS and BNA: the role of "Traditionalist" parties in Niger, 1948–60', *JAH*, XVI, 1 (1975b), 113–35.
2 Based on Fauvet (1959), 69–87; Schachter-Morgenthau (1967), 41–4 & 393–4.
3 *Ibid.*, 48–54.
4 *Ibid.*, 55.
5 Speech by Hamani Diori in Nat. Assembly, 18 August 1948.
6 R. Adloff & V. Thompson, *French-Speaking West Africa in Transition* (1958), 152.
7 Aristide Zolberg, 'The structure of political conflict in the new states of tropical Africa', *APSR*, LXII, 1 (1968), 70–87.
8 Jean-Louis Miège, *Expansion européenne et décolonisation de 1870 à nos jours* (1973), 358.
9 Inspired by Zolberg (1968), 71–2.
10 Ignace Colombani, 'R. pol. 1er sem. 1946, C. de Niamey', 31 July 1946, 8 (ASP Say).
11 *Ibid.*, 11.
12 Ignace Colombani, 'Revue trimestrielle, année 1947, 2e trim. C. de Niamey', 7 July 1947, 5 (ASP Say).

13 Serre (1950), 150.

14 By Deschamps (1963), 300.

15 See *inter alia* Pinon, 'R. de tournée de recensement du canton de Dessa', Tillabery, 12 July 1947 (ASP Tillabery); J. Toby, 'Circulaire à Messieurs les Commandants de cercle et chefs de subdivision', Niamey, 4 December 1948 (ASP Magaria); Colombani, 'Revue trim. 1947, 2e trim. C. de Niamey', 7 July 1947, 1–2 (ASP Say); I. Colombani, 'C. de Niamey. R. pol. 1946', 28 February 1947, 1 (AP Niamey).

16 C. de Maradi, 'R. ann. pour 1948', 31 January 1949, 8 (AP Maradi).

17 G. Tirolien, 'R. ann. SD Dakoro', Dakoro, 11 January 1950 (AP Maradi).

18 On the Hamallist movement after 1945, see J. Toby, 'Circulaire no. 107 APA/AM', Niamey, 16 May 1947 (AP Zinder); P. Lobry, 'R. de recensement', Say, 18 November 1951, 6–7; Pujol, SD Say, 'R. pol. pour 1948', Say, 24 January 1949, 1–2 (both ASP Say); J. Damery, SDC Niamey, 'R. ann. 1952', 7–8 (AP Niamey).

19 Vallet, 'R. tournée dans le Zermaganda', Tillabery, 16 September 1946 (ASP Tillabery); Pujol, SD Say, 'R. pol. pour 1948', 24 January 1949; Chief, SD Filingue (J. Espallargas) to *Commandant*-Niamey, Filingue, 13 September 1947 (ASP Dogondoutchi).

20 Michel Sellier, 'Lettre du chef de la SDC Niamey, au Commandant de cercle. Objet: droit foncier indigène', 27 February 1948 (ASP Say).

21 Secretary-General (H. Faure) to *Commandant*-Dosso, Niamey, 30 December 1946; Gov. (J. Toby) to Gov. Gal., Niamey, 16 November 1950 (ASP Magaria).

22 Acting Gov. (Ignace Colombani), 'Circulaire no. 175/APA', Niamey, 9 March 1950 (ASP Magaria).

23 See *inter alia*, Vallet, 'R. de tournée, canton de Simiri', Ouallam, 15 October 1947 (ASP Tillabery); Manal, 'R. tournée de recensement, canton de Tillabery, du 11.4. au 14.6.1950' (ASP Tillabery). According to Jean Rouch, some 7 per cent of the *total population* was absent in many parts of the West during the dry seasons between 1953 and 1956. See his 'Problèmes relatifs à l'étude des migrations traditionelles et des migrations actuelles en Afrique occidentale', *BIFAN*, XXII, 3–4 (1960c), 369–78, and 'Rapport sur les migrations nigériennes vers la basse Côte d'Ivoire', Mission ORSTOM-IFAN, roneotyped, 1957 (Library of the CNRSH).

24 C. Colonna d'Istria, 'R. tournée de recensement du canton de Kourteye', Tillabery, 10 January 1946, 6; *id.*, 'R. tournée, canton de Dargol', Tillabery, 1 September 1945 (both ASP Tillabery).

25 *Commandant*-Tillabery to Gov., 22 April 1947 (ASP Tillabery); Bailly, 'Recensement, canton de Myrriah', 1947 (CGD); L. Regnault, H. Himadou, Cornu, Allier & Tre-Hardy, 'Monographie du Cercle de Niamey', 1955, 26–7 (CGD); R. Fremineau, 'C.-rendu de tournée du canton de Gouré', 18 June 1952 (ANN). See also Henri Raulin, 'Communautés d'entraide et développement agricole au Niger. L'exemple de la Majya', *Etudes rurales*, 33 (1969), 15–26.

26 Séré de Rivières (1951), 46; Schachter-Morgenthau (1967), 396–7.

27 T. du Niger, 'R. pol. pour 1951' (signed R. Casimir), Niamey, 18 August 1952, 62 (AP Dosso).

28 Schachter-Morgenthau (1967), 88–9.

29 Chailley (1968), 507.

30 Oral sources.

31 See *inter alia*, 'R. tournée', Maine-Soroa, 26 December 1946 (ANN); SD Tessaoua, 'R. d'ens. 1946', 31 December 1946, 1–2 (ASP Tessaoua).

32 Based on oral sources; Schachter-Morgenthau (1967), 88–90; and Fuglestad (1975b), 123.

33 Inspired by Mortimer (1969), 68; and oral sources.

34 'Note annuelle, chefs indigènes: Barma Mustapha', Zinder, 1946 (AP Zinder).

35 G. Brouin, C. de Zinder, 'R. ann. d'ens. pour 1950', vol. I, Zinder, 5 February 1951, 21 (AP

Zinder); 'Chronique de la mission catholique de Zinder' (handwritten document consulted by courtesy of the parish priest of Zinder).

36 Bureau des APA, 'Elections générales du 10.11.1946', Nov. 1946 (Archives of the PPN/RDA).

37 Complete list in 'Procès-verbal de la séance du Conseil Général du 20.10.1947' (ASP Tessaoua).

38 H. Diori in Nat. Assembly, 30 July 1949.

39 Gov. to *Commandant*-Maradi, Niamey, 14 August 1947 (consulted by courtesy of Adamou Mayaki).

40 W. A. Lewis, *Politics in West Africa* (1965), 71–2.

41 Ernest Milcent, *L'AOF entre en scène* (1958), 41.

42 See for instance, Schachter-Morgenthau (1967), 84–94.

43 Paul Courtier, *La Quatrième République* (1975), 29–30.

44 I. Colombani, 'Revue trim. 1947, 2e trim. C. de Niamey', 7 July 1947, 5–6.

45 'Discours d'ouverture de la 2e session ordinaire du Conseil Général du Niger prononcé à Niamey le 4 Novembre 1950 par M. le Gouverneur Toby' (ASP Tessaoua).

46 Claude Ake, 'Explaining political instability in new states', *JMAS*, XI, 3 (1973), 347–59 (358).

47 J. M. Lonsdale, 'Some origins of nationalism in East Africa', *JAH*, XI, 1 (1968), 119–46.

48 C. de Zinder, 'R. pol. pour 1948', 1 (AP Zinder).

49 *Commandant*-Dosso, to Gov., April 1949 (ANN).

50 Pierre Brachet, C. de Tahoua, 'R. ann. pour 1949', 2–8 (AP Tahoua); 'R. au sujet des faits reprochés au chef de canton de Dungass, Abou Riri', Magaria, 2 September 1948 (ASP Magaria); G. Brouin, C. de Zinder, 'R. ann. d'ens. pour 1950', vol. I, 5 February 1951, 10–11 (AP Zinder).

51 Their point of view has been succinctly stated by Djibo Bakary in an open letter to Governor Toby, printed in *Reveil* (daily newspaper, Dakar), 22 January 1948, 4.

52 Oral sources.

53 See for instance, Gov. (J. Toby), 'Circulaire', Niamey, 22 May 1950 (ASP Gaya); G. Brouin, C. de Zinder, 'R. ann. d'ens. pour 1950', vol. I, 5 February 1951, 38–9.

54 Based on Gov., 'Circulaire', 22 May 1950 (ASP Gaya); J. Pinaud, 'R. de tournée, canton de Kantché', Magaria, 29 May 1945; Acting Gov. (I. Colombani) to *Commandant*-Zinder, Niamey, 23 August 1949 (both ASP Magaria); C. de Maradi, 'R. semestriel, 1er sem. 1945', 30 June 1945 (ASP Tessaoua).

55 Toby, 'Circulaire . . .', 4 December 1948 (ASP Magaria).

56 Acting Gov. (I. Colombani) to *Commandant*-Tahoua, Niamey, 8 December 1949; Gov. (J. Toby), 'Circulaire', Niamey, 2 October 1947 (both ASP Birnin Konni), 23 August 1950 (ASP Filingue), and 30 May 1951 (AP Tahoua); *JO-Niger*, 1 January 1946, 9; Secretary-General (J. Jarton), 'Arrêté no. 0293 APA', Niamey, 11 November 1949 (ASP Say); 'Discours prononcé par le Gouverneur Toby devant le Conseil Général du Niger à l'ouverture de la session budgetaire', Niamey, 30 October 1948 (ASP Tessaoua); Gov. to Gov. Gal., 16 November 1950 (ASP Magaria).

57 'P.-v. de la séance du Conseil Général du 9.11.1947', 4 (ASP Tessaoua); Le Maître, 'R. tournée, canton de Gouré', 5 January 1945 (ANN); Regnault *et al.*, 'Monographie du Cercle de Niamey', 1955, 33.

58 C. de Zinder, 'R. pol. pour 1948', 12 (AP Zinder).

59 Gov. to *Commandant*-Maradi, Niamey, 16 June 1947; *Commandant*-Maradi (J. Périé) to Gov., Maradi, 1 December 1947; 'Discours prononcé le 4 Avril 1949 au depart de M. Vilmin par le Vétérinaire Africain Ongoiba, désigné à cet effet par ses camarades et la population', Dakoro (all AP Maradi).

60 Serre (1950).

61 H. Diori in Nat. Assembly, 30 July 1949. The motion is reproduced in *Reveil*, 22 January 1948, 4.
62 Fuglestad (1975b), 128; oral sources.
63 *Idem.*
64 Bureau des APA, 'T. Niger. Résultat définitif des élections législatives du 27 juin 1948' (Archives of the PPN/RDA).
65 Hamani Diori, who hotly disputed the election of Condat, and asked for its invalidation, argued along these lines, Nat. Assembly, 31 September 1949.
66 Advanced by Ruth Schachter (Morgenthau), 'Single-party systems in West Africa', *APSR*, LV, 2 (1961), 294–307.
67 Ruth First, *The Barrel of a Gun. Political Power in Africa and the Coup d'Etat* (Harmondsworth, 1972), 56.
68 These terms are discussed in Fuglestad (1975b), 113–21.
69 T. du Niger, 'R. pol. pour 1951', 18 August 1952, 16 (AP Dosso).
70 Senate, 2 December 1948.
71 Mortimer (1969), 128.
72 *Ibid.*, 151; Schachter-Morgenthau (1967), 58.
73 T. du Niger, 'Revue des événements du 4e trim. 1950', 5; G. Brouin, C. de Zinder, 'Revue trim. 4e trim. 1950', Zinder, 20 January 1951, 1–2; Gov. (J. Toby), 'Circulaire no. 107 APA/AM', Niamey, 16 May 1947 (all AP Zinder).
74 Diori in Nat. Assembly, 5 February, 5 August & 30 July 1948; 20 October 1949.
75 Acting Gov. to *Commandant*-Niamey, Niamey, 23 March 1950 (ASP Say); *RJPUF*, XII (1958), 210–12.
76 Schachter-Morgenthau (1967), 193–9.
77 It should perhaps be added here that the lines of communication between the *évolués* of the PPN/RDA and the administration were never completely cut off during the 1947–51 period. According to oral information some of the more seasoned French school-teachers, in particular, seem to have served as go-betweens.
78 T. du Niger, 'Revue des événements du 4e trim. 1951', 12–13 (AP Zinder); Franz Ansprenger, *Politik im schwarzen Afrika. Die modernen politischen Bewegungen im Afrika französischer prägung* (Cologne and Opladen, 1961), 93; Mortimer (1969), 163; Milcent (1958), 51–2.
79 Pujol, SD Madaoua, 'R. ann. 1950', 15 January 1951, 11 (ASP Madaoua).
80 Nat. Assembly, 22 August 1951.
81 J. Toby, T. du Niger, 'R. pol. 1952', Niamey, 25 June 1953, 4–5 (AP Zinder).
82 Gov. (R. Casimir) to all *Commandants de cercle*, Niamey, 24 March 1952 (ASP Madaoua). But he does not seem to have been obeyed. See for instance, J. Guillemet, C. de Niamey, 'R. ann. 1952', 21 January 1953, 7 (AP Niamey); and oral sources.
83 J. Toby, T. du Niger, 'R. pol. 1952', 25 June 1953, 14–15 (AP Zinder).
84 J. Damery, SDC Niamey, 'R. ann. 1952', 4 (AP Niamey); *Commandant*-Dosso (Crouzille) to Gov., Dosso, 5 April 1952 (ASP Dogondoutchi).
85 R. O. Collins (ed.), *Problems in the History of Colonial Africa* (Englewood Cliffs, 1970), 281.
86 Elliot Berg, 'The economic basis of political choice in French West Africa', *APSR*, LIV, 2 (1960), 391–405 (392).
87 Hopkins (1973), 267.
88 Adloff & Thompson (1958), 284.
89 Berg (1960), 404; oral sources.
90 C. de Zinder, 'R. pol. pour 1948', 11 (AP Zinder); R. Sylvestre, 'Bull. de renseignements', Maradi, 23 April 1953, 4; R. Casimir, T. du Niger, 'Revue, événements, 2e trim. 1952',

Niamey, 23 July 1952, 18; J. Toby, T. du Niger, 'Revue, événements, 2e trim. 1953', 18 (all AP Zinder).

91 Cambillard, 'Etude du marché de textiles dans le territoire du Niger-Est', Zinder, 24 October 1956 (ASP Magaria).

92 R. Casimir, T. du Niger, 'R. évén. 2e trim. 1952', 23 July 1952 (AP Zinder); R. Falguerettes, C. d'Agades, 'Revue, 2e trim. 1953', Agades, 22 May 1953, 6 (AP Zinder); Acting Gov. (F. Raynier), 'Circulaire', Niamey, 31 May 1956 (ASP Madaoua); G. Brouin, C. de Zinder, 'R. écon. 1951', 3 February 1953, 36–7; Capt. Quemy, 'Situation politico-religieuse et sécurité générale au Niger-Est', July 1952, 1–2 (both AP Zinder).

93 Examples are provided by: C. de Maradi, 'R. ann. 1945', 31 December 1945, 5; P. Barlet, 'R. trim.', Maradi, 17 April 1951, 1 (both AP Maradi); and also by the various annual reports from Zinder signed G. Brouin, many of which have been and will continue to be frequently cited.

94 G. Brouin, C. de Zinder, 'R. ann. d'ens. pour 1950', vol. I, 5 February 1951, 11–14 (AP Zinder).

95 Oral sources; 'R. sur le recensement du canton d'Illela', Konni, 10 November 1946 (ANN); 'Recensement du canton de Dogueraoua', Konni, 21 September 1947 (ASP Madaoua).

96 Adloff & Thompson (1958), 71.

97 *Annuaire statisque de l'Union Française. Outre-Mer, 1939–49*, 126; Courtier (1975), 50–1.

98 Cambillard, 'Etude du marché de textiles . . . Niger-Est'.

99 Maurice Parodi, 'Histoire récente de l'économie et de la société française, 1945–1970', in G. Duby (ed.), *Histoire de la France*, vol. III (1972), 303–62.

100 *JO-RF. Avis et Rapports du Conseil Economique et Social*, 30 January 1953; Adloff & Thompson (1958), 264.

101 T. du Niger, 'R. écon. 1957', 5–7 (CGD); Ministère de l'Economie rurale (Service de l'Agriculture), 'R. ann. 1961. Première partie: statistiques', 3–4 (AP Zinder); Ministère des Affaires Economiques et du Plan, Service de la statistique, 'Bull. trim. de statistique, 1er trim. 1959', 4 (AP Say); Lancrenon & Donaint (1972), 34.

102 J. Toby, 'Discours . . . le 4 Novembre 1950' (ASP Tessaoua).

103 *Ibid.*; Pujol, SD Madaoua, 'R. ann. 1950', 15 January 1951, 1–15 (ASP Madaoua); 'P.-v. réunion du Conseil des Notables du C. de Dosso', 4 March 1951 (ASP Gaya); 'R. recensement, secteur de Tiengalla', Dosso, 22 October 1951 (ANN); C. de Zinder, 'R. ann. 1949', 1 (AP Zinder).

104 Police Commissioner-Zinder (G. Doutre) to Chief Commissioner-Niger, 13 February 1952, 1–14 (AP Zinder); J. Damery, SDC Niamey, 'R. ann. 1952', 25 (AP Niamey); R. Fremineau, 'R. tournée de recensement du canton de Yamia', Goure, 28 May 1952 (ANN); Gerber, C. de Maradi, 'R. ann. 1950', 31 January 1951, 5 (AP Maradi); G. Brouin, C. de Zinder, 'R. ann. d'ens. pour 1950' vol. I, 5 February 1951, 1–8 (AP Zinder); M. Perret, 'R. recensement, secteur de Tiengalla', Dosso, 22 October 1951 (ANN).

105 Beauvilain (1977), 21.

106 Larue, SDC Niamey, 'R. ann. 1954'; J.-J. Villandre, C. de Niamey, 'R. ann. 1953', 22 March 1954, 1–2 (both AP Naimey); C. de Goure, 'R. ann. 1953' (signed R. Winckler), 21 (AP Zinder); R. Gallinier, C. de Zinder, 'R. ann. 1953', 1 February 1954, 1–3 (AP Zinder); Acting Gov. (M. Augias), T. du Niger, 'R. pol. 1953' Niamey, 18 May 1954, 13–20 (AP Zinder); N. Julien-Viéroz, C. de Tahoua, 'R. trim.', 5 December 1953 (AP Maradi); *Le Démocrate* (organ of the UDN – roneotyped), 19 June 1954, 5–6.

107 'Synthèse Périodique (Service des Polices du Niger)', 28 February 1955, 12 (periodical pamphlet called 'Synthèse Périodique' or 'Synthèse Mensuelle' (referred to henceforth as SM) to be found in most archives in Niger).

108 Collins (1974), 209.

109 *Ibid.*, 50.

110 G. Besse, 'Rapp. sur l'Opération Hirondelle', Niamey, 20 July 1954, 1 (ASP Gaya); T. du Niger, 'R. sur l'activité des services', 1955, 22 (AP Zinder).

111 *Ibid.* It should be noted that the figures advanced by Y. Pehaut concern *exports*. See his 'Les Oléagineux dans les pays d'Afrique occidentale associés au Marché Commun. La production, le commerce et la transformation des produits' (thesis, University of Bordeaux III, 1973; Service de reproduction des thèses, University of Lille III, 1974), 759.

112 Figures from *L'Economie Ouest-Africaine (Bulletin de la BCEAO)*, 137 (1967); Adamou Mayaki, 'Les Problèmes économiques de la République du Niger', *Notes d'Information de la BCEAO* (June 1960); André Auclert, 'La Rentabilité de l'Opération Hirondelle. Rapport de mission au Niger du 10 septembre au 1er octobre 1955', Dakar (Direction Générale des Services Economiques et du Plan de l'AOF), 13 January 1956 (ASP Gaya).

113 *Outre-Mer 1958*, 229; J. Delpy, 'Le Développement économique de la République du Niger' (thesis, Faculty of Law, Paris, 1960), 72.

114 Besse, 'Rapp. sur l'Opération Hirondelle', 1; De Sablet, C. de Magaria, 'R. ann. 1956', 15 February 1957, 24–5 (ASP Magaria); Collins (1974), 74 & 77.

115 Lancrenon & Donaint (1972), 78.

116 Besse, 'Rapp. sur l'Opération Hirondelle', 2; Auclert, 'La Rentabilité de l'Opération Hirondelle', 25–7.

117 *Ibid.*, 25; *Annuaire statistique de l'Union Française. Outre-Mer 1939–49*, 225; P. Grasset, SD Tessaoua, 'R. ann. 1950', 31 January 1951, 6, and 'R. ann. 1951', 21 December 1951, 5 (ASP Tessaoua); C. de Maradi, 'R. ann. 1945', 31 December 1945, 29 (AP Maradi); Sellier, C. de Maradi, 'R. ann. 1954', 8 February 1955, 1–30 (AP Zinder); R. Galinier, C. de Zinder, 'R. ann. 1954', 15 February 1955, 25 (AP Zinder); J. Allusson, SD Maradi, 'R. trim. de renseignements', 22 November 1955, 11 (AP Maradi); *Marchés coloniaux*, 6 February 1954, 430.

118 Lancrenon & Donaint (1972), 78; Collins (1974), 94–9; Claude Raynaut, 'Circulation monétaire et évolution des structures socio-économiques chez les haoussas du Niger', *Africa*, XLVII, 2 (1977), 160–71.

119 Speeches by the Governor-General (Bernard Cornut-Gentille) on 7 March 1953 & 13 October 1954 (printed); R. Sylvestre, C. de Maradi, 'Revue 4e trim. 1952', Maradi, 13 January 1953, 2 (AP Zinder); Adloff & Thompson (1958), 264; Pehaut (1970), 55–9; Collins (1974), 138.

120 See Besse, 'Rapp. sur l'Opération Hirondelle'; Auclert, 'La rentabilité de l'Opération Hirondelle'; *Marchés coloniaux*, 13 December 1954, 492; J. Audu in the Assembly of the French Union, 24 May 1955; Pehaut (1970), 60–1; *id.* (1973/4), 760. For a much more critical appreciation of the *Opération Hirondelle*, see Guy Nicolas, 'Aspects de la vie économique dans un canton du Niger: Kantché', *Cahiers de l'ISEA*, 5th series, 5 (1962b), 104–88 (esp. 148).

121 Extrapolated from 'Procès-verbal de la Conférence des Commandants de cercle, Niamey, 20–25 avril 1955', (ASP Madaoua); and from *Inventaire social et économique des Territoires d'Outre-Mer de 1950 à 1955* (Ministère de la France d'Outre-Mer, Service des statistiques, 1957), 371; *Budget local du Niger*, 1947–56.

122 According to Ansprenger (1961), 105.

123 Berg (1960), 399.

124 T. du Niger, 'R. écon. 1957', 74 (CGD).

125 'Allocution prononcée par le Gouverneur R. Casimir à la séance d'ouverture de la deuxième session ordinaire de l'Assemblée Territoriale', Niamey, 20 November 1952 (ASP Magaria); *JO-RF. Avis et Rapports du Conseil Economique et Social*, 6 July 1954.

126 Oral sources.

127 *Budget local du Niger*, 1955–6–7.

128 Berg (1960), 399.

237

129 Speech by the Governor-General (B. Cornut-Gentille), on 7 March 1953 (printed).
130 R. Galinier, C. de Zinder, 'R. ann. 1954', 15 February 1955, 25 (AP Zinder); M. de Geyer d'Orth, 'Rapp. de tournée', Agades, 21 May 1953, 5–8; Chief, SD Dakoro (G. Azemia) to *Commandant*-Maradi, Dakoro, 30 March 1953 (AP Zinder).
131 C. de Zinder, 'R. pol. pour 1948', 31–2 (AP Zinder); 'P.-v. de la séance de l'Assemblée Territ. du 16.5.1952' (ASP Tessaoua); F. Borrey in Ass. French Union, 16 December 1949; Séré de Rivières (1951), 77–88.
132 T. du Niger, 'R. pol. pour 1951', 18 August 1952, 66–7 (AP Dosso).
133 G. Brouin, C. de Zinder, 'R. d'ens. 1952, partie pol.' Zinder, 10 February 1953, 34 (AP Zinder); C. de Goure, 'R. ann. 1953' (signed R. Winckler), 21 (AP Zinder); Pierre Menard, C. de Tessaoua, 'R. ann. pour 1956', 25 January 1957, 12 (ASP Tessaoua).
134 *JO-RF. Avis et Rapports du Conseil Economique et Social*, 31 August 1958.
135 C. d'Agades, 'R. ann. 1953', 24 (ANN); Barlet, C. de Maradi, 'R. trim.', 17 April 1951 (AP Maradi); General Raynal to Gov., Niamey, 13 June 1946 (ASP Birnin Konni); T. du Niger, 'R. pol. 1953', 18 May 1954, 48 (AP Zinder).
136 'La République du Niger', *Notes et Etudes Documentaires* (La Documentation française) (1958).
137 R. Casimir, T. du Niger, 'Revue des évén. du 3e trim. 1952', Niamey, 18 October 1952, 4 (AP Zinder).
138 Oral sources.
139 T. du Niger, 'R. pol. 1953', 18 May 1954, 49 (AP Zinder).
140 Georges Chaffard, *Les Carnets secrets de la décolonisation*, vol. II (1967), 271.
141 J. Dequecker, C. de Zinder, 'Revue trim.', Zinder, 20 June 1955, 5 (AP Zinder).
142 R. Casimir, T. du Niger, 'R. évén. 2e trim. 1952', 23 July 1952, 14 (AP Zinder).
143 T. du Niger, 'R. pol. pour 1951', 18 August 1952, 66–7 (AP Dosso).
144 T. du Niger, 'R. pol. 1953', 18 May 1954, 54–5 (AP Zinder); F. Raynier, T. du Niger, 'Revue des évén. 3e trim. 1954', 13 (AP Zinder).
145 Delpy (1960), 43.
146 T. du Niger, 'R. pol. 1953', 18 May 1954, 49 (AP Zinder); J. Toby, T. du Niger, 'Revue des événements du 1er trim. 1954', 14 (AP Zinder).
147 *Ibid.*, 15; Nat. Assembly, 11 September 1951.
148 Pehaut (1973/4), 759.
149 According to Nicolas (1962b), 119; Pehaut (1973/4), 757. See also the documents cited in note 130 above.
150 'La Migration des Peulhs vers le nord' (official report), Maradi, 27 March 1953 (AP Zinder).
151 *Ibid.*; Sellier, C. de Maradi, 'R. ann. 1954', 8 February 1955, 8–9, and C. de Maradi, 'R. ann. 1955' (both AP Maradi); M. de Geyer d'Orth, 'R. tournée chez les Kel Ferouane du 6.10 au 14.11.1952' (ANN); Dresch (1959); G. Brouin, 'Rapp. établi à la suite de la réunion des Commandants de cercle de Tahoua, Agades, Maradi et Zinder, au sujet des migrations peuls vers la subdivision nomade de Tahoua et le cercle d'Agades', Zinder, 7 April 1953, 2 (AP Zinder).
152 'Rapp. Commandant Gardaire, chargé des Affaires Musulmanes de la zone soudanaise. Tournée du 8 au 26 mars 1955' (ASP Madaoua); J. Maillocheau, SD Tanout, 'Revues trim.', 10 September & 15 November 1955 (AP Zinder).
153 E. Durand, C. de Tahoua, 'R. ann. 1956', 28 February 1957, 25 (AP Tahoua).
154 Oral sources and personal observations.
155 Brouin, 'Rapp. établi … réunion des Commandants'; J. Toby, T. du Niger, 'Revue des événements du 1er trim. 1954', 2–3; G. Brouin, C. de Zinder', 'R. écon. 1951', 3 February 1952, 2–3 (both AP Zinder); R. Pietrantoni, 'Monogr, SDC Tahoua', January 1955, 1–14 (AP Tahoua).

156 Brouin, 'Rapp. établi ... réunion des Commandants'; *Commandant*-Tahoua (Julien-Viéroz) to *Commandant*-Niamey, Tahoua, 31 March 1955 (AP Maradi); Dresch (1959).
157 *Annuaire statistique de l'Union Française. Outre-Mer 1939–49*, 234.
158 *JO-Niger*, 1 February 1946, 26–7; 1 January & 15 March 1951, 14 & 90–1.
159 Collins (1974), 94–9.
160 'P.-v. conférence des Commandants de cercle', Niamey, 20–25 April 1955, 7 (ASP Madaoua).
161 Chief, SD Magaria (L. Plagnol) to *Commandant*-Zinder, 20 July 1953, 1–2 (ASP Magaria).
162 Michèle de Saint-Marc, *Décolonisation et zone franc* (1964), 19.
163 Nicolas (1960 & 1962b); Raynaut (1977).
164 *Annuaire statistique de la France 1966* (INSEE), 128.
165 Collins (1974); Adloff & Thompson (1958).
166 Collins (1974), 77 & 222. See also *id.*, 'The clandestine movement of groundnuts across the Niger–Nigeria boundary', *CJAS*, X, 2 (1976), 259–78.
167 Nicole Echard, *Etude socio-économique dans les vallées de l'Ader-Doutchi-Majya* (Paris/Niamey, n.d.), 46–7; P. Falgueirettes, C. de Birnin Konni, 'R. ann. 1957', 20 February 1958 (ASP Birnin Konni).
168 Letter from Gov. Ramadier to Professor Gourou, Niamey, 28 December 1955 (AP Maradi); oral sources.
169 T. du Niger, 'R. pol. 1953', 18 May 1954, 18 (AP Zinder).
170 Delpy (1960), 122.
171 SD Magaria, 'R. ann. 1954', 36 (ASP Magaria).
172 *Comptes économiques 1961* (signed Adel Al-Akel, Niamey, Commissariat Général au Plan/Service de la statistique), 9 & 47; *Budget du Niger*, 1958-61.
173 *Comptes économiques 1961*, 48.
174 Delpy (1960), 101.
175 V. Roehrig, 'Evolution de l'enseignement au Niger', 4; Speech by Gov. Ramadier on 29 March 1955 (printed), 33–4.
176 *Comptes économiques 1961*, 12.
177 *Ibid.*, 9.
178 *Ibid.*, 13. In 1960 – after some sixty years of French colonization – 99.1 per cent of the population had no knowledge of the French language. *Etude démographique du Niger*, vol. II (1963), 6.
179 *Niger-Information* (government newspaper, Niamey), 20 January 1956, 2.
180 Jonathan Derrick, 'The great West African drought, 1972–1974', *AA*, LXXVI, 305 (Oct. 1977), 537–80.
181 See chapter 2 above, note 279 and chapter 3, note 191.
182 Lancrenon & Donaint (1972), 78.
183 Derrick (1977), 553–5. On the drought and famine of 1972–4, see also the various contributions in David Dalby, R. J. Harrison-Church & Fatima Bezzaz (eds.), *Drought in Africa. Sécheresse en Afrique*, vol. II (1977).
184 *African Research Bulletin*, XV, 7 (31 August 1978), 4779.
185 J. Lis, H. Sylwestrzak & W. Zajaczkowski, 'Ressources minières du Niger et perspectives de leur développement', *Africana Bulletin*, 24 (1976), 107–23.
186 The quotation is from Ann Seidman, 'The economics of eliminating rural poverty', in R. Palmer & N. Parsons (eds.), *The Roots of Rural Poverty in Central and Southern Africa* (1977), 401–21(410). Seidman is of course strongly opposed to the viewpoint she has summarized here.
187 Raynaut (1977); Nicolas (1962b & 1967). See also J.-C. Froelich, 'Les Structures sociales traditionelles et le développement', *Genève-Afrique*, VIII, 2 (1969), 36–46.

188 Milcent (1958), 66; Mortimer (1969), 202–7; Léo Hamon, 'Introduction à l'étude des partis politiques de l'Afrique française', *RJPOM*, XIII (1959), 149–96.

189 The first complaint from a *Commandant* dates from 1948: C. de Maradi, 'R. ann. pour 1948', 31 January 1949, 6 (AP Maradi). See also Sellier, C. de Zinder, 'R. ann. 1954', 8 February 1955, 89–92 (AP Zinder); Paul Bordier, 'Circulaire à tous services, bureaux, cercles et subdivisions', Niamey, 30 March 1957 (ASP Filingue).

190 Oral sources.

191 Schachter-Morgenthau (1967), 65.

192 *Ibid.*, 68.

193 Further details in François Luchaire, 'Les Institutions politiques et administratives des Territoires d'Outre-Mer après la loi-cadre', *RJPUF*, XII (1958), 221–94.

194 Based on G. Brouin, C. de Zinder, 'R. pol. 1951', 3 February 1952, 2–24 (AP Zinder); J. Damery, SDC Niamey, 'R. ann. 1952', 4–5 (AP Niamey); T. du Niger, 'R. pol. 1952', 25 June 1953, 6 (AP Zinder); T. du Niger, 'R. pol. 1953', 18 May 1954, 26–7 (AP Zinder).

195 J. Toby, T. du Niger, 'Revue des évén. 1er trim. 1954', 1–7 (AP Zinder).

196 Oral sources.

197 T. du Niger, 'R. pol. 1953', 18 May 1954, 26–7 & 50 (AP Zinder); 'P-v. conf. Commandants de cercle, 20–25 avril 1955' (ASP Madaoua); 'Conseil des Notables du cercle de Maradi. Séance du 11 juillet 1953' (ASP Tessaoua).

198 T. du Niger, 'R. pol. 1953', 18 May 1954, 5.

199 *Ibid.*, 4–5; Milcent (1958), 75; T. du Niger, 'Revue des évén. 1er trim. 1953', Niamey, 4 March 1953, 3–4 (AP Zinder).

200 J. Toby, T. du Niger, 'Revue évén. 2e trim. 1953', 1–6 (AP Zinder).

201 SM, December 1955, 2–3; & 31 May 1957, 5.

202 See for instance, J. Toby, T. du Niger, 'Revue évén. 3e trim. 1951', 4 (AP Zinder).

203 See for instance, 'P-v. de l'assemblée générale de l'UDN. Comité regional de Zinder', 18 May 1954 (AP Zinder); *Le Démocrate*, 17 November 1956.

204 J. Toby, 'Circulaire no. 176 APA à MM. les Commandants de cercle et subdivision', Niamey, 24 April 1954 (ASP Birnin Konni).

205 *Commandant*-Tahoua to chief SD Birnin Konni, Tahoua, 27 April 1954 (ASP Birnin Konni).

206 Of the local committees we know of – Zinder and Tessaoua – only one member was an *évolué*. See, 'P-v. ass. générale, UDN, Zinder', 18 May 1954 (AP Zinder); 'UDN. Section locale de Tessaoua. P-v. de l'assemblée générale', 18 September 1956 (ASP Tessaoua).

207 SM, 28 December 1955, 3–4. See also *Le Démocrate*, 17 November 1956; *Commandant*-Konni (P. Falgueirettes) to Gov., 15 November 1956 (ASP Birnin Konni); Regnault, Himadou, Cornu, Allier & Tre-Hardy, 'Monogr. C. de Niamey', 1955, 100–1 (CGD).

208 See for instance, N. Julien-Viéroz, 'Rapp. sur le déroulement de la campagne électorale et des élections législatives du 20 janvier 1956 dans la SDC de Tahoua', 6 January 1956, 1–2 (ASP Birnin Konni).

209 F. Fuglestad, 'Djibo Bakary, the French, and the referendum of 1958 in Niger', *JAH*, XIV, 2 (1973), 313–30 (316).

210 SM, 27 May 1956, 16–20; J. Toby, T. du Niger, 'Revue des évén. 1er trim. 1954', 15 (AP Zinder).

211 Chief, SD Madaoua (Henou) to *Commandant*-Tahoua, 27 January 1956; *Commandant*-Tahoua (N. Julien-Viéroz) to Chief, SD Madaoua, 8 February 1956 (both ASP Madaoua).

212 Election results in *Niger-Information*, 20 January 1956, 2–3.

213 'Comité local de l'UNIS. Procès-verbal de la réunion du 18 janvier 1953' (AP Zinder).

214 SM, 27 May, 25 October, 27 November 1956; SM (Note d'Information), 31 October 1956.

215 *Ibid.*, 27 November, 22 December 1956; Milcent (1958), 102–5.

216 Chaffard (1967), 272–3.

217 According to Chaffard (1967, 271–2), Djibo wanted to break his ties with the PCF and to join the Radical party of Pierre Mendès-France. But the latter's lack of interest provided Governor Ramadier with his opportunity. Ramadier 'blackmailed' Djibo into joining the SFIO by threatening to 'resurrect' a number of dormant charges against him.
218 Oral sources.
219 SM, 31 May 1957, 8.
220 Milcent (1958), 104–5; Chailley (1968), 480.
221 Bureau des APA, 'Résultats des élections du 30 mars 1957' (ASP Magaria).
222 Oral sources.
223 See for instance C. de Tahoua, 'Aperçu général d'ensemble', March 1958 (Military Archives of Zinder).
224 Chailley (1968); oral sources.
225 SM, 31 May 1957, 3.
226 *Ibid.*, 1 July 1957, 3.
227 See for instance *Afrique nouvelle* (newspaper, Dakar), 1 August 1958; *Azalaï, organe du MSA* (mimeographed newspaper, Niamey), 9 April 1958.
228 'Lettre du Sawaba au Général de Gaulle', Niamey, 15 September 1958 (ASP Tessaoua).
229 Fuglestad (1973), 324.
230 SM, 28 December; oral sources.
231 Fuglestad (1973), 325.
232 Abraham (1968), 791.
233 Oral sources.
234 For a discussion of the evidence, see Fuglestad (1973), 326–30.
235 Chailley (1968), 507.
236 Fuglestad (1973), 329.
237 High-Commissioner (Don Jean Colombani), 'Circulaire à tous mes Commandants et Chefs de Subdivision', Niamey, 23 November 1958 (ASP Gaya).
238 Complete results in 'Haut Commissariat de la République Française au Niger. Circulaire à tous Cercles et Subdivisions', Niamey, 22 December 1958 (ASP Tillabery).
239 This and the following section are based on Chaffard (1967); Finn Fuglestad & Richard Higgott, 'The 1974 coup d'état in Niger: towards an explanation', *JMAS*, XIII, 3 (1975), 383–98; *Le Monde*, 21–22 & 26 April 1974; oral sources.
240 *Ibid.* I have unfortunately been unable to consult Richard Higgott's completed PhD thesis on Niger politics.
241 I have taken this formulation from E. J. Hobsbawn.
242 Lancrenon & Donaint (1972), 69.

7. Conclusion

1 See for instance, Nathan Wachtel, *La Vision des vaincus. Les Indiens du Pérou devant la Conquête espagnole* (1971).

Glossary

alfaize	Title of the chief of Say
amatazza	Title of the chief of Keita
ameni	Assembly of all free men among the Tuareg
amenukal	Usually the head of a Tuareg confederacy
amiru	Title of ruler among the Songhay
anna/azna	Non-Muslim or 'animistic' Hausa
ardo	Petty Fulani chief
ar'holla	Title of the head of a Tuareg tribe
askiya	Title of rulers of the Songhay empire
azalaï	Huge caravan; in Niger refers exclusively to the caravans between the oases of Kawar and the sedentary south
baraka	Force/luck
birni	Walled Hausa town
bori	Possession dances
bugaje/buzu/bella	Hausa and Zerma for captives or slaves among the Tuareg
dallol	Fossil valley
durbi	Title of dignitary in Katsina and Maradi
dyulas	Indigenous traders
hauka	Possession dances (refers also to the members of the 'sect' practising these dances)
ighawellan	'Freed slaves' among the Tuareg
iklan	Domestic slaves among the Tuareg
imajeghen/amajegh	Tuareg 'noblemen'
imghad	Vassals of the *imajeghen*
ineslemen	Tuareg clerics
jihad	Muslim holy war
kanta	Title of the ruler of Kebbi
k'aura	Title of military chief (war-chief) among the Hausa
koy	Title of chief or ruler among the Zerma (e.g. *zermakoy, hikoy, gabdakoy, wonkoy, labukoy*)
lamido	Fulani chief
maï	Title of ruler among the Kanuri
mayaki	Title of war-chief among certain Hausa groups
saranuyia	Title of female ruler ('queen') among the Hausa
sarauta	The nobility, i.e. the 'office-holders' in a Hausa state
sarki	Title of ruler and/or dignitary among the Hausa

sarkin Musulmi	Title of head/ruler of the Sokoto Caliphate
talakawa	Hausa word for peasants, the rural poor (as opposed to *sarauta*)
tambari	See *amenukal*
zawiya	Centre of Sufi brotherhood

Bibliography

For abbreviations, see pp. 193–95.

DOCUMENTARY SOURCES

Niger
There are at the moment no classified and catalogued archives in Niger. Most 'archives' consist of huge piles of documents stored haphazardly in whatever drawers and/or lockers are available. Honourable exceptions include the archives of the *préfectures* of Maradi and Zinder, and the *sous-préfecture* of Tessaoua.

1. Archives Nationales du Niger
These holdings constituted before 1973 little more than bundles of mostly unclassified documents and files stored away in a dark room in the Supreme Court building. However, in 1973 a professional archivist was appointed Director of the Service des Archives, a Service which then formally came into being. One year later the archives were transferred to a newly completed building. The work of classifying the contents has progressed apace since then. However, at the time I last visited these archives (in 1978) there was still no catalogue or card-index of any sort. In fact, according to its Director, the Service des Archives will become fully operative only some time during the 1980s at the earliest. For further details, see Fuglestad (1978a).

2. Archives of the PPN/RDA, Niamey
Contain exclusively electoral results.

3. Archives of the préfecture of Dosso
Extremely poor.

4. Archives of the préfecture of Maradi
Contain quite a well-preserved and important collection of documents.

5. Archives of the préfecture of Niamey
Small but well-preserved collection.

6. Archives of the préfecture of Tahoua

7. Archives of the préfecture of Zinder
Well-preserved and very important collection of documents.

244

8. Archives of the sous-préfecture of Birnin Konni

9. Archives of the sous-préfecture of Dogondoutchi

10. Archives of the sous-préfecture of Filingue

11. Archives of the sous-préfecture of Gaya
Very important collection, but even in 1971–2 in a very advanced state of disintegration.

12. Archives of the sous-préfecture of Madaoua

13. Archives of the sous-préfecture of Magaria

14. Archives of the sous-préfecture of Say
Important and well-preserved collection.

15. Archives of the sous-préfecture of Tessaoua
Very important and well-preserved collection.

16. Archives of the sous-préfecture of Tillabery

17. Catholic Parish of Zinder
Contains the handwritten 'Chronique de la mission catholique de Zinder'.

18. Centre de Documentation du Commissariat Général au Dévelopment, Niamey
Contains only a few documents dating from the colonial period.

19. Library of the Centre Nigérien de Recherches en Sciences Humaines
Presently the Institut de Recherches en Sciences Humaines.

20. Military Archives of Zinder
Extremely poor.

France

1. Archives Nationales. Section Outre-Mer, Paris
Afrique III
Afrique IV
AOF XVI
Dahomey III
Soudan IV
Tchad I
Archives Privées 15 (Gaden papers)
Nouvelles series: Affaires Politiques, carton 167, 591, 592

2. Ministère des Armées. Etat-Major de l'Armée de Terre. Service Historique. Section Outre-Mer, Vincennes
Fonds AOF, section Niger I, III, V, VII

Bibliography

3. *Archives Nationales. Dépot des Archives d'Outre-Mer, Aix-en-Provence*
(i) Microfilms of the following series and sub-series of the Archives du Gouvernement Général de l'Afrique Occidentale in Dakar
D. Affaires militaires, 1763–1920
1.D. Opérations militaires, 1823–1920 (14 MI 293–8, 303–7)
4.D. Personnel militaire, 1779–1920 (14 MI 361 & 371)
F. Affaires etrangères, 1809–1921
3.F. Nigeria, 1889–1920 (14 MI 591–2)
6.F. Libye et Tripolitaine, Turquie et Italie, 1895–1920 (14 MI 607 & 619)
G. Politique et administration générale, 1782–1920
1.G. Etudes générales, missions, notices et monographies, 1818–1921 (14 MI 672)
11.G. Affaires politiques, administratives et musulmanes, Niger, 1897–1920 (MI 855–861, 864–5)
15.G. Affaires politiques, administratives et musulmanes, Soudan, 1821–1920 (14 MI 1047 & 1060)
17.G. Affaires politiques, AOF, 1895–1920 (14 MI 1077)
M. Tribunaux judiciaires (14 MI 1243, 1282, 1286–7)
S. Douanes et impôts (14 MI 1573–4)
(ii)Archives du Gouvernement Général de l'Afrique Equatoriale Française série D. Politique et administration générale, sous-serie 4.D. Rapports politiques, 1889–1954

Senegal

Archives Nationales du Sénégal, Dakar
Archives du Gouvernement Général de l'AOF, nouvelles séries: sous-série 2G. Rapports périodiques, 1895–1940 (vols. 13–14, 20–4, 26–33, 35–7, 40); sous-série 11G. Affaires politiques, administratives et musulmanes, Niger 1920 (vols. 7, 26–7, 31–3, 40)

Great Britain

1. Public Record Office
CO 446: Original Correspondence, Northern Nigeria, 1898–1913 (vols. 5, 11, 14, 15, 30, 38, 40, 52, 54)
CO 583: Original Correspondence, Nigeria, 1912–43 (vols. 16, 36, 56, 57, 58, 65)
CO 657: Sessional Papers, Nigeria, 1912–40 (vol. 1)
FO 2: Africa. General Correspondence (vol. 118)

2. Rhodes House, Oxford
Africa s. 62, s. 203, s. 230, s. 542, s. 547, s. 952
British Empire s. 62

Private collections
Victor Roehrig of Ottrott in Alsace and Léopold Kaziendé and Adamou Mayaki of Niamey gave me permission to consult manuscripts and documents in their possession.

GOVERNMENT PUBLICATIONS: PERIODICALS, STATISTICAL SURVEYS, OFFI-CIAL SPEECHES
Annuaire du Gouvernement Général de l'Afrique Occidentale Française (1912, 1915–16, 1917–21, 1922)

Annuaire statistique de la France 1966 (INSEE)
Annuaire statistique de l'Union Française. Outre-Mer, 1939–49 (Service des statistiques d'Outre-Mer/INSEE)
Budget local de la Colonie/du Territoire du Niger (annual)
Carde, Governor-General J. Speech in December 1927 (printed)
Comptes économiques 1961 (signed Adel Al-Akel, Niamey, Commissariat Général au Plan/Service de la statistique)
Contributions, taxes et redevances de toute nature perçues pour le compte du Budget local de la Colonie/du Territoire du Niger (annual)
Cornut-Gentille, Governor-General Bernard. Speeches on 7 February 1953 & 13 October 1954 (printed)
Etude démographique du Niger, vol. II (Ministère de la Coopération/INSEE, 1963)
Inventaire social et économique des Territoires d'Outre-Mer de 1950 à 1955 (Ministère de la France d'Outre-Mer, Service des statistiques, 1957)
Journal Officiel de l'Afrique Occidentale Française (26 July 1900, 6 January 1906 & 18 July 1925)
Journal Officiel du Haut-Senegal Niger (1 September 1906)
Journal Officiel de la République Française. Avis et Rapports du Conseil Economique et Social (30 January 1953, 6 July 1954, 31 August 1958)
Journal Officiel de la République Française. Débats parlementaires (Chambre des Députés, Conseil de la République, Assemblée de l'Union Française, Assemblée Nationale)
Outre-Mer 1958. Tableau économique et social des Etats et Territoires d'Outre-Mer (Paris, Service des Statistiques d'Outre-Mer, 1959)
Ramadier, Governor Jean. Speech on 29 March 1955 (printed)

NEWSPAPERS AND MAGAZINES
African Research Bulletin (XV, 7, 31 August 1978)
Afrique nouvelle, Dakar (1 August 1958)
Azalaï, organe du MSA, Niamey (9 April 1958)
Le Démocrate, Niamey (19 June 1954, 17 November 1956)
L'Economie ouest-Africaine. Bulletin de la BCEAO (no. 137, 1967)
Le Figaro, Paris (17 January 1923)
Marchés tropicaux, Paris (6 February & 13 December 1954)
Le Monde, Paris (21–22 & 26 April 1974)
Niger-Information, Niamey (20 January 1956)
Reveil, Dakar (22 January 1948)
Le Temps, Paris (10 July 1906 & 20 July 1917)

THESES, BOOKS, ARTICLES
Unless otherwise stated, books in English are published in London, books in French in Paris.
A.T. (Auguste Terrier?). 'Le Pays Zerma', *RCD*, 1 (1901), 28–30
Abadie, Colonel. *La Colonie du Niger* (1927)
Abdou Ibrahim. 'La Co-opération; un des facteurs fondamentaux de développement rural au Niger' (dissertation, Institut de Droit Rural et d'Economie Agricole, Paris, n.d.)
Abraham, R. C. *Dictionary of the Hausa Language* (1968)
Adamou Mayaki. 'Les Problèmes économiques de la République du Niger', *Notes d'Information de la BCEAO* (June 1960)
Adeleye, R. A. 'Rābīh b. Fadlāllah and the diplomacy of European imperial invasion in the Central Sudan, 1893–1902', *JHSN*, V, 3 (1970), 399–418
Power and Diplomacy in Northern Nigeria 1804–1906. The Sokoto Caliphate and its Enemies (1971)
'Mahdist triumph and British revenge in Northern Nigeria; Satiru 1906', *JHSN*, VI, 2 (1972), 193–214

Bibliography

Adloff, Richard & Thompson, Virginia. *French-Speaking West Africa in Transition* (1958)

Agbodeka, Francis. 'Sir Gordon Guggisberg's contribution to the development of the Gold Coast, 1919–27', *THSG*, XIII, 1 (1972), 51–64

Agg-Alăwjelj Ghubăyd. *Histoire des Kel Denneg*, edited and published by Karl-G. Prasse (Copenhagen, 1975)

Ake, Claude. 'Explaining political instability in new states', *JMAS*, XI, 3 (1973), 347–59

Alexandre, Pierre. 'Le Problème des chefferies en Afrique noire française', *Notes et Etudes Documentaires* (La Documentation française), no. 2508 (10 February 1959)

    'A West African Islamic movement: Hamallism in French West Africa', in R. I. Rotberg & Ali A. Mazrui (eds.), *Protest and Power in Black Africa* (1970), 497–512

Alhaji Hassan & Mallam Shuaibu Na'ibi. *A Chronicle of Abuja* (Lagos, 1962)

Alpers, Edward. 'Towards a history of the expansion of Islam in East Africa: the matrilineal peoples of the southern interior', in T. O. Ranger & I. N. Kimambo (eds.), *The Historical Study of African Religion* (1972), 172–201

Anene, J. C. *The International Boundaries of Nigeria 1885–1960. The Framework of an Emergent African Nation* (1970)

Anjorin, Abel Olorunfemi. 'The British occupation and the development of Northern Nigeria, 1897–1914' (PhD thesis, University of London, 1965)

Ansprenger, Franz. *Politik im schwarzen Afrika. Die modernen politischen Bewegungen im Afrika französischer prägung* (Cologne and Opladen, 1961)

Aron, Robert, with Elgey, Georgette. *Histoire de Vichy, 1940–44* (1954)

Arouna Hamidou Sidikou. *Sédentarité et mobilité entre Niger et Zgaret* (Niamey, 1974)

Asiwaju, A. I. 'Migrations as revolt: the example of the Ivory Coast and the Upper Volta before 1945', *JAH*, XVII, 4 (1976), 577–94

Austen, Ralph A. 'The trans-Saharan slave trade: a tentative census', in Henry A. Gemery & Jan S. Hogendorn (eds.), *The Uncommon Market. Essays in the Economic History of the Atlantic Slave Trade* (New York, 1979), 23–76

Ayandele, E. A. 'Observations on some social and economic aspects of slavery in pre-colonial Northern Nigeria', *Nigerian Journal of Economic and Social Studies*, IX, 3 (1967), 329–38

Ayasse, Lieutenant. 'Première reconnaissance N'Guigmi–Agadès–Bilma', *RTC*, 6 (1907), 553–82

Azèma, Jean-Pierre. *De Munich à la Libération, 1938–1944*, vol. XIV of the *Nouvelle Histoire de la France contemporaine* (1979)

Ba, A. Hampaté & Daget, J. *L'Empire peul du Macina* (Dakar, 1955/Paris, 1962)

Backwell, H. F. (ed.) *The Occupation of Hausaland. Being a Translation of Arabic Letters found in the House of the Wazir of Sokoto, Bokari, in 1903* (Lagos, 1927)

Baier, Stephen. 'African merchants in the colonial period. A history of commerce in Damagaram (Central Niger), 1880–1960' (PhD thesis, University of Wisconsin, Madison, 1974). Published in a revised version as *An Economic History of Central Niger* (Oxford, 1980)

    'Local transport in the economy of the Central Sudan, 1900–1930', paper presented to the Seminar on Economic History of the Central Savanna of Western Africa, Kano, 5–10 January, 1976(a)

    'Economic history and development. Drought and the Sahelian economy', *AEH*, 1 (1976b), 1–16

    'Trans-Saharan trade and the Sahel: Damergu, 1870–1930', *JAH*, XVIII, 1 (1977), 37–60

Baier, Stephen & Lovejoy, Paul. 'The desert-side economy of the Central Sudan', *IJAHS*, VIII, 4 (1975), 551–81

    'The Tuareg of the Central Sudan: gradations in servility at the desert edge (Niger and Nigeria)', in Suzanne Miers & Igor Kopytoff (eds.), *Slavery in Africa. Historical and Anthropological Perspectives* (Madison, 1977), 391–411

Baillard, Emile. 'Cartes économiques des pays français du Niger' (ca. 1899), reproduced in *Cartes Historiques de l'Afrique Occidentale* (Société des Africanistes, 1969)

Balandier, Georges. 'Les Mythes politiques de colonisation et de décolonisation en Afrique', *CIS*, XXXIII (1962), 85–96

Baroin, Cathérine. 'Effets de la colonisation sur la société traditionnelle Daza (République du Niger)', *JA*, XLVII, fasc. II (1977a), 123–32

   Les Marques de bétail chez les Daza et les Azza du Niger (Niamey, 1977b)

Barth, Heinrich. *Travels and Discoveries in North and Central Africa*, 3 volumes (1965, originally published in German in 1857–8)

Bary, Erwin de. *Le Dernier Rapport d'un Européen sur Ghat et les Touaregs de l'Aïr. Journal de voyage d'Erwin de Bary, 1876–77, traduit et annoté par Henri Schirmer* (1899)

Beauvilain, Alain. *Les Peul du Dallol Bosso* (Niamey, 1977)

Bello Alkali, Muhammad. 'A Hausa community in crisis: Kebbi in the nineteenth century' (MA dissertation, Ahmadu Bello University, Zaria, 1969)

Berg, Elliott. 'The economic basis of political choice in French West Africa', *APSR*, LIV, 2 (1960), 391–405

Bergo. 'L'Ecole William-Ponty', *Europe–France–Outre-Mer*, 368 (1960), 22–3

Bernus, Edmond. 'Les Touareg du Sahel nigérien', *COM*, no. 73 (1966), 5–34

   'Maladies humaines et animales chez les Touaregs sahéliens', *JSA*, XXXIX, fasc. I (1969), 111–37

   'Espace géographique et champs sociaux chez les Touareg Illabakan (République du Niger)', *Etudes rurales*, 37–9 (1970), 46–64

   'Drought in Niger Republic', *Savanna*, II, 2 (1973), 129–32

   'Les Composantes géographiques et sociales des types d'élevage en milieu touareg', in T. Monod (ed.), *Pastoralism in Tropical Africa. Studies Presented and Discussed at the XIIth International African Seminar, Niamey, December 1972* (1975), 229–44

   'L'Evolution des relations de dépendance depuis la période pré-coloniale jusqu'à nos jours chez les Iullemmeden Kel Dinnik', *ROMM*, 21 (1976), 85–99

Bernus, Edmond & Suzanne. *Du sel et des dattes. Introduction à l'étude de la communauté d'In Gall et de Tegidda-n-tesemt* (Niamey, 1972)

   'L'Evolution de la condition servile chez les Touaregs sahéliens', in Claude Meillassoux (ed.), *L'Esclavage en Afrique précoloniale* (1975), 27–47

Bernus, Edmond & Savonnet, G. 'Les Problèmes de la sécheresse dans l'Afrique de l'Ouest', *Présence Africaine*, 88 (1973), 113–38

Bernus, Suzanne. *Niamey: population et habitat* (Niamey/Paris, 1965)

   (ed. and commented upon by). *Henri Barth chez les Touareg. Extraits du journal de Barth dans l'Aïr, juillet–décembre 1850* (Niamey, 1971)

   'Recherches sur les centres urbains d'Agadèz et d'In Gall', *ROMM*, 11 (1972), 51–6

   'Stratégie matrimoniale et conservation du pouvoir dans l'Aïr et chez les Iullemmeden', *ROMM*, 21 (1976), 101–10

Bernus, Suzanne & Gouletquer, Pierre. 'Du cuivre au sel. Recherches ethno-archéologiques sur la région d'Azelich (campagne 1973–1975)', *JSA*, XLVI (1976), 7–68

   'Azelik et l'Empire Songhay. (Etat de la question de Takedda)', in *Fondation SCOA pour la recherche scientifique en Afrique noire. Troisième colloque international de Niamey, 30 nov.–6 déc. 1977*

Biobaku, Saburi & Muhammad al-Hajj. 'The Sudanese Mahdiyya and the Niger–Chad region', in I. M. Lewis (ed.), *Islam in Tropical Africa* (1966), 425–41

Bivar, A. D. H. & Shinnie, P. L. 'Old Kanuri capitals', in J. D. Fage & Roland Oliver (eds.), *Papers in African Prehistory* (1970), 289–302

Blanc, Edouard. 'Les Routes de l'Afrique septentrionale au Soudan', *Bull. Soc. de Géographie de Paris*, 7th series, 11 (1890), 169–216

249

Bibliography

Bonardi, Pierre. *La République du Niger. Naissance d'un état* (1960)
Bonte, Pierre. *L'Elevage et le commerce du bétail dans l'Ader-Doutchi-Majya* (Paris/Niamey, n.d. [1967])
   'Production et échanges chez les Touareg Kel Gress du Niger' (thesis, Institut d'Ethnologie, Paris, 1971)
   'Esclavage et relations de dépendance chez les Touareg Kel Gress', in Claude Meillassoux (ed.), *L'Esclavage en Afrique précoloniale* (1975a), 49–76
   'L'Organisation économique des Touareg Kel Gress', in Robert Creswell (ed.), *Elements d'Ethnologie*, vol. I (1975b), 166–215
   'Structure de classe et structures sociales chez les Kel Gress', *ROMM*, 21 (1976), 141–62
   'Les Kel Gress', in Edmond & Suzanne Bernus (eds.), *Les Touareg* (forthcoming)
Bonte, Pierre & Echard, Nicole. 'Histoire et histoires: conception du passé chez les Hausa et les Twareg Kel Gress de l'Ader', *CEA*, XVI, 1–2 (1976), 237–96
Boubou Hama. *Contribution à la connaissance de l'histoire des Peuls* (Paris/Niamey, 1968a)
   Kotia-Nima, vol. I (Niamey, 1968b)
Bouche, Denise. *Les Villages de liberté en Afrique noire française, 1887–1910* (Paris/The Hague, 1968)
Bourgeot, André. 'Les Echanges transsahariens, la Senusiya et les révoltes twareg de 1916–17', *CEA*, XVIII, 1–2 (1978), 159–85
Bovill, E. W. *The Golden Trade of the Moors* (1961)
Brenner, Louis. *The Shehus of Kukawa. A History of the Al-Kanemi Dynasty of Bornu* (1973)
Brévié, Jules. *Islamisme contre 'Naturisme' au Soudan français. Essai de psychologie coloniale* (1923)
Briggs, L. C. *Tribes of the Sahara* (Cambridge, Mass., 1960)
Brouin, G. 'Un ïlot de vieille civilisation africaine. Le pays de Ouacha (Niger français)', *BCEHSAOF*, XXI, 4 (1938), 469–79
Broustra-Monfouga, Jacqueline (formerly Monfouga-Nicolas). 'Approche ethno-psychiatrique du phénomène de possession. Le Bori de Konni (Niger). Etude comparative', *JSA*, XLIII, fasc. II (1973), 197–221
Brown, W. A. 'The caliphate of Hamdallahi' (PhD thesis, University of Wisconsin, Madison, 1969)
Brulard, M. 'Aperçu sur le commerce caravanier Tripolitaine–Ghat–Niger vers la fin du XIXe siècle', *Bull. Liaison Saharienne*, 31 (1958), 202–15
Brunschwig, Henri. *Le Partage de l'Afrique noire* (1971)
Bucaille, René. 'Une probable monnaie sahélienne de la période des grands empires', *NA*, 51 (1976), 74–7.
Buchanan, Angus. *Out of the World. North of Nigeria* (1921)
Calvocoressi, D. & David, N. 'A new survey of radiocarbon and thermoluminescence dates for West Africa', *JAH*, XX, 1 (1979), 1–29
Campbell, Dugald. *On the Trail of the Veiled Tuareg* (1928)
Castro, R. 'Examen des creusets de Marandet', *BIFAN*, XXXVI, 4 (1974), 667–75
Cazémajou, Captain. 'Du Niger vers le lac Tchad. Journal de route du Capitaine Cazémajou', *Afr.fr.*, 2–3, 5–10 (1900), 42–8, 87–91, 172–5, 207–10, 241–4, 280–9, 301–4, 335–7, 361–2
Chaffard, Georges. *Les Carnets secrets de la décolonisation*, vol. II (1967)
Chailley, Commandant. *Les Grandes Missions françaises en Afrique occidentale* (Dakar, 1953)
   Histoire de l'Afrique Occidentale Française (1968)
Chanoine, General (ed.?) *Documents pour servir à l'histoire de l'Afrique Occidentale Française de 1895 à 1899* (n.d.)
Chapelle, Jean. *Nomades noirs du Sahara* (1957)
Chatelain. 'L'Exode des Djerma de l'Andiarou vers le Dallol Bosso, le Djigui et le Fakara', *BCEHSAOF*, IV, 2 (1921), 273–9

Clauzel, J. 'Les Hiérarchies sociales en pays Touareg', *TIRS*, XXI, 1 (1962), 120–75

Cochémé, J. & Franquin, R. *A Study of the Semiarid Areas South of the Sahara in West Africa* (Rome, FAO/UNESCO/WHO, Interagency project on agroclimatology, 1967)

Cohen, Ronald. *The Kanuri of Bornu* (New York, 1967)

Cohen, Ronald & Brenner, Louis. 'Bornu in the nineteenth century', in J. F. Ade Ajayi & M. Crowder (eds.), *History of West Africa*, vol. II (1974), 93–128

Cohen, William B. *Rulers of Empire: The French Colonial Service in Africa* (Stanford, 1971)

Collins, John Davidson. 'Government and groundnut marketing in rural Hausa Niger: the 1930s to the 1970s in Magaria' (PhD thesis, Johns Hopkins University, Baltimore, 1974)

'The clandestine movement of groundnuts across the Niger–Nigeria boundary', *CJAS*, X, 2 (1976), 259–78

Collins, Robert O. (ed.) *Problems in the History of Colonial Africa* (Englewood Cliffs, 1970)

Colonial Office, *Annual Reports, Northern Nigeria, 1900–1911*

Coquery-Vidrovitch, Cathérine. 'L'Impact des intérêts coloniaux: SCOA et CFAO dans l'Ouest Africain, 1910–1965', *JAH*, XVI, 4 (1975), 595–621

Cordell, Dennis D. 'Eastern Libya, Wadai and the Sanūsīya: a Tarīqa and a trade route', *JAH*, XVIII, 1 (1977), 1–36

Courtier, Paul. *La Quatrième République* (1975)

Coutumiers juridiques de l'AOF, vol. III (1939)

Crowder, Michael. *West Africa under Colonial Rule* (Evanston, 1968)

'The 1914–1918 European war and West Africa', in J. F. Ade Ajayi & M. Crowder (eds.), *History of West Africa*, vol. II (1974), 484–513

'The 1916–17 revolt against the French in Dahomeyan Borgu', *JHSN*, VIII, 1 (1975), 99–116

Curtin, P. D. *Economic Change in Precolonial Africa. Senegambia in the Era of the Slave Trade* (Madison, 1975)

Dalby, David, Harrison-Church, R. J. & Bezzaz, Fatima (eds.) *Drought in Africa. Sécheresse en Afrique*, vol. II (1977)

Daniel, F. de F. 'The regalia of Katsina, Northern Provinces, Nigeria', *JSA*, XXXI (1932), 80–3

Daumas, General & Chancel, A. de. *Le Grand Désert. Itinéraire d'une caravane du Sahara au pays des nègres, royaume de Haoussa* (1875)

David, P. *La Geste du grand K'aura Assao* (Paris/Niamey, n.d.)

Maradi. L'Ancien état et l'ancienne ville des origines aux inondations de 1945 (Paris/Niamey, 1964)

Delavignette, Robert. *Freedom and Authority in French West Africa* (1950)

Delpy, J. 'Le Développement économique de la République du Niger' (thesis, Faculty of Law, Paris, 1960)

Derrick, Jonathan. 'The great West African drought, 1972–1974', *AA*, LXXVI, 305 (Oct. 1977), 537–80

Deschamps, Hubert. 'Et maintenant, Lord Lugard?', *Africa*, XXXIII, 4 (1963), 293–306

Deschamps, Hubert, Ganiage, Jean & Guitard, Odette, *L'Afrique au XXe siècle* (1966)

Destenave. *L'Occupation et l'organisation de la Boucle du Niger. Création de la région Est et Macina. Résumé des opérations par M. le Chef de Bataillon Destenave* (official report published by the Comité de l'Afrique française, n.d.)

Devisse, Jean. 'Routes de commerce et échanges en Afrique Occidentale en relation avec la Méditerranée. Un essai sur le commerce africain médiéval du XIe au XVIe siècle', part II, *Révue d'Histoire Economique et Sociale*, L, 3 (1972), 357–97

Diarra, Fatoumata-Agnès. *Les Femmes africaines en devenir. La femme zarma entre la tradition et la modernité* (1971)

Dickson, C. H. 'Account of Ghadames', *J. Royal Geogr. Soc.*, XXX (1860), 260

Djibo Hamani. *Contribution à l'étude de l'histoire des états hausa: l'Ader précolonial* (Niamey, 1975)

Bibliography

Donaint, Pierre. *Le Niger. Cours de géographie* (Niamey, Ministère de l'Education Nationale, 1965)

Dresch, Jean. 'Notes de géographie humaine sur l'Aïr', *Annales de Géographie*, LXVIII, 367 (1959), 257–62

Dufour, Jean-Louis. 'La Révolte touareg et le siège d'Agades (13 décembre 1916–3 mars 1917)', *Relations Internationales*, 3 (1975), 55–77

Dunbar, Roberta Ann. 'Damagaram (Zinder, Niger), 1812–1906: the history of a Central Sudanic kingdom' (PhD thesis, University of California at Los Angeles, 1970)

'Economic factors in the development of Damagaram (Zinder, Niger) in the nineteenth century', paper presented to the fourteenth annual meeting of the African Studies Association, Denver, Colorado, 3–6 November 1971

'Slavery and the evolution of nineteenth-century Damagaram (Zinder, Niger)', in S. Miers & I. Kopytoff (eds.), *Slavery in Africa. Historical and Anthropological Perspectives* (Madison, 1977), 155–77

Dupire, Marguerite. 'Situation de la femme dans une société pastorale (Peul woDaBe, nomades du Niger)', in Denise Paulme (ed.), *Femmes d'Afrique noire* (Paris/The Hague, 1960), 51–92

Echard, Nicole. *Etude socio-économique dans les vallées de l'Ader–Doutchi–Majya* (Paris/Niamey, n.d.)

'L'Habitat traditionnel dans l'Ader', *L'Homme*, VII, 3 (1967), 48–77

'Histoire du peuplement. Les traditions orales d'un village Sudye, Shat (Filingué, République du Niger)', *JSA*, XXXIX, fasc. I (1969), 57–77

'Histoire et phénomènes religieux chez les Asna de l'Ader', in CNRS, *Systèmes de pensée en Afrique noire* (1975a), 63–77

L'Expérience du passé: histoire de la société paysanne Hausa de l'Ader (Niamey, 1975b)

Echenberg, Myron J. 'Paying the blood tax: military conscription in French West Africa, 1914–1929', *CJAS*, IX, 2 (1975), 171–92

Evans-Pritchard, E. E. *The Sanusi of Cyrenaica* (Oxford, 1949/1954)

Farias, P. F. de Moraes. 'Review article: Great States revisited', *JAH*, XV, 3 (1974), 479–88

Fauvet, Jacques. *La Quatrième République* (1959)

Ferrandi, Jean. *Le Centre-Africain Français* (1930)

Fika, A. M. 'The political and economic reorientation of Kano Emirate 1882–1940' (PhD thesis, University of London, 1973)

First, Ruth. *The Barrel of a Gun. Political Power in Africa and the Coup d'Etat* (Harmondsworth, 1972)

Fisher, Humphrey J. 'The Central Sahara and Sudan', in Richard Gray (ed.), *The Cambridge History of Africa*, vol. IV (1975), 58–141

'The Eastern Maghrib and the Central Sudan', in R. Oliver (ed.), *The Cambridge History of Africa*, vol. III (1977), 232–330

'Leo Africanus and the Songhay conquest of Hausaland', *IJAHS*, XI, 1 (1978), 86–112

Fisher, Humphrey J. & A. G. B. *Slavery and Muslim Society in Africa. The Institution in Saharan and Sudanic Africa and the Trans-Saharan Trade* (New York, 1972)

Flint, John E. *Sir George Goldie and the Making of Nigeria* (1960)

Fonferrier, Captain. 'Etudes historiques sur le mouvement caravanier dans le cercle d'Agades', *BCEHSAOF*, VI (1923), 202–15

Foureau, F. *D'Alger au Congo par le lac Tchad. Mission saharienne Foureau–Lamy* (1902)

Documents scientifiques de la mission saharienne, mission Foureau–Lamy, vol. II (1905)

Froelich, J.-C. 'Essai sur les causes et méthodes de l'Islamisation de l'Afrique de l'Ouest du XIe au XXe siècle', in I. M. Lewis (ed.), *Islam in Tropical Africa* (1966), 160–71

'Les Structures sociales traditionelles et le développement', *Genève-Afrique*, VIII, 2 (1969), 36–46

Frolow, S. 'Note sur le climat de Niamey', *BCEHSAOF*, XIX, 1 (1936), 150–87

Fuglestad, Finn. 'Révolte dans le désert. Les mouvements de révolte chez les nomades du Sahara Nigérien (1915–1931)' (dissertation, Aix-en-Provence, 1971). Extracts published under the title 'Les Révoltes des Touareg du Niger (1916–17)', *CEA*, XIII, 1 (1973), 82–120

'Djibo Bakary, the French, and the referendum of 1958 in Niger', *JAH*, XIV, 2 (1973), 313–30

'La Grande famine de 1931 dans l'Ouest nigérien: réflexions autour d'une catastrophe naturelle', *RFHOM*, LXI, 1 (1974), 18–33

'Les "Hauka": une interprétation historique', *CEA*, XV, 2 (1975a), 203–16

'UNIS and BNA: the role of "Traditionalist" parties in Niger, 1948–60', *JAH*, XVI, 1 (1975b), 113–35

'Révolte et mort de Tegama, sultan d'Agadès (1920)', *NA*, 152 (1976), 96–101

'Archival research in Niger – some practical hints', *African Research & Documentation*, 16–17 (1978a), 26–7

'A reconsideration of Hausa history before the jihad', *JAH*, XIX, 3 (1978b), 319–39

'Earth-priests, "priest-chiefs", and sacred kings in Ancient Norway, Iceland and West Africa. A comparative essay', *Scandinavian Journal of History*, IV, 1 (1979), 47–74

'A propos de travaux récents sur la mission Voulet-Chanoine', *RFHOM*, LXVII, 1–2 (1980), 73–87

Fuglestad, Finn & Higgott, Richard. 'The 1974 coup d'état in Niger: towards an explanation', *JMAS*, XIII, 3 (1975), 383–98

Gadel, Commandant. 'Notes sur Bilma et les oasis environnantes', *Revue Coloniale*, VII (1907), 361–86

Gaden, H. 'Notice sur la résidence de Zinder', *RTC*, 2 (1903), 608–56 & 740–94

Gall, F. P. *Gazetteer of Bauchi province* (1920, reprinted 1972)

Gamory-Dubourdeau, Captain. 'Etude sur la création de cantons de sédentarisation dans le Cercle de Zinder et particulièrement dans la subdivision centrale', *BCEHSAOF*, VIII, 2 (1924), 239–58

Gann, L. & Duignan, P. (eds.) *The History and Politics of Colonialism in Africa*, vol. I (1969)

Garcia, Luc. 'Les Mouvements de résistance au Dahomey (1914–1917)', *CEA*, X, 1 (1970), 144–78

Gaulle, Charles de. *Mémoires de guerre*, vol. I (1954)

Gentil, Emile. *La Chute de L'Empire de Rabeh* (1902)

Gentil, Pierre. *Conflins libyens, lac Tchad, fleuve Niger* (1948)

La Conquête du Tchad (1894–1916) (roneotyped, Vincennes, 1971)

Gidley, C. G. B. 'Mantanfas – a study in oral tradition', *ALS*, VI (1965), 32–51

Gouilly, A. *L'Islam dans l'AOF* (1952)

Gouletquer, P. L. P. & Kleinmann, D. 'Structure sociale et commerce du sel dans l'économie touarègue', *ROMM*, 21 (1976), 131–9

Gouraud, Henri. *Zinder-Tchad. Souvenirs d'un africain* (1944)

Grandin, Captain. 'Note sur l'industrie et le commerce du sel au Kawar et en Agram', *BIFAN*, XIII, 2 (1951), 488–533

Grove, A. T. 'A note on the remarkably low rainfall of the Sudan zone in 1913', *Savanna*, II, 2 (1973), 133–8

Guillaume, Henri. *Les Nomades interrompus. Introduction à l'étude du canton twareg de l'Imanan* (Niamey, 1974)

'Les Liens de dépendance à l'époque précoloniale chez les Touaregs de l'Immanen (Niger)', *ROMM*, 21 (1976), 111–29

Guilleux, Charles. *Journal de route d'un caporal de tirailleurs de la mission saharienne (Mission Foureau-Lamy), 1898–1900* (Belfort, 1904)

Gunn, H. D. *Pagan Peoples of the Central Area of Northern Nigeria* (1956)

Hallam, W. K. R. 'The Bayajida legend in Hausa folklore', *JAH*, VII, 1 (1966), 47–60

Bibliography

Hamon, Léo. 'Introduction à l'étude des partis politiques de l'Afrique française', *RJPOM*, XIII (1959), 149–96

Hargreaves, J. D. 'The European partition of West Africa', in J. F. Ade Ajayi & M. Crowder (eds.), *History of West Africa*, vol. II (1974), 402–23

Harrison-Church, R. J. *West Africa. A Study of the Environment and of Man's use of it* (1969)

Hastings, A. C. *Nigerian Days* (1925)

Hébert, Jean. 'Révoltes en Haute Volta de 1914 à 1918', *NDV*, III, 4 (1970), 3–54

Hill, Polly. *Rural Hausa. A Village and a Setting* (1972)

Hiskett, M. 'The historical background to the naturalization of Arabic loan-words in Hausa', *ALS*, VI (1965a), 18–26

'The Song of Bagauda: a Hausa king-list and homily in verse', part 2, *BSOAS*, XXVIII, 1 (1965b), 112–35

The Sword of Truth. The Life and Times of the Shehu Usuman dan Fodio (1973)

Hodgkin, Thomas, & Schachter, Ruth. 'French-speaking West Africa in transition', *International Conciliation*, 528 (1960), 373–436

Hogendorn, Jan. 'The origins of the groundnut trade in Northern Nigeria', in Carl K. Eicher & Carl Liedholm (eds.), *Growth and Development of the Nigerian Economy* (East Lansing, 1970), 30–51

'The economics of slave use on two "plantations" in the Zaria emirate of the Sokoto Caliphate', *IJAHS*, X, 3 (1977), 369–83

Holden, J. J. 'The Zabarima conquest of north-west Ghana', *THSG*, VIII (1965), 60–86

Holt, P. M. 'Egypt and the Nile valley', in J. E. Flint (ed.), *The Cambridge History of Africa*, vol. V (1976), 13–50

Hopkins, A. G. *An Economic History of West Africa* (1973)

Horowitz, Michael M. 'Ba Karim: an account of Rabeh's wars', *African Historical Studies*, vol. III (1970), 391–402

Horton, Robin. 'Stateless societies in the history of West Africa', in J. F. Ade Ajayi & M. Crowder (eds.), *History of West Africa*, vol. I (first edn, 1971), 78–119

Hull, Richard W. 'The development of administration in Katsina emirate, Northern Nigeria, 1887–1944' (PhD thesis, Columbia University, New York, 1968)

'The impact of the Fulani jihad on interstate relations in the Central Sudan Katsina emirate: a case study', in D. McCall & N. R. Bennett (eds.), *Aspects of West African Islam* (Boston, 1971), 87–100

Hunwick, J. O. 'Religion and state in the Songhay empire 1464–1591', in I. M. Lewis (ed.), *Islam in Tropical Africa* (1966), 296–317

'The dynastic chronologies of the Central Sudan in the sixteenth century: some reinterpretations', *Kano studies* (new series), 1 (1973), 35–56

'Songhay, Bornu and Hausaland in the sixteenth century', in J. F. Ade Ajayi & M. Crowder (eds.), *History of West Africa*, vol. I (second edn, 1976), 264–301

Ibn Battûta. *Voyages d'Ibn Battûta. Texte arabe accompagné d'une traduction par C. Defremery et le Dr B. R. Sanguinetti. Réimpression de l'édition de 1854, augmentée d'une préface et de notes de Vincent Monteil de l'IFAN*, vol. IV (1968)

Iliffe, John. *A Modern History of Tanganyika* (1979)

Isichei, Elizabeth. 'The quest for social reform in the context of traditional religion: a neglected theme of West African History', *AA*, LXXVII, 309 (1978), 463–78

Jean, C. *Les Touareg du Sud-Est-l'Aïr. Leur rôle dans la politique saharienne* (1909)

Jenkins, R. G. 'Some aspects of the evolution of the religious brotherhoods in north and north-west Africa, 1523–1900' (MA dissertation, University of Birmingham, 1969)

Joalland, General. *Le Drame de Dankori. (Mission Voulet–Chanoine, mission Joalland–Meynier)* (1930, but written in 1905)

Johnson, Marion. 'The economic foundations of an Islamic theocracy – the case of Masina', *JAH*, XVII, 4 (1976a), 481–95

'Calico caravans: The Tripoli–Kano trade after 1880', *JAH*, XVII, 1 (1976b), 95–117

'By ship or by camel: the struggle for the Cameroons ivory trade', *JAH*, XIX, 4 (1978), 539–49

Johnston, H. A. S. *The Fulani Empire of Sokoto* (1967)

Kanya-Forstner, A. S. *The Conquest of the Western Sudan 1879–1899. A Study in French Military Imperialism* (1969)

Karimou, Mahamane. *Tradition orale et histoire. Les Mawri zarmaphones des origines à 1898* (Niamey, 1977)

Keenan, Jeremy. 'The Tuareg veil', *ROMM*, 17 (1974), 107–18

The Tuareg. People of the Ahaggar (New York, 1977)

Kersaint-Gilly, Félix de. 'Essai sur l'évolution de l'esclavage en Afrique Occidentale Française', *BCEHSAOF*, IX, 3 (1924), 469–78

Kirk-Greene, A. H. M. 'Introduction', to J. Burdon, *Northern Nigeria. Historical Notes on Certain Emirates and Tribes* (new edition, n.d.)

Lancrenon, François. 'La République du Niger', *Notes et Etudes Documentaires* (La Documentation française), nos. 3994–5, 12 June 1973

Lancrenon, François, & Donaint, Pierre. *Le Niger* (1972)

Landeroin, Captain. 'Du Tchad au Niger. Notice historique', in Ministère des Colonies, *Documents scientifiques de la mission Tilho, 1906–1909*, vol. I (1911), 309–537 & 538–52

Lange, Dierk. 'Progrès de l'Islam et changement politique au Kānem du XIe au XIIIe siècle: un essai d'interprétation', *JAH*, XIX, 4 (1978), 495–513

Last, Murray. *The Sokoto Caliphate* (1967)

Le Coeur, Charles. *Mission au Tibesti (Carnets de route 1933–34)* (1969)

Leroux, H. 'Animisme et Islam dans la subdivision de Maradi (Niger)', *BIFAN*, X (1948), 595–693

Leroy. 'Sécurité alimentaire au Niger' (unpubl. paper, CHEAM, 1949)

Levtzion, Nehemia. *Muslims and Chiefs in West Africa. A Study of Islam in the Middle Volta Basin in the Pre-Colonial Period* (Oxford, 1968)

Lewis, A. *Politics in West Africa* (1965)

Lhote, Henri. 'Le Cycle caravanier des Touaregs de l'Ahaggar et la saline d'Amadror. Leurs rapports avec les centres commerciaux du Soudan', *BIFAN*, XXXI, 4 (1969), 1014–27

'Recherches sur Takedda, ville décrite par le voyageur arabe Ibn Battouta et située en Aïr', *BIFAN*, XXXIV, 3 (1972), 429–70

Lis, J., Sylwestrzak, H. & Zajaczkowski, W. 'Ressources minières du Niger et perspectives de leur développement', *Africana Bulletin*, 24 (1976), 107–23

Lombard, Jacques. *Autorités traditionnelles et pouvoir européen en Afrique noire. Le déclin d'une aristocratie sous le régime colonial* (1967)

Lonsdale, J. M. 'Some origins of nationalism in East Africa', *JAH*, XI, 1 (1968), 119–46

Lovejoy, Paul. 'The role of the Wangara in the economic transformation of the Central Sudan in the fifteenth and sixteenth centuries', *JAH*, XIX, 2 (1978a), 173–93

'The Borno Salt Industry', *IJAHS*, XI, 4 (1978b), 629–68

'The characteristics of plantations in the nineteenth-century Sokoto Caliphate (Islamic West Africa)', *American Historical Review*, LXXXIV, 5 (1979), 1267–92

Lovejoy & Baier, see Baier & Lovejoy

Low, Victor. *Three Nigerian Emirates. A Study in Oral History* (Evanston, 1972)

Luchaire, François. 'Les Institutions politiques et administratives des Territoires d'Outre-Mer après la loi-cadre', *RJPUF*, XII (1958), 221–94

Lusignan, Guy de. *L'Afrique noire depuis l'indépendance. L'évolution des états francophones* (1970)

Bibliography

McNeill, William. *Plagues and Peoples* (1976, reprinted 1979)

Mademba, Bendaoud. 'La Dernière Etape d'un conquérant. Odyssée des dernières années du sultan Ahmadou de Segou, racontée par son cousin et compagnon d'infortune, Mohammadou Hassimou Tall', *BCEHSAOF*, IV (1921), 473–80

Mangeot, General P. 'Le Siège d'Agadès raconté par un prisonnier de Kaossen', *RCD*, 8 (1930), 479–82

Marshall, D. Bruce. 'Free France in Africa: Gaullism and colonialism', in Prosser Gifford & W. Roger Louis (eds.), *France and Britain in Africa. Imperial Rivalry and Colonial Rule* (New Haven & London, 1971), 713–48

Martin, B. G. 'Kanem, Bornu, and the Fazzān: notes on the political history of a trade route', *JAH*, X, 1 (1969), 15–27

Muslim Brotherhoods in Nineteenth-Century Africa (1976)

Mathieu, Muriel. 'La Mission Afrique centrale' (thesis, University of Toulouse-le-Mirail, 1975)

Mauny, Raymond. *Tableau géographique de l'Ouest Africain au Moyen Age d'après les sources écrites, la tradition et l'archéologie* (Dakar, 1961)

Métois, Captain. (No title) in *Afr.fr.*, 6 (1901), 203–4

Meek, C. K. *The Northern Tribes of Nigeria*, 2 vols. (1925/1971)

Tribal Studies in Northern Nigeria, vol. II (1931a)

A Sudanese Kingdom. An Ethnographical Study of the Jukun-Speaking Peoples of Nigeria (1931b)

'The Niger and the Classics: the history of a name', *JAH*, I, 1 (1960), 1–17

Mercier, Commandant. 'La Mission de ravitaillement du Tchad par Kano (janvier 1912–décembre 1913)', *RCD*, 7 (1914), 261–82

Meynier, O. *La Mission Joalland Meynier* (1947)

Meynier, General O. & Lehuraux, 'La Guerre sainte des Senoussya dans l'Afrique française', *RA*, LXXXIII, 2–3–4 (1939), 227–75 & 323–57

Michel, Charles. *Mission de Bonchamps. A la rencontre de la misson Marchand à travers l'Ethiopie* (1900)

Michel, Marc. *La Mission Marchand 1895–1899* (Paris/The Hague, 1972)

'Le Recrutement des tirailleurs en AOF pendant la Première Guerre Mondiale', *RFHOM*, LX, 4 (1973), 644–60

Miège, Jean-Louis. *L'Impérialisme colonial italien de 1870 à nos jours* (1968)

Expansion européenne et décolonisation de 1870 à nos jours (1973)

'La Libye et le commerce transsaharien au XIXe siècle', *ROMM*, 19 (1975), 135–68

Milcent, Ernest. *L'AOF entre en scène* (1958)

Mintz, Sidney W. 'History and anthropology: a brief reprise', in Stanley L. Engerman & Eugene D. Genovese (eds.), *Race and Slavery in the Western Hemisphere: Quantitative Studies* (Princeton, 1975), 477–94

Moll, Captain. 'La Situation politique de la région de Zinder', Zinder, 1 January 1901, printed in *Afr.fr.*, 1–2 (1902), 44–8 & 88–90

Monfouga-Nicolas, Jacqueline. *Ambivalence et culte de possession. Contribution à l'étude du Bori hausa* (1972)

Monteil, P.-L. *De Saint-Louis à Tripoli par le lac Tchad. Voyage au travers du Soudan et du Sahara accompli pendant les années 1890–91–92* (n.d.)

Mortimer, Edward. *France and the Africans, 1944–60. A Political History* (1969)

Muffett, D. J. 'Nigeria-Sokoto Caliphate', in M. Crowder (ed.), *West African Resistance. The Military Response to Colonial Occupation* (1971), 269–99

Museur, Michel. 'Un exemple spécifique d'économie caravanière: l'échange sel–mil', *JA*, XLVII, 2 (1977), 49–80

Murphy, Robert F. 'Social structure of the Southeastern Tuareg', paper presented at the Burg

Wartenstein symposium of pastoral nomadism, 15–26 July 1964, Wenner-Gren Foundation for Anthropological Research

Nachtigal, Gustav. *Sahara and Sudan*, vol. II (translated with an introduction by A. G. B. & H. J. Fisher, in press)

Naval Intelligence Division (Geographical Handbook Series). *French West Africa*, vol. II, *The Colonies* (1944)

Newbury, C. W. 'North African and Western Sudan trade in the nineteenth century', *JAH*, VII, 2 (1966), 233–45

Nicholson, Sharon. 'Climatic variations in the Sahel and other African regions during the past five centuries', *Journal of Arid Environments*, 1 (1978), 3–24

'The methodology of historical climate reconstruction and its application to Africa', *JAH*, XX, 1 (1979), 31–49

Nicolaisen, Johannes. 'Slaegt og samfund hos Tuaregerne', in Kaj Birket-Smith (ed.), *Mennesk-ets mangfoldighed* (Copenhagen, 1957), 110–25

'Essai sur la religion et la magie touarègues', *Folk. Dansk Etnografisk Tidsskrift*, III (1961), 113–62

Ecology and Culture of the Pastoral Tuareg (Copenhagen, 1963)

Nicolas, Francis. *Tamesna: Les Ioullemeden de l'est ou Touareg 'Kel Dinnik'* (1950)

Nicolas, Guy. 'Un village haoussa de la République du Niger: Tassao Haoussa', *COM*, 52 (1960), 421–50

'Circulation des biens et échanges monétaires au sud du Niger', *Cahiers de l'ISEA*, 5th series, 4 (1962a), 49–62

'Aspects de la vie économique dans un canton du Niger: Kantché', *Cahiers de l'ISEA*, 5th series, 5 (1962b), 104–88

'Une forme atténuée du "potlatch" en pays Hausa (République du Niger): le "Dubu" ', *Cahiers de l'ISEA*, 5th series, 10 (1967), 151–214

'Fondements magico-religieux du pouvoir politique au sein de la Principauté Hausa du Gobir', *JSA*, XXXIX, fasc. II (1969), 119–231

Dynamique sociale et appréhension du monde au sein d'une société hausa (1975)

Nicolas, Guy, Doumesche, Hubert & Mouché, Maman dan. *Etude socio-économique de deux villages hausa* (Paris/Niamey, 1968)

Nicolas, Guy & Mainet, Guy. *La Vallée du Gulbi de Maradi* (Paris/Niamey, n.d. [1964])

Nicolson, I. *The Administration of Nigeria 1900–1960. Men, Methods, and Myths* (Oxford, 1969)

Le Niger (published by the Gouvernement Général de l'AOF, 1931)

Norris, H. T. *The Tuaregs. The Islamic Legacy and its Diffusion in the Sahel* (Warminster, 1975)

Northern Nigeria. Correspondence relating to Sokoto, Hadeija and the Munshi Country. Presented to both Houses of Parliament by Command of His Majesty, August 1907 (HMSO, 1906, Cd. 3620)

Obichere, Boniface. *West African States and European Expansion. The Dahomey–Niger Hinterland* (New Haven/London, 1971)

O'Brien, Donald Cruise. 'Towards an "Islamic policy" in French West Africa, 1854–1914', *JAH*, VIII, 2 (1967), 303–16

O'Fahey, R. S. & Spaulding, J. L. *Kingdoms of the Sudan* (1974)

Olivier de Sardan, Jean-Pierre. *Les Voleurs d'hommes. Notes sur l'histoire des Kurtey* (Paris/Niamey, 1969a)

Système des relations économiques et sociales chez les Wogo (Niger) (1969b)

'Personnalité et structures sociales (à propos des Songhay)', in G. Dieterlen (ed.), *La Notion de personne en Afrique noire* (Colloques Internationaux du CNRS no. 544, 1973a), 421–45

'Esclavage d'échange et captivité familiale chez les Songhay-Zerma', *JSA*, XLIII, fasc. I (1973b), 151–67

257

Bibliography

'Captifs ruraux et esclaves impériaux du Songhay', in Claude Meillassoux (ed.), *L'Esclavage en Afrique précoloniale* (1975), 99–134

Olivier de Sardan, Jean-Pierre (ed. and trans.) *Quand nos pères étainet captifs. Récits paysans du Niger* (1976)

Oloruntimehin, B. Olatunji. 'Theories and realities in the administration of colonial French West Africa from 1890 to the first world war', *JHSN*, VI, 3 (1972a), 289–312

Onwuejeogwu, Michael. 'The cult of the "Bori" spirits among the Hausa', in Mary Douglas & P. M. Kaberry (eds.), *Man in Africa* (1969), 279–305

Osuntokun, J. 'Disaffection and revolts in Nigeria during the First World War, 1914–1918', *CJAS*, V, 2 (1971), 171–92

'The response of the British colonial government in Nigeria to the Islamic insurgency in the French Sudan and Sahara during the First World War', *BIFAN*, XXXVI, 1 (1974), 14–24

Paden, J. N., Morrison, D. G., Mitchell, R. C. & Stevenson, H. M. *Black Africa. A Comparative Handbook* (New York, 1972)

Palmer, H. R. 'Notes on the Korôrofawa and Jukun', *JAS*, XI (1921), 401–15

Sudanese Memoirs. Being Mainly Translations of a Number of Arabic Manuscripts relating to the Central Sudan and Western Sudan (1928/1967)

Palmer, Robin, & Parsons, Neil (eds.) *The Roots of Rural Poverty in Central and Southern Africa* (1977)

Parodi, Maurice. 'Histoire récente de l'économie et de la société française, 1945–1970', in G. Duby (ed.), *Histoire de la France*, vol. III (1972), 303–62

Pehaut, Yves. 'L'Arachide au Niger', in *Bibliothèque de l'Institut d'Etudes Politiques de Bordeaux, série Afrique noire*, vol. I, *Etudes d'Economie Africaine* (1970), 9–103

'Les Oléagineux dans les pays d'Afrique occidentale associés au Marché Commun. La production, le commerce et la transformation des produits' (thesis, University of Bordeaux III, 1973; Service de reproduction des thèses, University of Lille III, 1974)

Perham, Margery. *Lugard. The Years of Authority, 1898–1945*, vol. III (1960)

Périé, Jean. 'Notes historiques sur la région de Maradi (Niger)', *BIFAN*, I, 2–3 (1939), 377–400

Périé, Jean, & Sellier, Michel. 'Histoire des populations du cercle de Dosso (Niger)', *BIFAN*, XII, 4 (1950), 1015–74

Perron, Michel. 'Le Pays Dendi', *BCEHSAOF*, VII, 1 (1924), 51–83

Person, Yves. 'Du Soudan nigérien à la côte atlantique', in Hubert Deschamps (ed.), *Histoire générale de l'Afrique noire, de Madagascar et des archipels*, vol. II (1971), 85–122

'Dauma et Danhome', *JAH*, XV, 4 (1974), 547–61

Petragnani, Captain H. 'Turcs et Senoussistes au Fezzan pendant la grande guerre: histoire d'une révolution ignorée', *RCD*, 11 (1925), 508–26

Piault, Marc-Henri. *Histoire Mawri* (1970)

'Captifs du pouvoir et pouvoir des captifs', in Claude Meillassoux (ed.), *L'Esclavage en Afrique précoloniale* (1975), 321–50

Pidoux, Charles. 'Les Cultes de possession', *La Vie Intellectuelle* (December 1956), 42–60

Poncet, Yveline. *Cartes ethno-démographiques du Niger* (Niamey, 1973)

Poux-Cransac, Germaine. 'Tage Rabebe, chansons de Rabah', *JSA*, VII, fasc. II (1937), 173–87

Ranger, T. O. 'Territorial cults in the history of Central Africa', *JAH*, XIV, 4 (1973), 581–97

Rash, Yehoshua. 'Un établissement colonial sans histoires. Les premières années françaises au Niger, 1897–1906' (thesis, Paris, 1972a)

'Des colonisateurs sans enthousiasme: les premières années françaises au Damergou' (thesis, Paris, 1970), published in *RFHOM*, LIX, 1–2 (1972b), 5–69 & 240–311

Rattray, R. S. *Hausa Folklore, Customs and Proverbs* (1913)

Raulin, Henri. *Techniques et bases socio-économiques des sociétés rurales nigériennes* (Paris/Niamey, n.d.)

'Un aspect historique des rapports de l'animisme et de l'Islam au Niger', *JSA*, XXXII, fasc. II (1962), 249–74

'Travail et régimes fonciers au Niger', *Cahiers de l'ISEA*, 5th series, 9 (1965), 119–39

La Dynamique des techniques agraires en Afrique tropicale du nord (1967)

'Communautés d'entraide et développement agricole au Niger. L'exemple de la Majya', *Etudes rurales*, 33 (1969), 5–26

Raynaut, Claude. 'Circulation monétaire et évolution des structures socio-économiques chez les haoussas du Niger', *Africa*, XLVII, 2 (1977), 160–71

Rebérioux, Madeleine. *La République radicale? 1898–1914* (vol. XI of *Nouvelle Histoire de la France contemporaine* (1975))

Reibell, General. *L'Epopée saharienne. Carnet de route de la mission saharienne Foureau–Lamy (1898–1900)* (1931)

Renaud, Lieutenant. 'Etude sur l'évolution des Kel Gress vers la sédentarisation', *BCEHSAOF*, V, 2 (1922), 252–62

'République du Niger, La', *Notes et Etudes Documentaires* (La Documentation française) (1958)

Reuke, Ludger. *Die Maguzawa in Nordnigeria. Ethnographische Darstellung und Analyse des beginnenden Religionswandels zum Katholizismus* (Bielefeld, 1969)

Richardson, J. *Narrative of a Mission to Central Africa Performed in the Years 1850–51 under the Orders and at the Expense of Her Majesty's Government*, vol. II (1853)

Richer, A. *Les Oullimindens* (1925)

Riou, Lieutenant. 'L'Azalay d'automne 1928', *RCD*, 5 (1929), 281–5

Riou, Yves. 'La Révolte de Kaocen et le siège d'Agadès, 1916–17', roneotyped manuscript, Niamey, 1968

Rivet, Commandant. *Notice illustrée sur le Territoire Militaire du Niger et le Bataillon de Tirailleurs de Zinder* (1912)

Roberts, T. W. 'Railway imperialism and French advances toward Lake Chad 1890–1900' (PhD thesis, University of Cambridge, 1972)

Robin, J. 'Note sur les premières populations de la région de Dosso (Niger)', *BIFAN*, I, 2–3 (1939), 401–4

'Description de la Province de Dosso', *BIFAN*, IX, 1–4 (1947), 56–98

Robinson, C. H. *Hausaland or Fifteen Hundred Miles through the Central Sahara* (1896)

Robinson, R. E. & Gallagher, J. 'The partition of Africa', *New Cambridge Modern History*, vol. XI (1962), 593–640

Roche, Marcel. 'Note sur la sécheresse actuelle en Afrique de l'Ouest', in D. Dalby & R. J. Harrison-Church (eds.), *Drought in Africa* (1973), 53–61

Rodd, Francis (Lord Rennel of Rodd). *People of the Veil* (1926)

Rolland, Jacques-Francis. *Le Grand Capitaine* (1976)

Rossi, Ettore. *Storia di Tripoli e della Tripolitania dalla conquista araba al 1911* (Rome, 1968)

Rottier, Commandant. 'La Vie agricole en Aïr (Sahara central)', *RCD*, 11 (1927), 408–15

Rouard de Card, E. *Traités de délimitation concernant l'Afrique française* (1910)

Rouch, Jean. 'Les Sorkawa, Pêcheurs itinérants du Moyen Niger', *Africa*, XX, 1 (1950), 5–25

Contribution à l'histoire des Songhay (Dakar, 1953a)

'Rites de pluie chez les Songhay', *BIFAN*, XV, 4 (1953b), 1654–89

Les Songhay (1954)

Migrations au Ghana, 1953–55 (1956)

'Rapport sur les migrations nigériennes vers la basse Côte d'Ivoire', Mission ORSTOM-IFAN, roneotyped, 1957 (Library of the CNRSH)

Essai sur la religion Songhay (1960a)

La Religion et la magie Songhay (1960b)

Bibliography

'Problèmes relatifs à l'étude des migrations traditionnelles et des migrations actuelles en Afrique occidentale', *BIFAN*, XXII, 3–4 (1960c), 369–78

Rovagny, Albert. 'Villes d'Afrique: Niamey', *RCD*, 6 (1930), 329–37

Sabatier, Peggy. ' "Elite" education in French West Africa. The era of limits, 1903–1945', *IJAHS*, XI, 2 (1978), 247–66

Saint-Marc, Michèle de. *Décolonisation et zone franc* (1964)

Salifou, André. 'Le Damagaram ou Sultanat de Zinder au 19e siècle' (thesis, University of Toulouse, 1969, subsequently published in the collection *Etudes nigériennes*, 1971)

'Mallam Yaroh, un grand négociant du Soudan Central à la fin du XIXe siècle', *JSA*, XLII, fasc. I (1972), 7–27

'Les Français, Firhoun et les Kounta', *JSA*, XLIII, fasc. II (1973a), 175–96

Kaoussan ou la révolte senoussiste (Niamey, 1973b)

'La Conjuration manquée du sultan de Zinder (Niger), 1906', *Afrika Zamani*, 3 (1974), 69–103

'Quand l'histoire se répète: la famine de 1931 au Niger', *Environnement Africain*, I, 2 (1975), 25–52

Sauvy, Alfred. *Histoire économique de la France entre les deux guerres*, vol. I (1965) and vol. II (1967)

Schachter, Ruth. 'Single-party systems in West Africa', *APSR*, LV, 2 (1961), 294–307

Schachter-Morgenthau, Ruth. *Political Parties in French-Speaking West Africa* (1967)

Seck, A. & Mondjannagi, A. *L'Afrique occidentale* (1967)

Seidman, Ann. 'The economics of eliminating rural poverty', in R. Palmer & N. Parsons (eds.), *The Roots of Rural Poverty in Central and Southern Africa* (1977), 401–21

Séré de Rivières, Edmond. *Le Niger* (1951)

Histoire du Niger (1965)

Serre, Jacques. 'Monographie géographique du canton de Bambeye' (thesis, Aix-en-Provence, 1950)

Smaldone, J. P. *Warfare in the Sokoto Caliphate. Historical and Sociological Perspectives* (1977)

Smith, Abdullahi. 'The early states of the Central Sudan', in J. F. Ade Ajayi & M. Crowder (eds.), *History of West Africa*, vol. I (second edn, 1976), 152–95

Smith, Mary. *Baba of Karo. A Woman of the Muslim Hausa* (1965)

Smith, M. G. 'The Hausa system of social status', *Africa*, XXIX, 3 (1959), 239–52

Government in Zazzau (1960)

'The beginnings of Hausa society, A.D. 1000–1500', in J. Vansina, R. Mauny & L. V. Thomas (eds.), *The Historian in Tropical Africa* (1964a)

'Historical and cultural conditions of political corruption among the Hausa', *Comparative Studies in Society and History*, VI, 2 (1964b), 164–94

'A Hausa kingdom: Maradi under Dan Baskoré, 1857–75', in D. Forde & P. M. Kaberry (eds.), *West African Kingdoms in the Nineteenth Century* (1967), 93–123

Smith, Robert. Review of Smaldone (1977), in *JAH*, XIX, 2 (1978), 285–7

Soucadaux, J. 'Les Elites noires en AOF' (unpublished paper, CHEAM, 1941)

Sur le Niger et au pays des Touareg. La mission Hourst (1897)

Suret-Canale, Jean. *L'Afrique noire. L'Ere coloniale 1900–45* (1964)

Sutton, J. E. G. 'The aquatic civilization of Middle Africa', *JAH*, XV, 4 (1974), 527–46

'Towards a less orthodox history of Hausaland', *JAH*, XX, 2 (1979), 179–201

Swift, Jeremy. 'Disaster and a Sahelian nomad economy', in D. Dalby & R. J. Harrison-Church (eds.), *Drought in Africa* (1973), 71–8

Tchelle, Dr & Chamorin, Dr. 'La Méningite cérébro-spinale au Niger', roneotyped report, Niamey (World Health Organization, n.d.)

260

Tessières, Yves de. 'Une épisode du partage de l'Afrique: la mission Monteil de 1890–1892', *RFHOM*, LIX, 3 (1972), 345–410

Thiellement, André. 'Menaces de famine au Niger', in Pierre Gentil (ed.), *Derniers chefs d'un Empire* (1972), 45–52

Thom, Derrick J. 'The Niger–Nigeria borderlands: a politico-geographical analysis of boundary influence upon the Hausa' (PhD thesis, Michigan State University, East Lansing, 1970)
'The city of Maradi. French influence upon a Hausa urban center', *Journal of Geography*, LXX, 8 (1971), 472–82

Tilho, Jean. 'Variations et disparition possible du Tchad', *Annales de Géographie*, 37 (15 May 1928), 238–60

Toutée, G. J. *Dahomé, Niger, Touareg. Récit de voyage* (1897)

Trimingham, J. Spencer. *Islam in West Africa* (1967)

Tymowski, Michal. *Le Développement et la régression chez les peuples de la Boucle du Niger à l'époque précoloniale* (Warsaw, 1974)

United Nations Statistical Yearbook for 1977 (vol. XXIX)

Urvoy, Yves. 'Histoire des Oulliminden de l'est', *BCEHSAOF*, XVI, 1 (1933), 66–98
Histoire des populations du Soudan Central (Colonie du Niger) (1936)
Histoire de l'Empire du Bornou (1949)
'L'autorité du chef de famille, du chef de village et du prince chez les Hausa du Nord-Ouest', *BIFAN*, XXXIX, 1 (1977), 202–21

Verdier, R. 'Problèmes fonciers nigériens', *Penant*, 703–4 (1964), 587–93

Vikör, Knut S. 'The oasis of salt. The history of Kawar, a Saharan centre of salt production' (MA thesis, University of Bergen, 1979)

Vischer, Hans. *Across the Sahara from Tripoli to Bornu* (1910)

Wachtel, Nathan. *La Vision des vaincus. Les Indiens du Pérou devant la Conquête espagnole* (1971)

Wallace, William. 'Notes on a journey through the Sokoto Emirate and Borgu in 1894', *GJ*, VIII, 3 (1896), 211–19

Wilks, Ivor. *Asante in the Nineteenth Century: The Structure and Evolution of a Political Order* (1975)

Willis, J. R. 'The Torodbe clerisy: a social view', *JAH*, XIX, 2 (1978), 195–212

Zolberg, Aristide R. 'The structure of political conflict in the new states of tropical Africa', *APSR*, LXII, 1 (1968), 70–87

ORAL SOURCES

Nigeriens interviewed
The list is not exhaustive.

Abdou Aouta. Education: primary school. *Zermakoy* of Dosso since 1962

Abdou Gao. Mawri. Member of chiefly family. *Ecole Primaire Supérieure (EPS)*. Political itinerary: PPN/RDA. Chief of the cabinet of the President of the Republic, 1959–74

Abdou Salami Cisse. Primary school. *Alfaize* of Say since 1956

Adam Abdou. Zerma. Commoner. Ponty graduate. UNIS

Adamou Mayaki. Sudie. Son of the late Gado Namalay (*sarkin* Filingue to 1927). Graduate from Katibougou. PPN/RDA–UNIS–BNA. Former Secretary-General of UNIS. Former member of the Territorial Assembly, of the *Grand Conseil* in Dakar, and of the Assembly of the French Union (Versailles). Minister of Economic Affairs (1958–63), of Foreign Affairs (1963–5), Ambassador in Washington (1965–70), Préfet of Dosso (1970–1)

Ali Diaromeye. Fulani. Family of *notables*. Ponty graduate. PPN/RDA to 1951, then retired from politics. Member of the *Grand Conseil* (1947–52)

Bibliography

Amadou Issaka. *Sarkin* Kantche since 1954. Primary school. UNIS–BNA–MSA. Member of the *Conseil Général*/Territorial Assembly/National Assembly (1947–65). Minister (1965–74)

Amadou Yansambou. Zerma. Commoner. EPS. PPN/RDA. *Commandant*/préfet (1961–)

Ankoura Galadima. Hausa. Family of *notables*. Primary school. *Sous-préfet*

Any Mahamane. Hausa. Family of clerics. Primary and vocational school. UNIS. Member of the *Conseil Général* (1947–52)

Assane Sourghia. Songhay. Member of chiefly family. EPS. UNIS–BNA–MSA. Member of the Territorial Assembly (1952–8)

Barkire Niandou. Zerma. Member of chiefly family. Primary and vocational school

Boukary Bawa. Hausa. Family of *notables*. PPN/RDA. Member of National Assembly of Niger (1959–68). Mayor of Maradi 1968–

Boukary Sabo. Hausa. Son of the late Sabo Bawa (*sarkin* Mayahi 1932–50). Graduate from Katibougou. PPN/RDA. Minister (1965–74)

Courmou Barcougne. Zerma. Commoner. Ponty graduate. PPN/RDA. Minister of Finance (1958–70), of Foreign Affairs (1970). President of the *Conseil Economique et Social* (1970–4)

Damba Mainassara. Sudie. Commoner. Army officer. Commander-in-chief, Armed Forces of Niger, 1961–5

Dan Dicko Dan Kollodo. Son of the late Dan Kollodo (*sarkin* Katsina 1922–44). Educated at the University of Montpellier. Senior Lecturer, University of Abidjan. Minister of Education (1972–4)

Diamballa Yansambou Maiga. Songhay. Member of chiefly family. EPS. PPN/RDA. Minister of the Interior (1958–74)

Djibrilla Maiga. Songhay. Member of chiefly family. EPS. PPN/RDA–UNIS. Senator in Paris (1947–8)

Hamani Diori. Zerma. Commoner. Ponty graduate. PPN/RDA. Member of the French National Assembly (1946–51/1956–9). Prime Minister of Niger (1958–9). President of the Republic (1959–74)

Hamidou Sekou. Songhay. Commoner. Ponty graduate (later university). UNIS–BNA–MSA. Former member of the Territorial Assembly

Harou Kouka. Mossi/Hausa. Commoner. Ponty graduate. UNIS–PPN/RDA. Minister (1958–74)

Kaziendé, Léopold. Mossi. Commoner. Ponty graduate. PPN/RDA. Minister of Public Works and Mines (1958–70), of Industry and Commerce (1970–2), of Defence (1972–4)

Mahamane Tawaye. *Sarkin* Madaoua (1937–55, deposed and imprisoned in 1955). Primary school. UNIS. Member of the Territorial Assembly (1947–55)

Maidah Mamoudou. Hausa. Commoner. Graduate from Katibougou. PPN/RDA–UPN–PPN/RDA. Minister of Agriculture (1958–60), of Education (1960–3), of the Rural Economy (1963–70), of Foreign Affairs (1970–2), of Information (1972–4)

Maitournan Mustapha. Kanuri. Family of *notables*. Primary school. UNIS–BNA–MSA. Member of the *Conseil Général*/Territorial Assembly (1947–58)

Noma Kaka. Mawri. *Kona* (i.e. head of the village of Dogondoutchi) since 1970. Ponty graduate. Member of the Territorial/National Assembly (1958–65), Minister (1965–74)

Soumana Gouro. Fulani. Family of *notables*. Ponty graduate (and *Ecole de Vétérinaire* of Damako). PPN/RDA

Yaccouba Dan Bouzoua. Kanuri. Son of a former chief of the canton of Tanout. Primary school. UDN–MSA. Member of the Territorial Assembly (1957–9). Inspector of Labour since 1960

Yao Ibrah. Hausa. Family of *notables*. Primary school. UDN–MSA. Member of the Territorial Assembly (1957–8)

262

Yenikoye Alio. Sudie. Family of *notables*. EPS. *Sous-préfet*

Zado Niandou. Zerma. Commoner. Primary school. PPN/RDA. *Commandant de cercle/préfet* since 1960

Frenchmen interviewed

Batch, Laurent. Businessman, resident of Niger since 1947

Baudouin, J. Administrator. Deputy to the *Commandant de cercle* of Niamey, 1949–50; Deputy to the *Commandant de cercle* of Maradi, 1950; Acting Director of Economic Affairs, Niamey, 1950–2

Berlier, Monseigneur. Arrived in Niger in 1950; Catholic bishop of Niamey since 1961

Boquet, René. Administrator. Chief of the *subdivision centrale* of Maradi, 1947–50

Bordier, Paul. Administrator. Member of the *cabinet* of the Minister of Overseas France, 1950–1 and 1952–3; Governor of Niger, 1956–8

Brachet, Pierre. Administrator. Cadet Niamey, 1936–7; chief of the *subdivision nomade* of Tahoua, 1937–8; chief of the *subdivision* of Filingue, 1939 and 1941–3; *Commandant de cercle* of Tanout (1945–7), Zinder (1947–8), Tahoua (1948–51), Maradi (1958–60) and Birnin Konni (1960–1)

Brossard, Maurice. Administrator. Successively Deputy to the *Commandant de cercle* of Zinder, chief of the *subdivision centrale* of Zinder, justice of the peace of Zinder and chief of the *subdivision* of Tanout, 1948–52; chief of the *subdivision* of Magaria, 1952–3

Bruté de Remur, Louis. Teacher at the Catholic mission of Dogondoutchi, 1952–6

Caillard, J. Administrator. Deputy to the *Commandant de cercle* of Dosso, 1953–5; chief of the *subdivision centrale* of Zinder, 1955–8; *Commandant de cercle* of Dosso (1958–9) and Niamey (1959–60)

Cambazard, Jean. Magistrate. *Justice de Paix à compétence étendue* in Niamey, 1949–51

Colombani, Don Jean. Governor of Senegal, 1955–7; last Governor of Niger, 1958–60, and first French Ambassador in Niamey

Colonna d'Istria, Camille. Administrator. Deputy to the *Commandant de cercle* of Tillabery, 1945–6; chief of the *subdivision* of Tera, 1946–8; Director of the *Cabinet* of the Governor, 1949–50

Corbel, L. Teacher. Principal of the *Ecole régionale* (primary school) of Zinder, 1949–54

Crochet, Bernard. Administrator. Director of Economic Affairs, 1955–6

Dequecker, Jacques. Administrator. *Commandant de cercle* of Zinder, 1955–7

Durand-Viel, J. Administrator. Director of the *Cabinet* of the Governor, 1944–5; *Commandant de cercle* of Tahoua, 1946–8; Director of the Office of Muslim Affairs, 1948–9; Secretary-General (i.e. Lieutenant-Governor) of Niger, 1950–2

Espallargas, the late Jean. Administrator. Deputy-Director, then Director of the *Cabinet* of the Governor, 1942–3 & 1945–6; chief of the *subdivision* of Madaoua (1943–5), of the *subdivision centrale* of Zinder (1949–50); *Commandant de cercle* of Birnin Konni (1946–8), N'Guigmi (1951–2), Filingue (1958–9); Director of Political and Administrative Affairs, 1956–7 & 1959–60; Director of the *Cabinet* of the Minister of the Interior, Niamey, 1960–70

Fréminé, Robert. Teacher, then Director of the College of Niamey (embryonic secondary school), 1951–7; Minister of Education of the Territory of Niger, 1957–8

Gaillard, Albert. Administrator. Chief of the *subdivision* of Say, 1959–61; technical adviser to the Ministry of Finances of Niger since 1966

Hugot, Pierre. Administrator. Deputy to the *Commandant de cercle* of Goure, 1941–3

Julien-Viéroz, Noël. Administrator. *Commandant de cercle* of Agades (1952–3), Tahoua (1953–6)

Kervingant, Doctor. Director of the Health Service of Niger, 1948–51

Bibliography

Lacassagne, Henri. Administrator. Deputy to the *Commandant de cercle* of N'Guigmi (1949–51), Agades (1952–4)

Lacroix, the late Pierre-Francis. Administrator. Chief of the *subdivision* of Tera (1952–3), of Maine-Soroa (1953); Acting *Commandant de cercle* of Goure, 1953; Professor at the *Ecole Nationale des Langues Orientales*

Laroza, André. Administrator. *Commandant de cercle* of N'Guigmi, 1958–62; technical counsellor, Ministry of the Interior of Niger, 1963–70; Director of the *Cabinet* of the Minister of the Interior, 1970–4(?)

Lavenan, Paul. Administrator. Army officer, Zinder, 1939–40; Deputy to the *Commandant de cercle* of Dosso, 1946–7; Chief of the *subdivision* of Gaya, 1947–8; *Commandant de cercle* of Dosso (1948), Tillabery (1953–5); Director of the *Cabinet* of the Governor, 1950–2

Lennon, Jack. Administrator. Deputy-Director and Director of Economic Affairs, 1956–8

Luccioni, Ange. Overseas functionary. Chief of the *subdivision* of Maine-Soroa, 1956–7; Assistant to the Director of Economic Affairs, 1957–9; technical advisor to the Government of Niger, 1959–

Maillocheau, Jacques. Administrator. Deputy to the *Commandant de cercle* of Tillabery (1948–9), Dosso (1950–2); Chief of the *subdivision* of Tera (1949–50), of Gaya (1952–3), and of Tanout (1954–6)

Massu, Jacques. Army officer. Chief of the *subdivision* of Tibesti, 1938–41; Commander-in-chief, Fourth Brigade of French West Africa (with headquarters in Niamey), 1951–4. (Retired as five-star general)

Menard, Mrs Pierre. Widow of the late Pierre Menard, Administrator. Lived in Dogondoutchi (1950–2), Niamey (1953), Zinder (1953–5, 1960), Tanout (1956), Tessaoua (1956–7), Filingue (1960–1)

Nicolas, Francis. Administrator. Chief of the *subdivision nomade* of Tahoua, 1935–7 & 1938–9; army officer in Zinder, 1939–41; Director of Political and Administrative Affairs, 1947–8; *Commander de cercle* of Zinder, 1958–9

Quatorze, Jean. Administrator. Clerk in Niamey, 1941–3; Director of Political Affairs, Dakar, 1956–8

Raynier, Ferdinand. Administrator. Director of the *Sûreté* of French West Africa, 1952–4; Secretary-General of Niger, 1954–7

Riou, Yves. Administrator. Deputy to the *Commandant de cercle* of Tahoua (1936–8), Niamey (1938), N'Guigmi (1939–42), Zinder (1945); Chief of the *subdivision* of Filingue, 1938–9; *Commandant de cercle* of Tanout (1943–5), Goure (1946–9 & 1954–6), Dosso (1950–1), Tahoua (1951–3 & 1958–9), Filingue (1956–7); Acting Director of Political and Administrative Affairs, 1942–3; Acting Secretary General of Niger, 1953; Inspector of Administrative Affairs of the Government of Niger, 1959–65; Consul of France in Zinder, 1965–9; Consul-General of France in Niamey, 1969–73

Roehrig, Elizabeth. Teacher and Principal in Niger from 1938 to the early 1960s. Wife of:

Roehrig, Victor. Teacher and Principal in Niger from 1938 to 1967. Several times Acting Director of the Service of Education.

Rollet, Louis. Administrator. Cadet in Tahoua, 1941; Deputy to the *Commandant de cercle* of Tanout (1941), Zinder (1941–3); Governor of Niger, January to August 1958

Ruetsch, Bernard. Businessman. Resident of Niger since 1934

Sagnes, Jacques. Administrator. Deputy to the *Commandant de cercle* of Zinder, 1942–3; Inspector of Administrative Affairs, 1958

Sellier, Michel. Administrator. Deputy to the *Commandant de cercle* of Tahoua (1941), Birnin Konni (1942–3); Chief of the *subdivision* of Madaoua (1942), of Gaya (1945–7), of the *subdivision centrale* of Niamey (1947–8); *Commandant de cercle* of Niamey (1948–9 & 1950–2), Maradi (1953–5); Director of the *Cabinet* of the Governor, 1953

Séré de Rivières, Edmond. Administrator. Deputy to the *Commandant de cercle* of Tillabery

(1942–4); Chief of the *subdivision* of Filingue (1944–5), of Dogondoutchi (1945–6); Deputy-Director, Acting Director and Director of Political and Administrative Affairs, 1946–7 & 1948–51. *Chef de service* Ministry of the Interior (Niamey), 1959–62

Serre, Jacques. Administrator. Acting Director of Political and Administrative Affairs, 1947–8; chief of the *subdivision centrale* of Tahoua, 1948–9

Serre, Jean-Louis. Overseas functionary. Posted in Niamey (1950–1 & 1955), Tahoua (1951–2 & 1958), Birnin Konni (1953–5), Maine-Soroa (1955), Agades (1956–8) – Director of the *Cabinet* of the Minister of State for Nomadic Affairs, 1958–60

Taillandier, David. Administrator. Chief of the *subdivision* of Filingue, 1952–5

Verdié, Jean. Teacher at the *Cours Normal* in Tahoua, 1952–6

Villandre, Jean-Jacques. Administrator. *Commandant de cercle* of Dori (1946–7), Dosso (1947–8), Tillabery (1950–2), Niamey (1953–5); Director of the *Cabinet* of the Governor, 1948–9

The author has also had short conversations with Stephan JOSEPH, first Inspector of Labour in Niger, and with Dr Francis BORREY, member of the Assembly of the French Union, 1947–53, former leader of UNIS.

Index

BOOKS IN THIS SERIES

LaVergne, TN USA
08 September 2010
196259LV00003B/40/P